NICHOLAS II

Portrait of Nicholas II

NICHOLAS II

The Life and Reign
of Russia's Last Monarch

ROBERT D. WARTH

Westport, Connecticut
London

Library of Congress Cataloging-in-Publication Data

Warth, Robert D.
    Nicholas II : the life and reign of Russia's last monarch / Robert
D. Warth.
        p.   cm.
    Includes bibliographical references and index.
    ISBN 0–275–95832–9 (alk. paper)
    1. Nicholas II, Emperor of Russia, 1868–1918.   2. Russia—Kings
and rulers—Biography.   3. Russia—History—Nicholas II, 1894–1917.
I. Title.
DK258.W35   1997
947.08'3'092—dc21
[B]   97–5862

British Library Cataloguing in Publication Data is available.

Library of Congress Catalog Card Number: 97–5862
ISBN: 0–275–95832–9

First published in 1997

Praeger Publishers, 88 Post Road West, Westport, CT 06881
An imprint of Greenwood Publishing Group, Inc.

Printed in the United States of America

(∞)™

The paper used in this book complies with the
Permanent Paper Standard issued by the National
Information Standards Organization (Z39.48–1984).

10 9 8 7 6 5 4 3 2 1

Copyright Acknowledgments

The author and publisher gratefully acknowledge permission to quote from the following:

Excerpted from *Out of My Past: The Memoirs of Count Kokovtsov*, edited by Harold H.
Fisher with the permission of the publishers, Stanford University Press. Copyright 1935 by
the Board of Trustees of the Leland Stanford Junior University.

For excerpts from *The Memoirs of Count Witte*, ed. and trans. by Sidney Harcave. Copyright
1990. Reprinted by permission from M. E. Sharpe, Inc., Armonk, NY 10504.

Every reasonable effort has been made to trace the owners of copyright materials in this book,
but in some instances this has proven impossible. The editor and publisher will be glad to
receive information leading to more complete acknowledgments in subsequent printings of
the book, and in the meantime extend their apologies for any omissions.

Contents

Preface

During the nearly two decades that this biography has been underway, I have received moral and material assistance from many sources. Institutional support was provided by the University of Kentucky through leaves of absence and by travel funds from the research foundation. A grant from the Kennan Institute enabled me to explore the library and archival resources of Washington, D.C. Successive summer fellowships offered by the Russian and East European Center of the University of Illinois gave access to the excellent research facilities in Urbana. My trip to Moscow in the summer of 1992 was well timed, for the State Archive of the Russian Federation (the former Central State Archive of the October Revolution) had only recently become available to independent scholars.

Among individuals who have provided various kinds of assistance (aside from librarians and archivists), I thank in particular Samuel H. Baron, Robert F. Byrnes, William J. Chambliss, Ralph T. Fisher, Jr., Joseph T. Fuhrmann, Deborah Hardy, Mark Kulikowski, Alexander Rabinowitch, Mary J. Rehling, Andrei Simonov, Murat Taishibayev, George Tokmakoff, and Andrew Verner. I am especially grateful to my wife, Terry, who typed the original manuscript, among other necessary if mundane chores.

Transliteration from the Russian language always presents difficulties, but I have used the Library of Congress system, with some variations. Names are given in the Russian form except for those familiar to Western readers (thus Nicholas II, not Nikolai II).

Dates also present difficulties because Russia used the "old style" (Julian) calendar until the Bolshevik regime adopted the Western calendar on February 1, 1918. Russia was therefore twelve days behind the West in the nineteenth century and thirteen days in the twentieth. As is customary, I have used the "old style" for events prior to the calendar change, but to avoid possible confusion both dates are employed for events of international significance.

NICHOLAS II

1

Nicholas II as Tsarevich

On Sunday afternoon, March 1, 1881, Tsar Alexander II was returning to the Winter Palace in St. Petersburg after lunching with his cousin, the Grand Duchess Yekaterina. The day was drab and chilly, with snow clinging to the streets and sidewalks. The emperor's carriage, guarded by mounted Cossacks and followed by two sleighs containing security personnel, turned into the thoroughfare beside the Catherine Canal. About a hundred yards farther on, Nikolai Rysakov, a revolutionary terrorist, threw a round white object—a bomb painted white to blend with the snow—that exploded under the rear axle of the carriage. One of the Cossacks was wounded, and a small boy watching the procession was fatally injured. The emperor, apparently unscathed, insisted on stopping to investigate and speak to the would-be assassin. A second terrorist standing nearby, Ignatyev Grinevitsky, tossed another bomb which exploded at Alexander's feet. The deafening blast, audible for miles around, seared his face, shredded his flesh, and nearly severed his legs. Bleeding profusely and only semiconscious, the "Tsar Liberator" was taken back to the palace to die.

Among the relatives who watched the gruesome deathbed scene was "Nicky," the emperor's grandson and the future Nicholas II. Then a slight boy not yet thirteen, "deathly pale in his blue sailor's suit,"[1] he automatically became heir apparent upon his father's accession to the throne. The new tsar, Alexander III, was age thirty-six in the prime of life. A physical specimen of massive if somewhat ungainly proportions, he could reputedly tear a pack of playing cards in two and twist an iron poker into knots. The role of autocrat suited his character and personality, one of obstinate conviction, devotion to duty, and resolute will. His conventional education, modest intelligence, and stodgy conservatism did not, however, provide favorable auguries for an enlightened reign.

Alexander III, as one born to his task, quickly assumed the mantle of authority. Within minutes of his father's death he left the Winter Palace, escorted by a regiment of Don Cossacks, and returned to his residence in the less imposing Anichkov Palace. The obsequies for the martyred tsar were lavish and prolonged, but his son was equal to the trying ordeal, remaining "forceful, majestic, subduing sorrow and immune to fear."[2] The chief regicides, members of a small conspiratorial band of revolutionaries known as the People's Will, were rounded up with dispatch. Their leader, Andrei Zhelyabov, had been arrested even before the fateful day. Grinevitsky, mortally wounded by his own bomb, died within hours of the assassination. Rysakov, who escaped injury, informed on his comrades. Only eighteen, he was hanged with four others, including Zhelyabov and a female terrorist, Sofia Perovskaya. The spectacle, Russia's last public execution, was witnessed by a huge crowd in Semyonovsky Square. The hangman, sodden with drink, bungled his job: agonizing strangulation, not a neatly severed spinal cord, characterized the procedure.

Although the state provided an officially sanctioned measure of revenge upon the "tsar killers," the public's more brutal members exacted their own vengeance in a burst of primitive savagery. In St. Petersburg, students and other symbols of "radicalism" were badly mauled—in a few cases literally torn apart in the streets.[3] In smaller cities Jews were the favored scapegoat, and the unfamiliar Russian word *pogrom* entered the international lexicon as a grisly synonym for mob ferocity, especially when directed toward Jews and their property. The government did not encourage these attacks, but the moral climate of the new regime may be gauged by Alexander III's purported comment: "In the depth of my soul I am always happy when they beat the Jews. Nonetheless, it is not to be permitted."[4]

Like the abortive Decembrist Revolt of 1825 that had furnished a melancholy prelude to the reign of Nicholas I, the "Alexandrine Conspiracy" concluded an era of major reform and introduced a period of inept statesmanship and unabashed reaction that led inevitably—or so it seems in retrospect—to the collapse of the monarchy thirty-six years later. Of the many strands of history and tradition that had woven a pattern of loyalty and confidence between tsar and people, most of them were sundered by acts which, if not always deliberate or even mistaken, were ultimately the responsibility of the sovereign. Alexander III set an unfortunate precedent shortly after his succession by repudiating the modest beginnings of a constitutional order. His father, only hours before his death, had approved a cumbersome but promising scheme to allow elected representatives an advisory role in the legislative process. Respectful of that political legacy, Alexander III might have accepted the project had it not been for the intervention of Konstantin Pobedonostsev, the director of the Holy Synod (the lay official who, in effect, presided over the Russian Orthodox Church).[5]

Pobedonostsev, who had been Alexander III's chief tutor, acquired, perhaps deservedly, a sinister reputation in liberal and radical circles. Bigoted, insufferably pious, a desiccated and humorless ascetic, he was an unapologetic reactionary who detested parliaments and constitutions—an eccentric anachronism in an age of "progress." His redeeming traits were few and unobtrusive, but he was endowed with a keen mind, and he had acquired an immense store of learning, especially in the field of Russian legal and institutional history. A vigorous critic of the judicial system prevailing in the 1860s, he never again ventured to tamper with the status quo. His moral code was rigid and puritanical, yet it did not deter him from plagiarism and other acts of intellectual dishonesty. Even within his own lifetime a kind of "black legend" arose: that he had become the evil genius whose malevolent presence dominated the reign of Alexander III and carried over to that of Nicholas II. Although rule by proxy would not have been uncongenial, he never acquired a lust for power and failed to exploit opportunities that a more ambitious official would have relished. Nevertheless, he remained a force to be reckoned with, particularly in formulating religious and educational policy, but the height of his political leverage came as early as the spring of 1881. Thereafter his influence was sporadic, uncertain, and largely confined to the moral suasion that he exerted upon the last two monarchs. Even Alexander, however, was discomfited at times by his forbidding mentor, allegedly remarking, "One could freeze to death, just listening to him all the time."[6]

Alexander III needed no prompting from his dour counselor to set an unerring course toward religious and ethnic discrimination, imperial expansion, and "counter-reforms" that compounded the growing imbalance between popular aspirations and the rigid political and ideological straitjacket of his regime. Mistaken in his basic assumptions and misguided in most of his policy decisions, he nevertheless remained dedicated to his calling. Despite frequent vacations and periods of indolence, he labored faithfully in what he conceived as service to his country. Nor was his rule invariably perverse and retrogressive. He learned to delegate authority and could both recognize talent and reward it appropriately. He approved of greater educational opportunities, disregarding the potential danger of a literate population. He presided over an industrial boom that produced economic and social changes inimical to a political system based on absolute monarchy. He also took pride in Russia's role as a world power, without thrusting it into the perils of armed conflict. Indeed, it was as the "Tsar of Peace" that he was to end his reign.

Alexander undertook the management of his family as he did his country, as a stern yet benevolent patriarch. A good husband and father by the standards of Victorian morality, he was a model of sexual fidelity and had openly disapproved of his father's one egregious lapse from monogamy. His only obvious vice—excessive drinking—provoked no scandal, for he pursued it with quiet discretion. His gruff manner and overbearing personality was softened in some degree by a charming if frivolous wife, Marie Fyodorovna, the daughter of King Christian of Denmark. As petite and graceful as her husband was huge and ponderous, she bore six children while still a young woman.

Nicholas Alexandrovich Romanov, the future tsar, was born on May 6, 1868, the eldest of three boys (a fourth died in infancy) and two girls. The date marked the feast day of St. Job, celebrated in the Old Testament for his prolonged suffering. Nicholas was later to remark on the coincidence with a kind of superstitious fatalism, as if God's will had predestined him to a similar life of sorrow and tribulation.

Preoccupied with state affairs, Alexander devoted comparatively little time to his children. He apparently failed to provide the kind of emotional warmth that according to later and more sophisticated notions of fatherhood would ideally develop strong character and well-rounded personalities in his offspring. Timid as a boy, Nicholas grew up in awe of his domineering father, combining exaggerated respect with what seems to have been stifled resentment—something he learned to conceal at an early age. The proverbial charm and aloof serenity that cloaked his emotions were perhaps his most distinguishing personality traits. A lady-in-waiting who knew and loved "Nicky" from the time of his birth blamed Alexander's "heavy hand" for molding his heir into an "insincere, secretive and even double-faced" individual.[7] Was dissimulation—to use no harsher a term—an artifice that he cultivated in boyhood and perfected in manhood? Although the evidence is too sparse to render a confident judgment, it appears that his early environment was not conducive to developing a self-reliant and secure personality.

The Empress Marie, in contrast to her husband, tended to be overprotective with her children. She spoiled "Nicky," who was frail and sickly as a young boy. The tsarevich eventually became an active and healthy youngster, fond of such outdoor sports as riding, shooting, swimming, and fishing. But his emotional development was delayed if not stunted, and he retained childish traits well into adulthood.

Alexander, far from spoiling his sons and daughters, insisted on a household regimen that was spartan in its frugality and simplicity. Nicholas and his siblings slept on camp beds, arose early, took cold baths, and were not pampered at mealtimes. The salutary self-discipline that such austerity would presumably produce was largely dissipated, however, by a permissive attitude in other areas of their upbringing. They were indulged with lavish toys and recreational facilities, attended by servants and governesses, and taught by lenient and respectful tutors. Far worse from the standpoint of a "normal" childhood was the artificiality of their environment. Brought up in the hothouse atmosphere of Anichkov Palace (and after 1881 at Gatchina, some twenty-five miles south of St. Petersburg), they were isolated from the real world and accepted without question their privileged status and its perquisites. Nicholas, as tsarevich, was imbued with the mystique of royalty, and long before he inherited the throne he had been thoroughly indoctrinated in the sacred principle of autocracy and of the divine blessing that sanctioned the Romanov dynasty and the reigning monarch.

From the age of thirteen Nicholas kept a diary that, with some lapses, would faithfully chronicle his daily routine. Lacking in introspection or critical reflection, it nevertheless provides a factual if remarkably superficial record of his activities, the state of the weather, and details of family life. With the passing years Nicholas seldom departed from his basic format, although as tsar he occasionally indulged in comments of political substance.[8]

Nicholas' parents had somewhat haphazard educations, and neither displayed the slightest aptitude for intellectual pursuits, but they respected the idea if not the reality of learning. They provided an abundance of tutors for their children, but the selection process was unduly capricious, and the early appointees were scarcely models of academic achievement. Nicholas' first tutor was Aleksandra Ollongren, the wife of an army officer. She taught in a school for young ladies and may have been chosen by Marie Fyodorovna because of her Scandinavian name.[9] She was supplanted in 1878 by Grigory Danilovich, an "old dotard" with the rank of general who held ultra-conservative views and had directed a military school for cadets. An uninspired but conscientious pedagogue, he became known in court circles as "the Jesuit"; he trained his young charge "to adopt an impenetrable reserve," an "essential trait of his own character."[10] An Englishman, Charles Heath, a "gifted and charming man," was later appointed as a language tutor. Under his guidance Nicholas acquired a flawless command of English and a broadened interest in sports and athletic competition.[11] Other tutors were provided for French, which he mastered easily, and for German, which he found more difficult. Whatever his limitations as a scholar, he was undeniably a talented student of foreign languages.

Had Nicholas' education been confined to the collective knowledge imparted by Ollongren, Danilovich, and Heath, he would have suffered from a severe case of intellectual malnutrition. As he grew older his parents acknowledged the need for instructors with more impressive credentials, presumably on the advice of Danilovich, and perhaps Pobedonostsev, who became his chief tutor about 1883. An ambitious program of studies was projected, including science and mathematics, political economy, history, geography, literature, law, and military science. Such distinguished savants as Vasily Klyuchevsky, Russia's greatest historian, Nikolai Bunge, the minister of finance, Mikhail Kapustin, a professor of international law at Moscow University, and the omnipresent Pobedonostsev tutored Nicholas in their specialties, as did an array of prominent generals on arcane matters of tactics, fortifications, and military history. In addition, Vladimir Meshchersky, the editor of the reactionary newspaper *Grazhdanin* (The Citizen), though lacking proper academic qualifications and seemingly with no "official" standing as a tutor, expounded political ideas and interpreted current affairs, reinforcing Pobedonostsev's baleful influence.

After completing the prescribed curriculum—he did so in 1890—Nicholas should have been, at least in theory, the best-educated heir to the throne in the annals of the dynasty. But there were basic flaws in this idyll of scholastic achievement. One, serious though not crippling, involved the royal tradition requiring these eminent authorities to abstain from the normal dialogue of master and pupil: lectures and rote learning, not tutoring in any realistic sense, constituted the approved pedagogical method. Nor, except in special cases, were they permitted to examine their charge on his mastery of a subject. All might have been well had Nicholas proved an apt and industrious student; instead, passive, amiable, and easily bored, he endured most of his schooling as a chore thrust upon him, seldom awakening from his intellectual torpor. Indeed, he acquired a distaste for men of talent and intellect, an aversion that became more pronounced as he matured.

Nicholas' prolonged if rather shallow academic training was not entirely wasted. Aside from his fluency in the major Western languages, he acquired an interest in Russian history, especially the picturesque and antiquarian kind, and he was attracted, though somewhat superficially, to both Russian and French literature. As a pious devotee of the Orthodox Church—its verities had been inculcated since childhood—he also explored its history and doctrine with some attention, receiving instruction from a worthy cleric.

A brief but significant interlude in Nicholas' school years occurred on May 6, 1884. By dynastic custom an heir apparent reached his majority on his sixteenth birthday, observed in a formal ceremony in the Winter Palace. With his family, courtiers, and dignitaries of church and state in attendance, Nicholas swore an oath of allegiance to his father as emperor, raising his right hand while touching with his left the flag of the Cossack regiment of which he was an honorary member. A salvo of three hundred guns from the Peter and Paul Fortress marked the occasion. There were religious rites; also, Nicholas recited a military oath, impressing at least one observer that "for one so young he conducted these solemn and fatiguing duties in an admirable manner."[12]

Pomp and ceremony, especially military reviews, had become embedded in the Romanov tradition. Nicholas readily absorbed that tradition, as he did the idea of military service, his one discernible passion as an adolescent, which at the age of nineteen he was finally allowed to indulge. In June 1887 he joined a company of the elite Preobrazhensky Guards Regiment with the rank of second lieutenant and spent most of the summer training at Krasnoe Selo, an army camp near the capital. His solicitous mother wrote that she missed him *"terribly"* and urged him to "be polite and courteous with everybody, see that you get along with all your comrades without discrimination, although without too much familiarity or intimacy, and *never* listen to flatterers." Nicholas dutifully promised his "dearest darling Mama" that he would always try to follow her advice: "One has to be cautious with everybody at the start."[13]

No one imagined, though the pretense was no doubt maintained, that the tsarevich was just another junior officer. But his quiet and unassuming manner, assisted by the natural camaraderie of army life without the constraints of court etiquette, assured him ready acceptance if not instant popularity. He resided in a small but comfortable wooden bungalow built especially for him. His off-duty hours were pleasant and relaxing, and he quickly fell into the harmless yet vacuous life style of his aristocratic fellow officers. He enjoyed billiards and skittles (an early form of bowling) and an occasional game of cards or dominoes, but he apparently never developed an interest in chess, a cerebral recreation ideally suited to Russia's long and frigid winters. Heretofore an abstemious youth, he became a social drinker and sometimes, later in his army career, partook all too freely of alcoholic stimulation. He confessed in the privacy of his diary to getting "stewed" and feeling "owlish," and one of his companions later recalled truly formidable drinking bouts. "Perhaps no one," he charged, "could fail to notice that Nicholas Alexandrovich's body was already poisoned by alcohol, that his face was becoming yellow, and his eyes glittered unhealthily with bags underneath, as is usually characteristic of alcoholics."[14] Whether or not the diagnosis was accurate—no other observer has confirmed this alarming condition—Nicholas as a mature adult became a moderate drinker, usually confining himself to wine at mealtimes.

Nicholas returned to civilian life on August 11, 1887, and immediately sailed with his family to Denmark, where they were guests of his grandfather Christian IX at the Fredensborg Palace in Copenhagen. In the fall he resumed his daily routine in Gatchina and St. Petersburg. Although he had not yet completed his studies, his existence was for the most part carefree, even sybaritic. Elaborate dinners, fancy-dress balls, and frequent appearances at the opera, the ballet, and the theater were the normal diversions of one of his rank and privilege. He returned to military duty in the summer of 1888, serving as the commander of his company. Promotion was virtually automatic for members of the royal family. A notable diversion took place on July 15 at the square adjoining the Winter Palace, when the tsar and his entourage, including Nicholas, attended a lavish celebration honoring the nine-hundredth anniversary of the introduction of Christianity to Russia. (The original event, the conversion of Vladimir I of Kiev to Christianity, was semi-legendary, but custom decreed ostentation on even such contrived state occasions.) Completing his tour of duty in August, Nicholas renewed his schooling along with his lively round of social activities.

On October 17 an accident briefly marred the outward serenity of his sheltered life. While conveying his family from a vacation in the Crimea, the imperial train derailed near the village of Borki in Kharkov Province. The royal party, eating in the dining car at the time of the incident, was reportedly saved from injury or death by the tsar's herculean strength: the roof collapsed, and he managed to lift it just enough for his wife and children to escape unhurt. Others, chiefly servants and train personnel, were less fortunate; twenty-two died, and thirty-six suffered grave injuries. Alexander may have overextended his physical capacity, for it was generally believed in court circles that his kidneys were adversely affected by the enormous strain. A plot by revolutionaries was suspected, but investigation offered a more commonplace verdict: excessive speed had triggered the accident. Sergei Witte, who headed the Southwestern Railway, had previously expressed himself in blunt terms about the hazards of the imperial train operating at high speeds on a light roadbed. Alexander recalled the warning and rewarded him with the directorship of the Department of Railroad Affairs, a notable step in Witte's spectacular rise in government service.[15]

By 1889, as Nicholas approached his twenty-first year, he had received no training in affairs of state. His elevation to the throne seemed a remote event—his father was only forty-four at the time—and he evinced no interest in politics or governmental administration. Alexander regarded his son with a kind of benevolent disdain as naive and childish. To honor Nicholas' birthday, May 6, he nevertheless appointed him to the State Council and to the Committee of Ministers. Neither body had prerogatives apart from the sovereign will, but precedence conferred upon them a quasi-constitutional status and a continuity that lasted until 1905. Membership in the council, while largely ceremonial, did grant the privilege of discussing legislative matters in a formal setting. The committee, selected by and responsible to the tsar, constituted only a pale reflection of Western-style cabinets and seldom met in plenary session. However constricted their authority, both bodies dealt on occasion with major political and social questions, and they constituted a unique opportunity for the tsarevich to learn the royal trade. In the beginning Nicholas attended meetings with some regularity, but he was less a participant than a silent observer, shy and inexperienced, apparently as indifferent to his apprenticeship as he was to most of his academic studies. He resented the number of documents that he was expected to digest before each meeting, tacitly admitting in his diary to dereliction of duty: "I regularly limit myself to one or two of the most interesting topics, but the rest go right into the fire!"[16]

In the latter part of June 1889 Nicholas interrupted his brief acquaintance with political affairs for his third summer of military training. He served as a subaltern in the Hussar Guards Regiment, an elite cavalry unit, and returned the following summer as squadron commander. In the interim, to his immense relief, he completed his formal education ("Today" he wrote on April 28, 1890, "I concluded my studies finally and forever"). He also embarked upon a dalliance with a pretty ballet dancer, an involvement that proved more than a passing fancy. The sexual escapades of the grand dukes—indeed of the capital's male aristocracy—were conducted with reasonable discretion, but they were often accompanied with enough rumor and gossip to satiate the most prurient of appetites. Nicholas was both cautious and circumspect, as befitted his position, and obviously no sexual sophisticate. His first affair, as far as can be determined, had involved an operetta singer introduced by one of his uncles. The liaison ended abruptly when the police, supposedly at the tsar's behest, ordered her out of the capital.[17] He met the ballet dancer, Matilda Kshesinskaya, in March 1890, when the royal family attended a recital at her school. She was instantly smitten, and Nicholas responded by seeking her company when she danced for the officers at Krasnoe Selo in July. Nicholas' cryptic references to Kshesinskaya in his diary cast doubt on her account of a purely platonic relationship.[18] But they had no opportunity for privacy, according to her recollections, and did not meet again for over a year. Their prolonged separation was occasioned by Nicholas' "grand tour," an extended Middle Eastern and Asian journey that included Russia's vast wilderness domain of Siberia.

A trip to Europe would have been the conventional method of rounding out the tsarevich's education. Alexander, however, was no great admirer of Western civilization, and as a determined apologist for Russia's historic "mission," especially in the Far East, he very likely sought to instill in his son a similar view of his country's destiny. General Danilovich arranged the itinerary, with help from several consultants. The sizable party included Nicholas' brother Georgi, who traveled as far as India before ill health obliged him to return to Russia; his cousin, Prince George of Greece; Prince Vladimir Baryatinsky, a major general who served as the expedition's chief of staff; Prince Esper Ukhtomsky,[19] who became Nicholas' tutor on Asian civilization and was assigned the task of writing an official account of the journey; three young officer-companions; a water-color painter who joined the group in Trieste; and a naval surgeon, who joined in Cairo.

Nicholas and his suite left Gatchina by rail on October 23, 1890.[20] After a stop in Warsaw and a longer stay in Vienna, where the Emperor Franz Josef honored Nicholas with a personal visit at the station, the journey continued to the port of Trieste. The Russian cruiser *Pamyat Azova*, manned by a crew of 580 and escorted by two smaller vessels, awaited the party and conveyed them to Greece; there, sightseeing and the hospitality of the king and queen occupied several days before the voyage resumed. The Mediterranean cruise and the festive air aboard ship restored Nicholas, who had left Russia in a melancholy mood ("very sad and depressed," according to his diary),[21] to good humor. Disembarking near Cairo on November 10, Nicholas and his entourage began an extensive tour of Egypt's ancient monuments: the great pyramids, the Sphinx, the temple of Karnak, the tombs of the pharaohs, even a yacht trip up the Nile to the First Cataract. Camel rides, naked dancing girls, and an incognito visit to a bazaar furnished lively diversions, although the Russians found the unaccustomed heat oppressive. They rejoined the ship at the port of Suez and passed through the Red Sea in late November, pausing at Aden and reaching Bombay on December 11.

The British authorities in India were extravagant in their hospitality, with official dinners and receptions, hunting expeditions for tigers, leopards, antelope, and boar, trips by rail to the major cities, and an interminable round of visits to tombs, temples, mosques, and palaces, including the incomparable Taj Mahal. Sir Donald Mackenzie Wallace,[22] probably Britain's leading specialist on Russia, served as the designated escort throughout the seven-week tour. With the temperature sweltering and the novelty of his travels having worn off, Nicholas became bored and irritable, confiding his Anglophobia to the privacy of his diary: "It is intolerable to be surrounded by Englishmen" and "to see red uniforms everywhere."[23] Petulant remarks in a letter to his mother brought a gentle rebuke: he should set aside personal comfort and "be doubly polite and amiable and, above all, never show you are bored."[24]

On January 30, 1891, Nicholas sailed for Columbo and a week's excursion in Ceylon. There he encountered his cousin Sandro (Grand Duke Aleksandr Mikhailovich), who had been hunting elephants in the jungle, and complained that his trip was "senseless." "Palaces and generals are the same all the world over," he lamented, "and that's all I am permitted to see. I could just as well have stayed at home."[25] Nicholas took an excessively narrow view of his itinerary, if he has been quoted accurately, but he did have a valid point: his journey was more ceremonial than educational, though it was scarcely to be expected that the heir to the Russian throne could proceed as if he were an ordinary tourist.

At the next stop, Singapore, Nicholas managed an incognito tour of the city. On February 21 he departed for the island of Java, the proverbial jewel of the Dutch East Indies. There, among other novelties, a crocodile hunt was arranged, and he was credited with shooting at least one of the creatures, probably the stuffed specimen later displayed in the Winter Palace. He reached Bangkok, the Siamese capital, on March 8. Protocol demanded an official reception by King Chulalongkorn, and Nicholas dutifully wore the dress uniform of the Hussar Guards, hardly a comfortable garment in the stifling heat. The king's bounty was lavishly expressed by an assortment of exotic gifts, including a menagerie of baby elephants, tigers, monkeys, and birds, which presumably found sanctuary in a Russian zoo. The tour of Southeast Asia concluded in Indochina, where Nicholas was received by the French governor-general in Saigon with a graciousness appropriate to his rank and perhaps with a cordiality the more genuine due to the impending Franco-Russian alliance.

The expedition arrived in the British colony of Hong Kong on March 23. A visit to nearby Canton on the Chinese mainland was followed by a more extensive but tedious journey up the Yangtze on a Russian steamboat. It took almost a week to reach Hankow, where the Russian colony honored Nicholas with a banquet. Returning to the coast near Shanghai, he re-boarded the *Pamyat Azova* and set off for Japan. After a stay in Nagasaki during Easter week, he proceeded by water to Kobe and there took a special train to the former capital, Kyoto, still a venerable cultural shrine.

On April 29 Nicholas, his retinue, and Japanese officials visited the nearby resort of Otsu. As they returned through the city after an outing on Lake Biwa, Nicholas rode in a rickshaw near the head of a long procession of such vehicles. A heavy police guard lined both sides of the narrow street. Suddenly one of the constables on duty ran up brandishing a sword and struck at Nicholas. Aimed with deadly intent, the blow proved a glancing one, for the victim ducked in time; the blade sliced through his bowler hat, inflicting two cuts on his scalp. Nicholas prudently took flight. Two of the rickshaw bearers captured the assailant: one brought him down with a lunging tackle, while the other subdued him with blows from the fallen sword. Prince George struck the attacker with a bamboo cane, and in some accounts, including Nicholas' diary, he became the principal hero of the episode (the plethora of eyewitnesses multiplied the confusing and even contradictory versions of what actually took place).[26] The Russian naval surgeon, who had accompanied the party to Otsu, cleaned and bandaged the wounds, which were apparently bloody but less serious than had been feared. Later, back in Kyoto, several stitches were taken, and the cuts eventually healed without complications, aside from scars that were above the hairline and thus unnoticeable. According to rumor, perpetuated by later biographers, Nicholas suffered headaches for the rest of his life as a result of the attack, an implausible physical reaction to so minor an injury but a credible psychosomatic response to what must have been a deeply traumatic experience. On the other hand, a reliable witness has provided a reverse twist to the allegation: "I was told by the emperor himself that, after that incident, he had never again been troubled by the frequent headaches from which he had suffered since his childhood."[27]

The Japanese government and people were mortified by the near tragedy and sought to expiate the crime by public and private apologies to the victim, by letters of condolence to Alexander III and his wife, by the resignation of various officials deemed negligent, and by an intention to punish the would-be assassin with execution. In Russia the alarming first reports were soon modified when it became clear, at least to the royal family, that the injury was not serious and that no revolutionary conspiracy had been involved. Nicholas (as did others) dispatched a reassuring telegram to his parents, followed by a letter describing his experience in greater detail. His mother was shaken by the "horrible catastrophe" and ascribed his second narrow escape from death—the first being the accident at Borki—to divine intervention.[28] Nicholas, obeying a telegram from his father, retreated to the safety of the flagship, personally escorted from Kyoto by the Japanese emperor. Although disposed to continue his tour by a visit to Tokyo, he was overruled by another telegram from Alexander. Before leaving the harbor at Kobe he celebrated his twenty-third birthday with felicitations, festivities, and expensive gifts presented by his hosts.

The assailant, meanwhile, had been identified as Tsuda Sanzo, a former samurai with an exemplary record in military service and with the police force, though one of his colleagues spoke of him as an "irritable and savage man." He was not a religious fanatic, as reports circulated abroad described him, but a zealous "patriot" with tendencies that in Western psychiatric parlance were distinctly paranoid. He claimed that Nicholas had been discourteous to the emperor by failing to pay his respects before touring Japan. Also, the presence of Russian naval vessels in Kobe and the arrival of the tsarevich, added to past Russian "aggression," seemed evidence to him of a sinister plot against his country. The authorities, in seeking the death penalty for the crime, were thwarted by a legal code that made no provision for execution in cases of aggravated assault except upon members of the royal family. The Supreme Court upheld the sanctity of the law—the Russian royal family did not qualify—and sentenced Tsuda to life at hard labor (he died of pneumonia several months later while in custody). The two rickshaw bearers became instant if evanescent celebrities. They were decorated and granted small annual state pensions for life, while Nicholas bestowed a gift of 2,500 yen (about $1,250) on each of his benefactors, in addition to life pensions of a thousand yen annually conferred by Alexander III.[29]

Nicholas departed with assurances that he bore no grudge against the Japanese people or their government. Yet the experience left an emotional scar that found an outlet in contemptuous private references, both written and oral, to the Japanese as "monkeys"; and his imprudent—one might even say reckless—policy in East Asia of later years revealed not only a deeply rooted animosity toward Japan but an ugly streak of chauvinism hazardous to the national interest.

When he reached Vladivostok on May 12, Nicholas set foot on his native soil for the first time in nearly seven months. The city, founded in 1860 in the wake of Russian expansion at China's expense, was to serve as the eastern terminus of the Trans-Siberian Railway. The grandiose project to link Moscow and St. Petersburg with the shores of the Pacific was inevitable, given Russia's growing imperial interests in Asia. On March 17,

1891, Alexander III had issued a rescript announcing the enterprise and charging his son "with the duty of laying the foundation stone, in Vladivostok, of the Ussuri section of the Great Siberian Railway, which is to be built at State expense and under the direction of the Government."[30] Nicholas, in a formal ceremony on May 19 following outdoor religious services, shoveled dirt into a wheelbarrow and emptied it on the construction site. Later he laid the first stone of the future passenger station. Other official duties during his visit included appearances at a projected monument to the memory of Admiral Gennadi Nevelskoy, an explorer and empire builder of some forty years before, and at a new drydock then under construction that was named in Nicholas' honor.

On May 22, abandoning the comforts provided by the *Pamyat Azova*, Nicholas and his entourage set out on the long and fatiguing journey to European Russia via the overland route across Siberia. His transportation consisted of open carriages and river steamboats, and if the country was sparsely populated and its "cities" crude settlements of wooden huts and dirt streets, the arrival of the tsarevich was a memorable occasion for the patriotic inhabitants and the deferential local authorities. However lacking in the exotic flavor of foreign lands, Siberia was impressive in its enormous dimensions and unlimited resources. Except for the prolonged and tiresome interludes of travel, his journey became something of a triumphal procession of cheering crowds and official receptions. Indeed, the routine varied little from his previous experience, though Buryat tribesmen, Kirghiz nomads, and Cossack horsemen offered a vivid contrast to the people of more traditional Asiatic societies.

On August 4 Nicholas reached St. Petersburg. His overall impressions of the trip are not on record, but one may surmise that it sharpened his sense of self-importance and aroused his interest in Russia's "destiny" in Asian affairs. Prince Ukhtomsky, an ardent imperialist, had apparently lost no opportunity to convey his own sentiments to his impressionable young charge. Nicholas' readjustment to a "normal" life style was to outward appearances rapid and untroubled. He served his usual military stint—necessarily abbreviated because of his late-summer arrival—by commanding a detachment of the Horse Guards Artillery, and he renewed his affair with Kshesinskaya, though it was interrupted by a family visit to Denmark in the fall.

The year 1892 began auspiciously for Nicholas when he was promoted to the rank of colonel and given command of the First Battalion of the Preobrazhensky Guards. The position, however, was entirely honorific, at least until the following summer when he was again on active duty. Of more substance were two appointments made several weeks previously, apparently at the prompting of Sergei Witte shortly before he became minister of communications. The tsar, while still complaining of his son's "altogether infantile judgments," allowed himself to be persuaded that

Nicholas should assume more responsibility.[31] The tsarevich was accordingly entrusted with two chairmanships, that of the Siberian Railroad Committee, involving the financing and construction of the great railway, and of the Special Committee on Famine Relief, a major governmental effort to alleviate the suffering brought on by drought and crop failure in 1891–1892.

The famine committee was no mere political charade to disguise the government's reputed passivity in the face of crisis. Its members worked with a sense of dedication, and Nicholas, quiet but attentive, carried out his assignment with an earnest devotion to duty. Nonetheless, he was less assertive than his role seemed to require, and others with more practical experience took over the technical aspects of committee business.[32] An American diplomat who spoke to him on the subject, apparently late in 1892, was appalled when Nicholas "in an offhand easy-going way" dismissed the famine as a thing of the past to which he no longer devoted any attention.[33] Mass starvation had indeed eased considerably by this time, but cholera and typhus of epidemic proportions remained a grim legacy of famine conditions. Whether or not Nicholas was both callous and misinformed, as his interlocutor seemed to think, he recalled his committee service with nostalgic pride. "Those were the good times," he commented in later years.[34]

The Siberian Railroad Committee had become Witte's special project, designed to bypass the bureaucratic labyrinth of the State Council in order to develop Russia's enormous frontier. Having acquired an interest in East Asia, Nicholas accepted the chairmanship as something more than a routine assignment. His tenure, if considerably longer than that on the famine committee—he continued to serve during the first decade of his reign—was unremarkable, for elder statesman Nikolai Bunge managed most of the regular business in his capacity as vice chairman. But Nicholas did support Witte's attempt to encourage the migration of landless peasants to Siberia, a measure generally opposed by the landlords because it would reduce the supply of cheap labor. Nicholas also served on the Finance Committee, responsible for government credit policy, a body of whose existence he had previously been unaware, and on the State Military Council, whose deliberations were theoretically closer to his own experience.

Thus, contrary to the impression usually conveyed that Alexander III deliberately isolated his son from governmental affairs, Nicholas had ample if somewhat belated opportunities to pursue the royal craft. That he eventually came to the throne unprepared and lacking in confidence was more likely a result of character defects and emotional immaturity than of a dearth of on-the-job training. Observers outside the royal family were aware of the tsarevich's shortcomings. For example, Vladimir Lamzdorf, a foreign ministry official, commented in his diary in January 1892 with seeming accuracy: "The heir, 24 years old, presents a strange appearance, half child, half man, small in stature, slender, insignificant, although, as they say, he is stubborn and displays a surprising lightmindedness and lack of sensitivity."[35]

In 1893 Nicholas was sent on two ceremonial visits to represent his family at royal weddings, that of Princess Margaret of Prussia, the sister of Emperor William II of Germany, and that of Prince George, the Duke of York (later King George V of England). Upon his arrival in Berlin in January, Nicholas became the object of his cousin William's effusive hospitality and attentive flattery. The kaiser, chafing under the recent Franco-Russian diplomatic rapprochement, regaled his impressionable guest with harangues on the failings of the French government, supposedly a veritable cesspool of corruption and iniquity. Combining ignorance with naiveté, Nicholas not only accepted the strictures of his host with equanimity but eventually surpassed them with vehement denunciations of that benighted republic. Promising to approach his father on the French question, he was provided with a draft memorandum. Whether he kept his promise cannot be determined, but Alexander III in any case proceeded to consolidate an alliance with France, and William was chagrined and sorely displeased that his ambitious personal diplomacy had been so ineffectual.[36]

Nicholas' journey to England—he could have recalled little of his first visit at the age of five—came during the summer when the heat was "tropical." He nonetheless found London most congenial ("I never thought I would like it so much"). He stayed at Marlborough House, and Queen Victoria received him cordially at Windsor Castle, where she conferred the Order of the Garter, pronouncing him "charming" and "simple and unaffected."[37] Nicholas bore a startling resemblance to his cousin (the bridegroom), especially since both had grown fashionable Vandyke beards, and the two were constantly mistaken for one another. A member of Parliament, observing Nicholas when he visited the House of Commons, wrote that he "certainly did not give the impression of either mental or physical vigour. It was hard to realize that this slim, not very tall, and decidedly delicate-looking stripling was the son of the giant who could twist tin plates in the hollow of one of his brawny hands."[38]

Nicholas' parents, apprehensive about his affair with Kshesinskaya, and in any event persuaded that the royal heir should be safely married, had by 1893 made discreet inquiries about a suitable bride. The two handsome daughters of Prince Nicholas of Montenegro, then being educated in St. Petersburg, were considered likely prospects. But Nicholas proved indifferent. Nor did he respond favorably to a match with Princess Helène of Orleans, the daughter of the Count of Paris, the pretender to the French throne, or with Princess Margaret of Prussia. Neither candidate, moreover, evinced a willingness to adopt the Orthodox faith, a prerequisite for marriage into the Russian royal family.

With a stubbornness and tenacity seemingly at odds with his shy and retiring nature, Nicholas held out for an obscure but well-connected German princess, Alix of Hesse. A granddaughter of Queen Victoria, Alix had lost her mother at the age of six, and that childhood tragedy helped to mold a personality that struck many as reserved to the point of haughty aloofness. But among intimates she could be winsome and animated, and her striking good looks caught Nicholas' eye when they met for the first time in 1884. Their acquaintance was renewed and blossomed into a romance five years later when Alix returned to St. Petersburg to visit her sister Ella, who had married one of the grand dukes. Initial objections to the match by Nicholas' parents were overcome in part when a reluctant Alix, following her sister's example, offered to convert from Lutheranism to Orthodoxy. Perhaps the overriding consideration, however, was Alexander's failing health. Only forty-nine in 1894, he had aged noticeably, and during the summer his illness was diagnosed as nephritis, a kidney disease. In September, belatedly accepting medical advice to seek the more beneficent climate of the Black Sea, he moved to Livadia Palace in the Crimea. Nicholas had spent much of the summer with Alix in England but dutifully accompanied his father to Livadia. With anxious dismay the family witnessed the deterioration of Alexander's once-powerful physique. Father John of Kronstadt, a "miracle worker" of popular renown, came to offer spiritual consolation, and finally extreme unction; the tsar died with quiet dignity on the afternoon of October 20.

To Nicholas, a devoted but overly submissive son, the death of his father came not only as a crushing personal blow but a traumatic and bewildering alteration of his royal status. His accession to the throne was solemnized in a ceremony on the palace lawn, where a priest administered the oath of allegiance. (His formal coronation was delayed until 1896.) Nicholas was woefully unprepared, both politically and emotionally, to assume the burden of supreme autocrat. But the situation was not hopeless. His oft-quoted lament to his cousin Sandro ("I know nothing of the business of ruling. I have no idea of even how to talk to the ministers")[39] at least indicated a commendable self-awareness of his limitations. Contrary to the judgment rendered by later critics of the regime, particularly revolutionaries, Nicholas was not a simpleton, a man of subnormal intelligence. If he lacked sophistication and experience, and if his intellectual horizons were excessively narrow, he possessed a genetic endowment that probably surpassed that of his father: he was gifted with an excellent memory and had no difficulty in grasping the essence of a written memorandum or an oral report. Nor was he deficient in the social and cultural graces normally expected from one of his privileged upbringing. More important, he had an agreeable personality and a gracious manner that belied his exalted position. Even Witte, no admirer of the emperor, conceded that he had "a thoroughly good, kind heart" and that he was "remarkably well bred."[40] Nevertheless, with due allowance for his redeeming qualities, Nicholas was a distressingly shallow and irresolute young man whose success as a ruler would depend upon qualities other than good intentions and a willingness to work diligently in the service of his country.

2

The New Autocrat

The prolonged and elaborate ritual of a royal funeral overshadowed the beginning of Nicholas' reign. After a week's delay, apparently due to the weather and procedural difficulties, a cruiser escorted by ships of the Black Sea fleet conveyed Alexander III's remains to Sevastopol. There a special train continued the long journey to St. Petersburg. Frequent stops along the route allowed townspeople and peasants to pay their respects, the local clergy to pray for the deceased, and on occasion a choir to chant a requiem. In Moscow the emperor's coffin lay in state for a day and a night at the Cathedral of the Archangel Michael within the Kremlin walls. In the capital the funeral procession took four hours to reach the Cathedral of the fortress named for Saints Peter and Paul, the traditional repository of deceased Romanov tsars since Peter the Great. An exhausting round of religious ceremonies followed, with services twice a day for the family, dignitaries of church and state, and a sizable delegation of foreign royalty. The body was exposed to public view for a full week and, though the embalmers had presumably discharged their function with competence, they had had belated access to their subject; perfume and incense could not entirely disguise the odor of putrefying flesh.

The formal obsequies were at last completed on November 7. The period of mourning was relaxed a week later to permit the sovereign to marry. Custom dictated matrimony for Russia's rulers, and the engaged couple were in any event anxious to tie the legal knot. Nicholas had preferred a quiet ceremony in the Crimea but was persuaded that the occasion demanded public recognition befitting his status. The wedding took place in the chapel of the Winter Palace with restrained pageantry, and cheering street crowds welcomed the royal pair with generous spontaneity. It was noted that public security, so rigid under Alexander III, had been relaxed. The couple resided temporarily in the Anichkov Palace, foregoing a conventional honeymoon. Whatever his shortcomings as a ruler, Nicholas became a devoted if uxorious husband. To all outward appearances the marriage was a supremely happy one, and its fertility was amply demonstrated in due course by the birth of four daughters and a son.

The dowager empress retained a strong emotional hold on Nicholas and became his chief political adviser, at the same time tactfully declining to assume any degree of power in her own right. Her relations with her daughter-in-law, Alexandra Fyodorovna (Alix's new Russian name), were less harmonious, partly because of a personality clash and partly because royal protocol required precedence for the senior empress. Although the two women managed to preserve the amenities, Nicholas, to his chagrin, was sometimes torn between loyalty to his mother and deference to his wife.

In adjusting to the role of autocratic ruler, Nicholas proceeded cautiously, still hesitant and insecure but gradually learning to accept his responsibilities. He continued to suffer from a commonplace but persistent malady—a nervous stomach—at military reviews and other state occasions, but he eventually managed to overcome these distressing emotional symptoms. "Society"—that is the educated public—was customarily disposed toward optimism at the accession of a new ruler and waited anxiously for the signs and portents that would surely foreshadow a "progressive" resign. Nicholas' proclamation announcing his accession to the throne was carefully nonpolitical, yet it was considered "softer and less autocratic" than the pronouncements of Alexander III.[1] Bolder spirits among the public alluded to the possibility of a legislative assembly, the "crowning of the edifice," as it had become known during the great reforms of Alexander II in the 1860s. Nicholas himself offered few clues as to his political course and ideological convictions. Largely out of filial loyalty, he retained almost all of his father's ministers and advisers. One exception, General Yosif Gurko, the governor-general of Warsaw, was dismissed because of a "request" to the tsar that verged on an ultimatum. This action, coupled with an imperial reception for a delegation of Polish nobles, aroused unwarranted expectations that Alexander III's policy of Russification would be moderated. Another replacement, that of Apollon Krivoshein, the minister of transportation, was prompted by the appearance of financial impropriety.

The liberal press and a few public organizations, most notably zemstvo assemblies representing local rural government, openly advocated reform. In an address of welcome the "radical" Tver zemstvo respectfully proposed something akin to a constitutional regime. Drafted by Fyodor Rodichev, Ivan Petrunkevich, and other liberals, the document angered Nicholas, and he retaliated by ordering reprimands or more strigent punishment for those involved.[2] But a public rebuke revealing the depth of Nicholas' hostility to these gently worded promptings was reserved for his reception of noble and zemstvo representatives at the Winter Palace on January 17, 1895. He confessed to a "terrible fit of nervousness" beforehand. Regaining his composure but still ill at ease and speaking from a prepared text, he referred to zemstvo meetings "lured by senseless dreams" regarding participation in governmental affairs. "Let all know," he declared, "that while devoting all My energies to the good of the people, I shall safeguard the principle of autocracy just as firmly and steadfastly as did My unforgettable late Father."[3] The "manifesto" was brusque and gratuitously insulting, for the assembled guests had made no political demands and had gathered at the sovereign's invitation. The ill-chosen phrase, "senseless dreams," reverberated throughout the empire and did much to alienate the politically sophisticated.

The rumor flourished, never to be confirmed, that the speech had been drafted by Pobedonostsev, the supposed evil genius of the previous reign who retained his post as director of the Holy Synod. He firmly denied it: "I would never have expressed myself in such crude terms. My advice was to say nothing except commonplaces . . . and the Emperor had promised to confine himself to the obvious. I was amazed as anybody else when I heard that evening what had taken place in the Winter Palace, amazed— and horrified!" The empress herself, he claimed, had put Nicholas up to it. "She knows nothing. But she thinks she knows everything, and above all else she is pursued by the idea that the Emperor does not assert himself sufficiently, that he is not given all she thinks he ought to receive. She is more autocratic than Peter the Great, and perhaps as cruel as Ivan the Terrible. Hers is the small mind that believes it harbours a great intelligence!"[4] Whatever the circumstances, there is no reason to doubt that the speech clearly stated the sovereign's political intentions and the sincerity of his belief in the efficacy of autocratic rule.

A stinging reply, "An Open Letter to Nicholas II," appeared in hectographed form a few days later, reaching a wide audience through copies mailed to zemstvo chairmen, editors, and other opinion molders. Its author, anonymous at the time, was Pyotr Struve,[5] a prominent young Marxist, who warned that the government was "digging its own grave." "You have yourself, by your words and your conduct," he admonished the tsar, "set the public a question, the mere putting of which clearly and openly already constitutes a terrible menace to autocracy. . . . You have begun the struggle, and the struggle will not be long in coming."[6] Georgi Plekhanov, the émigré founder of Russian Marxism, sent a copy to Friedrich Engels, the venerable custodian of Marx's legacy, and commented in a letter that the "young idiot in the Winter Palace has rendered a great service to the revolutionary party by his speech."[7] But neither professional revolutionaries nor zemstvo activists presented a serious challenge to entrenched authority.

A more experienced and perspicacious monarch than Nicholas might well have been excused for complacency about the state of the empire. Russia was at peace, and no discernible adversary threatened the homeland or the balance of international power. Domestic stability prevailed despite peasant grievances, a small but increasingly restless working class, nationalist aspirations among the non-Russian minorities, and mounting political dissatisfaction among professionals and the intelligentsia.

Surrounded by servile courtiers and ministers hardly less obsequious, Nicholas continued to lead a sheltered and relatively placid life, though burdened with duties and functions new to his experience. Indeed, he would have been a paragon of statesmanship had he sensed the dynamic yet subtle changes that would soon render obsolete his familiar world of royal absolutism, abject loyalty to the throne, and static social order. To maintain that Russia had become an affluent society by 1895 would be preposterous. But it had reached a stage of economic development that permitted others besides the nobility and the bureaucratic elite to flourish well above the subsistence level. Generally characterized by status, education, leisure, and a comfortable standard of living, this essentially bourgeois class, to use the Marxist cliché, chafed at the restraints of an anachronistic and "feudal" policy. Even the traditional apathy and insularity of the peasantry was beginning to erode, not because the "idiocy of rural life" had radically altered but because economic pressure—most notably overpopulation and a shortage of fertile land—was sabotaging the pattern of agrarian society.

If Nicholas remained oblivious to the transformation of the "old" Russia and the presumed need for reform that had so swiftly estranged his critics, he did not entirely fit the stereotype of a simpleminded reactionary so confidently purveyed by the radical intelligentsia. His self-image was that of an accessible and compassionate monarch, a protector of the commonweal from enemies both foreign and domestic, a devout champion of the Orthodox faith, and an enlightened ruler who would bring justice, prosperity, and tranquility to his subjects. These assumptions may have been self-serving and profoundly mistaken, but they were heartfelt convictions that were shared, in a somewhat inchoate fashion, by a majority of the population. Admittedly capable of immense self-deception, a flaw in human nature that appears to afflict rulers more commonly than the ruled, Nicholas nevertheless took pride in his calling. He saw himself as an honorable man of principle and would have bridled at any accusation of hypocrisy or deceit. Ironically, no one contributed more to the destruction of that image than Nicholas himself, even allowing for the argument that an autocrat too can be a prisoner of events. Yet, quite aside from the obvious verdict that his good intentions seemed almost invariably to lead to bad results, he did not deliberately set out to estrange "society" or stubbornly to resist the march of "progress."

Nicholas' humanitarian and benevolent instincts were nowhere more pronounced than in his attempts to further education, particularly at the elementary level, where the war against illiteracy had to be waged. Informed that only half the eligible children in St. Petersburg were receiving instruction, he commented, "And this in the capital of Russia!"[8] That he placed so much emphasis on education cannot be reconciled with the views of a hopeless reactionary. Had he been an incorrigible die-hard he would likely have echoed the sentiments of the Russian ideologue who allegedly complained with cynical logic, "To scatter schools everywhere and fill them with embittered blockheads is like feeding people stones instead of bread."[9]

The misery and hardships of his people, whether peasants or nobles, also touched Nicholas, though how deeply is a matter of conjecture. Other than through government reports, he had virtually no direct knowledge of their sufferings. Except in cases of antigovernment disorders and revolutionary agitation, which he almost invariably proposed to punish with ruthless severity, he was kind-hearted, even sentimental, and genuinely concerned about public welfare. He earnestly desired better medical services and improved roads, and he was delighted, projecting his own piety, when informed of the religious zeal of the populace. He could less readily identify with complaints about bureaucratic fraud and mismanagement or with the alien world of commerce, industry, and finance. Indifferent and ill informed as to the growth and complexity of Russian capitalism, he nonetheless retained the services of Sergei Witte, the redoubtable minister of finance whose "system" sought to overcome the historic deficiencies of a backward industrial economy. That he recognized Witte's ability and endured his blunt manner and irritating conduct so long despite profound temperamental differences testifies to his patience and forbearance, though not necessarily his confidence in or approval of his willful subordinate.

If a true reactionary could be found among Nicholas' ministers and confidants, it was Pobedonostsev, who soon discovered that his former charge had little use for his opinions and advice except in matters dealing with the Church. But the Pobedonostsev "legend" sustained itself until his forced retirement in 1905. In theory the government's most important official was the minister of the interior; Ivan Durnovo, a bureaucratic nullity who had served in that capacity since 1889, was "promoted" to head the Committee of Ministers in October 1895. He was replaced by the well-meaning and vaguely liberal Ivan Goremykin, whom an associate depicted as clever, egotistical, and honest but placid and "incurably lazy."[10] These latter qualities secured sardonic references to "His High Indifference" among his colleagues. Another major post, that of foreign minister, witnessed a rapid turnover, with its first three occupants, Nikolai Giers, Prince Aleksei Lobanov-Rostovsky, and Mikhail Muravyov, dying in office. Giers had presided at least nominally over the negotiations leading to the secret Franco-Russian alliance concluded not long before Alexander III's death. Nicholas himself, disregarding his woeful lack of expertise in diplomatic matters, attempted in some degree to become his own foreign minister, ultimately with disastrous results. Witte too sought to aggrandize his governmental "empire" and competed quite successfully for nearly a decade with the legitimate foreign ministry.

Nicholas and Alexandra moved from their cramped quarters in St. Petersburg to Tsarskoe Selo (literally the "Tsar's Village") in the late summer of 1895. About fifteen miles south of the capital, the "village" consisted mainly of a vast and splendid estate with two palaces, artificial lakes, formal parks and gardens, fountains and statues, and groves of imposing trees. The royal couple resided in the Alexander Palace, the smaller of the two ornate structures built in the eighteenth century. Their personal quarters were refurnished in the heavy Victorian style of the day. Nicholas, as conscientious an administrator as his father, pored over state papers and received official callers in the privacy of his study. Ministers normally made weekly reports in person dressed in the "uniform" of their office, "a dark blue swallow-tail coat with gilt or silver buttons, a white tie and the insignia of the highest Russian Order they possessed."[11] His grand ducal relatives, especially the formidable brothers of Alexander III, were frequent visitors, with their intimidating manner and dogmatic advice. Nicholas, so his cousin claimed with pardonable exaggeration, "spent the first ten years of his reign sitting behind a massive desk in the palace and listening with near-awe to the well-rehearsed bellowing of his towering uncles. He dreaded to be left alone with them."[12] Nor were they the only offenders. According to General Pyotr Vannovsky, the war minister, Nicholas took advice from all comers: "grandparents, aunts, mama and anyone else; he is young and accepts the view of the last person to whom he talks."[13]

The imperial court and household employed a veritable army of officials, soldiers, retainers, and servants. Count Illarion Vorontsov-Dashkov, a distinguished aristocrat who had served in the Russo-Turkish War, presided over the ceremonial aspects of court life as chief minister until his forced resignation in 1897, reputedly at the insistence of Alexandra. Petty intrigue became a way of life among the imperial courtiers. Devoid of political sophistication, they craved only the perquisites of a monarch's favor—"a promotion at Christmas, a decoration on the Emperor's birthday, or a raise in salary when Easter came round."[14] With a huge staff theoretically at his beck and call, Nicholas declined to fill the post of personal secretary. The position might seem obvious and indispensable, but it infringed on his privacy and his conception of autocratic power. Even for purely family matters, such as acknowledging routine messages, he declined assistance. Nor would he permit the installation of a telephone in his study, preferring to read and annotate government reports or to render his judgment in brief memoranda. Only for drafting speeches and documents of a more general nature did he prove willing to delegate some of his authority.

Nicholas' idiosyncratic insistence upon safeguarding his autocratic privileges illustrated the irony of his position. Custom dictated that as supreme ruler he preside over the business of the state no matter how petty and inconsequential. Mired in the minutiae of day-to-day affairs, he received endless reports and recommendations that required resolution at the apex of power. Most decisions should have been made at a subordinate level. Yet the weight of tradition—and Nicholas' own sense of duty, grafted to his notion of royal authority—severely hampered his effectiveness as monarch and undermined the very power that he sought to uphold. The trivia of routine business threatened to drain the vitality if not the essence of absolute monarchy. On occasion he rebelled, or at least protested, against his "subservience" to the administrative machinery. But in the last analysis, he was, if not precisely a willing prisoner, unable and perhaps unwilling to sever the ambivalent ties that bound him to the dynastic absolutism of his predecessors.

The upkeep of Tsarskoe Selo and countless other obligations of the ruling sovereign required enormous financial resources. Nicholas was a wealthy man by conventional standards, but his expenses seemed invariably to outstrip his income. The government provided handsomely for the royal family, an annual appropriation of eleven million gold rubles ($5,500,000 at the official rate of exchange). Most of the imperial estates, including farms, forests, orchards, vineyards, and fisheries, had been acquired by Catherine II in the eighteenth century. Their intrinsic value was enormous, but mismanagement and graft is said to have reduced the yearly income to hardly more than two million dollars. Bank deposits in England and Germany of over a hundred million drew relatively modest interest, while frozen assets of rare diamonds and other jewels were valued at some eighty million. Altogether the tsar could expect annual revenues of ten to twelve million dollars. The maintenance of seven palaces and their fifteen thousand employees; support for five imperial theaters, the Academy of Arts, and the Academy of Sciences; generous yearly stipends to the grand dukes and duchesses; upkeep of hospitals, orphanages, and other state institutions; and endless demands for charitable contributions all conspired to drain the royal purse.[15] Less frugal than his father, Nicholas was nonetheless wary of frivolous expenditures. He once scolded his mother for interceding on behalf of a needy princess: "It would be a fine state of affairs indeed at the Treasury if, in Witte's absence (he is at present on a holiday) I were to give a million to one, two million to another, etc. All that has been accumulated—and what forms one of the most brilliant pages in the history of dear Papa's reign is the sound condition of our finances—would be destroyed in the course of a few years!"[16]

On New Year's Day of 1896 the royal family returned to the capital to inaugurate the winter social season. The interminable round of formal dances, banquets, and theater parties were essentially a product of duty and custom, since Nicholas and Alexandra were not by nature gregarious and convivial hosts. The festivities ended on the Sunday before Lent. By this time the lavish preparations for the tsar's coronation, traditionally held in Moscow, were being rapidly completed. Count Vorontsov-Dashkov, who had presided over the crowning of Alexander III, was again in charge, marshalling his forces in the exacting details of the royal celebration. Muscovites were encouraged to decorate and refurbish their city as thousands of visiting officials and dignitaries, in addition to more humble folk, arrived for the grandiose occasion. Although the rich and well born were overly represented in the formal agenda, ordinary citizens were not ignored: they were invited to a special fête, with food, drink, entertainment, and souvenir gifts from the sovereign. The opulent splendor that prevailed at government expense, contrasting so sharply with the oppressive poverty of the private sector, did not go unheeded by critics of the regime. But their grumblings received no public notice of any consequence, and the festive crowds and the air of pomp and pageantry offered reassuring "evidence" to those seeking it that the tsar and people shared a sense of solidarity and well-being.

The coronation ritual itself took place on May 14 in Uspensky Cathedral within the walls of the Kremlin. The metropolitans of St. Petersburg and Moscow, the senior prelates of the empire, presided over the resplendent and lengthy ceremony. Two minor incidents marred its solemnity. An intruder, "a man of very dark complexion, dressed in a suit of shepherd's plaid, with a black felt hat," advanced well into the church before the police seized him and hustled him off.[17] The other, equally trivial but potentially an evil omen to the superstitious, occurred when a jeweled chain from the Order of St. Andrew fell to the floor as Nicholas proceeded to the altar steps. Only those nearby noticed the mishaps, and they were pledged to secrecy to avoid public concern.[18]

On May 18 the long awaited popular reception took place at Khodynka Field on the city's outskirts. For days the *narod*, or common people, mostly peasants, had gathered on the vast plain. By early morning of the appointed day the crowd, estimated at over half a million, grew restless. Many were hungry and thirsty, anticipating the imperial largesse that promised food and kegs of *kvass* (a fermented beverage) to fill the engraved mugs soon to be distributed. Security measures were lax, with only a police detachment of some sixty men on hand. The officer in charge, alarmed by the size and mood of the crowd, sent urgent requests for reinforcements; by 6 A.M., only a squadron of Cossacks had responded. Row on row of wooden booths were piled high with the promised souvenirs and provisions.

Officials on the scene apparently made the fateful decision to hand out the gifts immediately rather than to wait until 10 A.M., the designated hour. Those in the rear pushed forward to receive their share, and within seconds a wild stampede swept aside the token force of police and mounted Cossacks. Military exercises had creased the terrain with trenches and other irregularities that proved fatal to hundreds who lost their footing and were trampled by the surging mob. Some of the Cossacks and their horses were allegedly "torn limb from limb" and "stamped into jelly." The officer in charge was said to have had "both arms torn from his body." With the remorseless power of an avalanche the human tide swept on, sustained by anonymous thousands unaware of the grisly scene that lay ahead. Within a few minutes, probably ten to fifteen at most, the frenzied rush had spent itself, and the maimed, the dead, and the dying littered the field as if a major battle had been fought.

Medical assistance was slow and haphazard. An unknown number of ambulatory victims were presumably cared for by friends or relatives. The more seriously injured were taken to hospitals, while carts and wagons, with bodies stacked like cordwood, transported the dead to mortuaries or to the Vagankovskoe Cemetery for mass burial. Official statistics placed the number of fatalities at 1,429, the injured in the thousands. Unofficial estimates were considerably higher, though the figure of four to five thousand dead is probably exaggerated.

Nicholas was informed of the tragedy without undue delay, but it is possible that the first reports sought to minimize the seriousness of the affair. In the afternoon he attended festivities adjacent to Khodynka, reputedly with bodies still piled under the reviewing stand, but gave no indication that he knew what had transpired. The full import of the disaster may not have been conveyed to him until after his public appearance. His impulsive reaction was to cancel the remaining ceremonies, other than to honor the dead, and to retire to a monastery for a period of mourning. But his uncles and various officials argued persuasively that a sovereign's duty should override personal feelings. Accepting their counsel, he attended the formal ball given that evening by the French ambassador, an important state occasion because of the Franco-Russian alliance. He also fulfilled other social obligations prescribed by the coronation schedule, climaxed by a great military review at Khodynka just eight days after the disaster. But he demonstrated his concern by attending services for the dead and by visiting injured patients in the hospitals. Financial help, including modest pensions, provided vital economic security to the victims or to their families, and he founded an orphanage for the children who had been left homeless.

The circumstances of the tragedy were probed by several investigating committees. The most thorough and "official," that chaired by Count Konstantin Pahlen, a member of the State Council, blamed Grand Duke Sergei Aleksandrovich, the governor-general of Moscow, and Vorontsov-Dashkov for their failure to arrange adequate crowd control. A jurisdictional conflict between the two, both jealous of their authority, had set the stage for the catastrophe. Nicholas declined to punish them, even with a reprimand, for the grand duke was one of his forbidding uncles and Vorontsov-Dashkov had become a friend and confidant. The Moscow police chief emerged as the principal scapegoat; he was dismissed, albeit with a handsome pension.[19]

The repercussions of the affair are difficult to assess. No popular outcry arose, and there was surprisingly little public criticism. Despite this seeming apathy there is evidence that "society," even political moderates, regarded the debacle as additional confirmation of the regime's incompetence and the tsar's callous indifference to the fate of his subjects. The latter charge is of course unjust: weakness and poor judgment should not have been taken for lack of compassion. Nor was Nicholas unmarked by the experience. His attitude of resigned fatalism, already pronounced, was accentuated. So too was a streak of stubbornness, heretofore concealed by timidity, uncertainty, and an amiability that sought to placate his mother, his uncles, and the court entourage. A new-found sense of authority appears to date from the Khodynka episode. Before the year was out he confronted one of his officious uncles, the Grand Duke Vladimir Aleksandrovich, who had disregarded instructions on military appointments. "The whole fault," he wrote, "lies in my stupid kindness. With the sole wish to avoid quarrels that spoil family relations, I give in again and again, until I am finally made the fool, without will power and without character. Now I do not simply ask, I command you to carry out my *previously expressed will.*"[20]

For much of the remainder of the year Nicholas performed basically ceremonial functions. The first of his post-coronation appearances took place in Nizhny Novgorod, at a great Exposition of Trade and Industry designed by Witte to impress the world with Russia's economic progress. The exhibits may well have demonstrated "spiritual and material growth" and cause for "patriotic joy," as Witte put it, but attendance remained sparse until popular entertainment was provided, adding a note of frivolity to the otherwise austere exposition halls. Nicholas and Alexandra toured the exhibition on July 17–20. Their initial visit was something of a fiasco because a violent thunderstorm flooded the grounds and "hailstones as large as pigeon eggs" smashed the glass in a number of pavilions. Witte claimed great success for his project. Yet its excessive cost and a pronounced lack of public enthusiasm, either for the exhibition or for the concept of industrialization, cast doubt on the popularity if not the wisdom of the finance minister's economic policy.[21]

Nicholas visited Emperor Franz Joseph in Vienna on August 15–17, largely as a courtesy call, for the two sovereigns had no serious political business. The opportunity arose, however, for the foreign minister, Lobanov-Rostovsky, who accompanied Nicholas, to begin negotiations with his Austrian counterpart, Count Agenor Goluchowski, that eventually led to an agreement on the Balkans. Unfortunately for Lobanov and the continuity of Russian diplomacy, he died suddenly on the imperial train as Nicholas returned home for the dedication of the Cathedral of St. Vladimir in Kiev.

Later in the month the new monarch paid his respects to his temperamental cousin, William II, at Breslau, where the German army was conducting maneuvers. The kaiser, who could flatter Nicholas outrageously, had already bombarded him with patronizing letters (in English) seeking, among other stratagems, to spur "Nicky's" ambitions in East Asia at the expense of Russian involvement in European and Middle Eastern affairs. Weakening the Franco-Russian alliance had become William's top priority, and he urged Nicholas to "keep those damned [French] rascals in order and make them sit still."[22] Nicholas successfully resisted the kaiser's blandishments, at least in Breslau, and went on to Denmark for a family visit.

A September journey to Scotland, where Queen Victoria presided at Balmoral Castle, was also planned as a family affair. But politics intruded in the form of Lord Salisbury, the prime minister and foreign secretary, who had two lengthy conversations with Nicholas. Also, the queen intervened about the situation in Turkey, where "affairs were very critical and some catastrophe was dreaded."[23] Just a month before, such a catastrophe had indeed occurred, a massacre of the Armenian population in Constantinople that pricked the moral conscience of Western public opinion without, however, provoking governmental action. Salisbury was less concerned with Turkish atrocities than with restoring some measure of harmony to Anglo-Russian relations. He considered the emperor "conciliatory, straightforward and honest" but of course "purely Russian in his views." Although their talks ranged over a broad spectrum of foreign policy issues, Turkey and its fate remained the focal point. Nicholas denied any territorial ambitions but upheld Russia's traditional goal of controlling the straits of the Bosphorus and Dardanelles: they were "the door to the room in which he lived, and he insisted he must have the key of that door." Salisbury hinted, bordering on indiscretion, that Britain's long-standing opposition might be withdrawn if, in conjunction with the other European powers, a suitable "arrangement" could be made. Presumably such a solution would involve territorial compensation at Turkey's expense. Surprisingly, Nicholas' reaction was at best lukewarm. He distrusted a revived "concert of Europe" that might again hand over the key to Russia's back door to its enemies. Nor did he relish Salisbury's idea that the sultan should be forced to accept reforms to avoid the imminent collapse of his empire.[24] On that point the callow young monarch proved a better prophet than the queen's illustrious minister, for Turkey, if not precisely a flourishing political enterprise, managed to retain its sovereignty and independence.

The "Russian occupation" strained Balmoral's accommodations to the utmost. Four laundry maids had to share a single bed, and "the footmen's quarters were as packed as the hold of a slave ship." But on his departure Nicholas presented the master of the household with a thousand pounds to be distributed among the servants. "Such Oriental munificence more than compensated for a few days' overcrowding."[25]

A stiff gale was blowing as the *Polar Star*, one of the imperial yachts, conveyed the royal party from Plymouth to Cherbourg. A relatively experienced sailor, Nicholas suffered less acutely from seasickness than his wife and his infant daughter, the Grand Duchess Olga. In France the reception exceeded all expectations in its warmth and exuberance. An absolute monarch visiting a young republic, particularly one with an unrivalled revolutionary tradition, hardly seemed a congenial match but the national interest, as interpreted by most Frenchmen and their chosen leaders, demanded such a welcome, and patriotism momentarily superseded devotion to republican principles. Nicholas had made it clear before his arrival, however, that he deplored manifestations of anti-German sentiment. His hosts did their best to dampen the ardor of revanchists still affronted by the humiliation of Prussia's victory over Napoleonic France in 1871. Nicholas had his customary "fit of nerves" before reaching Paris but soon recovered and thoroughly enjoyed the numerous public and private events arranged in his honor. He was especially touched by the ceremony that laid the foundation stone for a bridge across the Seine named in his father's memory. Aside from viewing the historical and cultural treasures of Paris, he toured Versailles and concluded his visit with a military review in Chalons. Political discussions were held to a minimum, but Foreign Minister Gabriel Hanotaux brought up the perennial Turkish question and gained Nicholas' agreement to Russian participation in a scheme by the European powers to exert greater control over Turkey's financial affairs.

From Chalons the royal family departed by train for Darmstadt, where Alexandra was reunited with her relatives and Nicholas had the satisfaction of a two-week respite from official duties. A host of problems, both foreign and domestic, awaited his return to Russia in October 1896.

3

Reform and Reaction

As the second anniversary of his reign approached, Nicholas II had grown accustomed to the privileges and obligations of his exalted rank. At the same time he lacked the inner serenity and self-assurance that should have accompanied a healthy ego. Tasting the aphrodisiac of unlimited power, sanctioned by a naive belief in his divine right to the throne, he nevertheless failed to set a steady course for the ship of state. As Aleksandr Polovtsov, a member of the State Council, gloomily observed a few years later, "The young tsar is more and more contemptuous of the organs of his authority, and begins to believe in the efficacious force of his own autocratic power."[1] In short, Nicholas reigned but did not rule, at least in the pragmatic sense of providing effective and knowledgeable leadership. The political vacuum thus created was filled by a kaleidoscope of ministers and advisers, all competing for the tsar's attention and favor.

The one stable element in this mélange of administrative rivalry was Sergei Witte. The finance minister, whose consuming passion to "modernize" Russia anticipated by several decades his Soviet successors, possessed the "arrogance and the humility of greatness."[2] Devious and energetic, brusque and unpolished, he never acquired the knack of treating his royal master with the tact and deference of an accomplished courtier. He "would sometimes allow emphasis to degenerate into vehemence, reinforce his arguments with resonant blows of his fist on the table, and raise his voice till it could be heard in the adjoining room."[3] But the inexperienced emperor, at first overawed by the obvious ability and commanding presence of his minister, tacitly accepted the economic program—and much of the foreign policy—that Witte so relentlessly pursued. Railroads, Witte's speciality, were to be the stimulus of Russia's new industrial expansion. The great Trans-Siberian line was well under way, though it met construction delays caused by natural disasters and staggering engineering difficulties, and deficient financing seemed to place the whole project in jeopardy. By the turn of the century the rail network, about two-thirds government-owned, had grown to nearly thirty-three thousand miles, an impressive gain from the 21,450 completed by 1894. In a spinoff effect, the production of the basic industrial commodities—iron, steel, and coal—rose dramatically, providing impetus to other sectors of the economy. To shelter the new industrial enterprises from foreign competition, tariff barriers were erected that aroused the ire of agrarian interests alarmed by the high price of farm machinery and equipment.

By providing a favorable investment climate Witte sought to establish a sound currency, ensure a surplus of exports over imports, and balance the national budget. He was able to secure foreign loans, chiefly from French banking houses, but his major financial reform involved the introduction of the gold standard. Proceeding cautiously, he first accumulated a gold reserve, a task that his predecessor had begun, and then by a series of administrative measures he discouraged speculation in paper rubles. Deciding upon monetary devaluation, he pegged the old ruble at two-thirds the value of the new gold ruble. Technical difficulties were surmounted by the spring of 1896, but a storm of criticism arose when the plan was announced, and the reform suddenly became a political issue. The government's Finance Committee approved; the State Council, concerned by the depressed condition of agriculture, objected. As the matter dragged on and Russia's credit position appeared to be endangered, Witte called upon the tsar to employ his autocratic prerogative. Nicholas responded forthrightly by convening a special session of the Finance Committee, which he himself chaired, on January 2, 1897, and the necessary order for gold coinage was issued, implemented by an imperial decree the next day. The indignant State Council registered a strong and even insulting protest, if the recollections of Polovtsov are accurate.[4] In retrospect, Witte's monetary reform may have been the most successful of his economic projects. Yet a price had to be paid for the gold reserve that accumulated in the treasury vaults: oppressive taxes, forced exports, and lowered living standards. "The Russian peasant," Witte's biographer concluded (alluding to a famous campaign speech in Chicago the year before), "could complain even more justly than the American farmer in these years that he was being crucified on the cross of gold for the benefit of bankers and industrialists and for the prestige of his country."[5]

By the close of the century Witte had achieved the pinnacle of his career as finance minister. An imperial rescript in February 1899 praised his work, and on January 1, 1900, he was elevated to the second-highest rank in the bureaucratic hierarchy. His "veritable kingdom," supposedly a "State within a State,"[6] flourished with no apparent obstacle to further accretions of power and influence. But even then there were signs and portents of future adversity. His policy of peaceful imperialism in East Asia soon fell athwart the sovereign's adventurist mood. His sanguine forecast of Russian industrial progress failed to materialize; indeed, a serious downturn in production by 1901 demonstrated flaws in his "system." The persistent crisis in agriculture, an area in which his competence could be questioned, became more acute. Witte, sensing his exposed position, shifted his front. Helpless to alter the somber trend of Russo-Japanese relations and unable to staunch the hemorrhaging of Russia's industrial base, he turned his attention to the needs of agriculture.

The problems associated with Russian poverty and backwardness, the legacy of an overwhelmingly peasant society, had not suddenly arisen in the Witte era. Nor did every facet of the finance minister's program invariably worsen the plight of the *muzhik* and of the agrarian sector. Somewhat belatedly Witte discovered that the economy could not be neatly compartmentalized and that industry would be unable to prosper in isolation from agriculture. He emerged as a strong advocate of the peasant, supporting measures to improve not only his well-being but also his legal, social, and educational status. Failure to act, he warned Nicholas as early as 1898, invited peasant disorder that might not be confined to the rural masses. He advised a top-level conference on agrarian affairs. Nicholas temporized, perhaps swayed by the contrary views of Minister of Interior Goremykin. At length, in March 1899 he broadened the scope of the inquiry by calling a special ministerial conference at which he presided in person. The discussion ranged over the whole Witte "system," and the finance minister had his say, admitting that his tariff policy could not long be sustained, "because high prices inevitably follow from it and the masses grow poorer while a few individuals grow rich."[7] Nicholas, in a published statement, formally endorsed Witte's agenda but in bland terms that could not have given his minister much satisfaction.

Witte again sought to enlist Nicholas' support in a thoughtful memorandum submitted in February 1900. He laced his plea for renewed industrial development with patriotic phrases, no doubt in the hope that while statistics and hard economic facts might fail, an appeal based on Russia's precarious role as a great power in the international arena might have the desired emotional impact. He ventured to suggest that leadership from the throne would be indispensable: "Only the sovereign master of the fate of the Empire, in his love for his humble and devout people, can draw up the bright guiding views which will lead to the common goal and inwardly harmonize all activities of the central and local government agencies." The ministry of finance would of course coordinate the government's effort.[8] If Nicholas bothered to read the report, he did not respond in other than a perfunctory manner. Respectful flattery and allusions to national pride could well have attracted his attention, but economic theory was not his forte, and he began to heed the voices of tradition who insinuated that Witte stood for alien and radical methods contrary to the will of God and his anointed tool, the supreme autocrat. As a pro-monarchist newspaper editor complained, "The Sovereign listens only to God, and only from God does he take advice, but because God is invisible he takes advice from everyone he meets: from his wife, from his mother, from his stomach . . . and accepts all this as an order from God."[9] Ironically, Witte too believed in the principle of autocracy, not as a force for reaction but as a means of propelling Russian society into the mainstream of Western civilization. It was with disappointment and something akin to despair that he was ultimately obliged to recognize that Nicholas could not properly fill his designated role.

Meanwhile Witte competed successfully in the labyrinthine intrigue of bureaucratic politics. But he had no recourse against the petty gossip and vicious rumors that slandered him and even traduced his wife with "revelations" about supposed indiscretions in the past. These personal attacks eroded his affability, and he did not invariably resist the temptations of excessive power. Always a wily politician, he formed an expedient and somewhat exotic alliance with Pobedonostsev. He likewise cultivated the dowager empress, securing a powerful ally at court. His maneuvers in opposing Goremykin's scheme to extend the zemstvo system beyond the central provinces led to his rival's downfall in October 1899.

The new minister of the interior, Dmitri Sipyagin,[10] was a conservative nobleman with few independent views who had become a personal friend of Witte's. Harmony between the competing domains of Finance and Interior was largely restored. Notwithstanding his mediocrity, both intellectual and administrative, Sipyagin was credited with what Witte termed "feminine intuition." He traveled widely through the empire in 1900; though he took no opportunity to observe the seamier aspects of Russian life, he astonished his hosts by maintaining that there was something radically wrong and that revolution was imminent. The nature of that "something" continued to elude him, however, and he offered no panacea other than rigid adherence to the tradition of absolute monarchy. Witte's financial generosity allowed Sipyagin to erect a monument to himself, the Fontanka Palace, as his official residence. His great ambition, to give a dinner party for the tsar, was frustrated by a whim of fate. On April 2, 1902, the day before the anticipated royal visit, he was shot and fatally wounded by Stefan Balmashov, a Socialist Revolutionary terrorist. An act of violence that was to be repeated many times against government officials, the murder represented to the extreme radicals a legitimate form of protest against a tyrannical regime. ("We consider it not just our right, but even our sacred duty," the terrorists proclaimed, "to avenge the blood of the people with the blood of the oppressors.") The assassin was eventually hanged, the first political execution of Nicholas' reign.[11]

Sipyagin left a diary that apparently depicted Nicholas in unflattering terms (privately he told Witte "with deep sorrow that one could not rely on the Emperor, that he was treacherous and untruthful"). Government officials sorted out his papers, and the diary was "borrowed" for the sovereign's perusal. It was returned to the widow in due course, but a portion had "disappeared." Presumably Nicholas himself had destroyed parts of the censorious document.[12]

The appointment of Vyacheslav Plehve to succeed Sipyagin was a blow to Witte, for the two had already conceived a mutual dislike. An experienced bureaucrat who had served as a police official under Alexander III, Plehve was, as even Witte conceded, "very intelligent, hard-working, business-like." Although few questioned his ability, his detractors accused him of overweening ambition and cynical opportunism. They ridiculed him as "a superlative clerk," and Pobedonostsev sourly observed to Nicholas that Plehve was "a scoundrel." (But then, as the old curmudgeon complained, "Who is not a scoundrel nowadays?" He customarily derided virtually all ministers as "scoundrels," "idiots," and "fools.") Pyotr Orzhevsky, an astringent colleague of Plehve's, gained minor renown for his bon mot that "even a dead fish can go with the current." None of these derogatory quips, however, nearly equalled the notoriety of Plehve's own phrase, ascribed to him by Witte, that Russia needed "a little victorious war to stem the tide of revolution."[13]

That Nicholas deliberately chose Plehve to help undermine Witte's "kingdom" appears unlikely. Angered by the assassination, he sought a "hardliner" who would crack down on civil disobedience. His stern mood was also reflected shortly afterward by the replacement of the "liberal" minister of education, Pyotr Vannovsky, by the "conservative" Grigory Zenger. Plehve faced a demanding assignment and set about it with a vigor and resolution that would have bewildered his predecessor. "I have been brought to the ministry of interior as a strong man," he confided to the French ambassador. "If I manifest the slightest hesitation in repression, I shall lose my *raison d'être*."[14] Aside from the revival of terrorism, he faced other serious troubles: demonstrations by students and factory workers, serious disorders in Finland, and most alarming of all, peasant revolts in the Ukraine. By the time Plehve took office, local Ukrainian authorities had quelled the rural disturbances; the interior minister's formal report prompted Nicholas to award the prestigious Order of St. Vladimir to the governor of Kharkov Province for his brutal efficiency and to dismiss the governor of Poltava Province for his sluggish performance.

Nicholas derived great pride and satisfaction from his supposedly close relationship with the peasantry. The historic and indissoluble bond between the "dark people" and the "little father" in St. Petersburg had become an article of faith in court circles and among Slavophile ideologists. That it had also acquired a mystique of its own and constituted a self-congratulatory rationale for autocratic rule escaped the notice of the sovereign and his apologists. Although by no means oblivious to the agrarian crisis, he knew almost nothing, at least from direct observation, about the peasants and their way of life. But neither did most urban residents, and even those radicals who professed to speak in the name of the peasant, members of the Socialist Revolutionary Party, were scarcely better informed than the rest of "society."

The men (and women) who made their living by tilling the soil should not be stereotyped, yet they tended to share the conservative insularity of their class and their rural environment. Ignorance and illiteracy, superstition and suffocating tradition, contributed to their plight, as did the burden of taxation and the redemption dues still owed because of the emancipation of the serfs in 1861. Nor did the village commune and its system of joint land tenure and strip farming offer much hope to the enterprising *muzhik* who sought more efficient methods of cultivation. In the forty years following emancipation the peasant population nearly doubled, an alarming increase that reflected better medical services (and perhaps a declining rate of infanticide) rather than a sudden spurt in fecundity. In brief, a shortage of fertile land—and higher prices for that available—coupled with a depressed grain market compelled the government to recognize that delaying tactics would no longer suffice. As for the peasants, few could ignore the grim reality of rural impoverishment in their daily lives. Nor did the landed nobility, except for a wealthy elite, necessarily enjoy the privileged status that their titles implied.

In January 1902 Nicholas finally acknowledged the problem by administrative action. Sipyagin was charged with the cumbersome duty of revising peasant legislation; he had scarcely begun his task before his assassination. A Special Commission on the Needs of Agriculture was also established under Witte's leadership. "I have appointed you chairman," Nicholas informed him, "because if you cannot do the job, nobody else can."[15] Witte proceeded with his customary efficiency and broadened the scope of the inquiry by soliciting opinion from committees of "local men." Eventually over six hundred of these bodies were formed, with some eleven thousand participants (but only 2 percent peasants), a "democratic" approach unwieldy and fraught with political implications. Some of the consultants were zemstvo members with "progressive" views, and they could not be expected to confine their discussions to agriculture alone. To ensure that their voices would be heard, zemstvo representatives convened in Moscow on May 23–25 and agreed to support a program of reform that ranged well beyond agrarian issues. Plehve, learning of the unauthorized meetings, reported them to the emperor, who reprimanded the participants and warned that further offenses would lead to their banishment from public life.[16] Despite the ill will engendered by this incident, Plehve went out of his way to conciliate the zemstvos—or at least those members not hostile to the monarchical ideal. He went so far as to enlist the sovereign in his cause. On August 30, while attending army maneuvers in Kursk Province, Nicholas assured a delegation of zemstvo leaders that they would have his "heartfelt favor" if they attended to "local economic needs" and, by implication, avoided meddling in politics.[17]

In his Kursk addresses—he also spoke to representatives of the nobility—Nicholas gave public notice that the problems of his rural subjects would have priority over the exigencies of industrial growth. His intentions received official recognition in an imperial manifesto of February 26, 1903, which had been hastily prepared by Plehve and his associates to coincide with Alexander III's birthday. Rather cynically received in bureaucratic quarters, it demonstrated that in the imperial pecking order Plehve had risen and Witte had declined. An ambivalent program emerged from the document: the government sought reform and the good will of the public while it remained fearful of drastic change that would upset vested interests and violate the principle of autocracy. As for specifics, it emphasized peasant interests and took a stand against the "constraining custom of collective responsibility." A statute soon followed that abolished the village commune's time-honored obligation for tax payments. The future of the commune itself was left in confusion. On the one hand the "inviolability of the communal organization of land ownership" was proclaimed, while on the other the desirability of establishing "means whereby individual peasants may more easily leave the commune" was given equal weight.[18]

Plehve's growing ascendancy was reconfirmed the following May when a special conference on provincial reform convened, Nicholas again assuming the chairmanship. Little was forthcoming other than a strengthening of the powers of the provincial governors, who were in essence creatures of the interior ministry. Plehve's relations with the zemstvo leaders, initially quite promising, deteriorated in mutual suspicion. Indeed, the whole spectrum of liberal opinion turned against him, less because of his policies than because he symbolized growing disenchantment with the tsarist regime. He carried an additional burden, inherent in his job but inevitably conveying a sinister image: jurisdiction over the Department of Police, including its security section, known popularly as the Okhrana. Russia, while not precisely a "police state" in the all-embracing and malevolent sense that the term later acquired, did subject its citizens to arbitrary arrest for political offenses. Yet the least attractive aspects of government "tyranny" were normally reserved for a small segment of the population: practicing revolutionaries, especially those who sought to challenge the state's authority with acts of violence.

The public could have adjusted to repression, even despotism; it could not abide vacillation and caprice. The government inspired anger and con-

tempt, seldom fear: "[Its] thunder rolled incessantly; but there was no lightning." Plehve's ambitious plans "dwindled to pettiness or evaporated into
thin air. The mountain brought forth nothing but mice."[19] Equally responsible for the government's low esteem, Polovtsov confided to his diary, was
the "unbridled license of the bureaucrats and their thoughtless fantasies,"
the "regimentation which is reaching ridiculous limits," the "arbitrary interference in every conceivable affair," and especially the "unfortunate
choice of companions by the empress, the grand dukes and duchesses, and
the choice of scoundrels surrounding them."[20] His harangue spared the
chief culprit, the emperor himself, who had acquired a bizarre assortment
of "scoundrels." They were headed by Aleksandr Bezobrazov,[21] his confidant on Far Eastern affairs, "Doctor" Philippe,[22] a French master of occult
"science," and his old mentor, Prince Meshchersky, who had renewed his
contacts at court through the good offices of Sipyagin. A well-informed
British journalist registered a similar complaint, that Nicholas would allow
"a band of casual, obscure, and dangerous men to usurp the functions of
his responsible ministers whose recommendations are ignored and whose
warnings are disregarded."[23]

That Witte's tenure lasted as long as it did surprised many observers.
His dismissal, so widely predicted, came during the summer of 1903 when
Nicholas finally acquired the courage of his convictions. The decision, according to the version circulated by Plehve, was made suddenly during a
Te Deum sung at the launching of a battleship. Nicholas told him—the
quotation may be inexact—that the "Lord put into my heart the thought
that I must not delay that which I was already persuaded to do."[24] The
blow fell on August 15 at the tsar's residence in Peterhof after Witte had
delivered one of his periodic reports. Ill at ease but speaking in kindly tones,
Nicholas expressed his concern that Witte's health had been impaired by
overwork and that he was accordingly shifting him to the chairmanship of
the Committee of Ministers. When the startled Witte grimaced, Nicholas
gratuitously explained that the "promotion" was "the very highest position
which exists in the empire." The appointment did indeed offer status and
prestige, but unfortunately it lacked the kind of political authority that he
had become accustomed to. Witte recognized immediately that he had been
cast aside, and he did not conceal his resentment. "I lost patience. So much
falsity and hypocrisy enrage me," he related in 1904. "I told the Tsar: 'I
don't understand why you play such a game with me. . . . You might just
as well have sent me to Siberia or the Caucasus.' " But that same evening
he was the grateful recipient of royal patronage, "a thick envelope containing 400,000 roubles." As for Nicholas, he breathed a figurative sigh of
relief, perhaps regretting that he had not done the stressful deed months,
even years, before.[25]

Witte later ascribed his dismissal to his rejection of the "dangerous policy" that the tsar pursued in regard to Japan. But the reasons were more

complex than differences on foreign affairs. Nicholas had never grown accustomed to Witte's overbearing manner, and he had serious doubts about Witte's loyalty to the monarchy. Plehve, among others, insinuated that the finance minister harbored, at the very least, radical ideas, and there were accusations that he was involved in a "Jewish-Masonic" conspiracy, a paranoid fantasy nurtured by extremists of the Right.[26]

A British observer who interviewed Witte not long after his dismissal noted that he "looked exhausted and much older than his 53 years." Witte defended his policy with vigor: "People accuse me of having done things too quickly. That I worked quickly is quite true, there was no time to be lost. A surgeon who perceives that a leg has to be amputated without delay does not spend three months in preparing his patient's mind for the operation. He sets to work at once and does what is required. That is what I did."[27]

Contemporaries did not view Witte's fall as evidence that his "system" had also collapsed. His replacement, Eduard Pleske, was a disciple of Witte, and it seemed not improbable that the tsar might still utilize the services of his deposed minister in some new capacity. But Witte took up his ceremonial post, isolated from the centers of power, and Pleske, ill even at the time of his appointment, was in no condition to resume the forlorn struggle for industrial expansion. No groundswell of public sentiment arose to vindicate the once-mighty favorite. Nor did a positive consensus emerge among economists, businessmen, officials, and other presumably well-informed citizens. If Witte was a prophet ahead of his time, only the judgment of posterity was to redeem him.

The tsarist scheme of government made no provision for a minister of nationalities. By default the growing restlessness of the non-Russian minorities within the empire was a problem that devolved upon the interior minister. Neither Plehve nor his predecessors conceived a nationalities policy other than the Russification program that Nicholas had inherited from his father. Whether through expediency or conviction, Plehve pandered to his sovereign's conception of an orderly and stable realm whose citizens shared equally in their rights and duties regardless of ethnic identity. The principle, while it may have been sound in theory, glossed over the reality of Russian hegemony over its "subject" peoples, together with concessions to autonomy that helped to bank the fires of nationalism. Some minorities, such as the Turkic Muslims of Central Asia, could well benefit from the "tutorial" role of the tsarist regime. Others—the Finns were the prime example—had acquired a special status within the empire and resented Russian efforts to alter that tradition in the name of equity and uniformity. However deplorable Russian domination might seem to the minorities, the concept of racial superiority, except in the special case of the Jews, played no part in official nationality policy.

Historically the Poles had been the most obstreperous of the nationalities. Superficially "Russified" after their revolt in 1863, they represented a proud and rebellious heritage, one that required the kind of tactful diplomacy that the Russian authorities for the most part disdained to employ. Nicholas demonstrated his good will by visiting Warsaw in August 1897 and by minor concessions to Polish sensibilities, including the erection of a statue in memory of Adam Mickiewicz, the great national poet. Many upper-class Poles openly advocated reconciliation with Russia, and Prince Aleksandr Imeretynsky, the urbane governor-general, seemed kindly disposed to these overtures. It therefore came as a shock to patriotic Poles when in 1899 his secret report to the tsar, stolen by revolutionaries and published in London, revealed that he had urged further limitations on Polish liberties. Much of the agitation against tsarist oppression was co-opted by competing socialist parties. Josef Pilsudski, the future leader of an independent Poland, epitomized the "national" aspect of socialism by denouncing Russia as "an Asiatic beast hidden behind a European mask."[28] Other socialists, of whom Rosa Luxemburg was preeminent, chose the Marxist path, subordinating Poland's struggle for nationhood to the overthrow of world capitalism.

Unlike the Poles, the Finns had never experienced true national independence. But the growth of Finnish nationalism had been retarded by the exemplary behavior toward them of the Russian autocrats, who since 1809 had ruled over the Finns as constitutional sovereigns with the title of grand duke. Finland, as a grand duchy, maintained virtual autonomy, including its own army and its own Diet, or legislative assembly. This unique if not wholly idyllic arrangement was placed in jeopardy in 1898 when the ministry of war, after prolonged deliberation on Russia's military security, recommended the abolition of the Finnish army and the conscription of eligible males into the Russian armed forces. An ominous portent, it was followed by the imperial appointment of Nikolai Bobrikov, a professional soldier and a determined "Russifier" as governor-general of Finland. He scorned the "vanity of a little nationality that has never played any role in history and has not enjoyed independence."[29] Bobrikov presented Nicholas with a ten-point program to "reform" the grand duchy, and the Finns were alerted to the prospect of their constitution being overridden or revoked. On February 3, 1899, an imperial manifesto, together with "fundamental statutes," upheld the right of the tsar to issue legislative decrees for the empire, including Finland, subject to advisory opinion by the Russian State Council and the Finnish Diet. The Finns were outraged, and over half a million citizens, more than a fifth of the population, signed a petition of protest. The Finnish Senate also remonstrated, respectfully but firmly, and Nicholas is said to have been moved to tears when the document was read to him. He remained adamant in his views, however, refusing to receive a Finnish delegation and rebuffing a distinguished group of foreign scholars who brought an appeal to St. Petersburg signed by over a thousand intel-

lectuals from twelve countries. "They have smeared my government," he
is reported to have complained of the petitioners. "I shall never forgive
them for that."[30]

The Finns suffered further indignities. In June 1900, after a committee
that included Bobrikov, Plehve, and Pobedonostsev had secretly worked
out the details, a manifesto declared Russian to be the language of official
business in Finland. The next year the long-pending military reform was
introduced and met passive resistance; nearly 60 percent of those eligible
evaded the first draft call. The Finnish cause found an unexpected friend
at court in the dowager empress, who drew the obvious parallels between
Finland and her own native land. Writing from Denmark on October 1,
1902, she pleaded with her son to dismiss "that evil genius" Bobrikov,
whose policy "is based on *lies* and *deceit* and leads straight to *revolution*."
Nicholas replied on October 20, grief-stricken over the death of his dog
("I must confess the whole day after it happened I never stopped crying");
he turned aside his mother's protest, predicting that in "two or three years
things will settle down there on a permanent basis." Conceding that "sedition" had begun with his own manifesto of 1899, he felt that the "common people" had been led astray by false rumors spread "from above."[31]
To Nicholas political disturbances were never a product of genuine discontent among the masses but the bitter fruit of agitators, malcontents, and
other evildoers, who for reasons unclear to him were bent on attacking
established authority.

The struggle to subdue Finnish nationalism—and to curb mounting civil
disorder—escalated once more on March 27, 1903, when an imperial rescript granted Bobrikov special emergency powers for a period of three
years. The hated "dictator" added insult to injury by further repressive
measures, and a revolutionary opposition, previously small and ineffective,
looked to more forceful means of resistance. Before the proponents of violence could strike at their oppressors, a lone assassin, Eugen Schauman,
the son of a distinguished public servant, shot and mortally wounded Bobrikov on June 3, 1904, in the Senate building in Helsinki. He then killed
himself, leaving a deferential letter to the tsar: "The method is violent, but
it is the only one. With knowledge of Your Majesty's good heart and noble
intentions I beg Your Majesty only to find out about the real state of affairs
in the Empire—Finland, Poland, the Baltic Provinces."[32]

If Nicholas failed to take the assassin's gentle admonition seriously, he
did recruit, at Plehve's suggestion, a less zealous replacement in Prince Ivan
Obolensky, the governor of Kharkov Province. No friend of civil dissent,
as his conduct during the peasant revolt had testified, Obolensky nevertheless retreated from the extremes of his predecessor. A wary truce was declared, in effect, until the turbulent events of 1905 inaugurated a new era
in the Russian empire.

As reprehensible and self-defeating as tsarist nationality policy proved to be, on balance it was hardly more "imperialist" than that of the Western powers. But the status of the Jews offered no ready comparison. No other issue during the reign of Nicholas II aroused such universal condemnation as Russian anti-Semitism and the perceived role of the government in its perpetuation. Although the wave of pogroms that had marred the advent of Alexander III's reign were not repeated in the two decades that followed, various official acts of persecution and discrimination against Jews aroused bitter resentment. Many younger Jews rejected the passivity and resignation of their elders. The most alienated joined the revolutionary movement, in whose ranks, Plehve claimed, a full 40 percent were Jews.[33] Some chose to emigrate, and a large proportion reached the United States, where the more articulate informed the American public about the travail of their people and the rigors of tsarist despotism. Still others chose the path of assimilation by ostensibly abandoning Judaism for the Orthodox faith. Finally, the new movement known as Zionism, which sought a Jewish national homeland, attracted an enthusiastic Russian following.

Unlike Nicholas himself, whose anti-Semitism was both virulent and uninformed—he almost invariably referred to the Jews as "Yids"—Plehve, Witte, and other ministers were relatively enlightened. They seemed to have little personal antipathy toward Jews and to recognize that continued discrimination could only be detrimental to public order and political stability. Plehve nevertheless condoned official anti-Semitism and later became the major scapegoat in an unexpected outburst of violence against Jews that erupted on Easter Sunday, April 7, 1903, in Kishinev, a Bessarabian city in the southwest corner of the empire. The first serious pogrom—and the most notorious—of Nicholas' reign apparently began when young hooligans, with cries of "Beat the Yids!", chased a number of Jews from a public square. Rock throwing, vandalism, and looting followed. The police declined to intervene, and the disorders escalated the next day. The orgy of violence encompassed mutilation, beatings, murder, rape, and arson, resulting in some fifty dead, about five hundred injured, and 1,300 homes and businesses demolished.

The reaction from abroad was one of anger and disgust. The inaction of the police and the delayed arrival of troops aroused suspicion that the government, if it was not the instigator of the massacre, had deliberately refrained from interference. Plehve, as the responsible minister, was denounced in much of the Western press, and several newspapers published a compromising "secret letter," later found to be spurious, that Plehve had allegedly written to the governor of Bessarabia. If the evidence absolves the government, including Plehve, of an anti-Jewish conspiracy at Kishinev, it is equally clear that the bureaucratic hierarchy, from the tsar down to the lowliest policeman, shared complicity in creating an atmosphere of Judophobia, an open invitation to violence.[34]

Despite its moral culpability, the government did not countenance mob violence, whatever the circumstances. Many officials recognized (though probably not Nicholas himself) that from a public-relations standpoint Russia had been dishonored in the eyes of the world. Plehve sought to repair the damage, with mixed success. The governor of Bessarabia and his deputy were replaced, and in Kishinev new officials were appointed who sought to prevent renewed disorders. Nor did the scores of rioters placed under arrest escape punishment, although their trials were delayed and the sentences imposed were unduly lenient (the harshest term was seven years at hard labor for murder).

The Kishinev pogrom added immeasurably to Plehve's already odious reputation among men of good will, both foreign and domestic. However undeservedly, he had clearly surpassed Pobedonostsev as a symbol of obscurantism and unrelieved reaction. He was too politically astute to be unaware of his low public esteem, but he remained serenely confident of royal favor. He was entirely too optimistic, however, in assuming that he could quash the numerically small but vigorous revolutionary movement with police action.

The Marxists, for their part, had fared poorly in their organizational efforts. A "founding" congress at Minsk in 1898 gave them little else than a name—the Russian Social Democratic Labor Party. The original delegates were soon arrested, and not until the summer of 1903 did a second congress, meeting this time in the safer haven of London, seem to provide the basis for a true party. But the flourishing and consolidated Social Democratic organization that the Russian Marxists expected to achieve in London never materialized. Two factions, not a unified party, emerged: a precarious "majority" (the Bolsheviks) dominated by Vladimir Ilyich Lenin, a doctrinaire revolutionary from the Russian heartland, and an equally uncertain "minority" (the Mensheviks) led by Yuli Martov, a Westernized Jewish intellectual. This distant squabble, a mélange of ideology, tactics, and temperament, baffled the rank and file in Russia. The schism nonetheless dragged on despite peace overtures and unity conferences. Marxist ideology, though outwardly ill suited to Russia's agrarian heritage, fascinated large sections of the radical intelligentsia. The urban proletariat, in theory the ultimate consumer of the new doctrine, responded on occasion with surprising militance, not to Marxism as such but to Social Democratic agitators who attempted to link political demands with economic issues. Strikes and demonstrations, sometimes erupting into full-scale riots, presented no immediate threat to the regime but signified that Russia's working class might indeed achieve a level of revolutionary consciousness seldom attained in the West.

In Plehve's view, the seditious activities of Social Democrats paled in comparison to the terrorist program of the Socialist Revolutionaries. A secret "Battle Organization," nominally under SR leadership, had been established in 1901 to strike at tsarist officialdom with the weapon of assassination. Sipyagin had been its first victim, and Plehve "inherited" the unenviable status of priority target (the emperor himself acquired temporary immunity when it was decided that the peasant masses would be alienated by an attempt on his life). Plehve had confidence in the repressive powers of the Okhrana, however, and not entirely without reason. A remarkable double agent, Yevno Azef,[35] one of many police spies in revolutionary ranks, had not only infiltrated the Battle Organization but emerged as its leader. This fortuitous arrangement seemed to assure Plehve's safety, and the police were successful in rounding up a number of the principle terrorists. Yet Azef, of Jewish origin, held Plehve responsible for the Kishinev massacre. He had also come under the suspicion of his revolutionary comrades and needed a spectacular coup to vindicate himself. Azef thus had ample incentive to betray his superior. A close watch on Plehve, while it yielded useful information, revealed no consistent pattern to his movements. Several plots had already miscarried, and the terrorists, under Azef's general supervision, assembled for still another attempt on July 15, 1904. The intended victim never failed to take elaborate security precautions and understandably had developed something of a "siege mentality,"[36] with an adverse effect on his personality. As his special carriage, convoyed by police agents, rolled along Izmailovsky Prospekt to the Warsaw Station, where he was to board a train for Peterhof and report to the tsar, four prospective assassins awaited him. One of the four, Yegor Sazonov, disguised in the uniform of a railway employee, ran toward the coach grasping something concealed in a newspaper. Despite a collision with one of the bodyguards riding a bicycle, he hurled a bomb that exploded with "a strange, heavy ponderous thud," demolishing the carriage and its occupant. A "thin column of grayish-yellow smoke, almost black at the edges," obscured the scene, wrote an eyewitness. "I thought that through the smoke I saw some black fragments."[37]

Other than members of his family, few mourned Plehve's death. Even in non-revolutionary circles satisfaction, if not elation, was the predominant sentiment. Nicholas, who attended the funeral and was falsely rumored to be gratified by his liberation from Plehve's "tyranny," was greatly distressed by the incident. "In the person of the good Plehve," he wrote in his diary, "I have lost a friend and an irreplaceable minister of the interior. How sternly the Lord visits us in his wrath. In so short a time to have lost two such devoted and useful servants! But it is His holy will!"[38]

Azef, now a hero to the votaries of terror, was too apprehensive about the reaction of his superiors in the Okhrana to enjoy his success. But with surprising gullibility they accepted his explanations and neglected to pursue the clues that would have led to his exposure. His bizarre career lasted four more years before Russia's most famous agent provocateur was unmasked. Sazonov, severely wounded by his own bomb, recovered and eventually received a life sentence at hard labor. The leniency of the court—execution had been expected—was indirectly due to the benevolent policy instituted by Prince Pyotr Svyatopolk-Mirsky, an experienced government official who succeeded Plehve.

The appointment received public acclaim and signaled an imperial retreat from the rigors of the Plehve era. The sovereign, while unprepared to initiate major concessions, recognized that government and society should heal the breach that prevented a common struggle against the foreign adversary. The "little victorious war" that Plehve allegedly solicited had come suddenly and unexpectedly, with Japan. The public might well have sustained the ordeal had it been mercifully brief, properly diminutive, and truly successful. But the robust Japanese forces conspired to thwart any Russian dreams of military glory.

4

Peace and Imperialism

Nicholas had come to the throne an unsophisticated patriot whose knowledge of foreign affairs was negligible. He saw himself as a man of peace, even when pursuing a diplomatic course that a more prudent ruler would have recognized as hazardous and of doubtful benefit to the national interest. Experience, especially the humbling and costly lesson of war with Japan, eventually taught him caution and grudging acceptance of his country's vulnerability in the predatory arena of world politics.

Foreign policy lay within the autocrat's prerogative, and Nicholas freely indulged himself throughout his reign. Indirectly, however, he acknowledged shortcomings in his diplomatic skills by frequent consultation with his foreign minister, his ambassadors, and others with privileged access to the court. His tolerance if not preference for charlatans and adventurers extended to grave matters of external policy, and his vacillating conduct and erratic decisions aroused misgivings and occasional alarm among his more conventional advisers. The foreign ministry itself was not a bastion of diplomatic expertise. Patronage and "connections" were the keys to appointment and promotion. Aside from the language requirement (a thorough knowledge of French), the examinations "were only a comedy." "Intrigue was the main influence in the examiner's choice of a future Talleyrand," according to a highly placed diplomat. "A word from this or that Grand Duchess had great effect."[1]

The first diplomatic crisis of Nicholas' reign occurred in November 1896. An outgrowth of the Turkish problem, the burden of his conversations with Salisbury and Hanotaux during the previous summer, it was precipitated on the Russian side by the ambassador to Constantinople, Aleksandr Nelidov. For years he had importuned his government to seize the straits of the Bosphorus from the feeble grasp of the Turks, and his pleas had been disregarded, if not entirely ignored. He had also become a vigorous spokesman for the Armenian minority—those of the Ottoman Empire, not Russia's—who were subjected to periodic massacres encouraged, perhaps instigated, by the Turkish government. Fresh evidence of Turkish debility won Nelidov a new hearing, and he rushed to St. Petersburg to present his case in person. Nicholas convened a secret conference for that purpose on November 23. The ambassador's plan involved an attack by the Black Sea fleet on the forts of the Bosphorus and a troop landing at the northern end of the Straits. Since Turkey approached a state of anarchy, "incidents" could be expected (or contrived) to furnish a plausible pretext for intervention. Only after the success of the enterprise would the question of compensation for the other powers arise. The minister of war and the chief of staff gave their enthusiastic endorsement, while the other officials, who may have had reservations, remained silent or gave perfunctory approval. Witte, seldom one to equivocate on matters of foreign policy, became the only dissenter. He argued that the scheme would eventually lead to a general European war and "undermine the excellent political and financial situation" bequeathed by Alexander III.[2]

Nicholas, who had kept his own counsel, announced his support of Nelidov at the close of the conference. The matter appeared to be settled, and the military and naval authorities in Odessa and Sevastopol were instructed to prepare the expedition. Witte refused to back down, enlisting the support of Pobedonostsev and the Grand Duke Vladimir Aleksandrovich. The dowager empress also intervened. Whether or not this potent lobby proved effective, Nicholas changed his mind and abandoned the project. Ironically, an assault on the Bosphorus would have been a comparatively easy task, for the Turkish defenses were in great disarray. Although the war that Witte predicted was unlikely, the diplomatic repercussions would have been far-reaching. The British were not favorably disposed to unilateral action of a military nature. Nor were the French willing to support their partner in such an endeavor: a defensive alliance, however loosely interpreted, could not be stretched to include an act of aggression.[3]

Once the Russian threat evaporated, the European powers, through their envoys in Constantinople, made unexpected progress in drawing up a reform program to be pressed on the recalcitrant sultan. In the spring of 1897, before that commendable goal could be achieved, a new crisis arose, a war between Greece and Turkey over the island of Crete. The Greeks, who had been the aggressors, were quickly routed but were saved from the consequences of their folly by the speedy intervention of the powers. An armistice was forced on the sultan, though formal peace terms were delayed and a detachment of Russian troops temporarily occupied Crete, along with those of five other nations. The dowager empress, whose brother was King George I of Greece, wrote to her son from Copenhagen complaining of the "dreadful" situation. Nicholas gave his mother little comfort, referring to the Greeks as a "degenerate people with unlimited pride," most of whose army officers were "members of secret revolutionary societies." "We did not start all this business," he declared, "and I can repeat, as before God, that my conscience is clear."[4]

Russia's setback on the Straits question was offset elsewhere in the Near East. Austria, unable to gain support for an anti-Russian coalition, decided to renew the tentative overtures made at the time of the tsar's visit to Vienna. The Emperor Franz Joseph, accompanied by Count Goluchowski, returned the call in April 1897 and was surprised by the warmth and splendor of his reception in St. Petersburg. A "gentlemen's agreement" concluded on April 18 called for the maintenance of the status quo in the Balkans, and a somewhat similar commitment became applicable to Constantinople and the Straits. The pact brought a large measure of stability to the Near East for the next decade and eased the difficulties of arranging a peace treaty between Greece and Turkey. "It was necessary," Russia's foreign minister explained, "for us to put the Balkans under a bell-glass while we concerned ourselves with more urgent affairs."[5]

The kaiser also received a lavish reception in late July. Arriving at the Kronstadt naval base, he was entertained at the illuminated gardens of nearby Peterhof and reviewed Russian troops at Krasnoe Selo. As a special token of respect he was commissioned an admiral in the Russian navy. Nicholas (virtually apologizing to his mother, who heartily disliked the German emperor, for his generous hospitality) pronounced the visit a success, with his volatile guest on the whole "very cheerful, calm and courteous."[6] William, for his part, was delighted and maintained that in exhaustive discussions he had reached "*complete agreement* with Nicky on all important political questions, so that together we have, so to say, disposed of the world." His anxiety about the Franco-Russian alliance had been allayed, and, he contended, a "restoration of Alsace and Lorraine to France by Russian aid is an absolute and *downright impossibility*." War with France and Russia was no longer to be feared: "Nicky and I again parted as friends who are united by a sincere affection and *absolute* confidence in one another." The kaiser's hyperbole frequently tended to outstrip his common sense. No wonder that his secretary of state, Prince Bernhard von Bülow, considered him a "neurasthenic" who suffered from insecurity and anxiety, "always oscillating between excessive optimism and excessive pessimism."[7]

Two weeks later the ceremonies honoring the Austrian and German monarchs were repeated for President Felix Faure of France. Nicholas was impressed by the "tactful" and "amiable" Frenchman. The populace greeted him warmly in the capital, and the intelligentsia enjoyed the republican aroma that he exuded along with the rousing strains of the "Marseillaise." A state visit with no far-reaching political implications, it did serve to give public recognition to the Franco-Russian alliance. Heretofore the Russians had backed away from so blunt a term as "alliance"; now the farewell toasts exchanged on board the French cruiser *Rothnau* conceded that the two nations were "friends and allies." Nicholas insisted, out of concern for German sensibilities, on adding a proviso that they were "equally resolved to contribute with all their power to the maintenance of world peace," while Faure, providing a somewhat different interpretation, referred to the "common ideals of civilization, right, and justice."

For the moment the European powers had reached a nervous equilibrium. Much of that newfound harmony was spurious, for it had been achieved on the basis of non-European issues: the Near East, with Turkey the weak "victim"; the Far East, with China in the role of an Asiatic Turkey; and Africa, with the powers busily engaged in consolidating the spoils of empire. Russia had made no serious attempt to join the race for African colonies, and after 1895 it subordinated even its European concerns to the penetration of East Asia. Nicholas, while personally sympathetic to the French during the Fashoda crisis in the Nile valley in the fall of 1898, offered no diplomatic support, and the British soon added the vast territory of the Sudan to their African domain.

Nicholas deplored "England's arrogant conduct" and was sorely tempted to intervene more forcefully in the Boer War, which broke out a year later between Britain and the settlers of Dutch ancestry in South Africa. He reassured Queen Victoria, for whom he had a special fondness, that Russia would not take advantage of Britain's difficulties,[8] but his real intentions were more bellicose. In a letter to his sister Xenia on October 9/21, 1899, he confessed his pleasure in contemplating that "it is entirely in my hands to decide the ultimate course of the war in [South] Africa." All he need do, he speculated, was to "telegraph orders to all the troops in Turkestan to mobilize and advance to the [Indian] frontier. That is all! No fleet in the world, however strong, can prevent us from striking at England at her most vulnerable point." But logistical problems, chiefly the absence of a railway line, deterred him.[9] To his mother, who was pro-British, Nicholas wrote more discreetly, while frankly stating his sympathy for the Boers: "I wish all possible success to those poor people in this unequal and unjust war."[10] To his "Uncle Bertie" (Edward VII), who had succeeded Victoria on the throne, he wrote a gentle remonstrance on May 22/June 4, 1901: "A small people are desperately defending their country, a part of their land is devastated, their families flocked together in camps, their farms burnt. . . . In this case, forgive the expression, it looks more like a war of extermination. . . . Does not your kind heart yearn to put an end to this bloodshed?" The king answered at some length, politely defending the British cause, and Nicholas apparently made no reply.[11]

The new Russian foreign minister, Count Mikhail Muravyov, taking his cue from Nicholas, lofted a number of trial balloons to test the atmosphere for an anti-British coalition. Finding the response meager, he all but abandoned the idea in an extensive memorandum of January 1900 that was circulated to the appropriate ministers.[12] Extracting diplomatic concessions from England seemed a more promising alternative—the Bosphorus remained a formidable lure—yet British naval power in the Mediterranean could not be disregarded. The only tangible gains at British expense came in landlocked areas: Persia, where Russian influence continued to expand, and Afghanistan, where Russian troops concentrated on the border as a means of pressuring the Kabul government.

Nicholas' major initiative in European affairs in the first decade of his reign lay outside the scope of formal diplomacy. It involved no less than a daring proposal, launched in 1898, to limit armaments and to preserve "universal peace." The public response, with few exceptions, was one of astonishment and guarded enthusiasm; private reaction, at least among the political elite, was one of cynical disparagement. Sophisticates derided the tsar's invitation "to a general rubbing of noses and exchange of fine sentiments on the subject of peace and goodwill among men."[13] That so bold a gesture emanated from "backward" Russia, hardly an international symbol of peace and justice, occasioned not only surprise in government circles but also indignation that the customary diplomatic feelers had not been forthcoming. It seemed stranger yet that the most autocratic of Europe's rulers had been the one to make such an appeal. The controversy surrounding Nicholas' motivation, generally ascribed at the time to his lofty idealism, remains even now the subject of debate. When, after the collapse of the monarchy, more information became available, the answer seemed obvious: Russia needed a moratorium on the arms race. As one scholar has put it, the idea was "conceived in fear, brought forth in deceit, and swaddled in humanitarian ideals."[14] Germany and France had already introduced field artillery capable of firing six rounds a minute, and the Austrians were preparing to do the same. Russia, whose guns could fire a mere single round a minute, faced a huge financial outlay at a time when Witte guarded the treasury with stern vigilance, convinced that the burden of armaments might "become more irksome than war itself."[15]

The genesis of Nicholas' idea, if indeed he could rightfully take credit for it, was far more complicated than an Austro-Russian rivalry over field artillery.[16] Russia's sponsorship of what was to become the Hague Conference began late in February 1898, when Minister of War Aleksei Kuropatkin prepared a memorandum advocating a ten-year pact with Austria to forbid the introduction of rapid-fire artillery in the army of either country. He was prompted by financial rather than humanitarian reasons, but when he conversed with Nicholas on the 28th he reversed his priorities by suggesting that the sovereign secure for himself a lasting place in history

by taking the "great initiative" of creating "a universal monument to posterity in that billions spent now on the army will be used to increase the
well being of the population, and even with total failure of this initiative
the sovereign will be surrounded by the aureole of peace."[17] Kuropatkin's
delicate flattery struck the right psychological note, for Nicholas fancied
himself not only an indulgent ruler but a benefactor of mankind. He told
Kuropatkin to discuss the matter with Muravyov, and the foreign minister
accepted the concept of a moratorium with alacrity while all but ignoring
its idealistic implications. But within three weeks Muravyov, in conjunction
with most of his colleagues in the Council of Ministers, had become a
convert to a more grandiose plan, that Russia "take the lead in convening
a conference of the great powers for the purpose of guaranteeing a reduction of expenditures on all armaments."[18] He attempted to convey a sense
of urgency by predicting dire consequences if the arms race continued—
bankruptcy and ghastly bloodshed. From February 28 until August 12,
when the celebrated peace manifesto finally appeared, uncertainty and hesitation afflicted the imperial will. The dowager empress and the Grand
Duke Aleksei Aleksandrovich both gave lip service to the "great initiative"
but opposed its implementation. Influence from the other direction came
in the form of a monumental publication encompassing six volumes, Ivan
Bloch's *The Future of War*.[19]

Bloch, a Polish Jew who had become a successful railroad entrepreneur,
combined both business and scholarship. A prolific writer on technical subjects, he broadened his interests and finally turned in his magnum opus to
the nature of modern warfare. The text of the first five volumes, much of
it compiled with the aid of research assistants, contained a staggering array
of statistical data, relevant historical lore, and massive information on military, naval, and economic matters. The final volume, essentially a summary, drew novel and startling conclusions that were to be substantially
verified in the savage ordeal of the First World War. Bloch argued that the
limited wars of the past were no guide to the future, given the advanced
technology, economic resources, and manpower reserves available to the
contemporary nation-state. War had become tantamount to national suicide. No friend of socialism, despite agreement on the evils of militarism,
Bloch raised the specter of revolution as the ultimate outcome of armed
conflict to settle international disputes. Such an argument carried special
weight with Nicholas, who was greatly impressed with Bloch's arguments
after granting him a lengthy audience, apparently in February 1898.[20] But
the evidence for a direct link between Bloch and Nicholas' proposal is
largely circumstantial.

Nicholas continued to procrastinate for much of the summer. His final
decision, made at the urging of his foreign minister, revealed serious concern about the hostile British reaction to Russia's inroads on the integrity
of China. An idealistic pronouncement might soften anti-Russian sentiment

in Great Britain. "Peace is more important than anything else," Nicholas commented, "if honor is not affected."[21] On August 12/24, 1898, Muravyov released the manifesto to the representatives of the powers at the foreign ministry, with the French ambassador given a reception two hours earlier than the others in deference to his country's special status as an ally. The text stressed the "preservation of universal peace and a possible reduction of the excessive armaments that place a heavy burden upon all nations" as corresponding fully to the "humanitarian and benevolent intentions of His Majesty the Emperor." Nations with envoys accredited to the imperial court were invited to a conference to "put an end to these incessant armaments and to seek means of diverting the disasters that threaten the entire world."

The governments addressed were reluctant to dignify such a fanciful appeal with words of praise, yet public opinion could not be flouted with impunity, and the invitation received favorable, if tepid, replies. France, caught unprepared, was shocked and dismayed, fearful that the projected conference would codify its loss of Alsace and Lorraine. Private assurances that the alliance would not be endangered—that in fact the tsar's project was fundamentally innocuous—finally placated the French. Germany, vital to the enterprise, presented a different problem. Counting on his cordial relationship with the kaiser, Nicholas sought his cooperation and was rewarded with an effusive response. William, thoroughly skeptical of the tsar's utopian fantasy, nevertheless complimented him for his proposal, "the most interesting and surprising of this century!" "Honor," he wrote, "will henceforth be lavished upon you by the whole world, even should the practical part fail through difficulties of detail."[22] The unofficial view of the British government was best expressed by the Prince of Wales, who denounced the scheme as "the greatest rubbish and nonsense I ever heard of. The thing is simply *impossible*!" He concluded that Muravyov, that "sly dog" and "subtle intriguer," had put the tsar up to it.[23] But the British agreed to attend, though it was well into October before they gave their formal consent.

Discouraged but tenacious, Muravyov launched a second appeal on December 30, 1898. The document abandoned the rhetoric about preserving "universal peace" for a specific eight-point program stressing measures to alleviate the horrors of war. Its band-aid approach offended pacifists and other members of the self-constituted peace lobby, intent on abolishing war altogether. Yet it seemed the only practical means of evading the shibboleth of national sovereignty, to achieve at least something more meaningful than an international debaters' forum. Persevering in spite of the cool response to this renewed solicitation, Nicholas authorized the foreign ministry to proceed with the arrangements. The Hague, as the capital of an appropriately small "neutral" country aloof from great power politics, was selected as the conference site. Twenty-six delegations participated, including all twenty of the European states. The Russians were led by Baron Yegor Staal, their ambassador in London, who was named conference president in recognition of the tsar's inspirational role. Nicholas was also honored by the date chosen to open proceedings—his thirty-first birthday, May 6/18, 1899.

To no one's surprise, except perhaps unofficial observers, the notion of limiting armaments and military budgets—disarmament did not even appear on the agenda—was dismissed with almost indecent haste. The Arbitration Commission, under the chairmanship of Fyodor Martens, a Russian expert on international law, conceived a tribunal for mediating disputes—voluntary of course—that caught the delegates' interest. Germany's stubborn opposition almost proved fatal, for the kaiser had admonished his representatives to bring "healthy realism to bear on the mass of Russian hypocrisy, twaddle, and lies."[24] Finally, however, he relented, albeit ungraciously ("I consented to all this nonsense only in order that the tsar should not lose face before Europe"),[25] and the powers signed a convention establishing the Permanent Court of Arbitration at The Hague. Agreement was also reached on various rules of war: the prohibition of poison gas and explosive ("dum-dum") bullets, the extension of the Red Cross convention to naval warfare, the improved treatment of prisoners, and others. Not quite the fiasco that had been so freely predicted, the Hague Conference represented a halting step toward international cooperation. But it made no discernible impact on global politics or upon the size and effectiveness of military and naval forces.

If Nicholas II achieved modest renown as a "peacemaker" in 1899, his image was badly tarnished in the years that followed. To many, including a significant number of his subjects, his relentless pursuit of Russia's "mission" in East Asia violated the humanitarian principles that he professed to stand for. Nicholas is unlikely to have perceived any contradiction. Other European countries had long since preempted large portions of Asiatic and Pacific real estate, either as imperial possessions or as spheres of influence. Latecomers to the scene besides Russia, notably Japan, Germany, and the United States, sought a share of the spoils. Geography constrained and to some extent dictated Russia's "manifest destiny," and the political vacuum created by floundering dynasties in China and Korea offered an irresistible temptation to expand without paying the usual penalty in diplomatic crises or military confrontation.

Japan had not been insensible to the weakness of its neighbors. The island kingdom, proving an apt pupil of the great powers, emerged in the 1890s as an industrialized nation with a small but efficient army and a growing navy. A conflict between Japan and China over the domination of Korea broke out in 1894; the Japanese achieved a shockingly easy victory, leading to exorbitant demands at the peace table. China had no choice but to comply, conceding Formosa, the Liaotung Peninsula in southern Manchuria, and relinquishing its historic claim to Korea as a tributary state.

Russia took the lead in urging the European powers to offer their "friendly" advice to Japan that the annexation of Port Arthur, the key to South Manchuria, would not be favorably regarded. The British held aloof, giving the Russians pause, but at special ministerial conferences in the spring of 1895 the misgivings of the new Russian sovereign, who advocated collaboration with Japan, were overcome. France, with reluctance, and Germany, with enthusiasm, joined Russia in a three-power remonstrance on April 11/23: Japan's claim to the Liaotung Peninsula "would be a constant menace to the capital of China, would at the same time render illusory the independence of Korea, and would henceforth be a perpetual obstacle to the peace of the Far East." Faced with this formidable coalition, Japan grudgingly retreated, receiving as compensation a larger war indemnity from China than previously demanded.

China could expect to pay a price for its deliverance. Russia, as its principle benefactor, had more serious aspirations than denying Japan a foothold on the mainland. Nicholas had originally sought only an ice-free port, but the success of Russian diplomacy now opened up new vistas, of which a "big brother" relationship with China seemed the most promising. The kaiser offered his services in keeping Europe quiet and guarding the Russian rear. The "great task of the future," he informed Nicholas on April 14, was to "cultivate the Asian Continent and to defend Europe from the inroads of the Great Yellow race. In this you will always find me on your side, ready to help you as best I can." He also offered to assist in "the question of eventual annexations" in exchange for Russia's support in acquiring a suitable Pacific port for Germany.[26]

Talk of "annexations"—even spheres of influence—was decidedly premature. But Sergei Witte, more adept if not more astute than his colleagues, recognized that old-fashioned gunboat diplomacy, while hardly obsolete, might be counter-productive as an avenue of Russian imperialism. He accordingly seized upon the Chinese indemnity—about $150,000,000 exclusive of Japan's "extra" compensation—as an entering wedge. China's officials were not oblivious to the perils of a financial bailout by its powerful neighbor and canvassed the prospects for a foreign loan. For various reasons the negotiations lapsed, and Witte stepped in with confident aplomb, though fully aware that the Russian treasury contained no surplus for such an arrangement. French bankers had capital to lend, however, and Witte, with speedy finesse, arranged a financial package signed in St. Petersburg on June 24, 1895. The loan agreement with China, in which Russian banks subscribed only a nominal sum—the French supplied the remainder—provided a low interest rate of 4 percent. In case of default China promised "additional security," and it also undertook to avoid financial obligations to foreign powers unless Russia received similar treatment. That the Russian government guaranteed this "private" loan offered further evidence that Witte had managed a political coup in the guise of a financial operation.

Before the French representatives dispersed, they were importuned with still another project conceived by the versatile finance minister. The new venture called for a Russian bank, drawing largely upon French capital, "to operate, on the broadest principles, in the lands of eastern Asia."[27] The French were intrigued, and when their government encouraged the scheme for the sake of the Russian alliance, Witte and his subordinates worked out the details with great care. The charter of the new institution, designated the Russo-Chinese Bank,[28] was formally approved on November 24, 1895. Of the original capitalization, six million goal rubles, French banks held five-eighths of the 48,000 shares, the Russian treasury the remainder. But the French received only three of the eight directorships, and Prince Ukhtomsky, one of Witte's assistants and still a friend of the emperor, became the Bank's first president. The charter granted the institution extraordinary rights: to issue currency and coin money, to collect taxes, to engage in business enterprise, to secure concessions for rail and telegraph lines, and to take part in other quasi-financial operations. Whatever long-range plans Witte contemplated for his new creation, his immediate purpose involved the Trans-Siberian Railway—that is, access to northern Manchuria and thereby a shorter route from the Lake Baikal area to Vladivostok. One of the Bank's unofficial functions, Witte informed Nicholas, would be the financing of "gifts" to Chinese officials responsible for granting the necessary rights of way. The cynical assessment of a Russian diplomat, that the Bank was "a hybrid politico-financial institution which in reality was but a slightly disguised branch of the Russian treasury,"[29] constituted in its way a tribute to Witte's daring initiative.

Despite Nicholas' approval, negotiations with Peking for a Manchurian concession were unduly delayed. The Chinese were themselves reluctant to proceed, the Russian minister in Peking reported, because their gratitude had begun "to weaken and give place to a certain vague feeling of apprehension and distrust" over possible demands of an exorbitant nature.[30] Witte also had to contend with internal opposition, for the opinion was expressed, by no means frivolously, that a rail route so far from Russian territory would involve political and military risks that could not be foreseen. Witte countered with the "economic" argument that "the very nature of things will oblige us shortly to carry through branches of this [rail] line into the depths of China."[31]

The decision of the Chinese government to send veteran diplomat Li Hung-chang to Russia, ostensibly to attend the tsar's coronation, finally brought matters to a head. Witte dispatched Ukhtomsky to intercept Li at the Mediterranean entrance to the Suez Canal, before the representatives of other powers could intercede, and to escort him to St. Petersburg via the Black Sea. Hard bargaining ensued during the spring of 1896, and Nicholas himself entered the discussions. According to Li, the tsar argued that "Russia owns vast territories which are but thinly populated. Therefore she will not trespass upon a foot of soil which is the property of others. Moreover, the ties which bind her to China are very intimate. Hence her only motive in desiring the junction of the railways through Manchuria is the quick conveyance of troops for the purpose of affording effectual help to China whenever the latter country is hard set." Nicholas also pointed out that China's resources were insufficient to build the railway and that it would be an effective solution to hand over the concession to the Russo-Chinese Bank, with suitable safeguards to protect China's rights.[32]

Nicholas naturally put the best possible construction on Russia's motives. Li could not but be impressed with the prospect of armed assistance in the event of renewed hostilities with Japan. Witte, who conducted most of the negotiations, spelled out in detail what Nicholas had barely hinted at—a secret defensive alliance between the two countries. Nor did the finance minister neglect a suitable monetary reward to secure Li's cooperation: three million rubles, to be paid in future installments.[33] That Li ever received the full amount is doubtful; in this instance his desire for a treaty may have outweighed his cupidity. China did need a protector, and a blunt refusal to accommodate the Russians in Manchuria might uphold territorial integrity at the expense of national security. Li insisted that the Russo-Chinese Bank, not the Russian government, handle the railroad concession, but a leasehold of eighty years proved acceptable, with China retaining the right to purchase the line at the end of thirty-six years. Witte's request for a rail link into South Manchuria was refused. Once the railroad negotiations had been settled, the two powers turned to the alliance, and on May 22, 1896, a secret treaty was signed in Moscow by Li, Witte, and Lobanov-Rostovsky. Binding for fifteen years, it required joint military action in case of Japanese aggression against China, Korea, or the Russian Far East.[34]

The inclusion of Korea in the treaty reflected Russia's growing interest in that troubled kingdom. A Japanese coup in Seoul the previous year had forced the Korean monarch to become a puppet ruler; several months later he fled to the sanctuary of the Russian legation. The balance of power then shifted in Russia's favor, and the Japanese, seeking a compromise, sent a distinguished elder statesman, the Marquis Yamagata Aritomo,[35] to attend the tsar's coronation and to strike a bargain with the Russians. In his talks with Lobanov-Rostovsky, Yamagata offered to divide Korea into Russian and Japanese spheres of influence. The proposal was rejected, for reciprocity of this kind did not seem advantageous in light of Japan's Korean difficulties. But agreement of a sort did emerge in the so-called Moscow Protocol of May 28, 1896, in which the two powers, perhaps with deliberate ambiguity, recognized the principle of Korean independence and supported the king's efforts to restore political stability. Future Russian policy was inconsistent with a strict construction of the protocol. Nor did separate negotiations at the time with a Korean mission in St. Petersburg harmonize with Lobanov's efforts. Nicholas, without consulting his foreign minister, and in a private audience with the chief envoy, is said to have promised continued protection of the Korean monarch.[36] The implication was unmistakable that Russia would seek to "protect" the king in the same manner that Japan had done during its brief period of ascendancy.

During the summer a vanguard of Russian military "advisers," later supplemented, arrived in Seoul to begin training an army of some four thousand and a royal bodyguard of eight hundred. In February 1897 the Korean monarch, more confident of his security, returned to his palace. At the time Russia's interest in Korea was wholly political, and the idea of economic expansion on the pattern of Manchuria had scarcely occurred to Witte or to other government officials. That attitude was to change, in part because of a concession granted in 1896 by the Korean government to Yuli Briner, a well-connected Vladivostok businessman of Swiss origin, to exploit vast timber resources in northern Korea. Briner, lacking the capital to develop his concession, sought financial assistance in St. Petersburg without much success. Through Andrei Rothstein, however, a director of the Russo-Chinese Bank, his obscure venture was later transformed into a notorious quasi-governmental scheme that reached the throne itself.

Meanwhile, after tedious delays, a contract had been signed in the late summer of 1896 between China's envoy and representatives of the Russo-Chinese Bank to construct the Chinese Eastern Railway across Manchuria. As a Russian topographical surveying expedition sought the best route, Witte renewed his attempt to secure a branch line into southern Manchuria. In the spring of 1897 he sent Ukhtomsky to China for negotiations, but despite the payment to Li Hung-chang of a million rubles as a first installment on the promised bribe, the mission ended in abject failure.

Russian pressure on China relaxed for a time. But in November a new era of "gunboat diplomacy" began when Germany seized the port of Kiaochow on China's Shantung Peninsula. The murder of two German missionaries furnished a convenient pretext, but the kaiser had taken preliminary soundings during his visit to Russia in the summer and received what he chose to interpret as Nicholas' tacit consent. He nevertheless telegraphed Nicholas about Germany's intentions and received a prompt reply on October 25: "Cannot approve or disapprove your sending German squadron to Kiaochow, as I have just learned that the harbor was ours only temporarily in 1895–96."[37] Satisfied that his royal cousin would not object, at least very strenuously, and shrugging off the two "insolent" telegrams of protest that Muravyov dispatched from St. Petersburg, William opted for a fait accompli. His tactics succeeded despite a temporary rift in Russo-German relations and the discomfiture of the Chinese. Muravyov submitted a memorandum to the tsar on November 11 advocating the occupation of a port on the Liaotung Peninsula, and Nicholas responded favorably, calling for a ministerial conference three days later.[38] Muravyov encountered strong opposition among his colleagues, especially from the voluble Witte, who deplored an unseemly scramble for territorial rights among the powers that might upset Russia's advantageous position. The other ministers sided with Witte to the extent of opposing an adventurist policy, a consensus that Nicholas eventually overruled, apparently under Muravyov's prompting. The foreign minister claimed—his evidence was unconvincing—that the British were about to seize one or more ports and that China had requested Russian intervention. The kaiser, when informed that Port Arthur would be Russia's objective, expressed his delight, realizing at once that the action would legitimize his own avariciousness. He telegraphed Nicholas with typical bombast: "Russia and Germany at the entrance of the Yellow Sea may be taken as represented by St. George and St. Michael shielding the Holy Cross in the Far East and guarding the Gates to the Continent of Asia. . . . My sympathy and help shall not fail in case of need."[39]

A Russian squadron dropped anchor at Port Arthur on December 7, 1897. Although no landing followed, the vessels constituted a weighty "presence" during the winter as the Russians sought to consolidate their toehold at Liaotung by diplomatic means. Witte virtually conceded defeat, and by February 1898 the military and naval chiefs, in addition to Muravyov, had obtained Nicholas' approval of less subtle means of pursuing Russia's "request" for a leasehold. Further bribes eased the negotiations, and agreement came on March 15.[40] The terms included a twenty-five-year lease on the Liaotung Peninsula and consent to Witte's coveted branch line between the Chinese Eastern Railway and Talienwan (Dalny, as the Russians began to call it). The irony of the transaction was not lost upon the Japanese, who had been ousted from southern Manchuria only three years before. Witte, though his own role was by no means blameless, considered the "seizure" of Liaotung to be the "fateful step, an act of unparalleled perfidy, that was to have the most unfortunate consequences." His offer to resign was summarily rejected by the emperor.[41]

Japan's resentment was mollified to some extent by a new agreement on Korea. Tokyo's offer to recognize the Russian sphere of influence in Manchuria in exchange for an acknowledgment of Japan's hegemony in Korea had been turned aside in St. Petersburg. A weak substitute was provided in the Nishi-Rosen Convention (named for the principal negotiators) of April 13. The two powers pledged noninterference in Korea's domestic affairs, and Russia promised not to "obstruct the development of the commercial and industrial relations between Japan and Korea." Baron Roman Rosen, the Russian minister to Tokyo, later declared his handiwork to be "rather lame and pointless,"[42] but it need not have been had Russia shown some interest in implementing its part of the bargain.

By the turn of the century the powers were content to pause and digest their gains; the process of "carving the Chinese melon" had stopped just short of outright partition. Russia, with more to digest than its rivals, busily engaged in railroad construction, outfitting Port Arthur as a naval base and developing Dalny as a commercial port. Public opinion in China, passive for the most part, hardly seemed to matter. But animosity toward the "foreign devils" rapidly escalated, especially among the so-called secret societies. The most prominent of these organizations, the Fists of Righteous Harmony (to use a popular but somewhat inaccurate English rendering), who became the "Boxers" in Western journalese, gained the most notoriety by employing the tactics of violence. A veritable open season on foreigners prevailed during the summer of 1900, and Chinese converts to Christianity also found themselves in grave jeopardy. (Nicholas considered Western missionaries "the root of all the evil; they, together with commercial pretensions, most of all excited the hatred of the Chinese for Europeans.")[43] When the legation quarter in Peking came under siege, an international military expedition was obliged to rescue the diplomatic personnel and their dependents. The Russian contingent totaled some four thousand, not including other units involved in the relief of Tientsin. In Manchuria, where approximately three thousand armed railway guards were outnumbered by the Boxers and Chinese regulars, the Russians had to withdraw until reinforcements could arrive.

In St. Petersburg divided if not contradictory counsels prevailed. Witte led a "peace party" of sorts, urging moderation toward China. Minister of War Kuropatkin voiced the sentiments of the military and naval "lobby" that Russia should intervene with vigor and dispatch. Muravyov temporized, disinclined to take an alarmist view or to "disturb the Tsar." During an early stage of the crisis he died suddenly, a rumored suicide but apparently the victim of an accident. Upon Witte's strong recommendation, Nicholas replaced him with Count Vladimir Lamzdorf, a veteran diplomat whose knowledge of international affairs was impressive but who is said to have lacked Muravyov's saving grace—common sense. "Narrow minded and small of soul," he was reputed to be a "pervert" (that is, a homosexual), partly because he showed great favoritism to the handsome young men in his entourage.[44] Another observer, even less flattering, labeled him an inveterate bureaucrat and hard working "anchorite" with "a puny intellect . . . and a merely book and paper knowledge of men and things of the outer world."[45] Witte naturally had a different view and praised his accommodating colleague, a "thoroughly decent, honorable man" who "knew his trade inside and out."[46]

Whatever his personal qualities, Lamzdorf seconded Witte's "soft" policy toward China and temporarily gained Nicholas' support. Russia, still posing as China's friend, sent a circular note to the powers on August 12 suggesting the withdrawal of all foreign troops from Peking now that order had been restored. The "happiest day of my life," Nicholas wrote his mother, "will be when we leave Pekin[g] and get out of that mess for good."[47] Russian forces, alone among the powers, did indeed withdraw from the "mess" in September except for a bolstered legation guard. They therefore avoided much of the odium attached to the murder, rape, and looting that disfigured the allied occupation of North China. The situation in Manchuria, however, defied a tidy solution. Russian atrocities against the indigenous population more than matched those in the south, and Lamzdorf protested to Nicholas about such brutal conduct. But the sentimental monarch who could shed copious tears over the death of his favorite dog remained unmoved. He was "gracious to the Minister, but often interrupted him saying that, after all, the Asiatics deserved the lesson which they had been taught."[48]

The capture of Mukden in September 1900 all but completed the pacification of Manchuria. Control of the railroad zones had become a military occupation by over 175,000 troops. In response, Chinese representatives began sporadic and protracted negotiations in which Witte or his subordinates figured prominently. Rumors flourished about secret agreements at China's expense, for the Russians now enjoyed great bargaining leverage. The British, still mired in the Boer War, were also made uneasy by a prolonged Tibetan mission to Russia that presumably sought to weaken China's claims to the "Forbidden Kingdom." Nicholas received the mission at Livadia Palace in the fall of 1900, and its members called on government officials in St. Petersburg the following summer. The Dalai Lama, the Tibetan ruler, had sent messages intended for the tsar, but the foreign ministry made the embarrassing discovery that no one could be found in the capital to translate Tibetan. Finally the dilemma was solved when a professor of oriental studies from Vladivostok, in the capital for a vacation, volunteered his services.[49] Although avowed expansionists, Ukhtomsky for example, were willing enough to include Tibet within the Russian sphere of influence, no one in authority, including Nicholas himself, entertained serious designs on that remote and mountainous region.

Russia's intention of establishing a protectorate over Manchuria aroused British, Japanese, and American opposition, encouraging the Chinese to offer stiffer resistance. For a short time in the spring of 1901 a "war crisis" developed in Japan, with super-patriots active in fomenting hostility toward Russia. Moderation prevailed in the end, though the Anglo-Japanese alliance of 1902 was posited directly on the perceived threat of Russia to the balance of power in East Asia. Some progress had been made in the Russian-Chinese negotiations when the aged Li Hung-chang died in October 1901, necessitating a fresh start. At last, on March 26/April 8, 1902, an agreement was reached in Peking to evacuate Russian troops from Manchuria in three stages over a period of eighteen months. There remained, to be sure, a gaping loophole: "that no disturbances arise and that the action of other powers should not prevent it." Nor was there mention of railway guards, who would presumably remain on duty. But Japan expressed satisfaction, and the first stage of the withdrawal was substantially completed on schedule. Thereafter the Russians made only a token effort, a reluctance to honor their pledge that reflected Witte's political decline and the triumph of the "war party" in St. Petersburg.

If the precise degree of bellicosity displayed by the tsar and his new circle of advisers is a matter of dispute, it is undeniable that they pursued a reckless policy that could only be regarded by the Japanese as dangerously provocative. First and foremost among the "clique" that temporarily enjoyed imperial favor was Aleksandr Bezobrazov. A retired captain of a Guards regiment and an experienced government official, Bezobrazov exuded self-assurance and a superficial charm that made him a persuasive advocate of Russian imperialism. Yet his wife, who presumably knew him better that anyone else, was puzzled by his prominent role: "Don't they realize that he is half-mad?"[50] Along with a friend and former officer, Vladimir Vonlyarlyarsky,[51] who had taken an interest in the Briner concession in Korea, he gradually unfolded an ambitious entrepreneurial scheme. They proposed that a Russian company exploit the vast natural resources of East Asia, and a memorandum on the subject reached Nicholas in 1898 through the influence of Count Vorontsov-Dashkov. Nicholas expressed interest in the project and sponsored an expedition to survey the timber and mineral resources of the original Briner concession. After repeated failures to acquire government patronage, Bezobrazov, in the name of what was now called the East Asiatic Development Company, submitted a new prospectus to Nicholas in March 1900 with an impressive list of future investors. Attracted by the lure of assured profits, though mindful of the diplomatic implications, Nicholas authorized the purchase of two hundred shares from his personal funds to be held in the name of Captain (later Admiral) Aleksei Abaza, a cousin and associate of Bezobrazov. But opposition arose from Baron Vladimir Frederiks, the minister of the imperial court, who considered it unseemly for the tsar to engage in private business and had the courage to say so. Witte also objected and recommended that the matter be shelved until the Boxer troubles had ceased. Bezobrazov "flew into a perfect rage" and indiscriminately denounced Witte, his Manchurian railroad, the "Jewish consistorium and the tricks of European diplomacy."[52]

Blocked by Witte and deserted by its prospective investors, the East Asiatic Development Company came to an ignominious end in 1902. Yet its liquidation was, paradoxically, "more like a mine-laying operation," for the chief promoter's political fortunes waxed as his financial prospects ostensibly waned. Witte's victory was distinctly of the Pyrrhic variety. He complained that Bezobrazov visited the emperor at least twice a week for hours at a time, telling him "all manner of nonsense and every sort of ephemeral plan."[53] In November 1902 Nicholas dispatched Bezobrazov on a mission to the Far East "of a very confidential nature" and ordered Witte to open a line of credit for him of two million rubles drawn on the Russo-Chinese Bank. The royal favorite, with a veritable blank check to draw upon, spent lavishly. Most of his projects were devoted to economic development in Manchuria, but "humanitarian" causes also attracted his largesse: forty thousand rubles to expand the Russian hospital in Mukden and thirty-five thousand to a Russian newspaper in Port Arthur for propaganda purposes. His discretion left much to be desired, for he conducted himself with arrogant confidence as the tsar's official emissary and seized every opportunity to publicize his dogmatic and chauvinist views.[54] Nicholas learned of his "overzealous" behavior and recalled him in March 1903. Bezobrazov, though still a power to reckon with, never quite regained his hold over Nicholas, who conferred upon him, as a kind of consolation prize, the rank of state secretary and appointment to the chancellery of the State Council.

On May 31, 1903, the defunct East Asiatic Development Company was resurrected in a new guise—the Russian Timber Company of the Far East. The charter, even more ambitious than its predecessor, contemplated exploiting not only timber but minerals, fisheries, furs, navigation, and "all types of other industrial and commercial enterprises" in eastern Siberia, Manchuria, and Korea. Bezobrazov, while not an investor, became its chief promoter, and Nicholas is said to have provided a subsidy of 250,000 rubles from private funds.[55] Logging operations on the Briner concession in northern Korea were already underway, with a work force drawn largely from demobilized soldiers. The Japanese, well apprised of the situation, understandably regarded the "commercial" venture as a stalking horse for Russia's strategic aims.

This quasi-entrepreneurial activity coincided with a new and independent spirit on Nicholas' part. That summer, apparently exasperated by conflicting advice and concerned that his autocratic power might lapse by default, he asserted himself with vigor and determination. In June, seeking to simplify the chain of command and declare his emancipation from ministerial constraints, he invested Admiral Yevgeny Alekseyev with supreme authority over all Russian forces in East Asia. That decision was confirmed on July 30 with the admiral's appointment as viceroy of the Far East, which in theory made him responsible for all military, naval, economic, and diplomatic affairs within the region. In practice the new arrangement worked poorly because of jurisdictional conflicts, and within a few weeks Nicholas expressed doubt about his handiwork. His concern should have been directed to the reaction in Japan, where the move was taken as further evidence of aggressive intentions. Gravely offended by Alekseyev's appointment, Kuropatkin offered to resign, but Nicholas temporized, declaring that he had no suitable replacement. Witte's downfall came on August 15, soon followed by that of Bezobrazov, who nevertheless retained his government post. But the notorious "adventurer," who no longer had personal access to Nicholas, found a measure of solace in having "zealously unmasked" the "mangy triumvirate" of "patented scoundrels" (Witte, Lamzdorf, and Kuropatkin).[56]

For much of the year 1903 Nicholas toyed with the idea, at least twice before broached by the Japanese, of abandoning further demands in regard to Korea in return for due recognition in Tokyo of Russia's supremacy in Manchuria. When negotiations between the two powers resumed in late July, Japan had backed away from its tentative proposal. An awkward problem in communication developed, with Nicholas abroad much of the time, Alekseyev in Port Arthur, Lamzdorf only intermittently in St. Petersburg, and Baron Rosen in Tokyo. Delay was inevitable, and it was well into September before a Russian offer suggested a compromise that would nevertheless place some restrictions on Japan's freedom of action in Korea. The response from Tokyo was conciliatory and included a proposition for a fifty-kilometer neutral zone on both sides of the Korean-Manchurian frontier. When Russia's counterproposal finally came in late November, it virtually ignored Manchuria, implying that Japan had no say in the matter. The Japanese were already suspicious of Russia's procrastination, detecting an attitude of condescension. The empress had become seriously ill in Russian Poland, and Nicholas remained incommunicado for some time, unable or unwilling to attend to state business.[57] That little Japan might choose an armed conflict with mighty Russia seems never to have occurred to him. Yet he was apprehensive. "It is necessary to telegraph Alekseyev immediately that I do not want war," he told Lamzdorf. "Get an answer."[58]

Back in the Russian capital, Nicholas acknowledged the seriousness of relations with Japan by calling a special conference on December 15. He presided, with Kuropatkin, Lamzdorf, and Admiral Abaza among those present. Decisions were made to keep the talks going and to readmit Manchuria to the agenda. Nicholas reiterated his opposition to war: it was "unquestionably impossible." "Time is Russia's best ally," he maintained; "Every year strengthens us."[59] An accounting of troops present in Manchuria and projected for Far Eastern duty would justify Nicholas' optimism, but potential naval strength, especially if measured by other criteria than simply available warships, favored Japan.

A Russian note on December 24 reintroduced the Manchurian question, but in a formulation unsatisfactory to Japan. What became Tokyo's final offer reached Rosen on December 31; it included the proviso that Russia "respect the territorial integrity of China in Manchuria" (Nicholas saw the phrase as an "impertinence"). The note also contained the warning—ominous in diplomatic parlance—that further delay in solving the impasse would be "extremely disadvantageous to the two countries." The Russians, as well they might, considered the message provocative and a virtual ultimatum. They responded, after leisurely deliberation, with minor concessions on January 22, 1904, in a message that arrived in Tokyo several days later. By this time further negotiations were irrelevant: the Japanese government had decided upon war. On the 24th Japan's minister in St. Petersburg announced the severance of diplomatic relations. For the first time Nicholas expressed anxiety about the possibility of war. That question, he remarked to Kuropatkin in an irritated tone, "must be clarified quickly. . . . If war then war; if peace then peace, but this uncertainty becomes unbearable."[60]

Both powers had already begun military preparations, but Japan accepted the onus of "aggressor" by initiating hostilities. Russia hardly fit the role of innocent victim, and an imposing array of "warmongers" from Bezobrazov to the tsar himself could be cited to bolster the Japanese case. Although Nicholas was sincere in his desire to avoid war, he had presided with stubborn ineptitude over an adventurist policy of expansion that intimidated a weak China but could not fail to infuriate a strong Japan. His contempt for Japan as a "barbarous country" and for the Japanese as "monkeys" proved a psychological block that prevented him from recognizing an accomplished and dangerous foe. The conflict stands as the classic example of imperialist rivalry and national aggrandizement run amuck.

5

War with Japan

Seeking the advantage of surprise, Japan withheld a declaration of war and struck at the powerful Russian squadron at Port Arthur. Near midnight on January 26/February 8, 1904, destroyers launched a bold torpedo attack, crippling two battleships and a cruiser. The operational implications were more serious than the temporary loss of three vessels: Russia was suddenly placed on the defensive, and its Pacific fleet never regained the initiative. Japan controlled the sea.

Nicholas was startled by the news from Port Arthur but maintained his poise, confident, as were most Russians, that the upstart Japanese would soon be taught a salutary lesson. He characterized the attack as no more than the "bite of a flea."[1] "So the war has begun," he wrote his mother. "May God be with us. . . . He will help our brave men to be victorious over the foe."[2] He was heartened by the patriotic fervor—superficial perhaps—that swept the country, fanned not only by Japanese "treachery" but also by racial prejudice that automatically consigned Orientals to an inferior status. Yet the war was far away, presenting no threat to the homeland, and an unbroken succession of Russian defeats could not fail to dampen popular enthusiasm.

Nicholas remained convinced of ultimate victory. Nor was he concerned by the problem of financing the war; reparations from the vanquished enemy would replenish an empty treasury. His conscience often troubled him for not sharing the "dangers and privations" of the army. He did the next best thing, as he saw it, by attending various morale-building functions and presiding at ceremonies to honor troops departing for the front. The soldiers were blessed by the clergy, and Nicholas and Alexandra presented tin icons of the recently canonized St. Serafim of Sarov.[3] Crusty old General Mikhail Dragomirov, who had been one of Nicholas' tutors on military affairs, registered disgust at the excessive piety: "They attack us with artillery and we pay them back with 'Te Deums'; they blow us up with mines and we defend ourselves with 'holy images.' "[4]

Russia faced staggering logistical problems in fighting a war in Manchuria (Korea was quickly overrun by the Japanese). The vital rail artery of nearly six thousand miles between St. Petersburg and Port Arthur was single-tracked for the most part, and not until September 1904 was the rugged section around Lake Baikal completed. In matters of military strategy Nicholas was uninformed, though not without basic theoretical knowledge. To his credit he rarely intervened in tactical decisions and never, as far as is known, in field operations. He failed, however, to delegate proper authority to General Kuropatkin, his uninspired choice to lead the army in Manchuria. Since Alekseyev still held sway with ill-defined but presumably supreme power as viceroy, the appointment assured a jurisdictional conflict. Kuropatkin advocated a strategic retreat until reinforcements could alter the military balance in Russia's favor, while Alekseyev sought to defend Manchuria against Japanese encroachment from Korea. The result was an ill-advised stand in April at the Yalu River, where the outnumbered Russians were badly mauled.

A similar and equally unsatisfactory "compromise" followed, as Port Arthur seemed likely to fall. Alekseyev ordered Kuropatkin's forces to advance southward to relieve the besieged naval base. The general, threatened by a flanking attack, considered the move "strategic folly" but reluctantly proceeded when Alekseyev received the imperial sanction. The offensive, inadequately manned and poorly executed, also ended in disaster.

Nicholas made a better choice in Vice Admiral Stepan Makarov to command the Pacific fleet. A distinguished naval officer with an international reputation, Makarov took charge at Port Arthur with firm authority and infused a new spirit of confidence in sailors and civilians alike. His bold and aggressive tactics also impressed the Japanese, who maintained an effective blockade at a respectful distance from the harbor and its shore batteries. Unfortunately for Russia's naval fortunes, Makarov was lost on March 31 when the battleship *Petropavlovsk*, returning from a night sortie, hit a mine, exploded, and sank immediately. Of the ship's complement of some seven hundred men only seventy survived. Among the dead was Vasily Vereshchagin, an eminent painter of battle scenes who had been on board to absorb the flavor of actual combat. Both men were mourned as national heroes. Nicholas attended a memorial service for Makarov and his crew in St. Petersburg, and his diary recorded the "grave and unspeakably mournful news." "God's will be done in all things," he concluded, "but we beg the Lord to be merciful to us poor sinners."[5]

Makarov's replacement, unable to reach Port Arthur because of the Japanese siege, was obliged to assume his command at Vladivostok. There a small squadron of cruisers could do little more than harass the enemy. Alekseyev, again backed by imperial authority, ordered the Port Arthur flotilla to break through the blockade for the sanctuary of Vladivostok. On July 28 the Russians made a gallant effort, but Japanese shell fire disabled the flagship, killing the commanding admiral, and the surviving warships limped back to port.

Kuropatkin's army in Manchuria, reinforced and resupplied, presented a formidable obstacle to further Japanese gains. It prepared for battle at the walled city of Liaoyang on the rail line between Port Arthur and Mukden. Morale was buoyed, especially among the officer corps, by the announcement that on July 30 the empress had given birth to a son, the long-anticipated heir to the throne. Nicholas was elated, noting in his diary the "unforgettable day" in which "God clearly showed us his blessing." "I am happier at the birth of a son and heir than at a victory of my troops," he wrote. "Now I face the future calmly and without alarm, knowing by this sign that the war will be brought to a happy conclusion."[6] Experience had taught Kuropatkin, who took the salute in a special parade honoring the new tsarevich, that the Japanese soldier was a bold and tenacious foe. His confidence ebbed in the face of intelligence reports that his forces were outnumbered. In reality he commanded 158,000 men, thirty-three thousand more than the enemy, and possessed a clear advantage in field artillery.

Kuropatkin declined to take the initiative, and his outlying units retreated in good order before a determined Japanese assault that brought them within striking distance of Liaoyang by mid-August. The Russians had converted the hilly terrain surrounding the city into a stronghold of minefields, barbed wire, and concentrated artillery fire. The Japanese suffered heavy losses in renewing their attack, and a more daring strategist than Kuropatkin might have carried the day with a timely counteroffensive. Further probing at Russian defenses exposed serious defects. Fearing that he might be outflanked and that a withdrawal to Mukden, forty miles to the north, might be endangered, Kuropatkin ordered a general retreat. On August 22 Japanese troops entered Liaoyang.

The decisive battle that would determine the fate of Manchuria, if not the war itself, had yet to be fought; the Japanese were nonetheless victorious by conventional standards of warfare despite Kuropatkin's protestations to the contrary. The esprit de corps of the Russian troops was suspect, the civilian population largely indifferent to the war effort, and the radical intelligentsia sufficiently alienated to welcome the government's discomfiture. Still optimistic, Nicholas sent an encouraging message to Kuropatkin: "The retreat of the whole army in such difficult circumstances and over the terrible roads was an operation excellently carried out in face of grave difficulties. I thank you and your splendid troops for their heroic work and their continued self-sacrifice. God guard you."[7]

The sovereign's graciousness offered solace to the embattled commander. But Kuropatkin sensed readily enough that a victory, even a meager one, was an obligation that he could not lightly dismiss. Tactically and temperamentally ill-suited to impetuous forays on the battlefield, he conscientiously performed his duty by launching an offensive at the Sha River, north of Liaoyang, on September 22. His army had been strengthened to over 200,000, surpassing the Japanese by a comfortable margin. Once more the "Kuropatkin syndrome" emerged: excessive caution coupled with indecision, poor communications, and a rigid command system that allowed little flexibility under combat conditions.

Perhaps more symptomatic of Russian failure than the deficiency of a single individual were the inherent weaknesses of the army as a whole. Raw courage, never in short supply, could not compensate for technical backwardness, poor training, and incompetent leadership by senior officers. The Russians absorbed forty-one thousand casualties—twice those of the Japanese—and retreated toward Mukden. Nicholas, finally persuaded that dual authority in Manchuria unnecessarily handicapped the prosecution of the war, relieved Alekseyev of his viceroyalty on October 12 and elevated Kuropatkin to the supreme command (though without the title that Alekseyev had held). He arrived at his decision after a "great inner struggle," and even without the wisdom of hindsight one may question the promotion of a man who had so amply demonstrated his mediocrity. Nicholas refused to be discouraged, and in a telegram to William II he vowed that Russia would fight "until the last Japanese is driven out of Manchuria."[8]

A winter lull on the Manchurian front did not include Port Arthur, where Japanese infantry had repeatedly tried and failed to take the fortified Russian positions. By November huge siege guns firing five-hundred-pound shells arrived from Japan and made a vital contribution to the renewed assault. On the 22nd the Russians lost a strategic hill overlooking the harbor, and Japanese artillery destroyed what remained of the squadron. Although the military significance of Port Arthur lapsed with the annihilation of the Russian warships, to the Japanese public the city had become a symbol of patriotic sacrifice. The siege continued, essentially for quasi-political reasons. By mid-December it became apparent to the defenders that further resistance was futile. Morale had plummeted, and lethargy borne of fatigue and discouragement was endemic; disease, principally scurvy, was rampant; the hospitals, chronically short of medical supplies, overflowed with some fourteen thousand patients. Food and ammunition, however, were not critically short, and able-bodied men could still be summoned to do their duty.

On December 19 General Anatoly Stessel, the garrison commander, proposed surrender talks to the Japanese, ignoring the opinion of his senior colleagues. The formal terms of capitulation were quickly arranged. On humanitarian grounds, Stessel's decision could not be faulted. Why indeed prolong a bloody and useless resistance? But his superiors in St. Petersburg took the view that he had violated his obligations as a professional soldier. Nicholas, who had received a personal telegram from Stessel about the supposedly desperate plight of the garrison, was indignant at the "premature" surrender when he learned of the available resources. Publicly he praised the troops for their courage, and in his diary he commended them as "heroes" who "have done more than could be expected of them." "Therefore," he concluded with fatalistic resignation, the defeat "must have been God's will!"[9] As for the offending general, he was court-martialed after the war and condemned to death. Nicholas commuted the sentence to ten years, of which Stessel actually served about a year.

As Russia entered the second year of the war, its prospects were bleak but by no means hopeless. Time, so Nicholas fondly believed, was still the best ally. A sizable and growing army in Manchuria remained combatworthy, while the Japanese possessed no equivalent reservoir of trained manpower—they had paid a costly price at Port Arthur, with estimated casualties at ninety-one thousand, including those incapacitated by disease. Russia, even though no longer a naval power in the Pacific, was not bereft of warships, nor were they entirely inaccessible. The Black Sea fleet, bottled up by the Turkish Straits, could play no effective role, but the Baltic fleet was intact if inconveniently remote from the scene of the action.

During the previous summer Nicholas had presided at a meeting of the Higher Naval Board. Bowing to the imperial will with only timid dissent, the Board decided that the Baltic fleet should be sent halfway around the world to relieve Port Arthur. Rear Admiral Zinovy Rozhdestvensky, whose distinguished appearance was not matched by impressive naval credentials, assumed command. Privately he expressed serious reservations about the chances of success for his mission, an attitude in marked contrast to his air of public confidence. His irascible temperament was strained to the limit by the countless tasks of supplying and outfitting his ships for the long voyage ahead. On September 28, 1904, the fleet, renamed the Second Pacific Squadron, departed from the Baltic port of Libau. At Revel, Nicholas had provided, literally, a royal sendoff, with personal visits to the battleships and a rousing speech promising vengeance on the "impudent enemy who has violated the tranquility of our Mother Russia." A young naval architect commented on "the Tsar's very ordinary and already worn face," the "dull expression of his pewter-like eyes," and the "contrived mask of his good-natured smile. . . . There was something un-naval about the way he wore his captain's uniform, and the way he walked showed his unfamiliarity with the deck of a ship."[10] Alexandra presented chalices to those vessels furnished with chapels, and priests sprinkled the guns and decks with holy water. In his diary Nicholas sought God's blessing on the fleet:

"Permit it to arrive safely at its destination and that it accomplish its grave undertaking for the happiness and benefit of Russia!"[11]

With seven battleships, eight cruisers, nine destroyers, and a variety of auxiliary vessels, the squadron was numerically more powerful than the fleet originally stationed at Port Arthur. But many of the ships were outmoded in design, speed, and firepower. The twelve thousand seamen, most of them fresh conscripts, lacked proper training, and the efficiency of their officers left much to be desired. More threatening, though its perils had yet to be disclosed, were the vicissitudes of an eighteen-thousand-mile voyage without Russian bases to offer a friendly haven.

Misadventure occurred sooner than expected: during the night of October 8–9, while crossing the North Sea, several ships fired on British fishing trawlers, mistaking them for Japanese torpedo boats. The resulting Dogger Bank incident inflamed the British press, and for a few days the hounds of war appeared to have been unleashed. Nicholas, conceding that the affair was "more than awkward" (though he referred in private to England's "impertinent behavior"), sent a conciliatory telegram to Edward VII deploring the death of "innocent fisherman" in this "sad incident" (he crossed out "regrettable"). He explained that warnings about the Japanese "hiring fishing smacks and other vessels" to attack the squadron had resulted in "great precautions" being taken, especially at night. Nonetheless, he took a stiff-necked approach, in that he withheld a formal apology because the "facts and circumstances" were not known. The king appeared willing to accept Nicholas' explanation, but "what has caused me and my country so painful an impression," he protested, "is that your squadron did not stop to offer assistance to the wounded as search lights must have revealed to your admiral that the ships were British fishing vessels." At length the forces of moderation prevailed. France offered mediation, and Russia submitted to arbitration by an international commission. Yet to Nicholas it was "our despicable enemies" who had "abandoned their arrogance" by agreeing to a compromise settlement.[12] Russia eventually paid $325,000 as compensation for a sunken trawler and two dead fishermen.

The squadron, shadowed by British warships, pushed on to the Spanish port of Vigo, where Nicholas sent a message of encouragement: "In my thoughts I am with you and my beloved squadron. I feel confident that the misunderstanding will soon be settled. The whole of Russia looks upon you with confidence and in firm hope."[13] From Tangier in North Africa the battleships proceeded along the West African coast, rounding the Cape of Good Hope, while the smaller vessels passed through the Suez Canal. A December rendezvous at Madagascar in the Indian Ocean, where French colonial officials maintained an indulgent neutrality, brought news of the fall of Port Arthur. Its mission rendered superfluous, the fleet should have been recalled: intact it could at least serve as a bargaining chip in peace negotiations. But to Nicholas and his advisers the honor and prestige of the navy had to be upheld. For ten weeks it lingered in the tropical heat of Madagascar for refitting and repairs, coaling and reprovisioning. In that time drunkenness, disease, and rancid food all contributed to a breakdown of discipline and a sullen mood verging on insubordination.

By January 1905 Russia's Manchurian forces had increased to nearly 300,000 men, deployed in a wide arc below Mukden. Fortifications and massive artillery support appeared to make the city impregnable, although the fate of Port Arthur served as a constant reminder of the enemy's offensive strength. The Japanese were again outnumbered, this time by close to 100,000 troops, and the disparity lured Kuropatkin into a probing operation some thirty miles southwest of Mukden. Under the command of General Oskar Grippenberg, the Russians were repulsed with heavy losses, many sustained because of the deadly cold. A scandal erupted, hardly conducive to spirited morale, when Grippenberg and Kuropatkin publicly accused each other of incompetence and worse.

The struggle for Mukden followed inevitably. The combatants, more than half a million, conferred a dubious distinction upon the battle: it became the biggest in the annals of warfare up to that time and a harbinger of future slaughter between mass citizen armies. Japanese strategy, typically more daring than the Russian, masked the main assault with a diversionary move to the east of the city. Kuropatkin's response was sluggish and poorly coordinated, but he recognized the threat of a giant pincer movement that might trap his armies. The Japanese suffered heavy casualties in their offensive, however, and the battle raged furiously for nearly three weeks. On February 25 the Russians withdrew from Mukden and retreated in disorder along the rail line into northern Manchuria. The Japanese were too exhausted and short of ammunition to deliver the coup de grace. His command decimated by the loss of nearly a third of his men—seventy-thousand casualties and twenty-thousand prisoners—Kuropatkin relinquished his post on imperial orders.

News of the Russian defeat reached Rozhdestvensky in Madagascar before the Second Pacific Squadron had resumed its voyage. The route lay across the Indian Ocean, some 3,500 miles without a port. Repairs and coaling operations would take place in the open sea. The fleet "disappeared" for three weeks; on March 28 it passed near Singapore, reaching Cam Ranh Bay in French Indochina on April 1. Before proceeding on the last leg of the journey, Rozhdestvensky was "reinforced" by a small and decrepit squadron sent from the Baltic. He chose the most obvious passage to Vladivostok, the Tsushima Straits between Korea and Japan. Before dawn on May 14 his darkened fleet was sighted by the enemy. The date marked the anniversary of the tsar's coronation, and commemorative services were held on the larger vessels. Aboard the battleship *Oryol* the chaplain "gabbled the prayers unceremoniously, his thoughts obviously elsewhere. The men's faces were sour, and rigid as in a cataleptic trance.

The members of the congregation crossed themselves jerkily, as if flapping away flies. To wind up, they raucously sang *Long Live the Tsar*, and dispersed, muttering unseemly protests."[14]

The battle was joined in the afternoon when Vice Admiral Togo Heihachiro's fleet bore down from the north. The Russians opened the long-range duel with erratic salvos, sometimes effective despite a high proportion of defective shells. The Japanese reply a few minutes later quickly established their superior marksmanship. Within half an hour Rozhdestvensky's flagship, *Prince Suvorov*, had been set afire and the battleship *Oslyabya* sunk, losing two-thirds of her crew. Although the Japanese did not emerge wholly unscathed, the battle was decided well before nightfall. Rozhdestvensky, suffering multiple wounds, left *Suvorov* before it foundered; the battleships *Alexander III* and *Borodino* shared a similar fate. The remaining ships attempted to escape to Vladivostok under the cover of darkness. Only a cruiser and two destroyers succeeded; the others, subject to the whims of naval warfare, were scuttled, sunk, interned, or surrendered.

The 4,830 Russian sailors killed or drowned, together with some seven thousand imprisoned, offered eloquent testimony to the extent of the debacle. The toll at Mukden had been far greater, yet Tsushima struck an emotional chord that the land battles could not equal. The shock was felt most keenly in St. Petersburg, and even Nicholas, who had never lost faith in ultimate victory, registered his dismay. The news "weighs heavily upon my soul, with pain and sadness," he confessed. "I fear we shall have to drain the bitter cup to the dregs," he wrote his mother. He remained stoical but became "deathly pale" in the presence of his cousin Sandro.[15]

Faced with unrest and domestic violence that bordered on open rebellion, Nicholas for the first time seriously considered peace negotiations. As early as the summer of 1904 Tokyo had launched discreet inquiries, to no avail. They were renewed following the surrender of Port Arthur, again without result, and once more after the fall of Mukden, when the Japanese became gravely concerned by their inability to mount another offensive in Manchuria. President Theodore Roosevelt of the United States, who had offered his services in the cause of peace, privately registered his disgust with the tsar as a "preposterous little creature," the "absolute autocrat of 150,000,000 people. He has been unable to make war, and he is now unable to make peace."[16]

The disaster at Tsushima allowed Roosevelt to renew his efforts. Among other initiatives, he instructed the American ambassador, George Meyer, to request an audience with Nicholas, and it was granted on May 25. Meyer made an eloquent plea for peace, and perhaps because Nicholas listened quietly, he was favorably impressed with the tsar's self-possession. Nicholas had only the day before expressed support for negotiations at a military conference in Tsarskoe Selo, and he concluded the meeting, which lasted about an hour, by consenting to the president's offer. "You have come at a psychological moment," he told Meyer. As yet "no foot has been placed on Russian soil; but I realize that at almost any moment they can make an attack on Sakhaline [Island]. Therefore it is important that the meeting should take place before that occurs." He cautioned that his decision must remain "absolutely secret" until Japan either accepted or declined to negotiate.[17] Roosevelt, hitherto pessimistic about a positive response from Nicholas, was gratified and promptly invited the belligerents to confer directly without intermediaries. Both powers accepted, though disagreement arose as to a conference site: Japan preferred Asia and Russia a European capital. Washington proved an acceptable compromise, but its execrable summer climate induced a search for a cooler alternative. The coastal city of Portsmouth, New Hampshire, became the final choice.

Settling these procedural details tried Roosevelt's patience, principally because of Lamzdorf's arrogant manner, and he complained that "Russia is so corrupt, so treacherous and shifty, and so incompetent, that I'm utterly unable to say whether or not it will make peace, or break off the negotiations at any moment." Two weeks later, in a similar vein, he excoriated Russia as "so soddenly stupid and the Government . . . such an amorphous affair that they really do not know *what* they want."[18]

Nicholas had unanticipated difficulty in selecting an experienced diplomat to lead the Russian delegation. He quickly vetoed Lamzdorf's suggestion that Witte be appointed and instead selected Aleksandr Nelidov, the ambassador to Paris. Pleading ill health, among other disabilities, Nelidov declined, and the next candidate, Nikolai Muravyov, the ambassador to Rome, likewise refused, also claiming illness as well as poor qualifications. The search went on, and Nicholas finally and with extreme reluctance consented to Witte. Fully aware of the sovereign's aversion to him, Witte accepted the appointment without enthusiasm but resolved to do his best. He considered Nicholas "spiteful" and unforgiving: "I warned him against the Korean and Manchurian adventures, against the delaying of the evacuation of Manchuria, and the deleterious system of conducting the negotiations with Japan."[19] Aware, too, that he might become the scapegoat should the negotiations fail, he commented to the minister of finance: "When a sewer has to be cleaned, they send Witte; but as soon as work of a cleaner and nicer kind appears, plenty of other candidates spring up."[20] Despite his misgivings, he recognized the prestige as well as the importance of his new assignment: vanity and ambition, not simply patriotic duty, provided a powerful incentive.

Never one to suffer fools gladly, Witte took an unduly acerbic view of his subordinates, if his recollections faithfully record his opinions at the time. He had not been involved in their selection and simply accepted them because of his self-avowed wish not to "offend anyone." In Baron Roman Rosen, newly appointed to the ambassadorship in Washington, he found a "decent man, a gentleman to his fingertips," but "with the average intelligence of a logical Baltic German" and "quite out of touch with what was going on in Russia." G. A. Planson, "a typically obsequious bureaucrat," had served under Alekseyev as a "servile executor of a policy that had led us into this war." Fyodor Martens, a retired professor and a distinguished expert on international law who enjoyed an "inflated" reputation abroad, was a "limited person" and "afflicted with a pathological vanity." D. D. Pokotilov, the minister to Peking, happened to be a Witte protégé and thus one of the few who escaped the wounding thrusts of Witte's caustic pen.[21] A number of the plenipotentiaries resented Witte's highhandedness and his unwillingness to delegate authority or make better use of their services.

Prior to the opening of peace talks, Nicholas attended an extraordinary conference of his own with William II, one that culminated in the secret treaty of Björkö. The preliminaries to this curious episode in international diplomacy may be traced to the friendship that William had so assiduously cultivated with his royal cousin. The two had met uneventfully at Danzig in 1901, at Revel in 1902, and at Wiesbaden in 1903. The Revel meeting, on the occasion of naval maneuvers, had prompted William's provocative signal from his yacht: "The Admiral of the Atlantic bids farewell to the Admiral of the Pacific." Nicholas authorized an innocuous reply and muttered: "He's raving mad!"[22] Unable to weaken the Franco-Russian alliance, William could at least observe with satisfaction that Russia's commitment in the Far East weakened its role in European affairs. He grew uneasy at the Anglo-French rapprochement in 1904 and leaped at the opportunity presented by the Dogger Bank incident. Nicholas complained to him of "English and Japanese arrogance and insolence," suggesting a three-power alignment of Russia, Germany, and France.[23] William responded with the draft of a Russo-German alliance. But Nicholas' resentment toward Britain lessened, and he was no doubt reminded by Lamzdorf of Russia's obligation to France. William, for his part, balked at the idea of informing the French government before signing an alliance.

The draft treaty, allowed to dangle, was not forgotten. The kaiser brought a revised version on his cruise in the Baltic during the summer of 1905, and with a show of spontaneity he arranged a private meeting with Nicholas at Björkö on the Finnish coast near Vyborg. There on July 10–11, as the two imperial yachts, the *Hohenzollern* and the *Polar Star*, lay at anchor, the two emperors enjoyed a cordial reunion. According to William's effusive account, Nicholas revealed a "deep personal anger at England" and labeled King Edward VII a dangerous and deceptive intriguer. The kaiser hastened to agree, and with the camaraderie engendered by antipathy toward a mutual adversary he broached the subject of the abortive treaty proposal. When Nicholas expressed renewed interest, William was prepared: "I have a copy, which I happened to have quite by chance in my pocket." Nicholas examined the text as William "offered a fervent prayer to God that he would be with us and guide the young ruler." Nicholas soon rendered his verdict: "That is quite excellent. I quite agree!" With a casualness that belied his excitement, William invited his fellow monarch to sign the document: "It would be a very nice souvenir of our interview." Nicholas did so without hesitation, and his naval minister, Admiral Aleksei Birilev, obligingly signed as a witness without reading the text. With all signatures properly affixed, the two rulers embraced, and Nicholas commented, "I thank God and I thank you; it will be of the most beneficial consequences for my country and yours; you are Russia's only real friend in the whole world. I have felt that through the whole war and I know it." As for William, he shed tears of joy that Germany would "at last be freed from the frightful Gallo-Russian pincers."[24]

This triumph of personal diplomacy, as both emperors conceived it, turned to disaster with an element of farce when responsible officials in Berlin and St. Petersburg learned of the treaty. The German chancellor, Prince Bülow, offered his resignation, ostensibly because William had inserted the words "in Europe" in the article providing for mutual assistance in case of attack on either ally by a European power (that is, Great Britain). Russia would be of little help to Germany in a war with England unless it threatened to invade India. But the problem remained theoretical, because only after keeping his guilty secret for fifteen days did Nicholas finally confide, not without embarrassment, in his foreign minister. Lamzdorf was appalled—he "could not believe his eyes or ears"—and succeeded in conveying to his royal master the grave blunder in signing a treaty that violated the spirit if not the letter of the Franco-Russian alliance. Annulment furnished the only solution, but it had to be done with some finesse. Nicholas informed the kaiser in late September that the treaty "ought to be put off until we know how the French will look at it." William's voluble response revealed his disappointment and irritation ("We joined hands and signed before God who heard our vows!").[25] Nicholas then dropped the other shoe by proposing an amendment to the treaty that would make it inoperative in the event of war between Germany and France. William, who still hoped to salvage something from the Björkö affair, at last conceded that his diplomatic handiwork had collapsed. "A completely negative result," he complained, "after two months of conscientious hard work and negotiations. The first failure which I have personally experienced!" And he commented with shrewd insight: "The Tsar is not treacherous, but he is weak. Weakness is not treachery, but it fulfills all its functions."[26]

Peace with Japan was concluded in the interlude between the signature and the repudiation of the Björkö treaty. Witte had left Russia with the tsar's ringing admonition against the payment of "one kopek in indemnity or the cession of one inch of land."[27] He gave lip service to these instructions while recognizing that compromise might prove necessary: Japanese troops had in June occupied Russian territory—Sakhalin Island—for the first time and possessed the military capability of seizing Vladivostok and other portions of the Maritime Province. As to an indemnity, he remarked sardonically that if the Japanese army reached Moscow "we might reconsider." Relying on a strategy of sincerity, frankness, and "complete simplicity without any conceit" to win over American public opinion, he also cultivated the press by his accessibility and outspokenness.[28]

President Roosevelt, as host, received Witte and his Japanese counterpart, Baron Jutaro Komura, on separate occasions and later formally introduced the two delegations. Witte impressed Roosevelt, but not favorably. "I cannot say that I liked him," he confided in a letter after the conference, "for I thought his bragging and bluster not only foolish but shockingly vulgar when compared with the gentlemanly . . . Japanese. Moreover, he struck me as a very selfish man, totally without high ideals." He was also accused of being "utterly cynical, untruthful, and unscrupulous."[29] For his part, Witte found Roosevelt a strong personality with good intentions but complained that their relations "were not particularly harmonious or cordial." Nor did Roosevelt and "other American statesmen" escape his censure for their "ignorance" and "naive" judgments.[30]

Although the delegations were housed in a resort hotel near Portsmouth, the conference sessions took place across the bay in Kittery, Maine, where spacious accommodations were provided at the Portsmouth Navy Yard. Despite electric fans, the Russians—and presumably the Japanese—often found the heat suffocating and the voracious mosquitoes no less insufferable. Journalists also swarmed about, almost as annoying as the mosquitoes, and Witte and his colleagues were bombarded with letters and telegrams offering advice, requesting autographs, and espousing a variety of dubious causes.

Formal sessions began on July 28/August 10 with an exchange of credentials and the presentation of the Japanese peace terms. Witte spoke in French most of the time, but his imperfect knowledge of the language led him to frequent lapses into Russian. Except for Komura, who spoke in Japanese, the other members of his delegation chose to use English. Translators inevitably slowed the pace of the negotiations.

Although Witte maintained as a matter of diplomatic strategy and for the sake of public relations that the war had been "no more than a minor unpleasantness," he was prepared to recognize that conquest bestows its own legitimacy upon political claims. He therefore accepted the principle of Japanese hegemony over Korea and the Liaotung Peninsula, including the South Manchurian Railway between Port Arthur and Changchung. Yet he haggled over details with such persistence that the Japanese grew exasperated with his pettifogging tactics. He rejected out of hand the cession of Sakhalin or paying an indemnity, and a telegram from St. Petersburg conveying imperial instructions added three more items to the taboo list. A stalemate seemed inevitable, especially since Nicholas had regained confidence in the stability of his regime and was under pressure form the "war party" to renew hostilities should the Japanese prove obdurate. As if to remind himself of his "duty," he noted on the margin of one of Witte's telegrams to Lamzdorf: "It was said—not an inch of land, not a ruble of indemnities. On this I shall insist to the end."[31]

On August 5 Witte offered a possible compromise on the major stumbling block: a partition of Sakhalin, with Japan to annex the southern half. Komura expressed interest, provided Japan received compensation for removing its troops from the north (in fact, an indemnity in disguise). When the expected refusal came from St. Petersburg and the talks verged on an open break, Roosevelt intervened. He approached the kaiser, who promptly urged Nicholas to compromise and arranged an imperial audience for Ambassador Meyer. Nicholas received him at Peterhof on August 10, and after a two-hour conference he surprisingly agreed to the division of Sakhalin. He remained adamant, however, about an indemnity, disguised or not, and declared that he would go to Manchuria and lead the army himself before submitting to such a demand.[32] Unsatisfied, Roosevelt renewed his appeal to Nicholas, pointing out that Japan would probably occupy Harbin, Vladivostok, and eastern Siberia if the war dragged on. Nicholas refused to budge and instructed Lamzdorf, "Send Witte My order to end negotiations tomorrow [August 16] in any case. I prefer to continue the war rather than await gracious concessions on the part of Japan."[33] Witte protested to Lamzdorf that such an order placed him in an untenable position—that Russia, not Japan, would bear the onus of deliberately wrecking the hope for peace.

The prospects for a settlement were clouded when the envoys gathered for the final session on August 16. Witte had already prepared a telegram announcing failure. Komura meanwhile received a message from Tokyo to conclude a peace treaty even at the cost of foregoing both an indemnity and the whole of Sakhalin. In a preliminary meeting with Witte, Komura, without disclosing the full extent of his government's concession, revealed that the demand for an indemnity or other compensation had been dropped. The formal agreement to sign a peace treaty, as both delegations assembled, thus came as an anticlimax. Witte composed an unctuous telegram to Nicholas informing him that "peace will be restored thanks to your wise and firm decisions and in strict conformity with the instructions of your Majesty." In reality Nicholas' "firmness" had been stubborn pride and his "wisdom" open to question, although his intractable stand on the payment of an indemnity was vindicated by the final result. In other respects, he had steadily retreated from his original position under Witte's long-range "guidance." Not only did he yield Russian territory, however inconsequential, but he also reversed himself in conceding to Japan the South Manchurian Railway and fishing rights in Russian coastal waters.

The treaty caught Nicholas by surprise, and he "walked around all day as if in a trance." Irritated that Witte had disobeyed him, he refrained from expressing his appreciation, yet he could not remain oblivious to the success of Russian diplomacy. Mollified by congratulatory telegrams, he decided on August 18 that Witte may have done well after all: "Only today have I begun to get used to the thought that peace will be concluded and that this is probably good because that is the way it ought to be."[34] His belated message to Witte on August 20 was hardly effusive but satisfied the amenities: "I express to you my thanks for the able, firm conduct of the negotiations which you worked out to a good issue for Russia."[35]

With further details to be worked out, the formal signing of the peace treaty was delayed until August 23/September 5. Prior to the final ceremony Witte had been uncertain of Japan's intentions and succumbed to depression and anxiety ("I spent a restless, nightmarish night, sobbing and praying"). With the signature duly affixed, he telegraphed Nicholas, "We all thank God for the end of the war and pray for you."[36] For his part, Nicholas had not entirely reconciled himself to the treaty. "In the palace," he noted in his diary, "there began a divine service on the occasion of the conclusion of peace. I must confess that I did not feel in a joyful mood."[37]

Witte expected to tour the United States to strengthen the good will toward Russia that he had presumably generated at Portsmouth but thought better of it when he suspected "insidious intrigue" against him in St. Petersburg. "It was, no doubt, insinuated within His Majesty's hearing that I was aiming at becoming the president of the Russian Republic," he grumbled.[38] Despite his altered plans he spent nearly a week in New York and Washington as an honored guest. Among other activities, he visited the stock exchange, received an honorary degree from Columbia University, and dined with Roosevelt at Oyster Bay. He also had several meetings with the wealthy financier J. P. Morgan, including a trip up the Hudson River to see the military academy at West Point. He pronounced the lunch and dinner aboard Morgan's yacht "the only two decent meals I had while in America."[39]

On August 30 Witte boarded a German vessel in New York for the journey across the Atlantic. In poor health, he kept his condition to himself to avoid the "malingerer" label that had been applied to Nelidov and Muravyov. "The trouble," he maintained, "centered in my lungs, and I kept myself going by adhering to a strict diet and receiving powerful cocaine massages, which completely upset my nerves."[40]

In France, Witte conferred with President Emile Loubet, among others, and was received by the kaiser (with the tsar's approval) at the royal hunting lodge in Romintern. The German emperor conferred on him the Order of the Red Eagle, an "extraordinary honor," and revealed to him the substance of the Treaty of Björkö.

Back in St. Petersburg on September 15, Witte was gratified to learn that the sovereign was now, at least outwardly, well disposed toward him. Nicholas talked with him at length and found him "very charming and interesting." Witte, perceiving his affable mood, asked him pointedly: "Your Majesty, do you still have any doubts about my loyalty to you and do you believe those who have tried to persuade you that I am a revolutionary?" Nicholas very likely harbored reservations about Witte's political views but politely replied: "I trust you completely and have never believed those slanders." Witte, who thought the "slanders" had come chiefly from Plehve, was grateful for the emperor's expression of confidence despite his admission that he was aware of the slanderous charges.[41] When Nicholas told his envoy that he was conferring upon him the title of count, he recalled that Witte "went quite stiff with emotion" and "tried three times to kiss my hand!"[42] In a formal letter conveying the honor, Nicholas gave overdue and apparently sincere recognition of Witte's services, praising him for having acquitted himself "brilliantly" and acting "firmly and with the dignity which befits a representative of Russia." Official opinion and much of the educated public concurred in this estimate of his performance, but staunch patriots jeeringly nicknamed him "Count Half-Sakhalin."

One of the incidental consequences of Witte's journey to the United States arose from a letter he conveyed from Roosevelt to the tsar which referred to the Russo-American commercial treaty providing reciprocal freedom of travel. The president pointed out that American Jews were virtually excluded from Russia, and he expressed the hope that this discriminatory policy would be rescinded in the interest of the mutual friendship that Witte's visit had furthered. When no action was taken, the Jewish "lobby" in the United States began a campaign to abrogate the treaty, believing that such a step would place pressure on the Russian government to alleviate the plight of its own Jews. This strategy succeeded late in 1911 when the State Department, reluctantly but under a virtual Congressional mandate, gave notice that the treaty would be terminated in a year's time. Russian officials considered the action unwarranted interference in their domestic affairs, and in consequence the lot of Russia's Jews may well have retrogressed, though persecution (at least in the form of pogroms) did not flourish in the final years of the tsarist regime. Informal arrangements between Washington and St. Petersburg prevented any serious disruption of commercial relations.[43]

Unlike Japan, where the Portsmouth treaty provoked three days of rioting in Tokyo, Russia—that is, grass-roots rather than governmental Russia—received the settlement with stolid indifference. Domestic politics, soon to erupt once more in a trial of strength with the autocracy, dominated popular concerns. Indeed, it was difficult to perceive that the national interest had been affected one way or the other by the war or its somewhat ambiguous conclusion. To be sure, Russia's expansion had been checked in East Asia and Japan's correspondingly encouraged, and there were voices in official circles, including the emperor himself, who for a time lent support to the idea of a war of revenge. But such sentiments were a reflection of old-fashioned chauvinism rather than a considered judgment based on military realities, and they soon ceased to have any practical application as the government refocused its attention on internal affairs.

6

Revolution: The Dress Rehearsal

The wisdom of hindsight, in particular the events of 1917, conferred on the "revolution" of 1905 an aura of legitimacy that it would not otherwise have acquired. The popular though unsuccessful assault on the tsarist redoubt, unprecedented in Russian experience, caught monarchists and revolutionaries alike by surprise. The mismanaged war with Japan presented the opportunity, and an astonishing militance seized the urban public, with turbulent echoes in the countryside.

The government, too, aside from diplomatic blunders exceeded only by military incompetence, nearly self-destructed. Experience, skill, and timing are desirable if not essential prerequisites for an autocracy that seeks to reform itself. Nothing stimulates the appetite for change, indeed revolutionary excess, more than liberalization by slogan and by half-measures designed as a sop to public opinion. And an autocrat who embarks upon such a perilous enterprise should be confident not only of his own powers but those of the ruling elite and its support mechanism, that is, the loyalty and efficiency of the armed forces. The tsar, bereft of Witte's guidance by his own choice and of Plehve's by assassination, lurched between reform and reaction, seeking to control the situation but constantly wallowing in the wake of unfamiliar events that continually surprised and distressed him.

The selection of Prince Svyatopolk-Mirsky to become minister of the interior in August 1904 was greeted as the harbinger of a liberal "spring." The appointment had been delayed as the candidates jockeyed for position, and the choice of a moderate was influenced in part by the dowager empress. Nicholas interviewed Mirsky and found his reluctance to accept the post something of a novelty, "the mark of a noble mind and a praiseworthy indifference to the race for office."[1] Although a colleague complained that Mirsky "lacked will-power and initiative," possibly because of poor health, and was "without administrative experience," such carping notes were rare.[2] The new minister was known to be unsympathetic to his predecessor and had gained a reputation for leniency as governor-general of the Vilna region. He aroused further enthusiasm by dismissing "reactionaries" who had served under Plehve and by announcing his intention of fostering "an attitude of sincere trust [of the government] in public and class institutions and in the people." Zemstvo assemblies, municipal dumas, and other organizations, in addition to private individuals, sent messages of congratulation and good will. Expectations of basic reform stirred once more. Unfortunately, such lofty hopes could not be sustained, as Mirsky's wife foresaw: "In Russia's present condition, under such a sovereign . . . no minister can do anything. Besides, the squabbles of Petersburg can ruin the reputation of a saint, let alone an ordinary mortal."[3]

Mirsky, despite his sincerity and a kind of muddled idealism that sought to offend no one, was disinclined to tamper with the structure of autocracy. If he managed to preserve his optimism amid the sudden groundswell of popular excitement, Nicholas himself grew uneasy, for he had encouraged gestures of conciliation to unify the war effort, not to dismantle imperial authority. Mirsky nonetheless forged ahead. He encouraged freedom of expression and cultivated the zemstvo liberals, ending the harassment and other disabilities to which they had been subjected even before the Plehve era. He also approved the extension of zemstvos to the border provinces and hinted that their representatives might be appointed to the State Council. Recognizing that the unsavory image of the Okhrana might tarnish his efforts toward "spreading sunshine and enchanting the public," he placed it under a supposedly autonomous assistant minister.[4] He also gave permission for an assembly of zemstvo leaders to be held in the capital.

On November 6–9, 1904, meeting in private homes, 104 zemstvo delegates gathered to chart a new political course. Despite the nominal secrecy of the proceedings, an unprecedented groundswell of public support materialized; over five thousand telegrams were sent offering encouragement and urging reform. An unrepresentative and largely self-appointed body—the delegates bore no specific mandate from their constituencies—it was heavily weighted toward "radicals" and moderate constitutionalists. The influence of traditional liberals, of whom Dmitri Shipov was the most prominent, had greatly diminished, though he was elected chairman on the strength of his past services. A sizable minority urged a resolution in favor of a constituent assembly, but in the interest of harmony with the government a compromise passed with near unanimity calling only for "freely elected representatives of the people" to guide the country toward "a new path of political growth marked by the establishment of the rule of law and cooperation between the government and the people."[5]

A delegation was chosen to call on Mirsky, who declined to receive it because of his determination to avoid granting any kind of official recognition. He did see Shipov, however, and accepted in late November a memorandum on the zemstvo demands that public opinion had already rendered obsolete. "Society"—at least its most vigorous spokesmen—had embarked upon a "banquet campaign" in imitation of the French revolutionaries of 1847–1848 who had successfully forced the abdication of King Louis Philippe. Russia's larger cities experienced a veritable epidemic of banquets in which intellectuals, professionals, and public men gathered to denounce the regime and to compose fiery declarations, usually calling for a constitution. Censorship having been also relaxed, there were audacious editorials and a proliferation of newspapers and journals. Nicholas refrained from interference, though he apparently blamed his minister for allowing the situation to get out of hand. The flood of resolutions and demands vastly irritated him. "I find this action insolent and tactless," he wrote on the margin of a telegram from the Chernigov zemstvo. "The zemstvo assemblies, whose jurisdiction is clearly defined by law, have no business to concern themselves with matters of state."[6]

Increasingly frustrated by the emperor's vacillating attitude, which seemed to approve reform in principle but seldom in practice, Mirsky sent a letter on November 21 asking that he be allowed to resign. The unexpected request shocked and angered Nicholas, who summoned the errant minister to Tsarskoe Selo and scolded him for his temerity. But Mirsky did not equivocate and spoke more boldly about the necessity of reform than Nicholas was accustomed to hearing. In the end, though the two apparently talked at cross-purposes much of the time and no concessions were extracted from the tsar, Mirsky promised to stay on: "There were tears, and I kissed his hand."[7]

His moral authority at least temporarily enhanced, Mirsky hastened to submit a report outlining his program.[8] He anticipated imperial support and sought a high-level meeting that would smooth the path for reform. Nicholas consented and presided over a special conference of ministers, State Council members, and designated guests, apparently held on December 2, 6, and 8. (No official account of the proceedings was kept, and the dates are in dispute.) The presence of several grand dukes added an ultra-conservative flavor to the proceedings. Nicholas, violating his promise to Mirsky, even invited Pobedonostsev with a personal note: "We are all confused. Help us bring order out of this chaos." Inadequately prepared and an ineffective speaker, Mirsky relied on "intuition mixed with a little sound common sense" and fared poorly in such distinguished company.[9] Pobedonostsev recalled his own struggle against the "constitution" proposed at the beginning of Alexander III's reign and warned against a repetition of that folly. The opposition of the venerable reactionary could be taken for granted—even Nicholas was prepared to discount his "senile chatter"— but Mirsky had counted on Witte to come to his aid. Instead, Witte played both volubly and persuasively on the tsar's anxiety that a constitutional order would be the ultimate outcome of major reform. He proposed a "compromise" solution that carried the meeting, largely because Nicholas approved it: to reject the plan to admit elected representatives to the State Council but to examine the other suggestions.

The matter was transferred to Witte's domain as chairman of the Committee of Ministers, and he seized the opportunity to assume the mantle of statesmanship once more with unconcealed pleasure. That he had engineered a minor political coup disgusted Mirsky's wife: "Only one feeling governs him—self love and a passion for power."[10] As for Mirsky himself, recognizing that his program had been emasculated, he allegedly left the conference "completely broken in spirit" and remarked gloomily to his collaborators, "Everything has failed. Let us build jails."[11]

Critics on the Right pointed out that Plehve had acted in office so as to divert public discontent from the government to himself, while Mirsky curried favor by shifting the blame for unpopular decisions on to the tsar. To the extent that this was true—the dichotomy was of course exaggerated—it simply meant that Plehve had been a convinced apologist for absolute monarchy whereas Mirsky harbored reservations about the system he was charged with upholding. Autocracy tends to fare poorly when its servants are insufficiently dedicated to its values and traditions. If Nicholas chose to resist granting concessions, he should have searched for another Plehve. But he vacillated and did neither.

The result was the imperial decree ("Concerning Plans for the Improvement of the Social Order") of December 12, 1904, which offered cosmetic remedies for governmental malpractice but stood firm against any erosion of autocratic power. "I will never agree to the representative form of government," he told Witte, "because I consider it harmful to the people whom God has entrusted to me."[12] Nicholas, following the "hallowed precepts" of his royal ancestors and "mindful of the sacredness" of the divine power thrust upon him, promised to improve the lot of the peasants, to assure justice and equality before the law, grant the zemstvos and municipal dumas a more significant role in local affairs, provide government insurance for factory workers, permit a greater measure of religious toleration, and to remove unnecessary restrictions on the press.[13] Had these assurances been forthcoming, with proper implementation, earlier in his reign they would have gratified the vast majority of his subjects. Coming when and as they did, extracted from a reluctant sovereign by mass protest and missing the vital ingredient of Mirsky's formulation, the promises were greeted with skepticism. Even for those accepting the pledge at face value, the inertia of the higher bureaucracy was so engrained that no one could predict when the reforms might be realized. The popular mood was also aggravated by an official announcement on December 14 that no more illegal meetings and demonstrations would be permitted, that zemstvos and dumas should confine their activities to legitimate functions, and that the press should cease its obstreperousness. Though the police apparatus enforced the edict with expedient laxity, public order was restored in most parts of the empire. Dissension and unrest persisted, however, especially among the minority nationalities. Many, perhaps most, middle-class liberals were further estranged, and the ranks of the revolutionary opposition swelled with new recruits.

Beset by problems of state both internal and external, Nicholas found comfort and solace in the annual commemoration on January 6, 1905, of Epiphany, a holiday that honored several traditions of early Christianity and was accompanied in the Orthodox faith by the ceremony of the "blessing of the waters." Respectful but spirited crowds gathered in the capital as Nicholas and his retinue proceeded to the Winter Palace for the celebration of a mass in the chapel. The royal party, together with dignitaries of church and state, then gathered under a canopy on the ice of the Neva River where the clergy, headed by the Metropolitan Anthony, pronounced the blessing as a cross was lowered into the water. An artillery battery stationed across the river fired the traditional salute as the ritual ended. One of the shells, to the consternation of the assembled guests, contained live ammunition which wounded a policeman and broke some windows in the palace. Nicholas, outwardly unperturbed, completed the ceremony. The affair received no local publicity—apparently the censors exercised vigilance—but reports reached the foreign press, and rumors swept the city that an assassination attempt had been made. An official inquiry disclosed nothing more sinister than simple negligence. The officers in charge received light punishment, soon followed by imperial clemency.[14]

Only three days later the incident was virtually forgotten in the wake of "Bloody Sunday," an event less shocking than Khodynka in the number of casualties but infinitely more serious for the future of the monarchy. The massacre perpetrated by the tsarist regime on January 9 had a lengthy and labyrinthine gestation period involving two onetime collaborators in "police socialism," Sergei Zubatov[15] and Father Georgi Gapon.[16] A sophisticated and zealous proponent of monarchism, Zubatov had joined the Okhrana in 1886, originally as an informant, and by talent and dedication rose to become chief of the Moscow office within a decade. In 1898 he composed a thoughtful memorandum arguing that the proper method of insuring the loyalty of the working class and of protecting it from revolutionary contamination lay in police-supervised labor organizations. His political superiors accepted the scheme on an experimental basis, even though trade unions were forbidden by law. Under the guise of mutual aid societies these organizations flourished in Moscow, Kiev, Odessa, and other cities.

Zubatov recognized that the workers had legitimate grievances and was not averse to agitation, even strikes, if the economic aspects of the dispute could be sealed off from their political implications. Plehve and other officials remained wary of the project, yet Zubatov was promoted in 1902 to head the Okhrana.

Seeking recruits to lead a police-sponsored union in the capital, Zubatov met an ambitious young priest name Georgi Gapon. Although criticized as "hare-brained, ignorant, [and] conceited,"[17] Gapon possessed the charismatic qualities of a born leader and had gained a reputation for humanitarian work among the poor. He hovered on the fringes of Zubatov's police network, reluctant to become a paid agent, and finally gained permission to found an independent union in the summer of 1903. Shortly thereafter Plehve abruptly dismissed Zubatov, who had unwisely become entangled in the power struggle between the interior and finance ministers. Invited to return to police service after Plehve's assassination, he refused successive offers and remained in retirement, still a convinced monarchist but embittered by the circumstances of his ouster.

Gapon, no longer under Zubatov's tutelage, though the two had parted on friendly terms, proceeded to build up a following among the city's workers. A newly opened clubhouse became a center of social and educational activities, and in time the proliferation of similar facilities testified to the popularity of the concept. The authorities kept a close watch on these developments, including the formal establishment of the St. Petersburg Assembly of Russian Factory and Mill Workers in 1904. Gapon cooperated fully and even accepted police funds—four hundred rubles on one occasion—to "divert suspicion." The money was entered on the books as an "anonymous gift."[18] How much his assistants—and ordinary members—knew about his peculiar relationship with the tsarist regime is uncertain, but he made no secret of his extensive contacts and regarded them as an asset to the organization. It would not have occurred to him that he had compromised his integrity or acted in any sense as an agent or dupe of the secret police. The "partnership" at first proved mutually beneficial: the government was bolstered by a presumably loyal and docile labor movement, and Gapon achieved modest renown while pursuing good works as a champion of the proletariat and a devoted servant of the church.

The harmony of complementary interests was in time eroded by Gapon's growing spirit of independence. His career might have ended as ignominiously as Zubatov's but for the appointment of Svyatopolk-Mirsky and the permissive atmosphere that then briefly prevailed. As the Workers' Assembly expanded in numbers and influence, employers and factory managers became apprehensive. When four of its members were dismissed at the giant Putilov Works, whose shipbuilding and munitions production made it essential to the war effort, Gapon perceived their discharge as a serious challenge to his organization. The dispute escalated as negotiations failed. A strike, joined by sympathetic workers from other enterprises, immobilized the plant in early January 1905. Gapon's idea of a petition to the sovereign for a redress of grievances found ready acceptance among his followers. "The tsar does not know of our needs, and we will tell him," he declared. "If he loves his people, he will grant them their humble supplications."[19] Government officials pressured him to end the strike, however, and Mirsky refused to see him. In an unpleasant encounter with the minister of justice, Nikolai Muravyov, he allegedly "behaved with such undue familiarity and so insolently that everyone was outraged."[20]

On January 6 Gapon made the unique suggestion that the petition to the tsar, still in the process of revision, be presented in person by a workers' delegation. The proposal won speedy approval in the Assembly, and preparations began for a mass procession, including women and children, to the Winter Palace. The petition itself, couched in the sacerdotal idiom that was unmistakably Gapon's, pleaded with the tsar in obsequious terms: "Do not turn Thy help away from Thy people. Lead them out from the mire of lawlessness, poverty, and ignorance. Allow them to determine their own future; deliver them from the intolerable oppression of the officialdom. Raze the wall that separates Thee from Thy people and rule the country with them." The document purported to speak for not simply the workers of the capital but the "entire toiling class of Russia." Its demands, though respectfully phrased, were surprisingly bold. The "essential" one called for "popular representation," with elections to a constituent assembly by "universal, secret, and equal suffrage." Others included an amnesty for political and religious offenders; freedom of speech, press, assembly, and religion; free and compulsory public education; equality before the law; and separation of church and state.[21]

Copies of the petition, bearing the title "A Most Humble and Loyal Address," were sent to the emperor and various officials. Gapon himself kept the original containing workers' signatures. Properly forewarned, the government accepted the impending confrontation with no sense of urgency or anxiety. Troops and police received their assignments, and Mirsky told his colleagues at a meeting on January 8 that the workers would be barred from the center of the city, particularly the palace square. Nicholas, at Tsarskoe Selo, was induced to rescind his order to place the capital under martial law. He complacently noted in his diary: "The workers are behaving peacefully so far. . . . The head of the union is some priest-socialist Gapon."[22] That the workers might choose to defy the constituted authorities never seems to have occurred to anyone in a position of power. For his part, Gapon added fuel to the flames by numerous speeches that roused his listeners to a frenzy. His tone had become increasingly apocalyptic despite his insistence upon an orderly demonstration and his reassurances as to the benevolent intentions of the tsar. Recognizing at the proverbial last minute that he had become a potentially dangerous firebrand, the government issued on the evening of the 8th an "absolutely secret" order for his arrest. But the wily strike leader, anticipating such a possibility, had already gone into hiding, protected by loyal workers.[23]

Sunday, January 9, dawned sunny but cold. Groups of workers in the suburbs and outlying areas of the city had already begun the long march to the palace square, where the various detachments were to rendezvous before 2 P.M. Troops blocked most of the canal and river bridges, necessitating extensive detours, and thousands crossed the ice of the Neva River. Others, less determined, retreated or simply dispersed and went home. Gapon led the biggest procession, including the Putilov strikers, and the leading echelon carried icons, portraits of the tsars, and a large cross. The singing of hymns and the national anthem, "God Save the Tsar," lent an imposing dignity to the occasion. At the Narva Arch, commemorating Russian victories in the Napoleonic wars, infantry and cavalry units blocked the way. Mounted troopers charged the crowd but were unable to scatter it. As the march resumed, soldiers with rifles at the ready confronted the workers, and the commanding officer gave the order to fire. The first two volleys were aimed above the crowd; those that followed took deadly effect at close range, causing perhaps a hundred casualties. Gapon, unscathed but in a state of shock, found refuge in a series of private dwellings.

The massacre, with minor variations, repeated itself on a smaller scale in other parts of the capital. The classic pattern of unarmed civilians versus trained soldiers "doing their duty" prevailed. At Troitskaya Square next to the Peter and Paul Fortress there were forty victims, according to the official figure, at least triple that number by other accounts. At the Winter Palace, where troops supported by artillery were massed, demonstrators gathered on the adjacent streets. Peaceful at first, they became more unruly as word of the carnage elsewhere arrived and wounded survivors appeared on the scene. By 2 P.M. the huge procession supposedly led by Gapon had failed to materialize, and the Tsar himself remained absent. A company of Guards then attempted without success to clear the nearby Alexandrovsky Garden. A cavalry charge against the main body of the crowd encroaching upon the palace square also proved futile. Most of the demonstrators either stood their ground or found another vantage point, and bolder spirits responded with jeers and derisive shouts. Finally, his patience exhausted, the Guards commander gave permission to open fire. After three warning bugle calls, a company of infantry raked the crowd with two rifle volleys, inflicting some thirty casualties. Many of the survivors, though cowed for the moment, poured into side streets and vented their fury by breaking windows and attacking officers and uniformed officials. In a kind of mopping-up operation, military detachments cleared the main streets with brutal efficiency, leaving still more dead and wounded. By nightfall a sullen calm, except for looting and a few minor disorders, had descended upon the stricken city.

Bloody Sunday—the appellation only gradually gained currency—shocked and outraged not only the Russian public but also world opinion. Sensational versions in the foreign press, many based on rumor and fabrication, invariably exaggerated the casualties. The heavily censored Russian press could print only government handouts that inevitably minimized the bloodshed. The final report raised the number of fatalities to 130, excluding those who had not been admitted to a hospital and others who later succumbed to their wounds. That approximately 150 were killed and several hundred were wounded seems an accurate estimate but is at considerable variance from the inflated statistics favored by most Soviet historians. Gapon himself placed the death toll at between six and nine hundred, with "at least five thousand wounded."[24]

The tragedy acquired a mystique of its own. The reality was gruesome enough, but public alienation reached such heights that the regime's foolish incompetence was perceived as a callous act of deliberate brutality. Nicholas, not inappropriately, became the instigator and therefore the chief scapegoat of the affair. His actual role had been one of studied passivity. A more capable ruler would have seized the opportunity to cultivate his image and cement his bonds with the St. Petersburg workers. The naive tradition of the tsar as the "little father" of his people ended abruptly, at least among the urban proletariat. Nicholas continued to reside at Tsarskoe Selo, curiously detached from the handiwork of his subordinates. He never fully grasped the political implications of the disaster, not withstanding conventional expressions of sorrow. "A distressing day!" he noted in his diary. "In Petersburg serious disorders occurred because workers wanted to go to the Winter Palace. Troops had to fire at different places in the city, and many were killed and wounded. God, how painful and terrible!"[25]

Persuaded that some conciliatory gesture was necessary, Nicholas considered a manifesto offering labor an opportunity to air its complaints. He withdrew it, however, in favor of a plan to receive a deputation of "reliable" workers. When the minister of finance pointed out how unrepresentative the selection process had become and that the "radical elements" were boycotting the "elections," Nicholas replied testily, "If this is so, no one can reproach me for being indifferent to the needs of the workers; they are to blame for having refused to come to me with confidence."[26]

On January 19 thirty-four reluctant delegates, essentially chosen by their employers, were escorted by police officers to the Winter Palace. There they were strip-searched, briefed on matters of protocol in the royal presence, and personally inspected by the newly appointed governor-general of the capital district, General Dmitri Trepov. Taken by train to Tsarskoe Selo, they waited respectfully in a hall at the palace until the emperor appeared and read a short speech that Trepov had originally drafted. Nicholas omitted from the text a reference to his "grief for the unfortunate, mostly innocent victims of the current disorders" and altered another passage to scold the workers for "having let traitors and enemies of the motherland lead you into error and delusion." He assured the gathering that he was concerned with labor problems and would do everything possible to improve conditions. "I believe in the honorable feelings of the working people and in their unshakable devotion to me," he declared, "and therefore I forgive them their guilt."[27] He promised a donation of fifty thousand rubles to families of the victims and spoke individually to most of the workers. Tea and sandwiches were served, and as the delegates withdrew Nicholas urged them to go back to their jobs with "God's blessing" and to convey his words to their comrades.

If the reception gratified Nicholas' sense of noblesse oblige, it angered the working class and was denounced as a provocation by opponents of the regime. Many of those who participated in the charade at Tsarskoe Selo were subjected to verbal if not physical abuse when they returned to the factories. The capital still resembled an armed camp. A general strike, joined by students, professors, journalists, and other members of the educated public, merged with the "liberation" movement in demanding reform and an elected national assembly. Outside St. Petersburg, strikes and demonstrations erupted in almost every industrial center. Violence occurred most frequently in the borderlands, where anti-Russian nationalism provided additional incitement to political disorder. Only in late January did economic necessity dictate a temporary end to the strike movement.

Nicholas deeply resented concessions torn from him by force or intimidation. He remained stubbornly convinced, despite overwhelming evidence to the contrary, that only a tiny segment of troublemakers, principally revolutionaries, intellectuals, and Jews, were engaged in a conspiracy against the throne and that he retained the loyalty and devotion of the common people. Even more fatuously, he blamed "English intrigues" for playing "a major role in instigating the rebellion of the Petersburg laboring masses."[28] Most professional revolutionaries of any reputation were safely abroad and evinced no compelling urge toward a hasty and possibly ill-timed return. Lenin was among them, reaching his homeland only in November when the revolutionary tide had begun to recede. A notable exception was Leon Trotsky, an independent Marxist with recent Menshevik affiliations, who had to exercise discretion upon his premature return and eventually retreated to the relative safety of Finland.

The only "celebrity" revolutionary was Father Gapon, whose conversion to the anti-tsarist crusade had been instantaneous on January 9. His vitriolic outbursts knew no bounds, and he assumed as his natural right the post of chief avenger of Bloody Sunday. Ill prepared for his new career— his intellectual depth and political skills were distressingly meager—Gapon found sanctuary abroad. In Geneva, a hotbed of émigré radicalism, he had flirted with the Social Democrats and joined the Socialist Revolutionaries. Later he became involved in an abortive gun-running expedition to Russia.

Frustrated and lured by the dramatic events in his homeland, he returned to St. Petersburg in November 1905. There, rather superfluous and increasingly at odds with the radical intelligentsia, he sought to rebuild his old following in the Assembly and to renew his government contacts. Enticed by the promises of the Okhrana and seduced by its financial rewards, he became enmeshed in a farcical game of cat and mouse with the authorities. (He possessed the feral instincts of a cat but ended up playing the mouse.) An embarrassment to his former comrades, he fell victim to an "execution squad" of Socialist Revolutionaries who, without a formal party mandate, hanged him in March 1906. Gapon's meteoric rise and fall was perhaps the most bizarre episode in the colorful saga of Russia's revolutionaries. Had he perished more opportunely, struck down by a soldier's bullet on that fateful Sunday, his place in the pantheon of martyred heroes in the struggle against tsarist tyranny would have been permanently enshrined.

By early February of 1905 the autocracy had subdued its more vociferous domestic foes but without a notable enhancement of its image. Prince Mirsky, depressed and discouraged, had renewed his attempt to resign shortly after the December decree. Nicholas had obviously lost confidence in him but, lacking an immediate replacement, asked that he remain for the time being. By some accounts, Witte would have been appointed to the vacant post if Nicholas had not suspected him of being a Freemason.[29] Mirsky loyally obeyed, absorbing more than his fair share of responsibility for Bloody Sunday. After further entreaties, he was allowed to retire without the courtesy of a seat on the State Council—an unprecedented rebuke—or the slightest token of appreciation. The extreme Right showered him with abuse, claiming that he was sympathetic to the Poles, "a friend of the 'kikes,' [and] a traitor whose policies had opened the door to revolution."[30] Nicholas may not have shared such irrational views, but he blamed his departed minister for the strikes and disturbances that had led to the fateful confrontation with tsarist authority.

Mirsky's replacement, Aleksandr Bulygin, was a wealthy landowner and former provincial governor who had been recommended by General Trepov. Considered a "pleasant and honest man" of "innate good nature," he, like most administrators of his rank and experience, proved deficient in those statesmanlike qualities that might renew the short-lived dialogue between tsar and people.[31] Even had he possessed the wisdom and determination to pursue such a goal, he would have encountered the intransigence of the sovereign, whose notions of reform lagged far behind public expectations. But Nicholas, for all his egregious flaws of character and judgment, was not without a sense of honor and royal obligation. He had made certain promises in his decree of December 12, and he fully intended to carry them out—"interpreted" of course in his own unique fashion. Nor did he retract his words about improved working conditions imparted to the delegation at Tsarskoe Selo. He selected Nikolai Shidlovsky, a senator and member of the State Council, to chair a special commission on the causes and possible remedies for labor unrest in the capital. Both workers and employers were to elect representatives to serve in the investigation. But the workers proved so obstreperous in their demands—many had fallen under the influence of the Social Democrats—that the elections were never completed, and on February 20 Nicholas ordered the dissolution of the commission. A renewed wave of strikes erupted.

Shidlovsky's ill-fated enterprise was essentially taken over by another commission already in existence under the chairmanship of Minister of Finance Vladimir Kokovtsov. Workers' representatives were excluded, but a genuine effort to provide remedies for labor grievances might have reached fruition had the industrialists who participated in plenary sessions not withdrawn their support. The commission languished in obscurity and futility, with only occasional meetings later in the year.

Other tentative reforms proceeded at a leisurely pace through the bureaucratic maze. Nicholas had received a profound personal shock when his uncle, the Grand Duke Sergei Aleksandrovich, was assassinated on February 4. As the longtime governor-general of Moscow, Sergei was thoroughly detested by the public as a die-hard reactionary. Not even his cousin could "find a single redeeming feature in his character," said to be "obstinate, arrogant, [and] disagreeable."[32] He became the second major victim of the terrorist Battle Organization and the first member of the dynasty to be killed since Alexander II. The assassin, an expelled student named Ivan Kalyayev, threw a bomb near one of the Kremlin gates, demolishing the grand duke's carriage and reducing its occupant to a "ghastly crimson mess."[33] Noting the "frightful crime," Nicholas attended a mass for his uncle but declined a journey to Moscow for the funeral service as too risky. Sergei's widow, the Grand Duchess Yelizaveta, visited the assassin in his prison cell and interceded with the tsar to spare his life. Nicholas might have done so had Kalyayev shown remorse and asked for clemency.[34]

Something of a self-imposed prisoner at Tsarskoe Selo, Nicholas chaired special sessions of the Council of Ministers—nearly moribund in recent years—on February 3, 11, and 18. Mirsky's idea of electing representatives to share in the legislative process was revived, though the unfortunate minister had already been consigned to memory. On February 18, to the confounding of his own ministers, who were scheduled to meet later that day, an imperial manifesto was published. Prepared in secret, the document was sufficiently "reactionary" to be ascribed to Pobedonostsev, but the question of authorship remains obscure. The manifesto upbraided disturbers of the peace, called upon loyal citizens to join the struggle against sedition, and reaffirmed the tradition of autocracy. And with a brazen candor that could not fail to insult public opinion, it maintained that the war with Japan was being fought "for the honor and glory of Russia and for the domination of the Pacific Ocean."[35] The negative impression created by this pronouncement was softened by a decree to the Senate granting the right of petition. Those with honorable intentions might henceforth submit, for the common good, proposals that would be examined by the Council of Ministers. In the same vein Nicholas reluctantly signed a rescript declaring that the new minister of the interior had been charged with implementing the tsar's decision "to assemble the most trustworthy men, possessing the confidence of the people and elected by them, to undertake the preliminary examination and consideration of legislative measures." As Nicholas saw it, he had preserved the dignity of the throne by admonishing unruly critics while graciously bestowing upon his subjects political rights that they had never known before. Whether the imperial horn of plenty thus presented was half full or half empty remained a matter for public scrutiny.

The Bulygin Duma, as the project for a consultative assembly came to be known, would have won overwhelming approval a decade earlier. In 1905, with popular expectations having rapidly outstripped governmental initiatives, Nicholas' "generosity" fit the classic mold of ill-timed reform: too little and too late. The ingratitude displayed by the politically literate did not necessarily extend to the rural masses, whose knowledge of ideology and governmental affairs was at best ill informed. Yet the peasants were not insensible to urban disorder, and faint stirrings of unrest in the countryside recalled the agrarian disturbances of 1902.

As Bulygin, with no sense of urgency, worked on his assignment, the army's defeat at Mukden and the naval disaster at Tsushima encouraged bolder demands upon the government. Liberal monarchists, satisfied with the modest concessions granted by the sovereign, were now considered ossified reactionaries. Virtually every organization representing the educated public, joined by the urban proletariat and ethnic minorities, clamored for a constituent assembly elected on the basis of universal suffrage and an ambitious program of social reform. In May, climaxing months of effort, chiefly by the "radical" Union of Liberation, representatives of fourteen professional and other interest groups founded the Union of Unions in Moscow. A separate zemstvo congress, though "conservative" in the context of the times and badly divided, voted to present a petition to the tsar. The socialists accepted the idea of a constituent assembly readily enough but looked forward to a "bourgeois" revolution that would make a clean sweep of the monarchy. In their view only an armed insurrection, not the genteel method of the ballot box, could dislodge the intractable autocracy.

Nicholas acknowledged the lesser of evils by receiving a zemstvo delegation at Peterhof on June 6. The occasion marked his first meeting with a representative body of the public, and he chose to be polite and conciliatory. Prince Sergei Trubetskoy, a distinguished scholar, spoke for his colleagues in a deferential vein, for which he later received sharp criticism from the Left. Just as the sovereign is above social distinction, the ruler of all his people, so must the forthcoming assembly "serve the interests of the whole realm and not of classes," he declared. "Your Majesty, return to the formula of Svyatopolk-Mirsky, that the renewal of Russia must be based on confidence." Nicholas responded with serviceable platitudes on the "unity between the Tsar and all of Russia" but indicated his determination to pursue the course of reform: "Cast aside your doubts. My will—the Tsar's will—to call together representatives from the people is unswerving. Attracting them to the work of the state will be done in an orderly fashion. . . . I hope that you will help me in this work."[36]

Anti-monarchists remained skeptical of the sovereign's good faith, and their suspicions were confirmed in short order. On June 20 Nicholas received a delegation of nobles from Kerch Province and assured them that the "consultative institution" he envisaged would be composed of the "two basic landed classes, the nobility and the peasantry, which from time immemorial have shared joy and grief with their Tsar." The next day, receiving yet another conservative delegation, he failed to contradict its plea to maintain the autocratic system.[37] With either singular naivete or calculated ambiguity—no one could be sure which—Nicholas pursued an enigmatic course that did much to diminish the residue of good will still available to the established order.

During the summer sporadic strikes and rioting, coupled with the first instances of major disaffection in the armed forces, stretched to the limit the government's capacity to maintain public order. The most notorious episode, unprecedented in the annals of the Russian navy, involved mutiny aboard the battleship *Potemkin*, the pride of the Black Sea fleet (to Nicholas "horrifying news . . . not to be believed!").[38] The mutineers, who commandeered the ship in mid-June after shooting several officers, found temporary refuge at Odessa, where virtual civil war had broken out. Their example, ending in failure, did not prove contagious, but problems of discipline and morale rendered the fleet suspect for several years to come.

These disturbances in outlying parts of the empire, while serious enough, created no sense of emergency in St. Petersburg. When Bulygin and his assistants, chiefly Sergei Kryzhanovsky, at last submitted a draft program for a State Duma, Nicholas convened a special conference at Peterhof on July 19.[39] Ministers and other high officials, five grand dukes, and the distinguished historian Klyuchevsky attended successive meetings to determine the electoral procedure and other details. An elite body, it nevertheless incorporated a variety of opinion, short of radicalism, and witnessed lively debates. But in general the "moderate" viewpoint, as represented by Bulygin and the Council of Ministers, tended to prevail. Nicholas assumed the chairmanship, and after each article had been subjected to thorough discussion, he reserved the right to make the final decision. The most hotly contested issue, whether legislation rejected by the Duma should be submitted to the emperor, was resolved in favor of autocratic power. Nicholas formally announced the statutes creating the Bulygin Duma on August 6 in a florid manifesto calling for the elected representatives to render "useful and zealous assistance . . . for the sake of Our common Mother Russia, to maintain the unity, security, and greatness of the State in addition to popular order and prosperity."

The public reaction ranged from indifference to derision, although it was conceded by many liberals that a representative institution, whatever its defects, provided an outlet for political discussion. The extreme Left, as was to be expected, scorned the project as irrelevant to revolutionary goals, but even the "bourgeois" Union of Unions championed a boycott. The complicated voting arrangements, weighted in favor of the presumably conservative landlords and peasants, appeared to insure a docile assembly divested of any legislative authority. Convinced that he had been generous to a fault, while admitting that details of the reform needed further elaboration, Nicholas ignored protests and allowed General Trepov, who also served as the chief of police, a free hand in suppressing dissent. Trepov was not content, however, with the efficacy of force and recommended measures to influence public opinion that Nicholas apparently found uncongenial and inappropriate.

The government, once buttressed by peace with Japan, seemed to regain self-confidence. Few would have predicted that the turbulence of the past few months was only a prelude to more serious disorders. Foreseeing no major problems requiring his presence, Nicholas, together with his family, departed from Peterhof on September 4 for a two-week cruise on his yacht.

With a spontaneity that had no obvious inspiration from revolutionary agitation, the urban and rural masses soon offered a direct challenge to governmental authority. Sporadic violence in the countryside gave way to a peasant *jacquerie* that threatened to dispossess the landowning gentry. In the cities the government's constant battle against subversion was undercut by a tactical blunder: the restoration on August 27 of autonomous rights for universities and other institutions of higher learning. Classrooms and auditoriums were converted into political rostrums where students and townspeople gathered with impunity to denounce autocratic rule. Strikes in Moscow coalesced into boisterous political demonstrations, with street fighting and numerous casualties. Railroad workers walked off the job, and by the second week of October the transportation system had ground to a halt. A general strike, unparalleled in Russian and even in world history, paralyzed the government in St. Petersburg and spread throughout the empire. Students and teachers, clerks and factory hands, ballet dancers and lawyers, even lower-grade civil servants, joined the strike movement and in so doing delivered a resounding vote of no confidence in the existing regime.

Alarm verged upon panic in government circles. Nicholas, who had returned to Peterhof on September 18, maintained his composure and continued his normal routine with a complacency that astonished members of his entourage. He was well briefed—perhaps too well briefed, for similar reports throughout his reign had dulled his political instincts, reinforcing his natural passivity and fatalistic disposition. Moreover, the accustomed ritual of autocratic power, in which adoring crowds and faithful retainers seemed daily reminders of his popularity, had long since convinced him that only a tiny minority of evildoers were stirring up the loyal masses. On October 12 he instructed General Trepov to pursue more vigorous means of quelling disturbances. The general, characterized by one of his enemies as "a quarter-master by education" and a "pogrom-maker by conviction," became a symbol of oppression with his notorious order to the St. Petersburg garrison: "Should the people resist, do not use blank cartridges and do not spare your ammunition."[40] But armed force could not crush strikes and passive opposition.

Although Nicholas found the experience personally distasteful, he had already turned to Witte for guidance. The two met at Peterhof on October 9, and Witte read a memorandum recommending reform, including a guarantee of civil liberties and "a move toward the path of constitutionalism."[41] The original document had been prepared by Vladimir Kuzmin-Karavayev, a moderate zemstvo leader. Since much of the report was rhetorical and ambiguous, Nicholas understandably found it confusing. Witte returned the next day to expound his own views, elaborating his ideas on reform and clarifying a possible course of action: military dictatorship. Alexandra also attended the meeting. "As on other occasions when I was in her presence," Witte noted sardonically, "the Empress sat stiff as a ramrod, her face lobster-red, and did not utter a single word."[42]

Unwilling or unable to make a firm decision, Nicholas telegraphed Witte on October 13 to "coordinate the activities of the ministers with the basic aim of restoring order immediately."[43] He thus muddied the issue, whether deliberately or not, by placing Witte in charge of a ministerial cabinet, ignoring the reform proposals and emphasizing a policy of repression. Once more in Peterhof—to which access from the capital was possible only by water—Witte explained the alternatives and declined to head the government until he had obtained imperial sanction for his program. Nicholas canvassed a variety of other opinions, both civilian and military, and at one point seriously considered the notion of casting his cousin, the Grand Duke Nikolai Nikolayevich, a professional soldier, in the role of military dictator. The grand duke vehemently rejected the suggestion and allegedly threatened to shoot himself if the tsar refused to back Witte's agenda.[44] Even the redoubtable Trepov urged moderation. Of his closest advisers only Baron Frederiks, the minister of the imperial court, advocated a policy of no compromise.

Faced with the prospect of civil war in the streets and pressured by the near unanimity of his counselors, Nicholas gave way. As he explained "those horrible days" in a letter to his mother, he might have found an "energetic soldier" to "crush the rebellion by sheer force," but that would have meant "rivers of blood." The other way involved granting "civil rights, freedom of speech and press, also to have all laws confirmed by a State Duma—that, of course, would be a constitution."[45] Ironically, had Nicholas held out another day or two, displaying that streak of stubbornness which he reserved for more trivial occasions, he would probably have emerged triumphant: revolutionaries and strike leaders were prepared to admit defeat just as the autocrat, convinced that he had no other choice, issued the October Manifesto.

Nicholas signed the document on the 17th. The conception was Witte's, but the original draft had been prepared by Prince Aleksei Obolensky, a member of the State Council, at Witte's request. The final version received the editorial attention of Obolensky, Witte, and Nikolai Vuich, the interim chairman of the Committee of Ministers. The manifesto, surprisingly concise for so momentous a departure in Russia's political history, promised "freedom of conscience, speech, assembly, and association," and it broadened the franchise, with the possibility of universal suffrage in the future, while granting to the State Duma legislative powers.[46] Nicholas recognized that he had violated his own principles and the tradition of autocracy that he had sworn to uphold. "After such a day," he remarked in his diary, "my head began to ache and my thoughts became confused. God help us and comfort Russia."[47] "There was no other way out," he confided to his mother, "than to cross oneself and give what everyone was asking for. My only consolation is that such is the will of God, and this grave decision will lead my dear Russia out of the intolerable chaos she has been in for nearly a year."[48]

Upon later reflection, Nicholas expressed resentment at Witte's insistence that no modification should alter the text of the October Manifesto. On the evening of the 17th, according to Nicholas, such an attempt was made by telephone, and Witte's answers "came in an excited tone of voice and in a form that was not very polite. They were to the effect that he had considered the whole thing most carefully and could make no concessions."[49]

To his immense personal satisfaction, for his vanity craved honors and rewards, Witte emerged as the chairman of the Council of Ministers. No longer a ceremonial post, the chairmanship gave him the freedom, subject to the tsar's approval, of selecting a cabinet that would secure public confidence and presumably work in harmony with an elected Duma. Yet he was not a prime minister, as he was loosely referred to, because his authority derived from the monarch, not from a political party or a legislative majority. He later portrayed himself as reluctant to take over his new post because Nicholas lacked confidence in him. "Now, as he had in sending me to Portsmouth, the Emperor was throwing me into the fire with a light heart, thinking to himself: 'If he survives, we can get rid of him later, but if he perishes, so be it. He is an unpleasant person: he does not yield on anything; he understands everything better than I, and this I cannot endure.' "[50]

Despite a seemingly auspicious start, Witte did not enjoy mass popularity or gain the respect of any large segment of public opinion. Nicholas, who might have been expected to generate a sense of gratitude if not enthusiasm for his senior minister, quickly grew disenchanted. As early as October 27 he complained that for "such a clever man" it was strange that Witte "should be wrong in his forecast of an easy pacification." He also deplored Witte's attempt to open a dialogue with prominent liberals: "I do not quite like his way of getting into touch with various extremists, especially as all these talks appear in the press next day, and as often as not are distorted."[51]

That Witte, whose frenetic pace has been likened to the "proverbial one-armed paperhanger with the hives,"[52] anticipated a smooth transition to a new political order is highly unlikely. But he was unpleasantly surprised by the strength and persistence of organized opposition. If moderates tended to accept the manifesto with elation and good will, radicalized workers and intellectuals, as well as sizable elements of the middle class, saw it as a sign of weakness and an excellent opportunity to press further demands. Revolutionaries, with more bravado than perspicacity, foresaw the collapse of the monarchy. Trotsky's comment on the tsar's dispensation summed up a wide spectrum of popular opinion: "It [the proletariat] wants neither the police hooligan Trepov nor the liberal stockbroker Witte, neither the wolf's jaws nor the fox's tail. It does not want a whip wrapped in the parchment of a constitution."[53]

Rumors, confusion, and unrest tinged with violence continued to reign in the cities, although the termination of the general strike in the capital on October 21 gave the government a partial reprieve from the peril of economic strangulation. Renewed insubordination in the armed forces presented the authorities with still another threat to internal stability. Both soldiers and sailors mutinied at Kronstadt, Sevastopol, and Vladivostok, and Nicholas deplored the "strong wave of subversive propaganda . . . sweeping through the Army."[54] But revolutionary consciousness remained sufficiently dormant among the rank and file to allow forceful intervention by loyal detachments. Punitive military expeditions ruthlessly quelled disturbances along the route of the Trans-Siberian Railroad, which could only gradually accommodate the troops returning from the Manchurian front. Similarly harsh measures subdued the villages, where peasant rebellion flared up in the fall and spilled over into 1906.

Nicholas became frustrated and discouraged by the sluggish progress of pacification. He fretted that his ministers "talk a lot, but do little," that everyone is "afraid of taking courageous action: I keep on trying to force them—even Witte himself—to behave more energetically. With us nobody is accustomed to shouldering responsibility: all expect to be giving orders, which, however, they disobey as often as not." He claimed to be doing his "very best" to ease Witte's difficulties. "But I must confess," he wrote, that "I am disappointed in him in a way. In everybody else's opinion he is a very energetic and even despotic man who straight away would try his utmost to re-establish order."[55]

In the arduous process of stabilizing his regime, only one development seemed to cheer Nicholas: the "strong reaction" to the "subversive elements" who "raised their heads" after the October Manifesto. A "whole mass of loyal people suddenly made their power felt," and he blandly assumed that they truly represented public opinion. "The impertinence of the Socialists and revolutionaries had angered the people once more; and, because nine-tenths of the trouble-makers are Jews, the People's whole anger turned against them. That's how the pogroms happened. It is amazing how they took place *simultaneously* in all the towns of Russia and Siberia." The government's critics had a sinister explanation for such "spontaneity," and Nicholas took note of it by declaring that the supposed complicity of the police was a "worn-out fable." Besides, not only Jews were victimized: "some of the Russian agitators, engineers, lawyers and such-like bad people suffered as well."[56]

However naive and simplistic his analysis—a ruler capable of such self-delusion was indeed fortunate to retain his throne—Nicholas did have a valid point. Not all of his subjects craved revolution or drastic reform. Peasant grievances focused on the landlords, seldom upon the tsar. That the muzhik could be relied upon, however, as a faithful servant of the state was a dangerous illusion that Nicholas accepted with grateful assurance. The cities were of course the hotbeds of sedition, but even the workers, supposedly united by class solidarity, according to the precepts of Marxism, did not uniformly share radical sentiments. And the dregs of urban society, the *lumpenproletariat*, furnished recruits for the "patriotic" mobs that attacked Jews and other ethnic minorities, intellectuals, and revolutionaries in the belief that they were protecting throne, fatherland, and Orthodoxy. Such were the "Black Hundreds," whose noxious blend of violence, anti-Semitism, and chauvinism bore a striking resemblance to the fascist gangs of a later time and a different place. Beginning in late October a wave of pogroms broke out in Odessa, Kiev, Tomsk, and dozens of other cities. As in the Kishinev massacre, the central government did not play a conspiratorial role, but the reluctance of the police to intervene demonstrated that a Black Hundreds mentality pervaded local officialdom to a scandalous degree. The Okhrana was later exposed as a major producer of anti-Semitic propaganda. The official in charge of the printing press allegedly bragged about the success of his operation: "We can handle a job of any size—a ten-man pogrom or a ten-thousand man pogrom, whatever you please."[57]

A dozen or more quasi-respectable fronts for hooligan action arose in 1905, the largest and most notorious of them the Union of the Russian

People.[58] The Union was founded on October 22 by Dr. Aleksandr Dubrovin, a St. Petersburg physician with organizational talent but obnoxious personal traits. An associate pronounced him a "vile parasite" and a "coarse, repulsive animal."[59] It was led by "establishment" figures who nevertheless sought a popular base with a more demagogic appeal than that offered by other reactionary organizations. Nicholas, though at times ambivalent about such vociferous "support"—the Union opposed the October Manifesto—sympathized with its aims and received a delegation headed by Dubrovin on December 23. He accepted badges signifying honorary membership for himself and his son, remarking that he valued the Union's help in overcoming Russia's enemies: "Unite the Russian people—I am counting on you." When a delegate ventured to ask, "Are we right, Sire, to remain loyal to autocracy?" Nicholas resorted to Delphic phrases: "Soon, soon the sun of truth will shine over the land of Russia, and then all doubts will disappear."[60]

On other occasions the emperor was less equivocal about his support of the Black Hundreds. He told Count Konovnizin, an apostle of anti-Jewish violence, "I know that Russian courts are too severe toward the participants in the pogroms. I give you my imperial word that I shall always lighten their sentences, on the application of the Union of the Russian People, so dear to me." During the next decade the Union submitted 325 petitions for amnesty on behalf of 476 individuals found guilty of participating in pogroms, and those whose conviction involved crimes against Jews were invariably pardoned.[61]

By the beginning of December 1905 the government had made modest headway in its struggle against "anarchy." Nicholas, while conceding that the "agrarian disturbances continue unabated," found reassurance in Witte's promise to "deal with the revolutionary movement energetically." "He understands," he reported to his mother, who remained in Denmark, "that the well-disposed elements in the country are not pleased with him and are getting impatient at his inaction. He is now prepared to order the arrest of all the principal leaders of the outbreak. I have been trying for some time past to get him to do it—but he always hoped to be able to manage without drastic measures."[62]

On December 3 the chief center of resistance to the government's authority in the capital, the St. Petersburg Soviet (or Council) of Workers' Deputies, was shattered with the arrest of some 230 members. Witte took credit for the successful coup, as did the newly appointed minister of the interior, Pyotr Durnovo. (Witte allegedly interrupted a meeting of the Council of Ministers to announce Durnovo's action, his face "chalk white" and his voice breaking in agitation: "All is lost." His words "had the effect of an exploding bomb," and the session hastily disbanded.)[63] Nicholas reported that "everyone was delighted" with the arrests. "Furthermore twelve newspapers have been suppressed and their editors will be prosecuted for the odious things they have printed. . . . All this of course gives Witte the courage to keep to the right line of action."[64]

A rump Soviet sought to carry on clandestinely, issuing the call for another general strike. The response was discouraging, but in other cities the flame of rebellion still flickered. An effective strike in Moscow on December 7 under the leadership of the local Soviet led to an armed insurrection. Although the workers' militia that challenged the government had little prospect of success, the fighting dragged on because doubts about the reliability of the Moscow garrison prevented its participation. With the arrival of the Semyonovsky Regiment from St. Petersburg, a final assault crushed the revolutionary workers on December 18. The rebel leaders fortunate enough to escape impromptu execution were imprisoned for later trial. Nicholas was gratified that the insurrection had been crushed, "thanks to the faithful determination of our glorious troops." He claimed that only ten soldiers were killed and that the rebel losses were "terrific" but difficult to determine "because many of the killed were burned to death in the houses, and most of the wounded were removed and are being hidden by their comrades."[65]

The fate of the Moscow uprising, perceived as an end to the turbulent events of Russia's revolutionary year, did not wholly complete the process of pacification. But the pockets of resistance that remained did not unduly strain the country's military resources, and the business of government could proceed in a manner approaching normality. "The bad elements," Nicholas observed, "have lost heart in the Northern Caucasus, in South Russia and in the Siberian towns."[66]

With the emergency over, Nicholas took an almost sadistic pleasure in the army's ruthless tactics. "Terror must be met by terror," he philosophized. In Siberia his generals were "to arrest all agitators and to punish them with exemplary severity." Uncharacteristically, he lost his temper when General Kazbich informed him in a personal audience that the serious political disturbances in Vladivostok had been quelled without bloodshed. "You should have shot them, General," he shouted, "shot them and not made speeches!"[67] On Witte's memorandum about "anarchists" inducing a strike of railroad workers, he noted: "Will it really be possible for these 162 anarchists to corrupt the army? All of them should be hanged."[68] Reading a report from the Baltic region, where a rebellious Latvian town had been spared on humanitarian grounds, Nicholas scribbled in the margin: "This is no reason. The city should have been destroyed."[69] Similar remarks of a vengeful nature were liberally sprinkled on other reports. His attitude fit the image of the bloodthirsty tyrant projected by the revolutionaries, a stereotype at odds with the kindly, gentle, and even timid Nicholas of private life. Yet the two personalities were not irreconcilable. Nicholas was hardly unique in his propensity to transform complex phenomena into meaningful abstractions and mankind into the evil and the virtuous. Thus "subversives," representing the ultimate in human depravity, obviously deserved no mercy, while family, friends, and acquaintances— even a dog—could arouse emotions of compassion and sorrow that derived from firsthand experience.

When "counterrevolution," as the government's adversaries saw it, finally triumphed, Nicholas had already begun to regret the October Manifesto and resent the man he held responsible for forcing his hand—Count Witte. Himself a convert to the efficacy of terror, he noted in January 1906 that Witte had "radically changed his views" since the Moscow revolt and "wants to hang and shoot everybody." "I have never seen such a chameleon of a man," Nicholas complained. "That, naturally, is the reason why no one believes in him any more. He is absolutely discredited with everybody, except perhaps the Jews abroad."[70] As in 1903, Witte's usefulness to the sovereign had virtually ceased, but it was politically inexpedient to terminate his services prematurely. Nicholas had the power, if not the audacity, to revoke the manifesto, and he must have been tempted to do so. Yet he had signed the odious document, and he proposed to honor his word. He made that clear in a reception for Rightist leaders on December 1, 1905: the manifesto, he declared, "is the full and convinced expression of my inflexible will and an act that cannot be altered."[71] Whether the embryonic constitution he had granted would lead to a limited monarchy with an effective legislature or simply provide a fig leaf for an unregenerate autocracy remained on the political agenda of the future.

7

The Duma Experiment

The Council of Ministers that Witte assembled late in October of 1905 did not meet "society's" expectations or enjoy public confidence. Bulygin and most of his colleagues had been allowed to resign. The infamous General Trepov was among them, only to be appointed palace commandant and to become the tsar's "absolutely indispensable" confidant at Tsarskoe Selo and Peterhof. Nicholas informed his mother that Trepov was "acting in a kind of secretarial capacity. He is experienced and clever and cautious in his advice. I give him Witte's bulky memoranda to read, then he reports on them quickly and concisely. This is of course a secret to everybody but ourselves."[1] According to Witte's hostile testimony, Trepov became "a cross between an irresponsible dictator and an Asiatic eunuch" and "wielded an overwhelming influence over the weak-willed Emperor." He emerged as "virtually the head of the government for which I bore responsibility. During my six months as premier I had to do battle with him over every question about which we disagreed."[2] Witte conferred too much credit on his rival, for Trepov sought only to serve the emperor as a sincere and loyal counselor, not to accumulate power in his own right.

Pobedonostsev, aged and ailing, was also a political casualty, supposedly discharged by Nicholas in a manner "highly characteristic of the heartlessness and unceremoniousness with which he is accustomed to treat his old servants."[3] But there were a few holdovers: Lamzdorf remained at the foreign ministry, and the ministers of war, marine, and the imperial court retained their posts as the sovereign's appointees. Witte's choice of Pyotr Durnovo, a "reactionary" official with police experience, to the key position of interior minister was both unfortunate and puzzling. Blackmail—with documents or letters that would have ruined Witte's career—has been suggested. He later admitted that the appointment had been "one of my major mistakes," yet as in the mass arrest of the St. Petersburg Soviet, the two worked in tandem to suppress revolutionary outbreaks.[4] At first Nicholas balked at Durnovo's candidacy, presumably because Alexander III had removed him from office in an earlier scandal. But he finally accepted him, initially as acting minister, and later expressed his pleasure at Durnovo's "splendid work." He also thought well of Mikhail Akimov, the new minister of justice, who had replaced the overly scrupulous Sergei Manukhin. But the rest of the ministers he labeled "people without importance."[5]

Nicholas was essentially correct in his judgment, for Witte had to rely heavily upon mediocre bureaucrats, not the "public men" that he courted with some diligence. He conferred with such distinguished political figures as Dmitri Shipov, Aleksandr Guchkov, and Pavel Milyukov and found them indisposed to accept a cabinet portfolio. Shipov, who represented the conservative wing of the zemstvo movement, was offered the position of state comptroller; Nicholas received him at Peterhof, an honor denied the other "liberal" candidates. Guchkov, nominally a wealthy industrialist and one of the founders of the Union of October 17 (the Octobrist Party), was seriously considered to head the ministry of commerce and industry. Milyukov, a professional historian and later head of the Constitutional Democratic Party (known as the Kadets), had a lengthy discussion with Witte but was never formally tendered a cabinet post. He asked Witte why the word "constitution" had been so explicitly avoided. In a "disappointed tone, tersely and dryly," Witte responded, "I cannot because the Tsar does not wish it." With that Milyukov abruptly ended the meeting: "Then it is useless for us to talk. I cannot give you any sensible advice."[6]

Although Milyukov was more tactless than other politicians of the Kadet and Octobrist parties, his abrasive style exemplified the profound distrust of middle-class liberalism toward the monarchy and its spokesmen. Durnovo having become a symbol of police state repression, the moderate oppositionists disdained collaboration as a matter of principle, choosing an adversarial relationship when expediency and compromise might have provided a rare opportunity for government and "society" to explore if not compose their differences. As in the brief "honeymoon" of Svyatopolk-Mirsky in the fall of 1904, the historic moment passed and could not be reclaimed, at least during Witte's ascendancy.

The prospects for an effective State Duma appeared discouraging, but the tedious process of elucidating the October Manifesto and designing the appropriate statutory law remained to be addressed. Priority went to the legislature and electoral procedures. Lesser bureaucrats supervised the paperwork, and higher officials gathered at regular intervals to review the documents. Draft proposals with recommendations were submitted to the emperor, who in December 1905 held a so-called Crown Council at Tsarskoe Selo for advice in making final decisions.[7] In contrast to the summer conference at Peterhof, which discussed the franchise for the stillborn Bulygin Duma, the winter meetings—there were three sessions in all—included Witte and the new cabinet appointees, four invited "public men," and only one representative of the grand ducal "lobby." Liberal opinion favored the magnanimous "four-tailed" formula of secret, equal, direct, and universal suffrage. Nicholas suspected that such prodigality would be the first step toward a democratic republic. "God alone knows how far people will go with their fantastic ideas!" he exclaimed to his mother. He found the sessions tiring and often boring: they "usually last not less than seven hours—simply awful!"[8] Witte's performance, though histrionic, was ambivalent and erratic, as if he could not bring himself to make a firm commitment on the franchise question.

The electoral law announced on December 11 was perhaps the most complicated ever devised by the mind of man. It retained the provision for indirect voting associated with the Bulygin Duma while extending the ballot to groups previously disfranchised. Only males (twenty-five or over) could vote, a form of gender discrimination then prevalent in democratic countries. Four categories of voters were recognized: landowners, burghers, peasants, and workers. The franchise was reasonably generous, yet there were exclusions that denied the ballot to landless peasants, nomads, soldiers and sailors, artisans, and various urban residents, including students and workers in small factories and commercial enterprises. Ethnic minorities were also slighted in weighting the votes for electors, who would make the final selection of deputies. In the case of industrial workers, it was a three-stage process; for communal peasants, four stages were required. The government made a conscious decision, understandably one of self-preservation, to rely on the more prosperous segments of society to protect its interests. Thus each elector in the provinces of European Russia represented two thousand landowners, four thousand urban residents, thirty thousand peasants, or ninety thousand workers.[9] Given the high rate of illiteracy and the dearth of political sophistication among the masses, the choice of indirect and weighted elections was to be expected. But the timing of the announcement was poorly chosen. The new law, a "progressive" measure considering the circumstances, was nearly invisible in the public excitement attending the rebellion in Moscow.

A second Crown Council met at Tsarskoe Selo on February 14 and 16, 1906. A somewhat more elite body than its predecessor, it included no public representatives, and the presence of a number of grand dukes and court figures added, in theory, to its conservative bias. The principal business of the conferees was to determine the nature of the State Council, a question that had already undergone thorough scrutiny by its chairman, Count Dmitri Solsky, who headed a special commission for that purpose.

Both Solsky and Witte agreed that the Council, heretofore "an organ of gracious listeners" composed of "venerable old men"[10] and not even mentioned in the October Manifesto, should become a body equal to the Duma in its legislative functions. But it should be so constituted that it would act as a restraint upon the other chamber. Since a substantial consensus had already been reached, Nicholas urged at the opening session that "superfluous" issues be avoided to expedite the matter at hand. The discussion could not be easily confined, however, and spilled over into a second session.[11] The disagreements that arose were largely procedural, Witte repeating his vacillating performance of the previous December. Nicholas, despite his impatience with his long-winded chief minister, seldom intervened except to make his decision known on disputed points. An imperial manifesto on February 20 formally spelled out the rights and duties of the two legislative houses. One-half the members of the State Council, as the designated "conservative" upper chamber, were to be appointed by the tsar, the other half to be elected by such elite groups as the Orthodox clergy, provincial zemstvos, academic institutions, and representatives of industry and commerce. The manifesto also called attention to a major restriction upon the legislative prerogative: the sovereign's right, at his sole discretion, to revise and amend the Fundamental Laws of the empire, which were the legal underpinning of the autocratic monarchy.

Because the October Manifesto and the decision of the Crown Councils had tampered with the structure of the basic law, still another conference, with four sessions in all, convened at Tsarskoe Selo in April 1906.[12] A preliminary revision of the Fundamental State Laws had been underway since December, and Nicholas displayed his resentment toward Witte by assigning the task to the secretary of the State Council. Witte did have an opportunity to review the draft document, consulting a number of legal experts in the process, and it was submitted to the Council of Ministers for formal discussion in March. The ministers accepted Witte's proposals and added a few of their own. The result augmented the sovereign's power at the expense of the Duma: the tsar maintained exclusive authority to direct foreign policy and command the armed forces, to declare martial law and other emergency measures, issue decrees safeguarding public order and social welfare, and administer the monetary system and control much of the state budget.

The April meetings, attended by substantially the same group of officials that had assembled in February, approved most of the recommendations of the Council of Ministers. But the process was far from automatic. Lively discussions, in which Nicholas participated, assured a thoughtful assessment of the issues even if anti-monarchist sentiment had been totally excluded. The "basic question," as Nicholas himself recognized, was his autocratic status. "I have been torn by doubts: do I have the right before my ancestors to alter the prerogatives of the power that I received from them?" While admitting that in view of the October Manifesto he could be charged with duplicity if he adhered to his old title, he nevertheless expressed his conviction that "80 per cent of the Russian people will be with me, will give me support, and will be grateful to me for such a decision. It is a matter for my own conscience, and I shall resolve it myself." This astonishing declaration alarmed even his staunch adherents. Durnovo and two of the grand dukes joined the "moderates" in agreeing that a monarch who granted a legislative assembly was no longer "absolute." Nicholas retreated in the end, conceding almost perfunctorily that his position was no longer that of an "absolute autocrat." Article 4 of the code thus read: "The All-Russian Emperor possesses the supreme autocratic power. Not only fear and conscience, but God himself, command obedience to his authority."[13] The new formula represented a concession on Nicholas' part, but his role as "autocrat" had not been relinquished despite clear evidence that his autocratic power had been circumscribed. He was thus able to divorce his function as monarch from the regular business of government—that is to reign but not rule.

The Fundamental Laws were published on April 23, 1906. Although they guaranteed civil liberties—somewhat tenuously since the government already restricted the rights conferred—their main thrust upheld the tradition of autocracy in relation to the Duma and the State Council. They amounted, in fact, to a disguised constitution, notwithstanding the regime's attempt to proscribe the loathsome term. The most controversial feature of the new "constitution" was Article 87, which granted the tsar the right to issue decrees with the force of law if neither legislative chamber was in session. Such measures were to be submitted to both houses within two months after they reconvened, but the potential for political mischief, a "legal coup d'etat" in Witte's phrase, was recognized at the time. More galling to the liberal opposition than specific articles of the code was the "insult" presented to the Duma, which met on April 27 without an opportunity to formulate or even to comment on the laws that regulated its functions and privileges. The animosity between the government and the First Duma was in some degree predetermined by the arbitrary dispensation of the Fundamental Laws.

April also witnessed Witte's "voluntary" resignation, marking an inglorious end to a distinguished career. The tsar's growing antipathy toward his pseudo–prime minister had been unmistakable. As early as January, Witte asked permission to step down, but Nicholas declined, citing the press of official business, especially pending negotiations for a foreign loan. A few weeks later a disagreement arose over the imperial appointments of the ministers of agriculture and commerce. Pleading "fatigue and poor health," Witte informed his colleagues about the prospect of his resignation, and Nicholas grudgingly yielded. Caught between his own reforming instincts that sought to appease public opinion and his efforts to placate

Nicholas and the "court party" by repressive measures to restore public order, he carried an intolerable burden of political responsibility and emotional stress. Yet he was also driven by vanity and an insatiable appetite for power which found expression in an arrogant manner that alienated even those who admired his enormous talent. His experience in 1903 had alerted him to the realities of royal perfidy, and he was certainly aware that his political stock had fallen to a new low. It is nevertheless probable that he indulged the fancy that Nicholas could not afford to dispense with his first servant. Indeed, Witte's services, if not indispensable, were estimable, and his last major achievement involved a long-term loan from France.

The Japanese war and internal disruption had placed the government on the brink of financial disaster. Russian diplomatic support for France during the early months of 1906 at the Algeciras Conference on the Moroccan question smoothed the path of the loan negotiations. Perhaps equally important, French public opinion was molded by means of handsome bribes dispersed to some fifty French newspapers, magazines, and news agencies by the Russian government.[14] A "Christian syndicate" provided the credit, for Jewish banking houses had refused participation ever since the Kishinev pogrom. The Rothschilds expressed interest if Russia would improve the treatment of its Jews, but Witte considered it improper to make such concessions for financial reasons. Nicholas allowed Witte a free hand, "contenting himself with the role of a spectator, but a deeply concerned one, watching a chess game."[15]

The final details were arranged in Paris by Count Vladimir Kokovtsov, who was subsequently rewarded by his appointment as minister of finance. He also, according to Witte, asked for eighty thousand rubles as a "gratuity" for his efforts. His request was rebuffed, but he did receive the prestigious Order of St. Aleksandr Nevsky. The loan signed on April 3, 1906, totaled 2,250,000,000 francs (843,750,000 rubles) at 5 percent interest. Technically it was an "international" transaction, for banking houses in five countries participated, but the French subscribed much the largest portion and guaranteed the Austrian share.[16] With financial stability achieved, the tsarist regime became more confident of its ability to rule and less respectful of its critics. The Social Democrats and Socialist Revolutionaries went so far as to announce their repudiation of all foreign debts should the government be overthrown.

His duty done, Witte began to press his resignation. He declared privately that his relations with the emperor had become "completely abnormal" and that if he stayed on he would "in effect serve as a puppet to General Trepov, Grand Duke Nicholas Nikolaevich, and a host of Black Hundreds figures who are now making their appearance on stage." On April 14 he sent a detailed letter to Nicholas. It provided a seven-point summary of his complaints, beginning with the state of his health: "I am worn out from the badgering from all sides . . . and have become so nervous that I cannot maintain the equilibrium required of a premier." He objected to Durnovo's "improper" policies which had resulted in antagonizing "most of the population" and led to voting for "extremist candidates" to the Duma as a form of protest. He was also displeased at becoming the target of "all those in Russian society who can scream and write, as well as by the extreme elements that have access to Your Imperial Majesty." He maintained that there were "other cogent reasons" for his resignation but declined to name them in the belief that those cited were sufficient to persuade the Tsar to accede to his "humble request." That evening he read the letter to the Council of Ministers, whose members received it as an unwelcome reminder of their own vulnerable positions. Several were inclined to follow his example but were dissuaded by his argument that it would create a precedent for a parliamentary form of government.[17]

Nicholas accepted Witte's resignation on April 16 in the form of a handwritten letter: "I thank you *sincerely* for your devotion to me and for the great zeal you have shown during the very difficult six months of your tenure." The loan he pronounced "the finest page in your list of accomplishments" and a "great moral victory for the government." An imperial rescript of April 22 informed the public, with due recognition of Witte's "determined and enlightened efforts," and it closed with a parting salute: "I remain inalterably well disposed toward you and sincerely grateful."[18]

Witte received a farewell audience with Nicholas, who was in an amiable mood—or pretended to be. Aside from a seat on the State Council and a knighthood in the Order of St. Aleksandr Nevsky (with diamonds), Witte was offered the ambassadorship to the first European country in which a vacancy occurred. He went abroad for a rest and later reminded Nicholas of his promise, as he had been instructed to do. He received no answer, but Baron Frederiks sent a message stating that His Majesty "expressed the opinion" that "given the present situation" your "return to Russia at the present time would be most undesirable." Witte was understandably infuriated by what amounted to exile at royal caprice and wrote an ill-tempered letter to Frederiks. The "exile" was rescinded in the fall, presumably with Nicholas' reluctant assent, and he once more enjoyed the privilege of an imperial audience without the slightest indication of ill feeling. Privately, however, Nicholas grumbled that it "would have been more sensible of him and convenient for me if he had stayed away." He complained of the "peculiar atmosphere full of all sorts of rumours and gossip and insinuations" that formed around Witte. "Some of the wretched papers are already beginning to say he is coming back to power, and that only he can save the country. Evidently the Jewish clique is starting to sow sedition again. . . . *As long as I live*, I will never trust that man again with the smallest thing. I had quite enough of last year's experiment. It is still like a nightmare to me."[19]

Retirement failed to mellow Witte or to restrain his intense ambition. He continued to speak out boldly in the State Council, and he intrigued unashamedly but without success for reinstatement at some level of bureaucratic expertise. He compiled voluminous memoirs, written at various health resorts while abroad to avoid the unwelcome attentions of the Okhrana. His death in 1915 reopened old wounds, and Nicholas commented that at last a dangerous source of revolt had been removed. To his wife he reported that a "truly paschal peace" reigned in his heart, and to the French ambassador he remarked, "Count Witte's death has been a great relief to me. I also regard it as a sign from God."[20] But his serenity must have been troubled, for the authorities sealed Witte's study and confiscated his papers. Through an adjutant who called on Countess Witte, Nicholas conveyed his interest in her husband's memoirs, which had been completed in 1912 and deposited for safekeeping in a French bank. An attaché of the Russian embassy in Paris searched the Witte residence in Biarritz in vain for the elusive manuscript.[21] Eventually published in Berlin after World War I, the memoirs were in great part a searing indictment of Nicholas and his reign. Witte therefore had the final word, but his recollections were so obviously self-serving and replete with errors of fact and interpretation—not to mention what could be considered deliberate falsehoods—that the historical confrontation between the two men may yet be recorded as a drawn battle.

Determined that the post-Witte cabinet would have his personal stamp, Nicholas made a clean sweep of the incumbents except for the posts of war, marine, and the court. He offered the chairmanship to Minister of Justice Akimov, who declined to accept. He then selected Ivan Goremykin, whom Witte disdained as a "bureaucratic nonentity" and who had failed to distinguish himself during his tenure as minister of the interior. The Okhrana chief in the capital described Goremykin as an "indolent person," uninterested in politics and asking only to be "bothered as little as possible."[22] But Nicholas, at least for the moment, preferred a faithful accolyte, not a prima donna: "Goremykin will not act behind my back, making concessions and agreements to damage my authority. I can be perfectly confident that I shall not be given any surprises or made to face any *faits accomplis*."[23] To the government's enemies, Goremykin symbolized a return to reaction. Yet the old bureaucrat did not turn his back on the reforms offered by the October Manifesto, nor did he repudiate the course set by his temperamental predecessor.

Interior Minister Durnovo, surprised and depressed by his own dismissal, was replaced by a relatively unknown figure, Pyotr Stolypin.[24] The latter's efficiency in quelling peasant disturbances while governor of Saratov had won recognition in St. Petersburg. At Goremykin's prompting, seconded by Trepov, Nicholas accepted Stolypin's candidacy but only with difficulty persuaded him—in effect, "commanded" him—to take over the post. Stolypin's courtly manner impressed Nicholas, and he later expressed his "love and respect" for the new minister while praising Goremykin for his recommendation.[25]

The veteran Lamzdorf, distrustful of the Duma and its intentions, was allowed to retire gracefully as foreign minister, supposedly "as a sop to public opinion for the Japanese war and as a means of getting rid of the last traces of that catastrophe."[26] He was replaced by Aleksandr Izvolsky, who had served most recently as minister to Denmark, a key position because of the dowager empress' sentimental regard for her original homeland. A moderate liberal in a cabinet dominated by conservative monarchists, Izvolsky accepted his assignment with reluctance. He found his new colleagues a "strange collection of functionaries," united by no common interest or program other than "their antipathy to the new order of things and to the very principle of representative government." Izvolsky's critics conceded his intelligence but regarded him as a "pompous snob" with "limitless ambition."[27]

Meanwhile the formal trappings of a semi-constitutional regime had taken a memorable step forward with the completion of balloting for the State Duma. The first such election in Russian history on a national scale, it took place in most parts of the empire from late February to mid-April. Illiteracy, apathy, and ignorance marked the cumbersome process, yet the opportunity to perform one's civic duty appealed to a broad spectrum of the population. The government, including Nicholas himself, was determined that the voting should be free from constraint and honestly conducted. Despite exceptions that were all too numerous, these conditions tended to prevail, and of the twenty million or more citizens who exercised their suffrage right (fewer than half of those eligible did so) a large majority signified their dissatisfaction with the status quo. The government and its spokesmen were surprised and dismayed by the result, for indirect voting and a decided bias toward rural inhabitants and the privileged had presumably erected a formidable barrier against "radicalism" in the lower house.

The Kadets and their allies, espousing a program of reform and much better organized than their rivals, emerged with a large plurality of 185 deputies. The more conservative Octobrists and their sympathizers gained only thirteen deputies, and the extreme Right was shut out entirely. The avowed revolutionary parties, the Social Democrats and Socialist Revolutionaries, officially boycotted the election on principle, though a number of local activists disobeyed the leadership. The social composition of the Duma did not accurately reflect the general population, but the distribution was broadly based. A third of the members were peasants and workers, a third professionals, state employees, and "intellectuals," and a third nobles, industrialists, and other property owners or managers. A well-educated group in relative terms, 42 percent had completed some college-level work. Since about the same proportion were under forty years of age, the Duma had an unusually youthful complexion.

Nicholas ascribed the disappointing outcome to the "excessive liberalism of the franchise law of December 11th, the inactivity of the conservative mass of the population and the complete non-interference with the election campaign on the part of the authorities, which is never practiced in other countries."[28] His analysis was not entirely mistaken, yet he failed to comprehend that public opinion, insofar as it was reflected in the polls, had returned an unfavorable verdict on his regime. What recourse did he have? He could legally prorogue the Duma, and some advisers urged that it was within his right to alter the electoral law to insure a more docile assembly. Nicholas rejected such counsel—or at least deferred it—while deciding whether his dignity would be compromised by receiving the deputies in an inaugural ceremony. Ultra-royalists argued that Goremykin should assume that function. "Conciliationists" suggested an address from the throne at the Tauride Palace, the Duma's new meeting place. Nicholas chose to follow the German precedent for the opening of the Reichstag and summoned the deputies to the Winter Palace.

On April 27, with the splendid pageantry reserved for solemn state occasions, the people's representatives gathered in the sumptuous St. George's Hall. As if to overawe the plebeian deputies, the officials, generals, and courtiers appeared in their most opulent regalia, and the ladies of the imperial family were "literally covered with pearls and diamonds." The legislators, far less affluent on the whole, dressed more "democratically": the middle class in business suits or formal attire; workers in simple blouses; peasants in boots and caftans; and the ethnic minorities frequently in colorful national costumes. This symbolic juxtaposition of "boundless Imperial luxury and the poverty of the people" struck one observer as "quite unsuited to the occasion" and an "ominous contrast" that "demagogues did not fail to comment upon."[29] Indeed, class antagonism was not confined to clothing, according to another witness: "Here an old general, there a bureaucrat, grown white in the service, could hardly conceal the consternation, the anger even, that the invasion of the sacred precincts of the Winter Palace by these intruders caused him." On the other hand, "the faces of the deputies . . . were lighted by triumph in some cases and in others distorted by hatred."[30] Baron Frederiks registered actual loathing: "The deputies? They give one the impression of a gang of criminals who are only waiting for the signal to throw themselves on the Ministers and cut their throats. What wicked faces! I will never again set foot among these people."[31]

Arriving in the capital on one of the imperial yachts, Nicholas prayed at length before the tomb of his father in the Peter and Paul Cathedral. Later, escorted by liveried footmen and court dignitaries, he made an impressive entrance before the assembled guests. After a prayer he took his place on the throne and then rose to read a brief speech of welcome. The banal wording and archaic style were innocuous, carefully avoiding any reference to a legislative program or to his own role as a "limited" autocrat. He did reassure the deputies that he would not renege on his promises: "I shall protect as immutable the course that I have set." He expressed his "firm conviction" that they would devote their strength in "selfless service to the nation" and that while the "enlightenment and welfare of the people" was necessary, the "spiritual greatness and prosperity of our land requires not only freedom but also order based on law." He concluded on a pious note, asking divine blessing upon his work, "together with the State Council and the State Duma." His remarks were greeted with enthusiasm on the Right and only tepid applause on the Left (that is, most of the Duma members). But the ceremony was considered a success in official quarters, and Nicholas departed for Peterhof by sea to resume his "exile" from St. Petersburg, still apprehensive about the danger of assassination.

The deputies, most of them conveyed by ferry boat on the Neva River, gathered at the Tauride Palace for the opening session of the Duma. Along the route crowds had taken up the cry of "amnesty!" The government had not been squeamish in ordering the arrest of suspected revolutionaries and other "subversives"; during the six months of Witte's ministry over fifty thousand offenders, according to one estimate, jammed the prisons or were banished to Siberia.[32] The issue of amnesty therefore ranked at the top of the Duma's agenda. Sergei Muromtsev, a founding father of the Kadet party and a distinguished legal scholar, was elected president by an overwhelming majority. Muromtsev promptly honored Ivan Petrunkevich, the veteran zemstvo leader, by inviting him to speak. Petrunkevich devoted his brief remarks entirely to a moving appeal for amnesty: "It is a debt of honor, a debt of conscience which demands that the first free words spoken from this platform he dedicated to those who sacrificed their lives and freedom to win political liberty for Russia." He cautioned his audience, however, to defer action until an "address to the throne" could be arranged, for amnesty remained within the emperor's legal prerogative. Following a short "inaugural" but concluding speech by Muromtsev, the lower house adjourned for two days.[33]

The Kadet leaders, enticed by the British model of a constitutional monarchy, sought to transplant it to Russia. The artificiality of their endeavor, if not immediately apparent, became more obvious when the "address to the throne" was completed. Largely prepared by Milyukov and two of his Kadet colleagues, the document called for the pardoning of political offenders, a cabinet responsible to the Duma, the abolition of the State Council, direct and universal suffrage, and land reform involving the expropriation of private estates. It received a thorough airing when the Duma resumed its deliberations and passed unanimously, after some revisions, when eleven deputies obligingly abstained. A delegation was chosen to present the "address" to the tsar, but Muromtsev's request on its behalf for an audience at Peterhof was refused. Nicholas, with justification, regarded parts of the Kadet program (for that was what the document amounted to) as an infringement of the Fundamental Laws. He was particularly incensed by the amnesty request because civil disobedience had not entirely ceased, nor had the Duma expressed regret for political assassinations in the past or condemned such acts in the future.

Since Nicholas—or his advisers—felt that it was entirely within his right to rebuff personal negotiations with the Duma but beneath his dignity to do so himself, what response should the government provide? Nightly sessions of the Council of Ministers convened in Goremykin's study to consider the problem. The chairman lacked a firm hand and conducted himself in a manner that seemed to say: "Babble as you will, for I shall act as I see fit." Stolypin nonetheless maintained an inscrutable silence; Minister of Finance Kokovtsov spoke at length with a confident air but ineffectually; and Izvolsky, who wore a monocle and reminded one of his associates of a pug dog, posed as an authority on parliamentary matters while exerting little influence. Only the minister of agriculture and the director of the Holy Synod took a forthright if malevolent view of the Duma as a revolutionary institution that ought to be dismissed or abolished. Eventually the minister of justice, Ivan Shcheglovitov, and the assistant minister of the interior, Vladimir Gurko, were charged with drafting official statements. Shcheglovitov's formulation was "humble, ingratiating, and remarkably vague," while Gurko's proposed answer was frank and "written in the language of authority." After more discussion a few minor changes were made in the Gurko draft to soften its tone, and the final version became available on May 12.[34]

Nicholas doubted the wisdom of a government declaration and despite his earlier fastidiousness briefly considered going to the Duma himself. He was dissuaded: a dangerous precedent might be established, impairing his image as supreme arbiter between the government and the country's representatives. As for the text prepared by the Council of Ministers, he preferred stronger and more decisive wording but found it acceptable as a token of the government's moderation toward the Duma. Foreseeing difficulties, he nevertheless declined to "run ahead of events." "It sometimes happens," he told Kokovtsov, "that a very severe attack of illness leaves a patient as by a miracle, although we should not look for miracles in such matters."[35]

Goremykin, accompanied by the Council of Ministers, appeared before the Duma on May 13. He read the government's reply in a voice that was scarcely audible, his hands shaking with nervous agitation. Offering cooperation on issues that did not exceed the Duma's authority, he frankly stated that its demands were unacceptable. He raised his voice only once in pronouncing the land reform "absolutely inadmissable" as a violation of property rights, a "fundamental rule of government throughout the world." He lifted his little finger for emphasis—perhaps, too, as a warning or a threat. Concerning an amnesty, the "welfare of the country would not be served in the present troubled times by pardoning criminals who have participated in murders, robberies, and acts of violence." Ignoring various points in the Duma program, he did promise to submit bills on primary education, taxation, and the local courts.[36]

The deputies listened in disgruntled silence. The great majority found the contents of Goremykin's speech distasteful, his attitude "haughty," and his tone "disdainful."[37] Vladimir Nabokov, a prominent Kadet who had steered the original "address" through the Duma with patient skill, rose to express the bitter disappointment of the assembly. "We do not have the beginnings of a constitutional ministry," he complained, "we have the same old bureaucratic watchwords." He concluded with the ringing and subsequently famous phrase, "Let the executive power bow before the legislative!"—to "deafening applause." As other speakers sustained the assault, Baron Frederiks urged his colleagues to walk out. But Goremykin, who sat quietly "smoothing his whiskers," took no initiative until intermission. The ministers then left in a body, and only Shcheglovitov returned. His conciliatory remarks did nothing to allay the mood of resentment and animosity. Several speakers called for the wholesale resignation of the ministry. Behind the scenes Milyukov chaired a caucus of Kadets and their allies to draft an expression of no confidence in the government. Brought to the floor of the chamber, the text expressed distrust of "a cabinet not responsible to the representatives of the people" and insisted upon its immediate resignation in favor of one enjoying the support of the Duma. With only token dissent—ten signed a separate declaration—the deputies passed the resolution, in effect a statement of defiance marking, as Milyukov put it, the "beginning of open struggle."[38]

Anxiety and apprehension pervaded both sides of the dispute, but only terminal victims of political naiveté could have expected the tsar's government to resign on command in proper parliamentary fashion. Goremykin conveyed a copy of the notorious resolution to the sovereign and invited the ministers to consider an appropriate policy toward the obstreperous lower house. With the possible exception of Izvolsky, who advised patience out of concern for European public opinion, they agreed that confrontation could not be avoided. The one point of difference centered on tactics: should the Duma be dissolved immediately or allowed to continue, at least on a temporary basis? In practice the government assumed an attitude of watchful waiting, and a kind of political gridlock ensued. The Duma overly indulged its right of interpellation—that is, to question and to investigate ministers or their subordinates concerning abuses of authority and other capricious acts. But the government proved adept at quasi-legal shadow-boxing to thwart the legislature. Even the deputies grew weary of an endless flood of inquiries, chiefly involving arbitrary arrest and detention, and sought without much success to limit debate to "urgent" cases.

In a number of instances the public was well served by the Duma's curious blend of officiousness and righteous indignation. When the official *Praviteltsvenny Vestnik* (Government Gazette) began publishing pro-tsarist telegrams from various monarchist sources, including unsavory Black Hundreds organizations, the Duma acquired a legitimate grievance. Such communications could not have appeared without support from the "highest circles," presumably the emperor himself, and they bore a suspicious uniformity that suggested collusion with local officials. An interpellation on May 16 protested these "testimonials" for their "audacious disrespect to the highest legislative institution." Goremykin's leisurely and ironical response, refusing to cooperate on the basis of a legal technicality, elicited a formal letter of complaint from Muromtsev and in turn another rebuff from the minister. A second interpellation only demonstrated the Duma's impotence in the face of governmental arrogance. Yet Stolypin and Shcheglovitov were far from intransigent, and despite the absence of the chief antagonist, Goremykin, the deputies nevertheless "adopted an exaggerated tone of impenetrable indignation" and hounded them with cries of "out" and "resign."[39]

On June 1 a pogrom broke out in Bialystok, a city in western Byelorussia, the most serious episode in a new wave of violence that had begun in the late fall of 1905. Up to eight hundred Jews were killed or wounded, and many businesses were plundered or destroyed. Several Jewish deputies sponsored an interpellation, and an investigating committee sent a mission to report on the situation at first hand. In answer to an earlier inquiry about questionable political activity by the secret police, Stolypin appeared before the Duma on June 8 and defended his ministry with vigor. He admitted that some individuals had exceeded their authority but claimed that such practices had already been curbed. He denied that local officials were involved in pogroms, a categorical statement that set off howls of protest. Prince Sergei Urusov, a Kadet who had had occasion to probe the Kishinev massacre while governor of Bessarabia, stated that while he did not impugn Stolypin's integrity, he found the minister's assertion less than convincing because no one could be sure that "unknown persons" would not be able "to seize parts of the state machinery with their dirty hands." The heated debate spilled over to the next session, and Stolypin's reply brought an uncomplimentary verbal barrage.[40] The Duma could only pass on to other business, after formally condemning pogroms and the officials who were presumably guilty of collusion.

A third major challenge to the government through interpellation concerned the death penalty, the occasion for the most unruly session in the proceedings of the First Duma. Having failed to achieve an amnesty, the Kadets led the struggle against the execution of political offenders. The government, reflecting the sovereign's view, saw the question as one of capitulation to terrorism—that is, an attempt to protect assassins and other apostles of violence from the consequences of their crimes. On June 19 Shcheglovitov spoke to the issue in measured tones, and the chief naval prosecutor followed with the reasoned argument that the Duma had virtually no legal authority to pursue the matter. When the chief military prosecutor, a man whose bloodthirsty reputation had preceded him, sought to take the floor, the outraged deputies shouted him down before he could utter a word. A recess became necessary to restore order. Count Pyotr Heyden, a respected Octobrist, scolded the assembly for its attitude toward free speech, a right that should not be denied even to "enemies." A Kadet who became a severe critic of his fellow legislators saw the incident as symptomatic of a more serious problem. This "was not an uncontrollable reflex that was regretted," he declared; "it was a pattern of behavior which the Duma considered it had a right to adopt and even justify morally, as protection of the 'Duma's dignity.' "[41] Defiantly, and with an eye to public opinion, a bill outlawing capital punishment was passed without dissent, but the State Council forestalled a dispute over its constitutionality by allowing it to expire in committee.

The open hostility between a "reactionary" monarchy and a "radical" legislative assembly did not preclude an occasional reconnaissance to test the adversary's resolve and conceivably to arrange a truce. The principal figure on the government's side in these semi-clandestine negotiations was, most improbably, General Trepov. That so staunch a symbol of authority and of alleged servility to the tsar would undertake such a mission suggested greater flexibility on his part than his numerous critics could possibly have conceded at the time. Yet accusations of duplicity were heard then and later, for it is credible, if unlikely, that he suggested the idea of a Kadet ministry as the surest means of demonstrating its incompetence to rule. A variation of this hypothesis assumes that he tried to sabotage a coalition cabinet, knowing that the tsar would soon quarrel with the Kadets and that he himself would emerge as a military dictator. On the other hand, such Machiavellian tactics demanded ingenuity and sophistication, whereas Trepov was a "very primitive politician" and "neither a coward nor a provocateur."[42]

If not with Nicholas' blessing, at least with his hesitant consent, Trepov first approached Petrunkevich, the venerable zemstvo liberal and Kadet floor leader, through a British correspondent named Lamark. Petrunkevich rejected the overture, stating that he would need authorization from his party. Trepov again used Lamark's services to contact Milyukov, who agreed to a personal meeting, and in mid-June the two conferred in secret at a St. Petersburg restaurant. The general was polite and businesslike, asking if Milyukov would take part in a "ministry of confidence." The Kadet leader replied that personalities were secondary to issues. Trepov conscientiously wrote down in considerable detail the conditions for such a cabinet, which included the demands already publicized as the Kadet program and contained in the Duma's "address" to the throne. He rejected only one item out of hand—a political amnesty. "The Tsar will never pardon the regicides!" he exclaimed, meaning the terrorists who had killed the Grand Duke Sergei and, given the opportunity, would presumably be delighted to assassinate other members of the royal family. The two "conspirators" departed on friendly terms, and Trepov went so far as to furnish his telephone number at Peterhof with an invitation to contact him soon. Milyukov "did not find it necessary, however, to take advantage of his kindness."[43]

A few days later—the date is uncertain—Kokovtsov delivered a routine report at Peterhof and was disconcerted when Nicholas, no friend of legislative initiative, told him, "I hear from certain sources that matters are not so bad as one might gather from the Duma speeches, and that if we only wait patiently and don't get nervous the Duma is sure to get down to work and see for itself that the state machine is not as simple as it first believed." Although Nicholas claimed to "have another opinion of it all," he had obviously been influenced by Trepov, if not others. Shortly thereafter he again confided in Kokovtsov by handing him a folded paper, with the remark, "Look at this curious document and let me hear your frank opinion as to the suggested composition of a cabinet to replace the one which is meeting with such decided opposition from the Duma." He disavowed Goremykin as the source, saying only that the list of names had been suggested by "outside persons who may be rather naive in their conception of state affairs" but who "sincerely seek a way out of present difficult conditions." Kokovstsov recalled that Muromtsev had been proposed to replace Goremykin, that Milyukov and Petrunkevich were candidates for Stolypin's post, and that other prominent Kadets were nominated for cabinet portfolios. Startled and dismayed, Kokovtsov asked Nicholas if he understood that by accepting such a list he would place the government in the hands of its enemies and change the regime to a monarchy of the British model. Nicholas listened attentively and inquired: "What should be done, then, to put an end to what is happening in the Duma and to direct its work into a peaceful channel?" Kokovtsov recommended dissolving the lower house and revising the electoral law. "We are not yet mature enough," he maintained, "to have a one-chamber constitutional monarchy of a purely parliamentary type, and I believe it my duty to warn you, Sire, not to attempt this new experiment from which there may be no return." The admonition seemed to make a deep impression on Nicholas, who gave Kokovtsov a firm handshake and declared: "Much of what you have just said I have lived through and suffered. I like to hear different opinions and I am not intolerant of what people tell me, although at times it is very painful to see the best dreams of my life shattered. . . . I shall never adopt a decision to which my conscience would not agree." And he asked his minister not to believe it "if you hear that I have *already* made this leap into the unknown."[44]

Trepov had not been alone in seeking a modus vivendi between government and opposition. Izvolsky ventured to poach beyond his legitimate domain by undertaking talks with Kadet leaders. Having won Stolypin's support, he resolved to submit a memorandum to the emperor and to resign if it met with ill favor. The document was composed by Nikolai Lvov, a deputy who had recently left the Kadets. It deprecated the "bureaucratic" Goremykin ministry as inspiring "the most profound distrust on the part of the masses." The Duma, faced with official hostility, had unfortunately been "torn from the fertile soil of practical legislative activity" and to some extent had become "a hotbed of revolutionary passions." An open rupture could be prevented by appointing a coalition cabinet to gain "the confidence and respect of the people." Muromtsev, "a man of cool disposition and positive mind," would be ideally suited to accept new duties as chairman of the Council of Ministers. Stolypin might continue to serve as interior minister, while Shipov and Milyukov should be seriously considered. The latter, despite "an immense ambition and a certain tendency toward intrigue," is "endowed with a very keen perception and an extremely clear political sense."[45]

On June 25 at Peterhof, Nicholas "listened with great benevolence" to Izvolsky's discourse on Russia's domestic situation and accepted the memorandum with a promise to study it carefully. He summoned his foreign minister to another audience a few days later and expressed sympathy toward some of the arguments in the Lvov memorandum. Izvolsky, waxing eloquent, sought to persuade him that a coalition ministry would bring order and authority to his regime: "Nothing so tempers radicalism as the responsibilities that come with power." Nor did European governments and public opinion regard the Goremykin cabinet with favor, which handicapped Russia's foreign relations and its credit standing. Nicholas, though impressed, raised numerous objections centering on his distrust of the Duma as a hotbed of extremists. In the end, without committing himself to a change of policy, he authorized Izvolsky to proceed with the negotiations and wrote a personal note to Stolypin granting permission. Both ministers held secret conferences with Duma leaders and compared results every night. Izvolsky's cousin, Aleksei Yermolov, was entrusted with obtaining support from his colleagues in the State Council.[46]

In late June—again the date is uncertain—Milyukov called on Stolypin at his summer home near St. Petersburg. Izvolsky was present but only as a silent but "honourable witness." Milyukov found Stolypin less congenial than Trepov and claimed that he "had no intention of giving me the chance to express myself on the substantive issues." The paramount issue to Milyukov was a Kadet ministry, with himself at its head. He acknowledged later to having "set very hard conditions," apparently in reference to his meetings with both Trepov and Stolypin, and his brand of doctrinaire liberalism obviously grated harshly on the latter. An official announcement characterized the conversation as having been "reported to His Majesty together with the judgment of the minister of the interior that the fulfillment of the wishes of the Kadet party could affect Russia's interests only in the most disastrous way, a judgment approved by His Majesty in its entirety."[47]

The idea of a coalition government still remained alive, if barely so. Stolypin consulted Muromtsev with inconclusive results and then sought contact with Shipov, the respected zemstvo leader, who had become an Octobrist deputy. By this time Stolypin, with the sovereign's acquiescence, was aiming at a "dissolution cabinet"—that is, a ministry sufficiently "liberal" to avoid a revulsion of public opinion when the time came to dismiss the Duma. Shipov at first spurned a meeting but thought better of it when he received an imperial "command" for an audience at Peterhof. Accompanied by Nikolai Lvov, and joined later by Izvolsky, he arrived at Stolypin's summer residence on the evening of June 27. Queried by his host, Shipov emphatically denounced the notion of dissolving the Duma as "unjust and politically criminal" and refused to be a party to it. Displeased but courteous, Stolypin changed the subject and asked if he would consider the chairmanship of a coalition ministry. Shipov thought it inadvisable without Kadet support. The conversation ended at three o'clock in the morning with Stolypin's remark that a decision about forming a new cabinet would be entirely the emperor's.

Later in the day Nicholas received Shipov with his usual civility, and the two were closeted for over an hour. He listened attentively, injecting an occasional question, as Shipov expressed his views on a wide range of topics with frankness tempered by respect. Shipov repeated his reasons for declining a government appointment, indicating that a condition excluding the Kadets would only antagonize the Duma majority. As for Milyukov assuming the leadership of such a ministry, his love of power and moral deficiencies disqualified him, in Shipov's opinion, yet he would be "exceedingly useful" as minister of the interior or of foreign affairs. Shipov recommended Muromtsev for the chairmanship, an appointment that "would be welcomed by broad public circles." He left Peterhof in good spirits, "deeply moved by the confidence and attention shown me."[48]

Shipov's optimism was sustained by reassurances from Izvolsky, Stolypin, and others that he had made a good impression on the emperor. Nicholas had indeed been swayed, at least momentarily, but he was more susceptible to the arguments of Stolypin and Kokovtsov. He told the latter, apparently at the end of June, that he "never intended to embark upon that distant and unknown journey which I was so strongly advised to undertake." "I did not say so outright to those who had suggested this idea," Kokovtsov records him as saying. They were "moved by the best intentions . . . because I wished to verify my own thoughts by asking the advice of those whom I trust. Now I can tell you that your opinion was supported by nearly everybody with whom I talked on this subject. I have no more misgivings nor have I ever really had them, for I have no right to renounce that which was bequeathed to me by my forefathers and which I must hand down unimpaired to my own son."[49] If this statement is to be taken literally, and there is no reason to doubt its essential accuracy, the elaborate negotiations of Trepov, Izvolsky, and Stolypin were doomed from the start. Even a more flexible attitude by Milyukov, Shipov, and Muromtsev would not have sufficed to create either a coalition or a Kadet ministry.

Nicholas, if in fact he indulged in an intricate charade about the feasibility of a non-bureaucratic cabinet, was more hesitant about dissolving the Duma. He obviously agreed in principle that it should be done but feared political repercussions. Goremykin, who had not, oddly enough, been privy to the negotiations initiated by either Trepov or Izvolsky, assumed the leading role, together with Stolypin, in persuading Nicholas that the life of the First Duma should not be prolonged. The government chose the agrarian question as the point to lay down the gauntlet to the recalcitrant deputies. No other ostensibly non-political issue besides land reform, affecting as it did over 80 percent of the population, was capable of arousing such bitter controversy. Without achieving a consensus on the problem as a whole, the Duma did, with near unanimity, approve the principle of expropriating large estates. The government announced its own program on June 20 in the official newspaper. The inviolability of private property was once again upheld, yet the document also included a penetrating attack on the traditional village commune, most notably in those regions where periodic redistribution of land allotments still prevailed. Concluding on a patriarchal note, the declaration called upon the peasantry "to know and to understand that satisfaction of its needs would come from peaceful work and the constant solicitude of the Sovereign Emperor, not from disorder and violence."[50]

Many deputies chose to regard the pronouncement as a deliberate provocation. Although neither the tsar nor his chief minister would likely have concurred, it was an ill-advised if legally permissible challenge to the sensibilities of the lower house. A suitable reply was hotly debated and passed less than overwhelmingly on July 6 in the form of an "appeal" to the public that bypassed the throne and retreated not at all from the Duma's conception of land reform. The impasse demanded a quick solution. The next day, with rumors already abundant in elite circles that dissolution was imminent, Goremykin and Stolypin were summoned to Peterhof. Baron Frederiks, highly agitated, tried to persuade them that the tsar should appear before the Duma with a stern warning before taking more drastic action. Both refused, pointing out the dangers of a personal confrontation between the monarch and the people's representatives.

Nicholas received Goremykin first and signed a decree of dissolution. He accepted the minister's resignation, apparently to Goremykin's immense satisfaction, and appointed Stolypin to the vacancy with the understanding that he would also retain the office of interior minister. The emperor stated that action against the Duma could no longer be postponed because it had become an instigator of rebellion: "I am obligated before God, before my country and before myself to fight, and I would rather perish than hand over without any resistance all power to those who stretch out their hands for it." At Stolypin's demurrer that he was inexperienced and unfamiliar with the ways of St. Petersburg society, Nicholas interrupted, referring to the icon before which he often prayed: "Let us make the sign of the Cross over ourselves and let us ask the Lord to help us both in this difficult, perhaps historic, moment." With the ritual performed, he embraced and kissed his new first minister.[51]

Military preparations were made to secure the capital, including an armed detachment stationed at the Tauride Palace. Goremykin, still technically the tsar's chief minister until a formal announcement of the change, supposedly retired for the night with strict instructions that he was not to be disturbed. A few hours later, according to a report that was widely believed but is impossible to authenticate, a special courier brought an imperial message that the order dissolving the Duma be temporarily rescinded, but the resourceful Goremykin did not receive it until the next morning. By that time, on Sunday, July 9, the decree had already been published and copies posted throughout the city. The doomsayers were confounded, for no open protests were discernible. The deputies who gathered for the scheduled session, finding the palace doors locked and well guarded, dispersed quietly and without incident. As Milyukov admitted, "All the dreams about how we would follow the example of the Roman Senate and remain 'seated' and not leave the Duma voluntarily were automatically reduced to ashes." An imperial manifesto, drafted by Stolypin and several associates, appeared on the same day justifying the government's conduct and promising the convocation of a new Duma on February 20, 1907, but with no date specified for a new election.[52]

Contrary to surface impressions, however, not all the deputies were intimidated. Milyukov had been reliably informed of the impending blow early in the morning, and on his bicycle he managed to contact most of the Kadet party's Central Committee. The members assembled not long after 8 A.M. in Petrunkevich's apartment, where Milyukov was charged with drafting an appeal to the public. They decided to adjourn to Vyborg, Finland, about eighty miles from the capital, a precarious sanctuary but relatively free from police interference. By late evening somewhat over two hundred Duma representatives, chiefly Kadets, had gathered there, at the Hotel Belvedere. A committee labored through the night revising the Milyukov draft; the document that emerged avoided an inflammatory call for direct action, in favor of passive resistance. ("Not a kopeck to the treasury or a single soldier to the army" was to be permitted, until the Duma re-convened.) Without time for adequate discussion—the Finnish authorities threatened to intervene—some 150 deputies signed it in haste, a number with serious reservations. Once back on Russian soil, the signators (including others who endorsed it later) were indicted for participating in a conspiracy to distribute a revolutionary manifesto. Tried late in 1907, 166 defendants were sentenced to three months in prison. But a more drastic punishment, the loss of political rights, barred the offenders from elective office. With the notable exception of Milyukov, the flower of the Kadet party was deprived of an effective voice in the legislative process.

Despite its "seditious character" (Stolypin's phrase), the Vyborg manifesto aroused little response from a public already emotionally drained by eighteen months of political strife. Even had it provoked a few sparks of popular enthusiasm, the recourse to civil disobedience, while theoretically sound, missed the mark: direct taxes figured only marginally in the state budget, and recruits for the army were not due until autumn. The spirit of rebellion, however, still infected the armed forces. During the third week in July revolt broke out anew at Kronstadt and in the fortress of Sveaborg near Helsinki. Perhaps more personally distressing to Nicholas, a mutiny occurred aboard the *Pamyat Azova*, "his" cruiser on the voyage to the Far East in 1890. "My heart bleeds to think of the disgusting things which have happened," he commented to his mother, claiming to be "very tired in mind, but fit in body."[53] At Peterhof he remained within earshot of artillery fire at Kronstadt, but no hint of emotion betrayed his placid demeanor. Izvolsky, who was present for a weekly report, alluded, somewhat presumptuously, to his extraordinary self-possession. Nicholas did not resent the observation, and his reply revealed the profound depths of his fatalistic piety: "If you see me so calm, it is because I have the firm, the absolute conviction that the fate of Russia, my own fate and that of my family, is in the hands of God, Who placed me where I am. Whatever happens, I will bow to His will, conscious of never having had a thought other than that of serving the country that He confided to me."[54]

These new disturbances proved ephemeral, as so often in the past. Despite a fresh outbreak of revolutionary terror, which served only to alienate moderates otherwise critical of the regime, the quiescence of the popular mood and the renewed confidence of the ruling elite demonstrated that the old order had not exhausted its political capital. Nor had its antagonists displayed a capacity for leadership that would attract a mass following. Bourgeois liberalism, if not precisely bankrupt, had been unable to broaden its slender constituency; its idealism bordering on utopianism, it proved unwilling to sacrifice integrity to the ignoble cause of political opportunism. Revolutionary militance had been equally unproductive, and in the end the frustration of impotence incited the partisans of violence to enter the blind alley of direct action against the symbols of authority. Yet Nicholas and his entourage, though not all of his ministers, mistook public apathy for a groundswell of popular support. A reprieve, not a vote of acclamation, was the most that the emperor's subjects would concede.

8

The Stolypin Era

Distinguished in appearance, a speaker of eloquence, and a confident and vigorous personality, Pyotr Stolypin assumed for five years the unenviable role of chief minister to a capricious royal master. His statesmanlike qualities and his emphasis on strong leadership and moderate reform within the context of a presumably limited monarchy, placed him in the Witte "succession." More tactful and deferential, however, than his predecessor in catering to the sovereign, in matters of form if not always of substance, he retained his office longer than any other chairman of the Ministerial Council in the "constitutional" era. The length of his tenure concealed to some extent the dissonances in his relationship with the tsar. His approach to the Duma revealed wariness if not distrust, and as his career matured he revealed a sense of self-righteousness and a core of political cynicism that allowed him to violate standards of moral and legal propriety with seeming indifference.

Under Stolypin the cabinet maintained a surprising continuity. Aside from Goremykin, two arch-reactionaries, the minister of agriculture and the director of the Holy Synod, were sacrificed to mollify public opinion. But within the imperial court the fate of General Trepov proved the most startling development. Presumably his opposition to dissolving the Duma and his "liberal" stand against a repressive policy alienated the tsar. Although he remained palace commandant, his political influence sharply declined. His health, probably not coincidentally, also suffered. On September 2 he died of a heart attack, according to the official verdict, yet rumors persisted that he had committed suicide. Apparently Nicholas intended to jettison him altogether. But "as usual in such cases," Witte maintained, he "tried to do so deviously, like a spider spinning a web for a fly. . . . Fortunately for the Emperor, Trepov's death saved him the trouble of administering the final blow."[1]

With seeming good faith Stolypin renewed his search for responsible "public men" who would modify the bureaucratic image that had gravely handicapped the previous ministry. Virtually ignoring the Kadets, he met Shipov, Guchkov, Prince Georgi Lvov, and others in what became another vain attempt to assemble a coalition regime. The prospective ministers were offended by Stolypin's reluctance to discuss his program in specific detail and regarded his invitation to join the cabinet as a mere exercise in public relations. Shipov and Lvov set rigorous conditions: that half the portfolios, including the interior ministry, be assigned to "public men," that the government prepare bills to be submitted to the new Duma immediately after its opening, and that capital punishment be suspended until the legislature acted on the matter. In a polite letter written on July 17, 1906, Stolypin rejected these demands and expressed his regret that he had "left an impression of a person who fears bold reforms and is a partisan of 'petty concessions.' "[2]

Nicholas received other candidates, including Guchkov and Nikolai Lvov, and after conversing with each one for an hour, he pronounced them "not fit to be ministers now," in a letter to Stolypin. "They are not men of action."[3] He also conferred with the more conservative Fyodor Samarin, who declined the directorship of the Holy Synod. Disgusted by their attitude, he observed to his mother, "They hold their own connections in higher esteem than patriotism, and seem to be guided by false modesty on the one hand, and fear of committing themselves on the other. We will manage without them, never fear!"[4] These abortive negotiations marked the last occasion when the government sought an accommodation with the opposition. Stolypin, in contrast to Nicholas, was depressed by the refusal of the moderates to accept ministerial portfolios, ascribing it to their doctrinaire attitude. They wanted freedom to criticize without assuming the responsibilities that go with authority. But Stolypin, too, was doctrinaire in his own way and disinclined to be flexible about political principles that in his view should not be bargained away.

On August 12 a group of terrorists who had withdrawn from the Battle Organization served notice of their intentions—there had been a respite from violence during the First Duma—with a particularly vicious deed: the bombing of Stolypin's summer home. Three individuals, two dressed as gendarme officers, had appeared in one of the waiting rooms, where citizens from all walks of life gathered to air their grievances with the minister personally. When the guards became suspicious the terrorists detonated bombs that demolished much of the residence in a terrific explosion. Stolypin, in his study, escaped unharmed, but the death toll reached thirty-three, including the perpetrators. He maintained his composure and assured two colleagues, who had rushed to the scene from the capital, that the tragedy would not alter his policy: "We shall continue to carry out our reforms. They are Russia's salvation." His fortitude as well as compassion for his daughter, who had been seriously injured, greatly enhanced his prestige. The outrage "did more than all his liberal measures to win him the sympathy of all classes who were not utterly sunk in the depths of revolutionary psychosis."[5] The Central Committee of the Socialist Revolutionaries formally disavowed the act, at the behest of Azef, who sought to "whitewash the Battle Organization in Stolypin's eyes."[6] But the terrorists, whatever their organizational affiliation, were not deterred from further atrocities, though none rivaled the carnage or publicity attending the Stolypin affair. Nor did the victims normally include innocent bystanders. On August 13 the murder by a lone female assassin of General Georgi Min, who had delivered the coup de grace to the Moscow insurrection in December 1905, saddened Nicholas, who offered his personal condolences and also attended the funeral. To ensure his own safety, Stolypin accepted the sovereign's invitation to move with his family to the Winter Palace.

True to his word, Stolypin resumed sessions of the Ministerial Council on the evening of the 12th with every intention of proceeding with his reform program. On the 14th a meeting was interrupted by a messenger conveying a letter from Nicholas to his chief minister urging prompt action to curb political crimes. He deplored the "ceaseless attempts and murder of officials and the daily reckless assaults that have led the country into a state of complete anarchy."[7] Stolypin preferred the normal judicial process but obeyed the royal injunction and prepared legislation to establish field courts-martial. Although he may have had personal scruples to overcome, it seems doubtful that he "rejected with horror the proposed new method of fighting the revolution."[8] A government decree of August 19 conferred upon the new military courts jurisdiction over revolutionary crimes of violence. The proceedings, to be held in secret, were designed to render speedy justice: sentences, normally the death penalty, were to be carried out within twenty-four hours. Hanging became the preferred method of execution, and the merciless finality of the "Stolypin necktie" (a phrase coined later by Fyodor Rodichev) aroused bitter resentment in liberal as well as radical circles. Guchkov, a minority of one among prominent oppositionists, accepted the anti-terrorist measures as "a cruel necessity," thereby prompting defections from the Octobrist party. Nicholas himself justified repression in much the same terms. "The courts-martial function independently of you and me; let them carry on in the full severity of the law," he wrote Admiral Fyodor Dubasov, who had just escaped a second assassination attempt. "There is and can be no other means of struggle against those who have become brutalized. You know me and know that I am not spiteful: I write to you fully convinced of the correctness of my opinion. It is painful and difficult but true, much to our sorrow and shame, that only the execution of a few can prevent seas of blood, and indeed have prevented them already."[9]

Reasonably secure from terrorist attacks at Peterhof during the late summer of 1906, Nicholas remained apprehensive nonetheless and considered himself a virtual prisoner. "How shameful it is, even to speak about it!" he wrote his mother. "After killing poor Min those anarchist scoundrels, encouraged by their success, came here to Peterhof to hunt for me. . . . The ringleaders were arrested yesterday." "I have been unable," he complained, "to go out riding or even outside the gate, and this in one's own home— at Peterhof, usually so peaceful! I blush as I write to you about all this, so ashamed am I for my country and so annoyed that such a thing could happen so near Petersburg." On August 31 he and his family embarked on an extended yachting cruise in the Baltic "to be away from his humiliation." They were guarded by a naval squadron, and Nicholas, well rested, regained his composure. Back at Peterhof in late September, he was gratified that the country seemed to have become "sober again" and that a "healthy reaction" toward "good order" had taken place. "Individual plots by anarchists are still to be expected." he reported, "but they have happened before and will not lead anywhere. The courts martial and the severe punishment they have inflicted for looting, robbery and murder are doing some good. It's distressing to have to have them, but unavoidable; and their effect is becoming evident."[10]

Nicholas may have been correct about lesser acts of violence, but the casualty rate itself did not bear him out. According to Stolypin's figures, recorded by a French journalist, 738 officials and 640 private citizens were killed by terrorists in 1906, and fatalities in these categories increased in 1907 to 1,231 and 1,768 respectively. The number wounded also rose during the same period. In 1908, however, the number of officials killed fell sharply to 365.[11] Based on information compiled by six major Russian newspapers, the special courts, which were disbanded in April 1907, condemned 1,144 defendants to death and imposed less drastic punishment on 779.[12] The government's draconian method, while it may have inhibited terrorism in the long run, had disappointing short-term results. The courts were allowed to expire, not for humanitarian reasons or in response to a public outcry but because their mandate under Article 87 of the Fundamental Laws would not have been renewed by the Second Duma.

If Stolypin's public image became, however unfairly, one of ruthless severity because of the government's anti-terrorist campaign and lesser measures of political repression, his other activities encompassed a wide range of social and political reform. Article 87 was invoked fifty-eight times to introduce provisional legislation prior to the convocation of the Second Duma. Many of these projects were of a technical nature and of peripheral interest even to the intelligentsia, the only group other than government administrators presumed to be knowledgeable on such matters. But a major reform, building upon years of discussion and preparation by Stolypin's predecessors, sought to confront head-on the perennial agrarian question. The government had been sorely troubled by the prevalence and intensity of peasant unrest in 1905–1906, though gratified by the failure of radical agitators to enlist the "dark people" in the broader revolutionary struggle. Various palliatives sought to ease the peasant burden: redemption dues from the emancipation settlement of 1861 were halved in 1906 and abolished altogether on January 1, 1907; interest rates were lowered and other concessions were granted to facilitate purchases through the Peasant Land Bank; and the remaining legal restrictions upon the *muzhik* were removed by a decree of October 5, 1906.

Finally, on November 9, 1906, came a bold assault on the traditional underpinning of rural life—the village commune. The new law (by tsarist decree) allowed heads of households the right to withdraw from the commune and to consolidate their land holdings, normally in scattered strips, into a single private plot. Stolypin thus inaugurated his famous "wager on the strong," an attempt to replace the primitive and inefficient "socialism" of communal ownership with a "capitalist" system of land tenure that in theory would develop a class of independent and prosperous farmers. As he put it more colorfully, "the government has placed its wager not on the drunken and the weak but on the sober and the strong—on the sturdy independent proprietor." Yet his aim was more ambitious than simply creating a class of "kulaks," or privileged farmers. Stolypin sought by economic means to instill in the peasantry a sense of civic virtue and to elevate it to full citizenship, not only with political rights but with conscious participation in society. "Private ownership," he had explained to the sovereign two years before, "is a written guarantee of order, because each small owner represents the nucleus on which rests the stability of public order."[13]

The Socialist Revolutionaries were dismayed, for their vision of a future socialist Russia had been based largely on an idealized commune. The Social Democrats, unresponsive to the mystique of peasant institutions, nevertheless recognized that the agrarian program endangered prospects for revolution. V. I. Lenin, who customarily scorned Stolypin as "the hangman," admitted that his adversary "understood the situation correctly: without breaking up the old system of land ownership the economic development of Russia cannot be guaranteed. Stolypin and the landlords boldly took the revolutionary path, ruthlessly destroying the old order, handing over the peasant masses as a whole to the mercy of the landlords and kulaks." He asserted that the party would "explain, propagandize, and spread to the masses the slogan of a joint uprising of the peasants with the proletariat as the *only* possible means to prevent the Stolypin method of 'rejuvenating' Russia."[14] But events failed to justify either apprehension on the Left or excessive optimism on the Right. The agrarian question proved intractable enough to become a major legacy of the tsarist regime.

Nicholas was generally content to play a passive role during the early phase of the Stolypin reforms. His anti-Semitism, however, was so deeply ingrained that he objected to lifting some of the discriminatory restrictions against Jews recommended unanimously by the Council of Ministers in October 1906. Two months later he wrote Stolypin that despite "convincing arguments" in favor of the proposal, "an inner voice keeps on insisting more and more that I do not accept responsibility for it. So far my conscience has not deceived me. Therefore I intend in this case also to follow its dictates. I know that you, too, believe that 'A Tsar's heart is in God's hand.' Let it be so. For all laws established by me I bear a great responsibility before God, and I am ready to answer for this decision at any time. I regret only one thing: that I am compelled to reject your decision on a matter to which you and your collaborators devoted so much time and labor." No other document emanating from Nicholas himself revealed quite so clearly the mystical piety that served to justify even unconscionable and outrageous decisions. Stolypin did not argue, as Witte might have done, and turned to other aspects of his program that did not violate his sovereign's "responsibility before God." But he did suggest that in order to avert any embarrassing repercussions—the press had got wind of the cabinet discussions—that the tsar's veto message be altered to a less astringent statement that would avoid repudiating his ministers. Nicholas accepted this artful solution.[15]

Nicholas' virulent brand of anti-Semitism extended also to "international Jewry," whose machinations had furnished "the real driving force behind the Russian revolution." He confided these sentiments to the German ambassador early in 1907 while expounding freely on the supposed characteristics of various nationalities. The English he pronounced "too egotistical," the French "too disorderly," while the Italians and Spanish were by implication of inferior stock. As for Russians, and Slavs in general, they had many good qualities but remained at a "lamentably low level" of culture. No doubt in partial deference to his visitor, he elevated Germans to the "highest level of civilization" and, surprisingly, praised Americans for "combining business ability with strict morality." As to internal affairs, the ambassador reported, he expressed his determination to "rule with an iron hand and views the future with confidence even if the next elections to the Duma again demonstrate that the Russian people do not have the maturity to appreciate the benefits that He has granted them."[16]

The government's relatively passive role in the election campaign to the First Duma was not repeated for the Second. An imperial decree of December 8, 1906, set the the elections for February 6, 1907. Stolypin issued instructions to local officials to refrain from interference with election campaigns except in cases involving anti-government agitation. But "irregularities" of all kinds, most of them apparently countenanced by Stolypin, took place on a broad scale. The Kadets, as the dominant liberal party, were singled out for various forms of administrative repression, and parties of the Right, including the unsavory Union of the Russian People, received financial aid from the ministry of interior's secret "reptile fund." The government's anxiety to secure a pliant Duma was thwarted by the voters themselves. They returned, through the cumbersome procedure of indirect voting, an assembly more "radical" in the extremes of Left and Right than its predecessor. The Trudoviks (or "Laborites"), a peasant-oriented caucus with a socialist ideology, captured a plurality of seats with 104. The Social Democrats dropped their boycott as self-defeating and gained sixty-five deputies, most of them Mensheviks. The Socialist Revolutionaries also abandoned their boycott tactic and returned thirty-seven. The Kadets were reduced to ninety-eight seats, while the Octobrists increased to forty-four.

By the tsar's decree the Second Duma convened on February 20, 1907, with many citizens taking an unofficial holiday. Thousands of telegrams exuding good will and brimming with encouragement indicated widespread public interest. No special ceremonies marked the occasion, but Nicholas did send a brief message of greeting which the conservative deputies acknowledged with enthusiasm by rising to their feet with shouts of "Long live the sovereign emperor!" Nicholas found the opposition's silence offensive: "What a colossal blunder it was of the Left not to rise when the Right cheered!" In a note to Stolypin he remarked that the "conduct of the Left is typical, if not to say indecent." A Kadet, Fyodor Golovin, was elected to the presidency, and Nicholas, though he tried to postpone the "tedious affair," dutifully received him. "My general impression," he commented, "is that he is a completely nonentity!" As for the Duma, "it will soon be evident how far . . . [it] intends to get down to serious work or to squander its time and small prestige in useless chatter and abuse."[17]

Stolypin did not share the sovereign's ill-concealed malice toward the Duma. In contrast to the studied indifference of Goremykin, he presented an ambitious legislative program to the deputies on March 6. Speaking with forceful dignity and manifest sincerity, he impressed even his detractors and achieved credibility with moderates, including many Kadets. Yet the opposition benches remained silent as the Right thundered its applause, for party principle demanded an adversarial relationship with the government. Alienation from the monarchy and its apologists had become too deeply ingrained to permit reconciliation on the strength of a single speech. The revolutionaries, concerned only to ply their trade, were scornful of the Duma itself except as a forum for agitation. In their eyes Stolypin was a mere lackey of tsarist oppression whose "reforms" amounted only to superficial tinkering with a hopelessly corrupt and reprehensible system. A Menshevik deputy from Georgia, Irakly Tsereteli, responded with a slightly disguised revolutionary appeal, and the tone was set for the rancorous partisanship that all too often characterized the debating style of the Second Duma. When Stolypin rose once more to rebut his critics, he emphasized the government's desire for legality and mutual understanding: "The language of hatred and malice cannot serve that end. I will not resort to it." The regime welcomed "exposure of any irregularity whatever," but public disorder would not be countenanced. "All your attacks are calculated to provoke a paralysis of mind and will in the government," he concluded with a deft rhetorical flourish. "They can all be reduced to two words addressed to the government: 'Hands up.' To these two words, gentlemen, the government, confident of its integrity, calmly answers with only two words: 'Not intimidated.' "[18]

Stolypin's firm but conciliatory leadership won the respect of the liberal intelligentsia, though there were misgivings and reservations. They could not overlook political reality: the tsar, not his chief minister, held the reins of power. Vasily Maklakov, a key figure among conservative Kadets, provided Stolypin with moral if not wholehearted parliamentary support. Renewed overtures to Milyukov again misfired because he refused to sanction without party approval an unequivocal denunciation of terrorism. In reporting to Nicholas, Stolypin was initially optimistic, commenting that the "mood of the Duma is very different from last year's, and during the entire session not one shout or whistle was heard." But by March 14 he complained that "verbal eruptions of an inflammatory nature continue in the State Duma, but as to work no sound is heard." By April 9 his disillusionment had progressed to cynicism, and he wrote Nicholas that the Duma left the impression of being "grey and lackluster." The deputies, he charged, were unprepared to work in the committees. "The Duma is 'rotting at its roots,' and many leftists, seeing this, wish for dissolution now in order to create the legend that the Duma would have performed miracles, but the government became fearful and spoiled everything."[19]

Nicholas came under pressure to dismiss the Duma soon after it convened. The Union of the Russian People, the most active lobby of the extreme Right, mounted a telegram campaign that Nicholas obliquely acknowledged by praising the Union for its support of the monarchy and public order. His court entourage also began to favor the idea of dissolution. As of March 29 Nicholas thought such action premature, but his future intentions were clear enough: "One must let them do something manifestly stupid or mean, and then—slap! And they are gone!"[20]

An incident that qualified for Nicholas' definition of both stupidity and meanness occurred on April 16, when an Armenian Social Democratic deputy, Arshak Zurabov, outraged conservatives by delivering a speech that "insulted" the honor of the army. With the Duma in recess to deal with disorder on the floor, Stolypin telephoned Golovin for firsthand information, explaining that the emperor had heard of the address and would not hesitate to dismiss the assembly. The Council of Ministers agreed that dissolution, while inevitable, should be postponed to allow the final draft of a new electoral law to be completed. Nicholas, though "stunned" by the Zurabov affair, accepted the decision but inquired of Kokovtsov with rhetorical indignation: "What will happen next? Is there need for any further proof that we can no longer tolerate such action unless we are prepared to be swept away by the storm of revolution?"[21] Despite Nicholas' impatience, the Duma continued to meet for another five weeks.

The royal birthday was celebrated by a reception at Tsarskoe Selo on May 6. The chief topic of conversation among the ministers and court officials involved the Duma session to be held the next day, at which the government was to be interpellated by Rightist deputies about a plot, already exposed, against the tsar's life. The conspiracy, with Stolypin and others as additional targets, had resulted in the arrest of twenty-eight Socialist Revolutionary terrorists on April 1 (Nicholas, ill informed as to revolutionary labels, referred to them as "very prominent anarchists").[22] Anticipating a show of patriotic self-congratulation that the tsar's life had been spared, the extreme Left boycotted the Duma at the appointed hour as Stolypin explained the circumstances of the attempted crime. Eighteen of the terrorists were tried and convicted, and three were hanged.

Two additonal interpellations, introduced when the oppositionists returned to their seats, concerned an incident that was to serve as the government's pretext to disband the Duma. On May 5 the apartment of Ivan Ozol, a Menshevik deputy from Riga, had been searched by police on information provided by a secret agent that it had become a meeting place for agitators attempting to subvert the armed forces. Stolypin responded that the action had been lawful, that criminal activities had indeed taken place on the premises, and that he could not be blamed if some of those implicated were members of the Duma. The Social Democratic faction, previously indifferent to rights of the legislature, protested that the inviolability of the deputies had been imperiled (they had been briefly detained, then released). A Duma majority sided with the Social Democrats on the principle of parliamentary immunity, and Stolypin bided his time, continuing his investigation and negotiating with Golovin.

Alarmed by rumors of the Duma's imminent dissolution, Golovin requested an audience with the tsar and was received at Peterhof on May 19. On this occasion Nicholas was less cordial than during their previous meetings, three in all. Golovin reported on the Duma's work and minimized the disorders that had occurred. Nicholas resented any attempt to excuse the rowdy behavior of the deputies: "What! The president of the Duma really does not have the authority to expel from the sessions a member of the Duma?" Golovin explained that he had no such authority and went on to express his distress at the personal attacks that had been directed toward him. Nicholas responded sympathetically, noting that public servants were always subject to severe criticism. It occurred to Golovin that the tsar saw himself as just such a "public servant." Despite Nicholas' comment that the electoral law would have to be altered, the Duma president left the meeting in an optimistic mood.[23] He was soon to be disillusioned.

Stolypin informed Nicholas on May 30 that within two days he would request the Duma to waive the rights of fifty-five Social Democratic deputies, of whom "fifteen of the more criminal members" were to be arrested immediately. Failure to comply would be grounds for the Duma's dissolution; a manifesto to that effort would be forwarded for Nicholas' signature.[24] On June 1, at a closed session of the Duma, Stolypin made good his promise. His aggressive tactics caught the deputies by surprise, and a prolonged debate lasting beyond midnight produced only a delaying action: a committee of twenty-two, with a Kadet plurality, was elected to consider the government's case and report the following evening. The committee examined the prosecutor's evidence conscientiously and came to the tentative conclusion that the accused had not been engaged in unlawful acts. The committee was unable, however, to render a definitive verdict within the time limit, and the Second Duma closed its final session in the near certainty that it would not meet again. Despite a late evening intercession with Stolypin by a delegation of four Kadet leaders, a visit unauthorized by the party, the government proceeded to carry out its threat. Nicholas waited impatiently for the legal details of dispersing the "accursed Duma" to be completed. In an impulsive note to Stolypin, he demanded "decisiveness and firmness": "There must be no delay, not a minute of hesitation! The bold are favored by God."[25]

The decree of dissolution on June 3 aroused little public reaction other than manifestations of elation on the part of the extreme Right. The offending deputies, except for those in hiding or in self-imposed exile, were arrested and tried in closed proceedings in November 1907. The majority received sentences ranging up to five years in prison; ten were acquitted. That the Social Democrats were committed to a revolutionary struggle with the government could not be denied; that they were also preparing an armed uprising, let alone that the Duma faction had been seriously implicated, strained credulity. With Stolypin providing the initiative, the authorities were not concerned with legal niceties but ran roughshod over their strident adversaries with full confidence that public opinion would sustain them or at least remain apathetic.

The fate of the Second Duma and its contingent of Marxist revolutionaries was overshadowed by the government's bold assault on the constitution—that is, the Fundamental Laws—by altering the electoral procedure without the consent of the legislature. An imperial manifesto, also issued on June 3, justified the government's conduct by condemning the Duma for its lack of cooperation, and announced that the new electoral law would help preserve the "true" Russian spirit in its legislative deliberations. Stolypin, as his critics were quick to point out, had achieved a veritable coup d'état. By manipulating the franchise he virtually ensured that future Dumas would be politically conservative and thus amenable if not necessarily subservient to the executive power. At the same time he rescued the Duma from its enemies, many of whom were prepared to abolish it altogether or to transform it into an advisory body.

Nicholas wavered but preserved sufficient independence from the court "camarilla" to follow Stolypin's lead. He acknowledged, however, the plaudits of the far Right and thanked the Union of the Russian People with "heartfelt gratitude" for its assistance. "I am confident," he telegraphed Dubrovin, "that now all the truly faithful and affectionate sons of the Russian homeland will unite still more closely, and as they continually increase their numbers they will assist me in bringing about a peaceful renewal of our great and holy Russia and in improving the goodly way of life of her people. Certainly for me the Union of the Russian People will be a trustworthy support, serving everyone and ever an example of legality and order."[26] Witte, who with good reason considered Dubrovin's organization a "gang of paid thugs," commented that the telegram "revealed all the poverty of political thought and sickliness of soul of the autocratic emperor."[27]

The electoral law had been fine-tuned in different versions over a period of months by Sergei Kryzhanovsky, Stolypin's assistant. The final text was rushed to Tsarskoe Selo late at night by a versatile courier, who contrived to enter the palace "in a manner known only to himself." He found the sovereign in a corridor on his way to bed, extracted the vital signature, and returned the document to the capital, where it was published without the legally required prior approval by the Senate.[28] The finished product retained the feature of indirect voting (with minor exceptions) and heavily weighted the suffrage in favor of the landed nobility and affluent urban residents. In the government's rationale, future Dumas would be elected by "the more cultivated strata of the population." The representation of the ethnic minorities was drastically reduced, and the number of deputies shrank from 518 to 442. One elector represented approximately 250 landowners, a thousand wealthy businessmen, fifteen thousand lesser bourgeoisie, sixty thousand peasants, and 125,000 workers.

Stolypin's handiwork constituted a sharp setback for the European parliamentary ideal so admired by the liberal intelligentsia. "Reaction" had triumphed, according to the opposition, and the revolutionary cause nearly expired in frustration and despair as the monarchy appeared to regain the confidence and stability of a decade before. But "progress" did not suddenly perish in a wave of mindless repression: the Third Duma met and achieved its statutory limit of five years; the emperor, however discontented, continued to rule as a quasi-constitutional monarch; civil liberties, though by Western standards severely limited, were secure enough to allow in most cases the free exercise of opinion; and the cultural pursuits of the intellectual elite, expecially in art, literature, and music, flourished with renewed vigor.

The Third Duma was elected in September and October of 1907. Public apathy and the arbitrary disqualification of both eligible voters and liberal candidates shifted the political spectrum even further to the Right than the electoral law would have mandated in any case. Fulfilling the government's expectations, the representation of the radical Left was sharply reduced. The Kadets emerged with only fifty-four deputies, the Octobrists obtained a plurality of 154, and the extreme Right for the first time captured a significant number of seats.

Without official fanfare, other than a conventional greeting from the tsar, the new Duma convened on November 1. Nikolai Khomyakov, an Octobrist prominent in the zemstvo movement, was elected president with near unanimity. The prospect of agreeable if not harmonious relations between tsar and Duma seemed excellent. But Nicholas remained aloof, protesting that it was "too early" when Stolypin suggested that he receive the deputies. "It has not yet proven itself worthy," he explained, "nor fulfilled expectations in the sense of my hopes for its cooperation with the government. Premature actions and precedents on my part should be avoided."[29] He became sorely offended when the deputies embroiled themselves in a symbolic but politically charged controversy over his sovereign powers. A majority agreed that a message of loyalty and respect to the emperor would be appropriate, but they differed on the proper wording. The Right held out for a reference to the "autocrat," while the Kadets insisted upon an allusion to the "constitution." In the end, when the "autocratic" formulation was rejected by a formal vote, 114 Rightists sent their own communication. Nicholas acknowledged their telegram with a benevolent response, while the salutation of the Duma majority drew an austere reply: "I am prepared to accept the sentiments expressed; I await your constructive work."

On November 19, however, he received Khomyakov at Tsarskoe Selo with polite amiability. The softening of Nicholas' attitude toward the Duma may be credited in large part to the tactful influence of Stolypin, who received the support of a majority of the deputies. The temper of the new assembly was revealed by its decision to suspend Fyodor Rodichev for fifteen sessions because of his attack on the suddenly popular chief minister. Stolypin cultivated a working relationship with Guchkov, the Octobrist leader, and forged an alliance with the moderate Right. But the radical Right, constituting some fifty deputies who responded to the gamy ideology of the Black Hundreds, regarded him with suspicion as a closet liberal and a potential threat to the monarchy. As for Nicholas' role in Duma affairs, he remained content to delegate authority to Stolypin, avoiding political involvement unless his prerogatives, real or fancied, seemed to be challenged. As a gesture of good will, he received approximately three hundred deputies of the Center and Right at Tsarskoe Selo in January 1908.

The crux of Stolypin's legislative program involved his agrarian reform of November 1906. Its implementation, with no serious opposition by the Third Duma and the State Council, should have led to further parliamentary victories, but in the few years that remained to him Stolypin spent his political capital with only meager results. His one major triumph, upon sober reflection, could not furnish a long-term solution to Russia's agrarian woes. Only about a tenth of the households in European Russia had chosen private farms over communal holdings by the final year of the old regime. Even 100 percent conversion to Western-style agriculture would not have altered the structure of peasant life in so short a time. Rural backwardness in all its manifestations could not be remedied by government fiat, nor did the proverbial land-hunger of the muzhik find release in the Stolypin reform.

The government's majority in the Duma, seemingly automatic, foundered as early as 1908. Paradoxically, the Octobrists, patriotic to a man and eager to provide for the national defense, proved irritating to Stolypin and his conception of an appropriate policy toward the armed forces. Guchkov, who fancied himself an expert on military affairs, chaired the Committee of Imperial Defense, a creation of the Third Duma with a self-imposed mission to investigate and improve the strength and performance of the army and navy. Under the committee's influence the Duma unexpectedly rejected a government request for credits to build four battleships for the Baltic fleet. The vote represented not anti-naval sentiment but anxiety as to the competence of the ministry of marine and skepticism that overall military planning had achieved a more competent level than that displayed in the war with Japan. In a letter to Stolypin on May 25, Nicholas expressed his indignation at the Duma's "blind and wholly unjustified diversion of credits for the reconstruction of the fleet. . . . And this," he lamented, "on the very eve of the arrival of the English king" (Edward VII, due at Revel in three days for an official visit).[30]

Stolypin eventually sidestepped the issue by invoking the previous year's budget for the projected battleships, but Guchkov meanwhile broadened the offensive with a speech to the Duma on May 27 that caused a minor sensation. He deplored the "irresponsible" nepotism and favoritism that permeated the highest echelons of the armed forces, including members of the royal family. The Grand Duke Nikolai Nikolayevich, who headed the Council of Imperial Defense, was singled out in unmistakable fashion, though not by name.[31] The minister of war, General Aleksandr Rediger, admitted that the criticism was justified and claimed that reform was underway. Stolypin privately expressed agreement; "Even the tsar considered the removal of the grand dukes from their posts," he allegedly told Guchkov. "But after your speech I am afraid that their position has been strengthened, since the sovereign would not like to create the impression that he acts under your commands."[32] Nicholas had already conceived an intense dislike for Guchkov, and this public airing of so sensitive an issue raised the level of his animosity. Stolypin, whose Duma majority rested upon Guchkov and the Octobrists, found himself in an awkward position. Obviously his loyalty to the throne had to take precedence. Nevertheless, Guchkov's "exposé" obtained results that could scarcely have been matched by personal diplomacy: the grand duke resigned, the Council of Imperial Defense was abolished, and other royal kinsmen relinquished their sinecures or were relegated to honorary positions. Nicholas later dismissed General Rediger "because twice in the Duma he not only failed to answer Guchkov's speeches but even agreed with him and thus did not defend the honor of the army."[33] Nicholas cautioned the new war minister, General Vladimir Sukhomlinov, to discontinue his predecessor's cooperation with the Duma: "Why should you argue with them; you are my minister." And a few days later he added: "I created the Duma so that it would advise me, not order me."[34]

This minor political skirmishing was succeeded by an actual ministerial crisis in 1909. But instead of a mildly obstreperous Duma, Stolypin had to contend with the State Council and its reactionary allies. Pyotr Durnovo, the former interior minister, Vladimir Trepov, brother of the recently deceased palace commandant, and Count Witte, still desperately seeking leverage for a return to power, furnished a core of intrigue within the Council. More royalist than the emperor, they zealously guarded the imperial prerogatives against the parvenu usurper, Stolypin. And Stolypin himself had grown less circumspect in dealing with his enemies. The pressures of his office were constant and the state of his health bordered on the precarious, yet he had acquired a taste for power and was "loath to let it slip from his hands."[35]

A power play arose over a routine bill to provide funds for a newly created naval general staff, a group of young officers under the jurisdiction of the ministry of marine who were dedicated to improving the efficiency of the navy. The Duma passed the necessary appropriation, including its endorsement of the official list of personnel. The State Council objected that the lower house had exceeded its statutory authority by validating an administrative as well as a budgetary measure, thereby infringing upon the legal authority of the monarch. The bill was rejected in July 1908. When the Duma, refusing to compromise, reaffirmed its decision, the Council again debated the issue in March 1909. Stolypin missed the session because of illness, but allusions were made to his supposed collaboration with the Octobrists to limit the rights of the emperor. By a margin of eighty-seven to seventy-five the Council reversed its previous vote, reflecting governmental pressure behind the scenes.

Stolypin won a hollow victory. The rumor spread that Nicholas might veto the bill and institute a cabinet shakeup. Returning from a convalescence in the Crimea, Stolypin was gratified to see his ministerial colleagues rally to his support. He was received at Tsarskoe Selo on June 22 and tried to allay Nicholas' concern that the Duma might seek to limit his rights. Nicholas protested that the Duma had already done so under a strict interpretation of the Fundamental Laws, "although, of course, one should not exaggerate the danger of such a violation." Stolypin was encouraged to believe that after further deliberation the tsar would accept the bill, for his parting words had been: "One cannot accuse this Duma of a desire to seize power, and there is no need to fight with it." Stolypin's surprise was all the greater, therefore, when he received a brusque letter from Nicholas three days later repudiating the controversial legislation. "Remember that we are living in Russia and not abroad or in Finland," he admonished. "Therefore *I do not consider the thought of anyone resigning*. Of course there will be talk about this in Petersburg and Moscow, but the hysterical cries will soon diminish. I charge you, together with the ministers of war and marine, to work out within a month the necessary rules to clarify the present vagueness in the examination of military and naval bills." And he repeated his warning: "I categorically reject in advance a request by you or anyone else to be relieved of his office."[36]

Nicholas had delivered a thinly disguised reprimand while preventing his minister from retaliating in the only way open to him. Outwardly Stolypin retained his composure. "On receiving such a letter I should tender my resignation," he commented to Kokovtsov, "but this I shall not do, as I do not want to pain the Tsar because of his momentary displeasure, which, evidently, was caused by some outside person."[37] Recognizing the limits to his authority—and that of the Duma—he cautiously backed away from his "alliance" with the Octobrists. Guchkov's sway over his own party had faltered, and dissension, previously concealed, led to a realignment in the Duma. A moderate Right coalition succeeded the Octobrists as the most powerful faction. Stolypin, not one to scorn the politics of expediency and self-interest, welcomed the new balance of power. Nor did he emerge empty-handed from his crisis of confidence with the sovereign. Nicholas granted him the privilege of recommending members of the State Council, a dispensation that led to the appointment of several moderates instead of the candidates favored by the extreme Right.

Nicholas' testy reminder that his imperial rights could not be disregarded, although chiefly directed toward the "liberals"—that is, Stolypin and the Duma—represented also a setback to the "reactionaries" who had been urging him to resume his autocratic role. Without undue violence to his conscience, Stolypin proceeded with a more cautious regard for royal sensibilities. He backed away, for example, from the Duma consensus that freedom of religious belief should have a more forceful legislative mandate. One of his speeches emphasized the emperor's duty to uphold the dogma of the Orthodox Church, implying that the "national spirit" should not be subordinated to the abstract theory of religious toleration.

Stolypin had already deferred, indeed pandered, to the tsar's conviction that Russification of the ethnic minorities should be given a higher priority in conducting the business of the empire. His patronizing brand of nationalism was succinctly expressed in answer to the complaint of a Polish deputy in the Duma: "Come over to our point of view, admit that the greatest blessing is to be a Russian citizen; bear this name with the same pride that the Romans once bore their citizenship, and then you will call yourselves first-class citizens and receive all your rights!"[38] The respite granted to the Finns because of the chaotic events of 1905 had ceased. An imperial decree of May 20, 1908, subordinated the Finnish administration to the Council of Ministers, and in 1910 legislation stripping Finland of much of its autonomy passed easily in the Duma and in the State Council. The debates constituted, with honorable exceptions, an unedifying demonstration of Russian chauvinism. Stolypin himself referred to the Finns as a "stubborn, hardheaded race," unduly "obstinate in their opinions."[39]

Stolypin's "conservatism," especially his nationalist bent, won over a portion of his Rightist critics. In January 1910 the government introduced a bill to establish zemstvo institutions in six western provinces, with legislative safeguards to insure the dominance of Russian landowners over their Polish counterparts in the election process. With forceful candor, Stolypin upheld the necessity "to declare openly and without hypocrisy that the western region is and will always remain Russian." Against the opposition of Kadets and Left Octobrists, the bill, slightly amended, passed the Duma by 165 votes to 139 the following May. The State Council postponed its debate on the question until the new year. Stolypin anticipated no serious resistance to his project despite the delay, but to forestall possible machinations by die-hard monarchists who resented the whole concept of zemstvos as a matter of principle, he let it be known that the "highest spheres"—that is, the tsar himself—desired the legislation. Durnovo and Trepov, whose hostility to Stolypin had never waned, resented these tactics and conveyed their doubts about the bill in a letter to the sovereign. Both were received in private audiences at Tsarskoe Selo, and Nicholas expressed his conviction that Council members were free to vote as their conscience dictated. These sentiments did not long remain secret, but Stolypin was caught by surprise when on March 4, 1911, a key provision of his bill failed of approval by twenty-four votes. That the outcome represented a fair test of the bill's merits is unlikely. The "reactionaries" had acquired wide support, a response based at least in part on Stolypin's pressure tactics, and an indeterminate number of councillors were influenced by Count Witte, whose political impotence found release in petty intrigue.[40]

Shocked and angered by what he regarded as a personal and political conspiracy by his enemies, Stolypin secured an audience with the emperor the next day and precipitously offered his resignation. Taken aback, Nicholas temporized. He could not have been unaware of his own contribution to the fiasco and no doubt sensed the rebuke concealed by his minister's impassioned, if civil, discourse. Stolypin proposed a way out of the impasse, one that amounted to an ultimatum: he would withdraw his resignation if Nicholas would recess the legislature and enact the zemstvo bill as a statute under the emergency powers of the Fundamental Laws. Also, as a lesson to his adversaries, he sought the temporary banishment from the capital of Durnovo and Trepov by imperial order. These were presumptuous conditions indeed for a servant to demand of his master, especially one so prickly on the subject of autocratic privilege. Stolypin remained intransigent, rejecting any compromise and disregarding Kokovtsov's observation that the tsar might yield to such tactics but would never forgive their perpetrator.

The denouement remained unresolved for four days as family members and court favorites sought the imperial ear. The dowager empress and at least two of the grand dukes espoused Stolypin's cause, while the tsaritsa and Prince Meshchersky were convinced opponents. Stolypin himself accepted his dismissal as a foregone conclusion until he accepted an invitation to call on Marie Fyodorovna at Gatchina. There he chanced to see Nicholas, who did not speak but wiped away tears with a handkerchief. Later that evening, presumably March 9, he received by courier an "amazing letter" of sixteen pages in which a penitent monarch allegedly recognized his errors, confessed his lack of candor, and requested that the petitions of resignation be withdrawn.[41] Whether such a lengthy and contrite message was ever written is questionable, but Nicholas did dispatch a much shorter letter that amounted to an oblique apology. He praised Stolypin for his "loyalty to me and to Russia" and for his "courageous support of Russian political principles on the borders of the state [which] induces me to retain you at all costs. . . . Can you really continue to be stubborn? Of course you will not. I know in advance that you will agree to remain." He summoned Stolypin for an audience the next day and closed the letter with a firm expression of confidence: "Remember—my trust in you has remained as complete as it was in 1906."[42]

Nicholas accepted Stolypin's terms without reservation and added a concession that apparently had not been discussed before: the right to nominate and replace thirty members of the State Council on January 1, 1912. Stolypin's misgivings about the tsar's reliability and good faith were such that he requested a written record of the agreement. Nicholas provided the document, writing on a large sheet of note paper with a blue pencil. The conditions were quickly fulfilled: the legislature was suspended for three days beginning on March 12, the zemstvo bill became law by imperial decree, and Durnovo and Trepov were given "leave" until the end of the year.

Stolypin again had achieved a shallow triumph. The State Council, seething with animosity, gained a measure of revenge by overwhelmingly rejecting the zemstvo bill before adjourning. The Duma expressed bitter resentment at this disruption of the parliamentary system. The Octobrists were particularly incensed, and Guchkov, their former leader, resigned his Duma presidency in protest. Both chambers of the legislature eventually submitted interpellations questioning the legality of the government's action. Stolypin's defense before the lower house on April 27 occasioned a major political spectacle, and his explanations were declared unsatisfactory by a vote of 203 to eighty-three.[43] Even his support in the "highest spheres" had begun to falter. Nicholas, easily offended in normal circumstances, could not forget the indignity that he had suffered in appeasing his minister. Stolypin, increasingly fatalistic, recognized the untenability of his position. "The Emperor will not forgive me if he has to fulfill my request," he had confided to Kokovtsov during the height of the crisis in March. "But that is a matter of indifference to me since I well know in any case that I am being attacked from all sides and that I shall not be here much longer."[44]

Under pressure at court, Nicholas resolved to lift the ban on Durnovo as early as April. Trepov resigned from government service and was granted a generous pension of six thousand rubles annually. Stolypin wrote plaintively on May 1 pointing out that Durnovo's "tireless activity" would prove "an inexhaustible source for constant disturbances of Your Majesty," but the letter was ignored.[45]

Exhausted, dispirited, and suffering from a heart ailment, Stolypin spent most of the summer at his estate in Kovno Province in northwest Russia. He nevertheless, according to a close associate, managed to compile a "monumental work concerning his proposed transformation of the state administration of Russia and his goals for passage of a whole series of reforms."[46] The project was to be submitted to the tsar in the fall. In Stolypin's absence Kokovtsov assumed the burden of acting chief minister.

By late summer the signs of imperial disfavor toward Stolypin were unmistakable. The minister journeyed to Kiev for ceremonies honoring the fiftieth anniversary of the emancipation of the serfs, of which the highlight was to be the dedication of a monument to Alexander II. In a gloomy mood, he remarked to an aide that he would not likely return to the capital as chairman of the Council of Ministers.

On September 1, 1911, Stolypin attended an operatic performance at the city theater. During the second intermission, standing with his back to the stage, he was suddenly confronted by a young man who fired two shots at him at close range. One bullet struck him in the chest, ultimately proving fatal. The emperor himself was an eyewitness and left a dramatic account in a letter to his mother. "We heard two sounds as if something had been dropped," he wrote. "I thought an opera-glass might have fallen on somebody's head, and ran back into the box to look. . . . Women were shrieking, and directly in front of me in the stalls Stolypin was standing. He slowly turned his face towards us and, with his left hand, made the sign of the cross in the air. Only then did I notice that he was very pale and that his right hand and uniform were blood-stained. He slowly sank into his chair and began to unbutton his tunic."[47]

Stolypin was taken to a clinic, where he died on September 5. An autopsy is said to have revealed that "all his vital organs had been severely overstrained" and that the physicians were "unanimous in affirming that his end was at hand."[48] Nicholas meanwhile continued his ceremonial duties and also visited the clinic, but Stolypin's wife would not allow him to see her semiconscious husband. Returning from a visit to Chernigov on the morning of the 6th, he paid his respects to the widow, "sank to his knees before the body of his faithful servant and offered prayers for a long while." Over and over he was heard to repeat the words, "Forgive me."[49] He attended a memorial service but left for his palace at Livadia before the elaborate funeral and burial at Pechersky monastery. Three monuments were built in Stolypin's memory; that in Kiev bore as an inscription his famous words condemning the revolutionary Left: "You need great upheavals; we need a great Russia."

The assassin was quickly identified as Dmitri Bogrov, a former law student who had had revolutionary contacts and later became an agent of the Okhrana. The police rescued him from a possible lynching at the theater and questioned him extensively but without a thorough investigation by the appropriate political authorities. A military tribunal closed to the public condemned him to death, and he was hanged on September 11. A belated Senatorial investigation revealed gross negligence on the part of important police officials, of whom some were reprimanded or dismissed. Despite Kokovtsov's objections, an imperial order prevented criminal proceedings against them. Nicholas explained his reasoning in the case to Aleksandr Spiridovich, a colonel in the gendarmes: "I see him [the responsible official] at every turn; he follows me about like a shadow and I simply cannot see this man so crushed with grief; surely he did not want to do any harm and is guilty of nothing except his failure to take every measure of precaution."[50] Bogrov's seemingly hasty execution and the possibility of police complicity in the affair raised suspicion that Stolypin had been the victim of an Okhrana conspiracy. The truth appears to be less sinister: that Bogrov was mentally unstable, that he acted on his own initiative, and that he sought the expiation of self-sacrifice for his betrayal of the revolutionary cause.[51]

Stolypin's martyrdom raised his reputation immensely in the eyes of his contemporaries. Later judgments, less influenced by his tragic fate, depended largely upon the political persuasion of the observer. Monarchists and other conservatives, despite the final estrangement of tsar and minister, generally held him in high esteem. Lacking a more convincing hero, many seized upon him as the one man who could have saved the regime in spite of itself. At the other extreme, liberals castigated him as an enemy of constitutional government, and radicals dismissed him contemptuously as an apologist for tsarist tyranny. But the labels applied by both admirers and detractors have not contributed to a sound historical verdict. Although a man of vision and statesmanlike qualities, Stolypin could not have "saved" Russia from the twin catastrophes of war and revolution even had a more flexible and "progressive" ruler occupied the throne. The obstacles he faced were formidable, his authority severely limited, and his term of office relatively brief. He dissipated his own strength by impolitic decisions, alienating potential supporters of both Left and Right. His tendency to personalize political conflict, especially pronounced in 1911, may have resulted in great part from failing health. As for the Duma and the State Council, the inability of either body to work amicably with the government during the "reactionary" years 1908 to 1911 reflected unfavorably upon the fragmented nature of "society" as well as the inexperience and political isolation of the liberal bourgeoisie.

9

Rasputin and His Predecessors

Nicholas' insistence on the status and privileges of an autocrat blended awkwardly with a personality and temperament that found their chief nourishment in privacy and the pleasures of family life. The charismatic qualities of leadership that might have enhanced his reign—or at least his popularity—were alien to his nature, and it never occurred to him that public opinion constituted a valuable political commodity that monarchs as well as democratic rulers would do well to cultivate. Yet he never shirked his duty as he saw it. The tedium of government reports and royal audiences was supplemented by frequent ceremonial appearances that invariably confirmed his belief that he remained a beloved father figure to his subjects; and he accepted without question, just as his ancestors had done, that the Russian empire was essentially the patrimony of the Romanov dynasty.

Nicholas maintained his interest in sports and recreational activities throughout his life. Hunting remained a prime leisure pursuit, with his tally of slaughtered animals (usually game birds, rabbits, and deer) carefully noted in his diary. Perhaps his favorite indoor pastime was reading, especially evening sessions with his family in which he or Alexandra would read aloud to the children. His personal library near his study was well stocked with the latest books, chiefly novels and popular literature, but he retained a fondness for selected Russian classics. Photography became a major hobby for the whole family. The hundreds of photographs extant provide a unique record with their self-imposed invasion of royal privacy. The new art of motion pictures attracted Nicholas' attention, more favorably in the latter part of his reign. He was initially suspicious of their power for evil: "I have pointed out more than once that these cinematographic sideshows are dangerous establishments. The scoundrels might get up to God knows what . . . since people, I'm told, flock there to watch any rubbish."[1]

Although Nicholas aged rapidly in his last years, particularly during World War I, he enjoyed good health for most of his reign. A major exception occurred in November 1900 when he was stricken with typhoid fever while in the Crimea. Alexandra insisted on nursing him herself, an arduous task that left her nervous and exhausted. His condition was deemed critical enough to necessitate a high-level conference whose participants, including Sipyagin, Witte, Lamzdorf, and Frederiks, decided that Nicholas' brother, the Grand Duke Mikhail, would legally succeed to the throne in the event of a fatal outcome. Nicholas' recovery resolved the immediate problem, and the birth of Alexis in 1905 provided a new heir apparent.[2]

Nicholas shared with Alexandra a deep piety, but his was tinged with profound fatalism, expressed verbally as a kind of incantation in times of adversity: "God's wishes shall be fulfilled."[3] Both were also drawn to spiritualism and manifestations of the occult, reconciling without any apparent difficulty these beliefs with their Christian heritage. Witte used the phrase "Orthodox paganism" to describe Alexandra's religiosity, and it would also be applicable to Nicholas. They regularly attended lengthy religious services on Sundays and holidays, usually at the chapel of the Alexander Palace in Tsarskoe Selo. Special observances were reserved for Holy Week at Easter, and beginning in 1900 they customarily spent the hallowed day at the Kremlin in Moscow. The rites and customs of the Orthodox Church were scrupulously observed. During the six weeks of Lent, for example, "no meat appeared on the Imperial table." Obviously the form rather than the content of Christian doctrine appealed to the royal couple, and if they were aware of what in the West came to be called the "social gospel"—the biblical teachings of Jesus as applied to the problems of society—there is no indication that they acted upon it other than by charitable contributions and by benevolent gestures befitting the moral obligations of noblesse oblige.

Probably the best-authenticated episode illustrating the peculiar blend of piety and superstition exhibited by the tsar and tsaritsa is that involving the canonization of Serafim of Sarov.[4] St. Serafim (1759–1833), as he was officially designated in 1903, entered the monastery at Sarov in Tambov Province while still in his teens. He later withdrew to a forest hut and spent many years in solitary prayer, meditation, and study. In his old age, after returning to the monastery, he advised, blessed, and reputedly healed thousands of pilgrims attracted by his saintly reputation. The idea of canonizing Serafim is unlikely to have occurred to Nicholas without prompting. Whatever the source of his inspiration—most likely Father John of Kronstadt—he consulted Pobedonostsev in the summer of 1902 and requested that a decree of canonization be submitted in a few weeks. Pobedonostsev strongly implied that such haste was unseemly, for the candidate's life and qualifications had to undergo a rigorous and lengthy scrutiny. According to Church tradition, an attested miracle and an uncorrupted corpse were deemed, if not essential, weighty evidence of a sanctified state. Alexandra, who had accompanied her husband, remarked that "everything is within the Emperor's province." Nicholas conceded that the process should not be rushed but ordered that it be carried out by the next year.

The necessary formalities were completed sooner than the normal two or three year period, and in late July 1903 the imperial family, along with a large contingent of grand dukes and duchesses, important court and Church officials, and up to half a million pilgrims and curiosity-seekers, converged on the town of Arzamas and the Sarov Monastery. Nicholas had provided financial assistance to refurbish the monastery, to construct a shrine for the saint's remains, and to prepare for the ceremony of reburial. After mass in the cathedral, Nicholas and various dignitaries bore the elaborate coffin in a solemn and majestic procession. Other rituals and ceremonies followed during the tsar's four-day visit. He shared a meal with the monks of the cloister, greeted the nobility of the local and adjoining provinces, and attended the daily religious observances. In walking to Serafim's hermitage in the forest he was nearly mobbed by enthusiastic crowds and had to be rescued by two members of his retinue, who hoisted him on their shoulders and carried him safely across a footbridge just before it collapsed beneath the weight of his zealous admirers. The incident could have had serious consequences, but he was deeply moved by the popular adulation he received at Sarov. It confirmed his own self-image as a noble and benign monarch, and he believed that in their mutual devotion to St. Serafim, tsar and people were as one.

Alexandra, too, reveled in the atmosphere of mass piety and miraculous deeds (a number of "cures" were claimed for ailing pilgrims, but one of her maids of honor, a victim of paralysis, showed no improvement). She prayed at Serafim's grave and bathed in the healing waters of a sacred spring. Her pregnancy and the birth of Alexis a little over a year later seemed to confirm the efficacy of sanctified ground. Nicholas was wholly persuaded: "I have indisputable evidence of the holiness and miraculous power of Saint Serafim; I am certain that no one can ever shake my faith in that power."[5] Sarov became to the Orthodox faithful the equivalent of Lourdes as a shrine for Catholic pilgrims.

Nicholas' appearance at Sarov was a matter of public record, but his interest in the occult was strictly a private affair. The immense notoriety of Grigory Rasputin—even today his name evokes an image of salacious scandal—has overshadowed his predecessors, as colorful an array of charlatans, "holy fools," and miracle workers as ever graced a medieval court. Unlike Rasputin, whose hold on the royal couple, especially Alexandra, was based on his alleged success in alleviating the hemophilic attacks of the Tsarevich Alexis, the early favorites seem to have provided solace of a different kind. With one or two exceptions, the earliest came from the ranks of the *yurodivy*—that is, simple-minded "prophets" supposedly touched by divine wisdom. Alexandra's initial failure to produce a male heir may have prompted a search for supernatural intervention. At any rate, by 1900 a steady procession of bizarre creatures ("monks, mad saints, pilgrims and holy beggars")[6] were received at Tsarskoe Selo, and some remained in residence for several months or longer. Their physical and mental disabilities were, in popular tradition, added proof of their extraordinary powers.

According to Sergei Trufanov (better known as the monk Iliodor, an anti-Semitic demagogue of formidable proportions), the first of the court favorites was known as Matronushka the Barefooted.[7] A retarded peasant woman of nearly eighty, she was reputed to predict future events with uncanny accuracy. Nicholas dispatched couriers to locate her—she was discovered in a St. Petersburg slum—and installed her in the imperial household, where he and Alexandra "would spend hours listening to her insane gibberish, in which she predicted a future male heir to the throne." A similar case was that of Pasha Sarovskaya, who lived at a monastery in Tambov Province and was rumored to be a hundred years old. More stubborn than Matronushka, she spurned offers of imperial hospitality, and in the summer of 1901 Nicholas and Alexandra sought her out at the cloister. Pasha was not overly cordial, according to the story, but did give Nicholas a stocking that Alexandra preserved as a sacred relic.

A third favorite, Vasily Tkachenko, was also of peasant background, an aged and illiterate ex-soldier from the Kuban region with an addiction to vodka. He acquired a patron in the Grand Duke Mikhail Nikolayevich, the youngest brother of Alexander II and a connoisseur of the "saintly" and supernatural. Through the grand duke he gained access to Nicholas and supposedly offered advice on the armed forces during the revolutionary events of 1905. While on pilgrimages he would send telegrams to Nicholas and Alexandra, and with their replies in hand "he intimidated more than one governor and minister." His career at Tsarskoe Selo was presumably terminated after a drunken fight with a cabman.

Still others, some of whose names are unknown, were received at the court. Seemingly one of the least obnoxious was a pilgrim from an abbey on Lake Ladoga known only as Miron. Described as a "harmless, quiet old man, beloved of children and kind to animals," he was guileless and unassuming, offering Christian homilies and soothing prayers. According to a British journalist of the time, the "most capable and honest" of the numerous "spiritualists and clairvoyants" at the court was N. A. Demchinsky, a "distinguished meteorologist" who published a daily weather forecast for a prominent St. Petersburg daily. He predicted fine weather for various official ceremonies and had the good fortune to see his calculations confirmed. Witte had earlier employed him as a "hired pen," and Nicholas sought to utilize his talents as a political adviser. But Demchinsky apparently made the mistake of ignoring the grand dukes and Minister of Interior Plehve. Denounced as an imposter and his memoranda disregarded, he was quietly dropped from royal favor early in 1903.[8]

A far more abrasive type was a demented epileptic, Darya Ossipova, who had achieved an awesome reputation in her native village for her prophecies and "miracles." Brought to the court by a general in the imperial entourage, she terrified Alexandra by her awesome curses. Yet the birth of Alexis coincided with her residence, and she therefore gained some credibility as a true miracle worker. She was nevertheless succeeded by one Antony, a *strannik* (literally, "wanderer") said to have been a favorite of the Black Hundreds and to have functioned as a "political magician and clairvoyant in the days of the first Duma."[9] An even more mysterious figure, a hypnotist whose name is recorded as Onore, was known for his "miraculous cures of nervous diseases." He had studied the shamanism of the Altai peoples and established a practice in St. Petersburg catering to the wealthy and influential. He was introduced into the "Rasputin group," apparently by Prince Putyatin of the court entourage, a "specialist on saints and fiends" and "the secret messenger between the court and the Black Hundreds." Onore was an honored guest in the "most reactionary drawing-rooms" and is said to have hypnotized Alexandra and attended her during her nervous attacks.[10]

Among the *yurodivy* the most grotesque—certainly the most conspicuous—was Mitya (or Mitka) Kolyaba. Born about 1865 and a resident of the famous Optina-Pustyn Monastery near Kozelsk (thus also known as Mitya Kozelsky), he was severely handicapped from birth: crippled, retarded, epileptic, deaf, half-blind, nearly mute, and with stumps in place of arms. He communicated "by guttural cries, stammerings, grunts, roars, squeaks, and a wild waving of his stumps." The monks regarded him as an oracle and prophet, and his reputation reached St. Petersburg. He was brought to the capital about 1901 with his "interpreter" and held "seances" with Nicholas and Alexandra. Failing to enlighten them about the birth of an heir, he drove the empress to hysteria with his "ear-piercing roars and frightful gesticulations." The duration of his stay at Tsarskoe Selo is uncertain, but he later became a bitter rival of Rasputin, conspiring against him with Iliodor and Hermogen, the bishop of Saratov. All three were punished, the "miraculous idiot" the least severely by the loss of his position as court soothsayer. Reportedly still alive and active in 1915, he was "obliged to disappear for a time to escape the vengeance of his terrible adversary" (i.e., Rasputin) and lived "among a small and secret, but fervent, sect" while "biding his time."[11]

The simpletons so prevalent at Tsarskoe Selo (and in select society circles in the capital) by no means exhausted the imperial taste for the occult. Two Frenchmen of native intelligence and "learning" of an esoteric kind shared the emperor's favors with the *yurodivy*. The first, Nizier Anthelme Philippe,[12] better known in Russia as "Doctor" Philippe, enjoyed a prominent place at the court for nearly three years. Born of peasant stock in Savoy in 1849, he moved to Lyons as an adolescent and worked in his uncle's butcher shop. A solitary youth with arcane interests, he attended the local medical school with the intention of becoming a public health officer. But he was obliged to withdraw when he began to effect sensational "cures" by the practice of "occult medicine," allegedly treating his patients with "psychic fluids and astral forces." The orthodox physicians of Lyons registered their indignation, and Philippe was convicted and fined on three occasions for practicing medicine without a license. He later acquired an assistant with a proper medical degree.

Philippe's reputation attracted an increasingly select clientele. Two Russian visitors persuaded him to journey to Cannes, where he was introduced to the "Montenegrin princesses," Militsa and Anastasia. They had married into Russian royalty and were zealous votaries of the occult as well as confidantes of the empress. In September 1901, with their patronage, Philippe was received by the Russian sovereigns at Compiègne on the occasion of their visit to France. The French "magician" was so impressive that he was invited to Russia and became an honored guest at Tsarskoe Selo. Unlike his sometimes raucous competitors, he comported himself with tact and discretion. "Once or twice a week," according to the retrospective account of the French ambassador, "he carried out experiments in hypnotism, prophecy, incantation, and necromancy" in the royal presence, and numerous decisions were communicated to Nicholas "by his dead father, Alexander III."[13] His supporters claimed even more astonishing feats: on one occasion he calmed a storm while aboard the tsar's yacht, and on another he detoured the wind at a military review. Still more awesome was his reputed ability to render himself invisible.

Philippe was provided with an appropriate rank, that of counselor of state (equivalent to a general), but he craved respectability as a licensed physician. The Russian ambassador in Paris was told to make inquiries, and one of the grand dukes interceded with the president of France. The French government, though eager to please its ally, drew the line at illegality. A solution was ultimately found: Minister of War Kuropatkin, whose jurisdiction included the Military Medical Academy in the capital, arranged at the emperor's request for a medical degree to be conferred on Philippe. The proud new "doctor" consulted a tailor and appeared at court in the uniform of an army physician.

The empress was still anxiety-ridden about her failure to provide a male heir, and Philippe claimed the ability not only to predict the gender of the embryo but to determine it "by combining the most transcendental practices of hermetic medicine, astronomy, and psychurgy." Under the influence of her French mentor, combined with a powerful wish-fulfillment fantasy, Alexandra conceived a pseudo-pregnancy, the falsity of which was discovered only when the court physicians examined her. Despite his egregious blunder, Philippe did not immediately lose favor. But Alexandra's confessor, the archimandrite Feofan, may have stirred doubts, and by the spring of 1903 Philippe's role had been partially undermined by malicious gossip.

Meanwhile, in Paris, the head of the Okhrana's foreign operations, Pyotr Rachkovsky, investigated Philippe's record and submitted a detailed report exposing him as a charlatan. (Minister of the Interior Sipyagin had advised Rachkovsky to throw the report in the fire.) Philippe retaliated by employing his dwindling influence with Nicholas, who presumably read the document, and Rachkovsky was summarily dismissed (though rehired in 1905). The birth of Alexis rendered the Frenchman's services in that domain superfluous, and Nicholas belatedly recognized that "a court cabal was using the magician to influence him in the exercise of his sovereign powers." Philippe was, in effect, honorably discharged and, though laden with gifts, he returned to his homeland disappointed and chagrined. Misfortune soon followed. His lowly status after the giddy heights of royal favor seems to have fueled a growing paranoia—or it may be that his feelings of persecution were amply justified. Rachkovsky bore him a grudge and apparently used his contacts with the French authorities to harass the unfortunate magus: the police kept him under surveillance, his mail was opened, and the press ridiculed him. The loss of his beloved daughter was an added emotional shock. He died in 1905, probably of heart disease, about a year after leaving Russia. His devotees asserted, if Witte's testimony is accurate, that "he bodily ascended to heaven, his work on earth completed."[14] Alexandra recalled that he had presented her with an icon attached to a little bell that warned her when "evil people" were present.

Another Frenchman, a disciple of Philippe known as Papus,[15] played a less significant part in Russian court life than his "spiritual master." Yet in European occult circles he was better known than Philippe. Originally Gérard Encausse, he was born in Spain in 1865, though brought up and educated in Paris. He eventually received a medical degree in 1894, but his formal studies had been interrupted when he became fascinated with such occult "sciences" as magic, alchemy, and astrology, and the literature of the cabala and the tarot. Briefly a member of the Theosophical Society, he later became grand master of the Martinist Order, a pseudo-Masonic organization. Under his pseudonym he published popular works and lectured on occult subjects. Like Philippe, he established an unconventional medical practice that became highly successful. In 1896, when Nicholas again visited France, Papus sent him a letter of greeting heavily larded with "mystic" homilies which the Russian ambassador acknowledged in the emperor's name.

In 1901 (the precise date is uncertain) Papus visited Russia, ostensibly to found a "school of psycho-physiology." That such an institution was actually founded is doubtful, but he did organize a lodge of the Martinist Order in St. Petersburg in which Nicholas and other "very high personalities" supposedly became initiates. He also arranged for the Russian translation and publication of his most popular book, an elementary text on "occult science." He was introduced to Nicholas by the Grand Duke Nikolai Mikhailovich, who had become friendly with Papus in France. Although Nicholas and Alexandra were duly impressed, he returned to his homeland and did not make a second visit to Russia until October 1905. Since the date coincided with the climax of revolutionary disturbances in that year and Philippe was no longer available for "psychic" advice, one may surmise that he made the journey by imperial invitation. A seance was arranged at Tsarskoe Selo, and Papus, by "an intense concentration of will and a prodigious expenditure of fluid dynamism," contacted the spirit of Alexander III. Nicholas allegedly received a message to carry on the struggle against the revolution.

Papus made his third and final visit to Russia in February 1906 and corresponded with the royal couple until 1915 or later. No friend of Rasputin, he warned the empress in a letter about the evil influence of the unsavory "holy devil" of popular legend: "From the cabalistic point of view, Rasputin is a vessel like unto Pandora's box, and contains all the vices, crimes, and lusts of the Russian people. Should this vessel break, we shall immediately see these horrible contents spilled all over Russia." Rasputin regarded Papus as a charlatan, and when Alexandra read the letter to him he reportedly replied, "Why, I've told you that many times. When I die, Russia will perish."[16]

Papus served in the medical corps of the French army and died in October 1916 of tuberculosis and other complications. In addition to his prolific writings on the occult, the notorious anti-Semitic forgery *The Protocols of the Elders of Zion* has been ascribed to his pen. Although there is no reliable evidence to that effect, it is possible that he provided material to an anti-Semitic French journalist, Jean Carrère, for a series of articles published in the *Echo de Paris* in the fall of 1901 under the pseudonym "Niet." The articles posited a sinister financial conspiracy—Jews were involved—to disrupt the Franco-Russian alliance; Witte is said to have provided a bribe of twelve thousand francs to prevent the appearance of more such "revelations."[17] Unlike Philippe, whose Russian career can be documented with some precision, Papus and his activities at court remain enigmatic. To fill the vacuum one authority on the occult has provided an ingenious but implausible quasi-political role for the French "sorcerer": that along with

Philippe and the "Montenegrin group" he represented the "Martinist" faction in an obscure intrigue in which the *Protocols* and anti-Semitism figured prominently.[18]

The last of the pre-Rasputin favorites, Pyotr Badmayev, was probably the most gifted. With the exception of Papus (and perhaps Demchinsky), he was unique in acquiring a higher education and in not confining his talents to matters of the occult. Born in eastern Siberia in 1851 of Buryat Mongol ancestry, he adopted the Orthodox faith and studied oriental languages at St. Petersburg University. He also acquired an interest in Tibetan medicine and became an active practioner after completing his studies in 1875. Until 1893 he worked in the Asiatic department of the ministry of foreign affairs and enjoyed the patronage of Witte and Prince Ukhtomsky. He also maintained close ties to the royal family under both Alexander III and Nicholas II. An advocate of "railroad imperialism" at the expense of China, he remained outside the Bezobrazov circle but contributed to the chauvinist atmosphere around Nicholas that helped to bring on the war with Japan. But it was as a de facto court physician that he made himself all but indispensable. His friendship with Nicholas lasted longer than any other court favorite, including Rasputin himself, if one excludes the period of about 1905–1906, when he appeared to lose influence because he had compromised himself as a foreign policy adviser. He provided medication for Alexis (without success) and may also have ministered to Nicholas and Alexandra. Whether or not his herbs, drugs, and "magic remedies" amounted to "a kind of alchemy flavored with sorcery," he maintained an exotic and well-stocked pharmacopoeia and is said to have preferred to treat "nervous diseases, mental afflictions, and the baffling disorders of feminine psychology."[19]

The rise and fall of Rasputin, an oft-repeated tale, still exerts its fascination upon the general public.[20] A Siberian "holy man" of peasant background (but never a monk, as is still widely believed), he acquired influential patrons in the Church and in 1905 became a resident of St. Petersburg. Through the "Montenegrin princesses" he was introduced to the royal couple on October 31 of that year. The two sisters supposedly vouched for the "miracle worker" in extravagant terms: "He is marvelous. He is a new saint. He cures all ills. He is a simple peasant from Siberia, but . . . God never entrusts His power to the spoiled children of sophistication."[21] Nicholas recorded the event matter-of-factly in his diary: "We became acquainted today with Grigory, a man of God from Tobolsk province." Rasputin made a good impression but did not become a court favorite until a year or so later, presumably after several meetings had taken place. Nicholas recommended him to Stolypin in a letter of October 16, 1906, and suggested that he might be received to bless the minister's invalid daughter (crippled in the terrorist bombing some two months before) with an especially holy icon. A meeting with family members occurred, apparently in Stolypin's absence, and the injured daughter thought so little of the visitor that she had the room fumigated with cologne after his departure.[22]

Rasputin's relationship with Nicholas and Alexandra involved a consummate blend of familiarity and deference. He never made demands or presumed too much yet spoke to them as equals, assuming the role of a clever and articulate but humble servant of God. To Nicholas he symbolized the folk wisdom of the peasant masses, while to Alexandra he seemed a divinely inspired figure with supernatural powers. The tsarevich's hemophilia, a well-guarded family secret, presented Rasputin with the opportunity to demonstrate his proficiency as a "healer" and thus strengthen his emotional bond with the royal couple. Through extraordinary luck, hypnosis, or psychological influence he provided relief for Alexis on a number of occasions when internal bleeding placed the boy's life in danger.

Rasputin established his own "court" in the capital, receiving petitioners from all walks of life and enjoying a profligate lifestyle that featured alcohol abuse and sexual promiscuity. His enemies grew in proportion to his notoriety. The most formidable was Stolypin himself, who received derogatory reports from the Okhrana. A meeting between the two was arranged in 1908, probably at the emperor's request, and Stolypin recalled the episode as wholly unpleasant: "He ran his pale eyes over me, mumbled mysterious and inarticulate words from the Scriptures, made strange movements with his hands, and I began to feel an indescribable loathing for this vermin sitting opposite me."[23] Stolypin, unaware of the personal reasons for Rasputin's success at court, persisted in making disparaging remarks about him during his audiences with the tsar. Encouraged by Nicholas' reluctance to pursue the matter, he ordered the banishment of the *starets* from the capital for five years. But the order was soon rescinded. Only imperial authority could have overruled Stolypin, and he absorbed the lesson readily enough: to ignore Rasputin in his official capacity and to avoid mentioning him in his meetings and correspondence with the tsar. Nicholas put it quite bluntly in their last conversation on the subject: "I know and believe you are truly loyal to me. . . . Everything you say may even be true. But I must ask that you never speak to me again about Rasputin. In any event, I can do nothing at all about it."[24]

Rasputin, however, did lose favor for a time in 1911, without Stolypin's intervention. A report on his "orgies," supplemented with compromising photographs, reached Nicholas, and he granted "permission" to the errant favorite to embark on a pilgrimage to Jerusalem. Abroad for four months, Rasputin was in effect forgiven for past transgressions upon his return and restored to the good graces of the royal family. Alexandra's devotion to him never wavered, but Nicholas harbored reservations that he seldom expressed to his wife.

10

A Final Reprieve

Russia's transition to the post-Stolypin era, though scarred by the violence of assassination, was otherwise uneventful. Kokovtsov succeeded to the post of ministerial chairman on September 6, 1911, at an imperial audience in Kiev. He also retained his position as minister of finance. Nicholas intended to appoint Aleksei Khvostov, the provincial governor of Nizhny Novgorod, to the vacated portfolio of interior minister, but Kokovtsov persuaded him that Aleksandr Makarov, an experienced police official who had served under Stolypin, would be a better choice. Nicholas received Makarov at Livadia and expressed his confidence that under the new appointee the ministry would solve the internal problems clamoring for attention and cease dissipating its energies on political squabbles.[1] This posthumous slur on Stolypin's reputation was blunt but of questionable accuracy.

Kokovtsov, though no disciple of Stolypin, stressed continuity and refrained from bold initiatives. He insisted that the Council of Ministers retain its authority in matters of foreign policy. His nationalist bias was less pronounced than his predecessor's, and he declined to press vigorous measures of Russification. By his prompt and forceful action in the aftermath of the Stolypin murder he forestalled a threatened pogrom in the Kiev area, for Bogrov was perceived as Jewish despite his family's conversion to Christianity.

However courageous Kokovtsov had been in averting possible bloodshed, another Kievan affair, the infamous case of Mendel Beilis,[2] did not provoke his intervention. The mutilated corpse of a twelve-year-old Christian boy had been discovered in Kiev in March 1911, the victim of a criminal gang, as subsequent investigation revealed. Beilis, an obscure Jewish clerk, was arrested four months later and charged with ritual murder. The local prosecutor, supported by police officials and extreme right-wing elements, maneuvered the indictment. But the case could not have proceeded without encouragement from governmental authority at a higher level. Nicholas, as far as is known, countenanced the prosecution but did not become actively involved. His Judophobia encompassed a belief in a Jewish world conspiracy and the reality of ritual murder, yet his gullibility had its limits. When presented with a copy of the fraudulent *Protocols of the Elders of Zion*, apparently in 1908, he had at first been entranced by its revelations ("What depth of thought! Everywhere one sees the directing and destroying hand of Jewry!") and its utility as anti-Jewish propaganda. But an inquiry authorized by Stolypin revealed the spuriousness of the document, and Nicholas accepted the report: "Drop the *Protocols*. One cannot defend a pure cause by dirty methods."[3]

Minister of Justice Ivan Shcheglovitov became the key figure in bringing the Beilis case to trial. His motivation remains obscure, though one may speculate that ideological zeal and political expediency were major incentives. After imprisonment for over two years, the defendant finally reached a courtroom in the fall of 1913. The prosecution had the advantage of an unsophisticated jury, chiefly composed of peasants; the defense was bolstered by lawyers of national reputation and the good will of the educated public. The verdict of not guilty was tarnished by the jury's avowal that Jewish religious practice might have been involved. The tsar concurred. "It is certain that there was a ritual murder," he commented. "But *I am happy* that Beilis has been acquitted, because he is innocent."[4] If the case hardly matched the notoriety and political bitterness of France's Dreyfus Affair, to which it has often been compared, it ranked as a scandal of international proportions and epitomized to many the moral squalor to which the tsar's government had been reduced.

In his competent, diligent, and uninspired fashion, Kokovtsov presided over a government that was increasingly in disarray. Even Stolypin had found it difficult to achieve stability, much less unanimity, in the Council of Ministers. His successor, insofar as he attempted the task, discovered that it was all but impossible. The ministers presided over semi-independent fiefdoms, reporting to the sovereign separately, much as they had before the October Manifesto, and largely indifferent to their chairman. Minister of Agriculture Krivoshein may have aspired to become chairman himself; he cultivated royal favor, including that of the Empress Alexandra, as well as influential "agricultural and industrial circles." Eventually he is said to have superseded Kokovtsov as "the most important person in the Council of Ministers."[5]

As was his custom with new appointees, Nicholas treated his chief minister with gracious indulgence when Kokovtsov journeyed to Livadia in early October of 1911. An ornate limestone palace in the Italianate style had replaced the old wooden structure earlier in the year, and Nicholas proudly escorted his visitor on a tour of inspection. He readily accepted Kokovtsov's nominees for the State Council, including several whom Stolypin had recommended. As for his martyred predecessor, Kokovtsov was shocked when Nicholas spoke of him with deep resentment: "He died in my service, true," Nicholas allegedly explained to Kokovtsov, "but he was always so anxious to keep me in the background. Do you suppose I liked always reading in the papers that *the President of the Council had done this . . . the President of the Council has done that*? Don't I count? Am I nobody?"[6]

The Empress Alexandra, whose interest in affairs of state had grown more rapidly than her political sagacity, expressed a wish to Kokovtsov that he never range himself "with those horrible political parties which only hope to be able to seize power or to subjugate the government." The minister's tactful reply, that his position was more difficult than Stolypin's and that he would not submit to the dictates of any group, was interrupted by Alexandra's complaint that he ascribed too much importance to Stolypin's activities and personality. "Find your support in the confidence of the Tsar—the Lord will help you," she told him. "I am sure that Stolypin died to make room for you, and this is all for the good of Russia." Kokovtsov departed for the capital on October 8 sorely troubled by the indifference to Stolypin's tragic end that he found in the imperial entourage and with newfound insight into Alexandra's "peculiar, mystic nature."[7]

The royal family remained in Livadia until mid-December of 1911. Their belated return to St. Petersburg coincided with the first widespread publicity concerning Rasputin, whose unsavory reputation had now acquired a sinister ring. Insinuations in the press that he had become a confidant at court and that he exercised influence over government appointments spread to the Duma, where a number of references to "dark forces" enlivened the rumor mill. Both Kokovtsov and Makarov were apprehensive, fearing imperial disfavor unless they could restrain the offending newspapers. Private diplomacy failed to alleviate the problem. Nicholas alluded to the matter in an audience with Kokovtsov, recommending censorship legislation, but his minister demurred because of the outcry that would surely arise from the Duma.

Intermediaries urged Kokovtsov to meet Rasputin, an opportunity he declined until he found himself drawn more closely into the growing scandal. Makarov received a disagreeable note from Nicholas in January 1912 demanding that he "take firm measures to bring the press to order." Kokovtsov advised him to resign if the sovereign persisted after the inadvisability of such measures had been carefully explained. He hoped that Rasputin could be pressured to return to his home village and in an oral report managed to convey to Nicholas his dismay that such an evil influence was undermining the prestige of the monarchy. Nicholas interrupted: "This disgusting affair must be ended and I shall take decisive steps to do so. I shall tell you of them later, but in the meantime let us drop the subject. It pains me extremely." Nicholas had reference to an investigation of Rasputin that he had authorized Mikhail Rodzyanko, the Duma president, to undertake.[8]

On February 13, 1912, Kokovtsov was received by the dowager empress, who wept bitterly about the Rasputin affair and promised to speak to her son about him. "My poor daughter-in-law does not perceive that she is ruining both the dynasty and herself," she lamented. "She sincerely believes in the holiness of an adventurer, and we are powerless to ward off the misfortune which is sure to come." Kokovtsov was amazed to receive a letter from Rasputin on the same day inviting him to a meeting. His first impulse, to ignore the letter, gave way to reasons of state—and perhaps to curiosity. He decided that his position obliged him "not to avoid a man who had perturbed all Russia" and that he would be able to give his personal impression to Nicholas at their next audience. "Also I was afraid I might incur the Tsar's displeasure for refusing to see a man who had requested an interview. Finally, I hoped to be able to show Rasputin that he was digging a grave for the Tsar and his authority."

Kokovtsov received Rasputin on February 15 in his study and was "shocked by the repulsive expression of his eyes, deep-set and close to each other, small, gray in color." Apparently the meeting was brief, and Rasputin had little to say; but he did promise to leave St. Petersburg. "In my estimation," wrote Kokovtsov, "he was a typical Siberian tramp, a clever man who had trained himself for the role of a simpleton and a madman and who played his part according to a set formula. He did not believe in his tricks himself, but had trained himself to certain mannerisms of conduct in order to deceive those who sincerely believed in all his oddities." He reported his encounter to Nicholas at the first opportunity, condemning Rasputin's "disreputable behavior" and those who sought his protection and assistance. Nicholas gazed out the window during his minister's brutally frank appraisal, an unmistakable sign of royal displeasure. Rasputin kept his word, though he returned to the capital in less than a month's time. Kokovtsov, whom the press incorrectly credited with an order of deportation, was gratified to find that Nicholas was as "kind and gracious as usual" at his next report and did not mention the painful subject.[9]

Another facet of the Rasputin scandal emerged when copies of six letters written several years before to the royal favorite by the empress and her children fell into private hands. Although the letters were entirely innocent, several indiscreet passages, read out of context and without a knowledge of Alexandra's florid and emotional style, could have been given a salacious interpretation. Makarov took it upon himself to track down the original letters and purchased them, evidently for a reasonable price. Kokovtsov advised him to hand them over to Alexandra with a truthful explanation, but Makarov chose to present them directly to Nicholas, who thrust them in his desk drawer with a sharp gesture indicating vast irritation. Kokovtsov's prediction that the unfortunate minister would be rewarded with dismissal came to pass, though it was delayed until the end of the year. Makarov's attempt to influence the elections to the Fourth Duma were not crowned with success, and Nicholas revived an earlier grievance: "He has let the press get completely out of hand and has absolutely refused to proclaim a law which would give the government authority to check the excesses in which the newspapers have been indulging. Even now, when the Duma is not in session and when we might invoke Article 87, he still refuses. So, I have decided to let him go."[10]

Meanwhile Rodzyanko proceeded with his investigation of Rasputin and obtained an audience with Nicholas on February 26, 1912. The Duma president delivered a stinging denunciation of the *starets*, citing in particular his intrigues in the Holy Synod, his sexual exploits, and his supposed adherence to the *khlysty*, a sect popularly believed to engage in orgiastic rituals. Nicholas listened patiently, interjecting an occasional question while nervously lighting cigarettes and throwing them on the floor unsmoked. Rodzyanko concluded by imploring him "to banish this villainous rogue" and thus "dispel the fears which assail those who are loyal to the Throne." Nicholas remained silent for a time and then replied: "No, I cannot promise you that. Nevertheless, I fully believe all you have told me."[11]

Rodzyanko pursued his inquiry and compiled a comprehensive dossier. He requested another audience with Nicholas on March 8 and was informed through Kokovtsov of a refusal: "I am unable to receive him, nor do I see any necessity for so doing, as I received him a week and a half ago." Nicholas found the Duma's conduct "deeply revolting," especially Guchkov's speech on the budget of the Holy Synod, the occasion for an attack on Rasputin as a "mysterious tragi-comic figure, like a specter of the underworld or a survivor of the darkness of centuries past." The tsar concluded, "I shall be very glad if my displeasure is made known to these gentlemen; I am tired of always bowing and smiling to them."[12]

Anticipating political difficulties in the Duma should Nicholas prove intractable, Kokovtsov persuaded him to write a conciliatory note to Rodzyanko pleading lack of time prior to his departure for Livadia and promising an audience upon his return. "It is better not to tease those gentlemen," Nicholas admitted. "I shall find another opportunity for telling them what I think of their behavior." Rodzyanko was mollified, especially since Nicholas requested a written report on Rasputin, but a number of Duma deputies expressed irritation that the royal schedule had on other occasions proved flexible enough to accommodate a variety of individuals pursuing apparently trivial matters.

On April 4, 1912, the façade of public tranquility was shattered by the Lena goldfields massacre.[13] Several thousand miners, striking to protest appalling working conditions amid the rigors of the Siberian climate, had faced the deadly fire of a military detachment called to the scene. Over two hundred workers were killed and many wounded, a toll exceeding the casualties of Bloody Sunday. The Duma seethed with excitement. Makarov appeared before the deputies with a slanted report that blamed the victims for the disaster. His cynical conclusion, "Thus it has been, so it will always be"—that is, the state would invariably suppress any popular uprising—shocked the public and rallied support for an impartial investigation. The Duma established its own committee, while the government chose a panel chaired by Sergei Manukhin, the former minister of justice. Nicholas personally approved the appointment, commending Kokovtsov's choice: "I know Manukhin well; he is very radical but a scrupulously honest man, and will not be corrupted. If we were to send some Adjutant General, people would pay little heed to his conclusions and would say that he was protecting local authorities. You have reasoned most cleverly."[14] Both inquiries focused on the callous attitude of the company management as the root cause of the affair, leading to major improvements for the miners. Working-class militance revived in the aftermath and, though assuming less formidable proportions than in 1905, it sustained a strike movement that lasted until the outbreak of war in 1914.

Reporting to the emperor at Livadia during the third week in April, Kokovtsov spoke frankly about the incompetence and "unprincipled conduct" of the war minister, General Sukhomlinov. The army, he maintained, was in a "terrible condition," poorly organized and "badly managed." As for the general, "Some laugh at him, some despise him, and with such a chief one cannot prepare an army for victory." Kokovtsov offered to resign if Nicholas disagreed, but instead he received a tepid vote of confidence. Sukhomlinov remained at his post, allegedly because the sovereign found him an ingratiating courtier and an amusing raconteur.[15] Kokovtsov resented profligate expenditures, especially the extravagant and often superfluous depredations of the war minister. Nicholas blandly conceded the point: "You are quite right," he told Kokovtsov at a later date, "the money will not be used and our armaments will not improve. In your conflicts with Sukhomlinov you are always right." Yet he proceeded to defend the errant minister on pseudo-patriotic grounds: "I should never forgive myself if I refused any military credits, even one ruble. . . . Let us hope that from now on things will improve with every new day, and should Sukhomlinov again say that you have refused him credits I shall tell him that I do not wish to hear such statements, that the responsibility is his, not yours."[16]

But "things" did not improve and in fact became a good deal worse. The able assistant war minister, General Aleksei Polivanov, was dismissed on April 27 by imperial order, presumably because of Sukhomlinov's complaint that Polivanov had funneled information to Guchkov for attacks in the Duma on the military establishment. Nicholas readily accepted a kind of quasi-Slavophile view prevalent among his ministers and advisers that the Russian people would overcome any national emergency. Since Kokovtsov felt that war would be a catastrophe for Russia, his warnings were considered unpatriotic, if not a sign of personal cowardice. The sorry state of the armed forces would not be evident until 1914.

As the Third Duma neared the end of its five-year term, Kokovtsov urged the tsar to set a date for a formal reception of the deputies. But Nicholas pleaded lack of time, an excuse that had become almost a reflex when unpleasant duties were to be performed, and his minister assumed the disagreeable task of reminding him that he had already pledged to receive the Duma members. Kokovtsov drafted a conciliatory speech, and on June 12 Nicholas read a slightly amended version to the assembled deputies at Tsarskoe Selo. He ventured to complain that they had not conducted their work "with that composure which alone assures a just and dispassionate fulfillment of legislative duties." His one major departure from the original text constituted a reprimand: "I was much distressed with your opposition to the matter of parish schools, which is particularly dear to me as having been bequeathed to me by my unforgettable father." Most of the deputies were offended, and to avoid an embarrassing rejection of financial aid to the parish schools Rodzyanko took it upon himself to withdraw the bill from the Duma's agenda. Later that summer, during the observances honoring the centenary of the battle of Borodino against Napoleonic France, the tsar snubbed Rodzyanko, a churlish reminder of the ill-fated school bill and the neglected report on Rasputin.[17]

The "conservative" Third Duma, despite its durability, had in the end fared only slightly better than its forerunners in forging a bond between the monarch and the people's representatives. Recognizing that a discriminatory franchise could not guarantee a submissive Fourth Duma, the government employed a variety of illegal and questionable tactics during the new election campaign. Assistant Minister of the Interior Aleksei Kharuzin, described as "intelligent, very ambitious, and inordinately pleased with himself," supervised these activities and "did not hesitate to break both the letter and the spirit of the law if he could further his career by so doing."[18] Aside from subsidizing the right-wing press and supporting conservative parties and their candidates, the government strove to defeat "undesirables" by trumped-up indictments, by intimidating electors, manipulating electoral districts, and other arbitrary acts. Jews were routinely excluded on various technicalities. Provincial governors also played a major role in electioneering chicanery, and the Holy Synod mobilized the Church hierarchy so effectively that an astonishing 81 percent of the electors were allegedly members of the clergy.[19] For all its effort the government won at best a precarious victory. The emperor's bête noir, Guchkov, was defeated, and the Octobrists, already in serious disarray, were reduced from 150 deputies (in 1907) to ninety-five. Yet the solid pro-monarchist majority that had been anticipated—a combination of Nationalists and extreme Rightists—did not materialize, and the deputies of the Center and moderate Left did not suffer appreciable losses. The reelection of Rodzyanko as Duma president signified that the balance of political power remained in equilibrium.

The opening session of the Fourth Duma took place on November 15, 1912. Rodzyanko provided an inaugural address which most of the Rightist deputies boycotted. He later requested and was granted an imperial audience. Nicholas appeared ill at ease and, contrary to his usual custom, stood throughout the twenty-minute reception. He objected to Rodzyanko's reference to "constitutional" government in his speech, and the president referred to the "numerous acts of injustice" during the election campaign. Otherwise the amenities were preserved, and Nicholas later received the Duma members—even many Kadets attended—with a display of cordiality.[20]

The major change in the government coinciding with the new Duma involved Makarov's replacement by Nikolai Maklakov as minister of the interior. A "fat, rubicund, cheerful man, a typical provincial dandy," Maklakov had been governor of Chernigov Province and was personally known to the tsar. He was also an intimate of Prince Meshchersky, whose influence at the court had revived conspicuously after Stolypin's death. Kokovtsov opposed the appointment, and the possibility of ministerial conflict presented Nicholas with a pretext to eliminate Kokovtov by offering him the post of ambassador to Germany. Pleading a lack of diplomatic experience and a reputation for championing peace that ill-suited the "nationalist" mood in government circles, he begged off the assignment and retained his dual role in the cabinet.[21] Obviously, as had been the case with Witte and Stolypin, he no longer enjoyed the full confidence of the sovereign, and his departure became only a matter of time.

During the latter half of 1912 the Rasputin scandal quieted. Nicholas apparently did not take Rodzyanko's report seriously; in any case, he took no action. The press, lacking fresh revelations, no longer featured the *starets*, who maintained a low profile by avoiding the capital. His ministrations were eagerly sought in October, however, when Alexis suffered internal bleeding during the family's residence at Spala, the royal hunting lodge in Russian Poland. Official announcements informed the public of the gravity of his condition without disclosing the nature of the illness. At the height of the crisis Rasputin telegraphed the empress from Pokrovskoe: "God has seen your tears and heard your prayers. Do not grieve. The Little One will not die. Do not allow the doctors to bother him too much."[22] Whether by coincidence or not, the hemorrhaging ceased a day later, and Alexis slowly recovered, reconfirming his mother's belief in Rasputin's supernatural powers. Nicholas, who acknowledged that his wife "bore the ordeal better than I did," remained curiously ambivalent about Rasputin and appeared to regard him less a man of God than a symbol of the common people with whom Nicholas retained strong sentimental ties. "He is just a good, religious, simple-minded Russian," Nicholas explained to the palace commandant on one occasion. "When in trouble or assailed with doubts I like to have a talk with him, and invariably feel at peace with myself afterwards."[23] To Kokovtsov he justified his conduct on somewhat different grounds: "Rasputin is a simple peasant who can relieve the sufferings of my ailing son by a strange power. The Empress's reliance upon him is a matter for the family, and I will permit no one to meddle in my family affairs."[24]

Early in 1913 rumors of Rasputin's reappearance in St. Petersburg began to circulate in the Duma. The newly appointed Maklakov called on Rodzyanko at the tsar's behest to ward off a possible revival of the scandal on the floor of the assembly. The president had an opportunity to reassure Nicholas in person: "The spirit which animates the Duma is wrongly interpreted; all mention of Rasputin has died down, there is no question of any interpellation." On February 21, inaugurating the celebrations marking the three hundredth anniversary of the Romanov dynasty, Rodzyanko had his first and only meeting with the celebrated "holy devil." Offended by the lowly place assigned to the Duma's representatives for services at Kazan Cathedral in the capital, he managed to obtain a more advantageous position, only to discover that it had been preempted by Rasputin. A bizarre scene followed in which Rodzyanko felt that he was being hypnotized, "confronted by an unknown power of tremendous force." "I suddenly became possessed of an almost animal fury," he reported; "the blood rushed to my heart, and I realized I was working myself into a state of absolute frenzy." He made a formidable appearance—not for nothing had he described himself as "the biggest and fattest man in Russia"—and Rasputin's self-confidence began to erode. The Duma president, calling him a "vile heretic" and "notorious swindler," threatened to have him thrown out, and the cowed *starets* finally "slunk away."[25]

The festivities attending the tercentenary were national in scope. During the spring Nicholas and his family toured the historic cities of old Russia associated with the ancestral lands of the Romanovs. Court officials conceived the journey as a public relations triumph, a rare opportunity to demonstrate the mutual devotion of tsar and people. But the crowds were sparse and lacking in enthusiasm, drawn more by idle curiosity than homage to the royal couple. Only at Kostroma, after a trip by steamer down the Volga, did the sovereign receive a spirited welcome. The ceremonies ended in Moscow on May 25, and except for a procession through Red Square to the Kremlin the public was excluded, apparently for security reasons. To monarchists the observances represented a renewal of faith in their country and its proud heritage. Ultra-royalists, unfulfilled by the ideology of conventional patriotism, urged the tsar to resume his rightful place as supreme autocrat and reduce the Duma to an advisory role.

As for the general public, at least to many of its more articulate spokesmen, the commemoration did little to raise the prestige and moral authority of a regime that if not yet bankrupt seemed determined to resist any outpouring of popular sentiment or political accommodation. This growing alienation found expression in the mood of apathy that greeted the imperial manifesto marking the anniversary, a lackluster homily that did little more than proclaim the virtues of the motherland. No major concession, such as a sweeping amnesty for political offenders, was forthcoming, nor did Nicholas unbend sufficiently to offer words of conciliation and compromise. The opportunity for gestures toward national unity and the general welfare disappeared in an interminable round of ritual and pageantry.[26]

The disharmony of Russian society was nowhere more striking than in the estrangement of government and Duma. Strained under Stolypin's leadership, the relationship became antagonistic under Kokovtsov. Much of the difficulty arose because neither the Council of Ministers nor the Fourth Duma could keep its own house in order. Kokovtsov faced a "patriotic" and reactionary faction led by Maklakov and to which Nicholas gave undisguised encouragement. Complaining of his "isolation and helplessness," he recommended cabinet shakeups in vain, for Nicholas supposedly "paid heed to Meshchersky's hints that it was contrary to the spirit of the Russian régime and suggestive of parliamentarism to make ministerial changes on the advice of the Chairman of the Council." Nicholas refused to consider parting with such conservative stalwarts as Minister of Education Lyov Kasso, an advocate of "firm government"; Minister of Transportation and Communication Sergei Rukhlov, a self-made man who had "risen from the bottom of the Russian peasantry"; Shcheglovitov, "a guardian of the law who was always ready to subordinate justice to politics"; or Krivoshein, "a consummate politician who at that time enjoyed the favor of the Tsar, the Duma, the zemstvos, and the press." Kokovtsov, though tempted to submit his own resignation, refrained from doing so "because I felt I had a duty to perform in moderating both our domestic and our foreign policy and because I was absolutely unwilling to force upon my gracious and considerate Sovereign the unhappy task of choosing between the other ministers and me."[27]

It could be argued that a more assertive leader—a Witte or a Stolypin—would have forced the issue one way or the other. But Kokovtsov, while justifying his conduct, recognized his limitations. He confessed that in his dealings with the tsar he may have "exhibited unpardonable weakness." In the case of the legislature, he conceded, somewhat obliquely, that he made mistakes ("I was later assured that I was not clever enough to handle the Duma as the late Stolypin had done"). His relations with the deputies, he admitted, were "very cool and formal and often hostile, though outwardly most cordial and correct." Nevertheless, he insisted that he "tried to steer a straight course." "I solicited favor from no one," he claimed, "shunned all intrigue, and bided my time till the Duma made some order out of its party chaos."[28]

Kokovtsov, if deficient in diplomatic skills and constrained by his royal superior, accurately assessed the disorganization and fragmentation of the lower chamber. The deputies of the Right, the government's natural allies, distrusted Kokovtsov and found common cause with his enemies in the cabinet. For his part Kokovtsov failed to develop a legislative program of any consequence. Such a negative policy reflected Nicholas' distrust of the Duma and his support for Maklakov and Shcheglovitov in their campaign in the spring of 1913 to curtail its rights and prerogatives. The result was a near deadlock, producing a mood of negligence and indifference on the part of the deputies and a high rate of absenteeism.

On May 12, 1913, an incident occurred in the Duma that triggered a prolonged political conflict and reinforced the breach between government and legislature. The affair began when Kokovtov, who prided himself on, if nothing else, achieving a balanced budget, replied with undue asperity to critical remarks made by Nikolai Markov, whose credentials as a legitimate "reactionary" were unsurpassed. Markov retaliated later on by linking the minister of finance to "bribery" and "theft." The charge, both vague and unsubstantiated, should have led to appropriate disciplinary measures against the speaker. But the acting president, Prince Vladimir Volkonsky, contented himself with a mild reproof. Since the Duma declined to intervene, the Council of Ministers resolved to boycott further sessions until Markov apologized. The tsar approved the decision while resisting the advice of Maklakov and Shcheglovitov to dissolve the Duma. Despite frequent meetings between Kokovtsov and Rodzyanko, the impasse continued during the summer recess.[29]

Late in July the imperial family departed on a Baltic cruise, and in early autumn they took up residence at Livadia. The political intrigue in the capital mounted in the tsar's absence. Maklakov again took the initiative by pressing for a bolder solution to the governmental "crisis": the dissolution of the Duma, its conversion to an advisory role, and the abolition of the Council of Ministers. He also proposed the restoration of preliminary censorship and restrictions on reporting speeches delivered in the Duma. Meshchersky joined the campaign by publishing in *Grazhdanin* (The Citizen) his "diary," a series of attacks on Kokovtsov for assuming the post of "grand vizier" and transgressing on the emperor's legitimate domain. The government, he declared, had succumbed to "parliamentarism," a "Western-European innovation" that should be eliminated. Maklakov's plan to curb the "unbridled" freedom of the press was doomed to defeat because Kokovtsov needed "the plaudits of the Duma." It was high time, Meshchersky argued, that the tsar learned who his true servant was and who was serving "the Rodziankos and the Guchkovs."[30]

Kokovtsov, then at Livadia, became highly indignant. Baron Frederiks advised him to protest to the tsar, but Kokovtsov felt that it would be useless. Nicholas was "in the habit of reading everything Meshchersky wrote," and rumor had it that *Grazhdanin* was the only newspaper that he read on a regular basis. Kokovtsov protested instead to Maklakov as the morally guilty party, receiving only an evasive reply for his pains. Far from retreating, *Grazhdanin* escalated its attacks on Kokovtsov; toward the end of the year they became so offensive that he could foresee his dismissal—it was Mershchersky's policy "to trample in the mud only those whose days had already been numbered."[31]

Meanwhile on October 14 Maklakov appealed directly to the tsar to allow the government more leverage in its relations with the Duma, including a decree of dissolution if necessary. A majority of the deputies, scheduled to resume their deliberations in November, were clearly in an uncooperative mood. Nicholas not only agreed with Maklakov but advocated a change in the statutes to allow the State Council a greater role in the legislative process. "Since we have no constitution," he contended, the Duma's right of veto should be dropped. "The presentation to the sovereign of the opinions of the majority and the minority for his choice and confirmation will be a good way of returning to the previous tranquil course of legislative activity, and moreover in the Russian spirit."[32] But what appeared to be a renewed government offensive reminiscent of Stolypin's coup in 1907 did not materialize. Kokovtsov had departed for western Europe on official business, principally the negotiation of another loan from France, and the Council of Ministers took no action. Tension over the Markov cpisode finally dissipated when the errant deputy, pressured by Shcheglovitov and others, offered his apology to the Duma.

Upon returning from his trip abroad, Kokovtsov again went to Livadia, unwilling to become a sacrificial victim of Maklakov and his allies. The ostensible reason for the audience was Maklakov's recommendation to the tsar that Boris Stürmer, a Rightist member of the State Council, be appointed mayor of Moscow. Nicholas, as courteous as always in receiving Kokovtsov, did not express his customary gratitude for his minister's labors, which had involved extensive negotiations in foreign capitals. He deferred consideration of the Stürmer matter until the next day and then informed Kokovtsov, who had been prepared to resign over the issue, that he had decided against the appointment so as to avoid possible offense to the citizens of Moscow. Seizing the opportunity of enlarging his modest victory, Kokovtsov registered intense dissatisfaction with the Maklakov "faction" and the disunity in the Council of Ministers. Nicholas preferred to think that Maklakov's mistakes were caused by inexperience, whereas Kokovtsov maintained that Mershchersky and his newspaper were at the root of the intrigue. Nicholas listened patiently but remained unconvinced, and Kokovtsov hinted that someone else might be better suited to preserving ministerial unity. Nicholas backed away from that implication, and the two parted on outwardly friendly terms. But Kokovtsov sensed the sovereign's irritation regarding the Stürmer matter and felt certain that his dismissal was imminent.

The chairman's position had indeed been undermined despite royal protestation to the contrary. The final blow, however, came from an unexpected quarter: the triple issue of temperance, alcoholism, and the state liquor monopoly. Excessive consumption of alcohol, especially vodka, had long been a major social problem, and it became more acute during the years of relative prosperity preceding World War I.[33] Temperance societies and other critics of official policy insisted that the evil arose from the state liquor stores, which profited from the trade to such an extent that they provided approximately a quarter of the government's revenue. Nicholas shared that sentiment in no small degree and found in Minister of Agriculture Krivoshein an enthusiastic advocate of drastic measures to curb the drinking habit. Kokovtsov, less a social reformer than a parsimonious guardian of the public purse, bowed to the imperial mandate and introduced an innocuous bill in the Duma bearing the title, "Some Changes in the Statute on the State Sale of Strong Drink." A fierce debate followed, and in December 1913 the State Council considered a more restrictive bill championed vociferously by Count Witte, who, ironically, had been instrumental in the establishment of the liquor monopoly in December 1894. Witte's sudden emergence as a protector of public morals had no doubt been induced by his dislike of Kokovtsov and his desire to curry favor with the tsar, who might yet return him to the ministry of finance or some other form of bureaucratic responsibility. Kokovtsov, while admitting Witte's "many exceptional talents," regretted that his "moral sense was completely atrophied." Nicholas appeared to share that opinion: "Was it not he who administered the liquor monopoly for ten years?" he asked rhetorically.[34]

In an audience on January 21, 1914, Kokovtsov, together with President Akimov of the State Council, endeavored to persuade Nicholas that a temperance campaign would be circumvented by illicit alcohol and result in decreased revenue. Only "by raising the moral and material level of the people," he argued, "could the evil of drunkenness be overcome." Nicholas remained unmoved, and Kokovtsov later surmised that his dismissal had already been decided. Akimov passed on the rumor that Mershchersky was behind the temperance measures, supposedly because of Rasputin's wishes (the royal favorite, certainly no model of sobriety, had reputedly said, "It is unbefitting for a Tsar to deal in vodka and to make drunkards out of honest people," and "The time has come to lock up the Tsar's saloons").[35] Such "information" may have induced Kokovtsov to conclude that a sinister plot had been hatched to remove him from office.

That Nicholas had chosen to part with Kokovtsov, if not obvious on the 21st, became more evident on the 24th. He was "exceptionally gracious" when he received his minister, an ominous signal in such circumstances. Kokovtsov's momentary discharge was an open secret among the political elite by the time the blow fell on January 29. Nicholas decided to inform him by letter because it was "easier to select the right words when putting them on paper than during an unsettling conversation." Always tactful on these occasions, he denied any "feeling of displeasure" as his motive, citing instead a "long-standing and deep realization of a state need." He had become convinced that "combining in one person the duties of Chairman of the Ministers' Council and those of Minister of Finance or of the Interior is both awkward and wrong in a country such as Russia." Moreover, the "swift tempo of our domestic life" and the "striking development" of the economy required "definite and serious measures" that should be "entrusted to a man fresh for the work." "During the last two years," Nicholas continued, "I have not always approved of the policy of the Ministry of Finance." He concluded by expressing his gratitude for Kokovtsov's devotion and for his "great service" in improving Russia's credit. "I am sorry to part with you who have been my assistant for ten years. Believe also, that I shall not forget to take suitable care of you and your family."[36] An imperial rescript announced Kokovtsov's "resignation" for reasons of health, offered public recognition of his work, and elevated him to the rank of count.

Tsar and minister met for a final report on January 31, and their parting was emotionally painful for both. Although bitterly affronted by his discharge and convinced that "intrigue" if not a full-blown conspiracy had been responsible, Kokovtsov remained deferential and asked to be forgiven if he had displeased his sovereign. He did venture to complain about receiving "such high honors" while his "past policies [were] so roundly condemned," and Nicholas responded with what amounted to an apology. Kokovtsov recalled the previous offer of the ambassadorship to Germany and indicated that a similar post in France would be to his liking. Nothing came of his initiative. By way of a financial settlement, Nicholas suggested "an appropriation of two or three hundred thousand rubles" and was astonished when Kokovtsov refused it as a matter of principle, asking only for an adequate pension.

The fall of Kokovtsov, though unlamented by public opinion, represented another milestone in the gradual retreat from the "constitutionalism" inaugurated in 1905–1906. The so-called Third of June System that Stolypin had introduced by his coup in 1907 never provided the kind of harmonious relationship between government and Duma that had been anticipated. Both Stolypin and Kokovtsov were frustrated in their endeavors, and not the least of their handicaps was the emperor himself. Nicholas could not long endure both talent and independence in his chief ministers;

if Kokovtsov had demonstrated no great precociousness in either direction, he had not proved a servile instrument of the royal will. The temptation to turn the political clock back to the less complicated days of unrelieved autocracy must have had an overpowering and nearly irresistible appeal to Nicholas. Yet he did not succumb despite an overabundance of flatterers, sycophants, and political primitives in his retinue whose ideology had never advanced beyond the concept of absolute monarchy as the epitome of responsible statesmanship. In resisting these ultra-royalists, he nevertheless shared many if not most of their assumptions and conveniently ignored, when it suited him, his obligations as a quasi-constitutional ruler.

The ambitious Krivoshein had long been the favored candidate among "insiders" to succeed Kokovtsov. Unfortunately for his aspirations, he suffered a serious illness late in 1913. Although he recovered, sustained in part by regular deliveries of holy water from the shrine of St. Seraphim of Sarov, a gift of the empress, he declined to be considered for the ministerial chairmanship. He found solace in playing the role of power broker, hovering behind the scenes and manipulating "the destiny of the puppets on the political stage."[37] He presumably influenced the appointment of Ivan Goremykin for a second tour of duty at the head of the Ministerial Council. That the aged Goremykin—then seventy-four but even older in appearance—would be summoned from retirement came as a distinct shock to "society." He accepted his duties with a conspicuous lack of enthusiasm. "I am like an old fur coat," he lamented to Kokovtsov. "For many months I have been packed away in camphor. I am being taken out now merely for the occasion; when it is passed I shall be packed away again till I am wanted the next time." Few expected him to be more than an interim replacement, but the venerable bureaucrat remained in office for two years. Departing from precedent with calculated deliberation, Nicholas did not confer upon him a regular cabinet portfolio, guaranteeing that Goremykin could not establish an administrative power base.

To fill the vacancy at the ministry of finance—there were no other appointments at cabinet rank—Nicholas chose Pyotr Bark, a Krivoshein protegé and the assistant minister of commerce and industry. He was also, according to gossip, "a man who did not shrink from rubbing elbows with Rasputin." While no longer a young man, he at least conformed far more closely than Goremykin to the royal proviso of "a man fresh for the work." An imperial prescript of unusual candor assigned to him the temperance campaign that Kokovtsov had so blatantly shirked. "I was greatly saddened," Nicholas declared, referring to his extensive domestic tour in 1913, "to observe heartrending scenes of the people's infirmities, of poverty-stricken families and neglected homes—the inevitable consequences of besotted lives. . . . I am firmly convinced that I have an obligation to God and to Russia to introduce without delay certain basic changes in financial management for the benefit of my beloved people. The health of the treasury must not be based on the destruction of the spiritual and economic vitality of my loyal subjects."[38] If Nicholas conveniently overlooked other reasons for poverty and infirmity, the temperance crusade did get under way, albeit at an exceedingly cautious pace. Bark eventually reported progress, particularly in the villages, but sophisticated urbanites treated the campaign with derision, and the Duma rejected an appropriation of 300,000 rubles to finance temperance societies.

Under Goremykin's halting direction the dismal state of the government-Duma relationship continued to deteriorate. He made a significant contribution to the process by announcing that henceforth the deputies could direct questions only to individual ministers, not to the chairman. Maklakov displayed more initiative than his nominal superior, though his major venture was not only unproductive but inimical to the regime's dwindling stock of moral authority. He proposed to indict Nikolai Chkheidze, a Menshevik deputy from the Caucasus, for delivering a "subversive" speech in the Duma. A successful prosecution would have ended or severely curtailed the right of parliamentary immunity, clearly an illegal act, and the tsar ultimately intervened to halt the proceedings. Maklakov's influence at Tsarskoe Selo suffered no ill effects, however, and he enjoyed great popularity with the royal family as a kind of court jester, displaying a special talent for mimicry and amusing stories. Elsewhere, according to Rodzyanko, he was "universally despised."[39]

The diffusion of ministerial authority that Nicholas fondly believed would enhance his own power and prestige—his "coup d'etat of January 1914," as he complacently put it—proved disappointing. He himself was largely to blame, for he declined to exercise direct leadership, either by appeals to public opinion or by authorizing Goremykin and Maklakov to conciliate the legislature. To Nicholas the Duma had always seemed to play an adversarial role, and now that the opportunity had seemingly arrived to refurbish the autocracy to something resembling its pre-1905 status, he lacked the political skill and intestinal fortitude to proceed. Rodzyanko had not been far wrong in December 1913 when he startled the emperor by informing him that there was no government. "The nation feels bewildered," he explained. "Each Minister has his own opinion. The Cabinet is generally split into two parties, the Council of the Empire forms a third, the Duma a fourth, and your own will is unknown to the nation. This cannot go on, your Majesty; this is not Government, it is anarchy."[40]

Nonetheless, "anarchy" not only prevailed but grew worse after the imperial "coup." By June 1914 the tsar became sufficiently alarmed at the legislative logjam to convene a ministerial conference. The unprecedented meeting took place at Peterhof on the 18th, and Nicholas revived the old scheme to relegate both the Duma and the State Council to advisory status. Surprisingly, and with near unanimity, the cabinet balked at such a radical move, and even such stalwarts of the Right as Goremykin and Shcheglovitov were firm in their opposition. Only Maklakov backed the proposal, though he too had his doubts. Unwilling to defy his own ministers, Nicholas retreated. "Quite enough," he said. "Obviously the question should be dropped."[41]

The warning signals of a great European conflict had by this time become too ominous to ignore. Russia's second war within a decade was to bring temporary national unity and postpone the "anarchy" that monarchists of the Rodzyanko persuasion so dreaded. Even the emperor, anxious to subordinate politics to the war effort, was prepared to accept the Duma as an asset instead of a liability.

Approaching the
Great War

Russia emerged from the conflict with Japan weakened but hardly pros-
trate. Its navy, aside from the isolated Black Sea fleet, had been annihilated,
but its army, though severely mauled, was still capable of suppressing mutiny and insurrection. Other than the Björkö treaty, a royal aberration that
had no lasting consequences, foreign policy reverted to fundamentals. In
practice this meant a renewed dedication to the French alliance and a shift
in emphasis from Asiatic to European affairs.

The retirement of Lamzdorf in April 1906 and his replacement by Aleksandr Izvolsky constituted the major change in diplomatic personnel. The
new foreign minister, who advocated better relations with England and a
rapprochement with Japan, anticipated opposition from the tsar. The idea
of avenging Russia's defeat retained great emotional appeal to extreme nationalists, and initially Nicholas counted himself among them. Gradually,
however, as passions cooled and as Izvolsky's discreet tutelage began to
take effect, Nicholas accepted the reorientation of foreign policy that led
in time to the Triple Entente of Russia, France, and Great Britain.

The negotiations that ended over half a century of Anglo-Russian antagonism had a lengthy gestation period. Perhaps the turning point came during Izvolsky's residence in Copenhagen when King Edward VII, on the
occasion of a family visit in the spring of 1904, held a friendly discussion
with the Russian minister. Alluding to the recent Entente Cordiale that
resolved the long-standing differences between England and France, the
king proposed a similar arrangement with Russia. Izvolsky reported the
initiative in some detail, but Britain's benevolent neutrality toward Japan

and the state of public opinion in both countries precluded any immediate action. Nicholas did acknowledge the king's overture, if indirectly and with unwonted emotion. "Taught by bitter experience in the years 1856 [the Crimean War] and 1878 [the Russo-Turkish War]," he wrote the British sovereign, "there is not a man in the whole of Russia who would tolerate another country mixing in this affair of ours and Japan's. This seems to be quite just, my dear Uncle Bertie. No one hindered England at the conclusion of her South African War. I hope you won't mind my telling you this so frankly, but I prefer you should hear it privately from me than in any other way." The king returned a soft answer through the newly appointed British ambassador to St. Petersburg, Sir Charles Hardinge. He commended Izvolsky as "a man of remarkable intelligence" and repeated his desire for a "satisfactory settlement regarding many difficult matters between us."[1]

Meaningful negotiations remained in abeyance until the spring of 1906, although Nicholas expressed his desire to host King Edward at Tsarskoe Selo. There the two monarchs might publicly sign an agreement whose provisions would be arranged beforehand.[2] Nothing came of the proposal, but meanwhile the two countries found common cause at the Algeciras Conference by supporting France in its dispute with Germany over the disposition of Morocco. In May, Sir Arthur Nicolson, who replaced Hardinge as ambassador, called on Izvolsky and set in motion the long and intricate bargaining process. Nicolson's first impressions of the Russian minister were not flattering: he found a vain and ambitious man whose reputation as an aristocratic dandy was embellished by faultless tailoring, a monocle, and the scent of cologne. Closer acquaintance modified his opinion, and he came to admire Izvolsky's "alert, quick and subtle" intelligence, his "perfect knowledge of the English language," and the loyalty and honesty that characterized his negotiating style.[3] It has been plausibly suggested that in Izvolsky's case "a fine intellect was mated with a rather shoddy soul."[4]

Progress was exasperatingly slow at first. The Straits question was on the agenda but without prospect of resolution; at length three other areas of friction emerged as the focus of a prospective accord: Tibet, Afghanistan, and Persia. "Nicolson," according to his biographer, "adopted the methods of a humane and highly skilled dentist dealing with three painful teeth. He would work for a bit on Afghanistan, proceeding delicately but firmly; at the first wince of pain, he would close the cavity with anodynes, cotton wool and gutta percha" and then go on to Tibet at the next sitting. Finally winning Izvolsky's full confidence, he brought "his three tasks to a simultaneous state of readiness without at any moment having jabbed the nerve."[5]

By mid-summer of 1906, however, Nicolson's diplomatic expertise appeared to be irrelevant. Through no fault of his own, several minor incidents marred Anglo-Russian harmony. An article in the *Times* offended the tsar, and the dissolution of the First Duma aroused indignation in England, climaxed by the prime minister's well-publicized remark, "The Duma is dead, long live the Duma!" The discouraged ambassador noted in his diary that Izvolsky's "former eagerness has been replaced by silence and apparent indifference. The Emperor is wounded. Two months ago there was every hope, and now very little."[6] The talks were all but suspended for a time, and in October Izvolsky journeyed to Paris and Berlin to gauge the diplomatic climate. Reassured that Germany would not take offense at an Anglo-Russian understanding, he returned to the confidential discussions in a more relaxed mood. He "keeps his eye constantly fixed on the Berlin thermometer," Nicolson commented, "and will carefully note any change of temperature."[7]

Tibet proved the least troublesome of the three areas of imperial rivalry. Traditionally, China held a vague suzerainty over the isolated and nearly inaccessible country, but by 1904 the British had established a virtual protectorate without admitting that they had done so. The tsar offered no serious objection to Britain's predominance in Tibet, though Izvolsky raised the argument that Russia had a "spiritual" interest because of its Buddhist subjects who regarded the Dalai Lama as their religious leader. Nicolson and his superiors conceded the point, and the final version of the agreement embodied a number of other compromises while retaining the essentials: that both parties would respect Tibet's territorial integrity, refrain from interference in its internal administration, and acknowledge Britain's "special interest" in regulating its external affairs. In short, neither power looked upon the region as one of vital strategic importance, but insofar as Tibet might become a pawn in international politics it was clearly assigned to the British sphere.

Afghanistan was a different matter, although, like Tibet, its location and mountainous terrain seemed to guarantee its immunity from great-power disputes. Nevertheless, it guarded the back door to India and thus remained a source of apprehension to Great Britain, perennially alert to Russian machinations. Nicolson reminded Izvolsky that in the recent past Russia had given assurances that Afghanistan lay outside its sphere of influence. Neither the tsar nor Izvolsky contemplated altering the status quo, yet there were irritating delays, and the Russian draft was not forthcoming until early May of 1907. The British counter-proposals revised the whole document, and a fresh beginning had to be made as far as the wording of the text. By August, Izvolsky had gained the tsar's approval provided a ministerial council gave its unanimous consent. At the crucial meeting strong opposition developed, and minor concessions had to be made by the British before the ministers would accept the new formulation. Russia endorsed Britain's ascendancy in Afghanistan, including a proviso that its political relations would be conducted through London. Other articles granted freedom of commercial opportunity and incorporated a guarantee—not without a convenient loophole—that

Britain would not interfere with Afghanistan's internal administration or attempt to annex or occupy its territory.[8]

Persia presented the most formidable obstacle to Anglo-Russian reconciliation. Animosity over the shah's kingdom had been sharp and persistent for much of the nineteenth century.[9] By 1900 the British had realistically admitted that Russia dominated northern Persia and was hardly less influential in the country as a whole. That position of strength, considerably weakened since then by war and revolution and by Germany's pretentions in the Near East, allowed Nicolson appropriate bargaining leverage. Izvolsky accepted the idea of spheres of influence with alacrity but balked at the specific British proposal. Not until February 1907, after he had overcome objections from the "military party," did he consent to discuss the geographical details of a partition. A British attempt to claim the Persian Gulf as a "special interest" offended Izvolsky, but a separate declaration to that effect appended to the main body of the text satisfied both governments.[10] The two powers promised to "respect the integrity and independence of Persia," and if the document studiously avoided the ugly phrase "spheres of influence," it did spell out the territorial settlement with some precision. Russia was allotted northern Persia, including the capital, Teheran; Britain received a smaller portion in the southeast to guard the gateway to India and Afghanistan; and a large neutral zone encompassed desert terrain and nearly all of the Persian Gulf coast.

Final negotiations were interrupted in late July 1907 when Izvolsky accompanied the tsar to a meeting with the kaiser off the Baltic coast at Swinemünde. The two monarchs had not met since Björkö, and the legacy of resentment from that occasion had not entirely dissipated. Nicholas, for his part, allegedly "felt anxiety all the time as to what might be unexpectedly sprung upon him."[11] He and his foreign minister informed William of the impending arrangements with England, and the kaiser professed to find it unobjectionable. Encouraged anew by the German reaction, Izvolsky resumed his talks with Nicolson, and the two diplomats signed the convention on August 18/31, 1907.[12] The terms, though "secret," could not be long concealed. Within three weeks the press had access to the main points, and Izvolsky feared "an avalanche of criticism" from military quarters and from "reactionaries." He was agreeably surprised when it failed to materialize in any sizable volume. Liberals, among whom Izvolsky included himself, were especially inclined to approve, if only because a closer relationship with England and France seemed likely to improve the climate for Russia's parliamentary development.

Russia also sought to improve its relations with Japan. Izvolsky, in talks with the Japanese minister to St. Petersburg, Baron Motono Ichiro, settled minor problems involving commerce, navigation, and fisheries. An agreement to arrange spheres of influence in East Asia with greater precision than in the Treaty of Portsmouth proved more elusive. France eventually played a major role as intermediary, and on July 17/30, 1907, Russia and Japan signed two conventions, one public and the other secret. The latter incorporated the core of the pact: Outer Mongolia was assigned to Russia, Korea to Japan, and Manchuria was divided between the two, the boundaries between north and south carefully defined. Later treaties, again largely at China's expense, solidified the entente between St. Petersburg and Tokyo; Japan boldly annexed Korea outright in 1910.[13]

The year 1907 encompassed still another facet of tsarist diplomacy, although it was quite unremarkable compared to the successful negotiations with Britain and Japan. The long-delayed second Hague Conference met during the summer and finally completed its business in October. Unlike the preparations for the 1899 affair, Nicholas II assumed only a ceremonial role in the preparations for 1907. President Roosevelt had taken the initiative as early as 1905 but graciously deferred to the Russian emperor. Privately he observed that Russia had been "really responsible for the devastating war which has occurred since the last Hague Conference" and noted the "grim irony" that Nicholas "should now take the lead in a proposition looking toward world peace."[14] Ironically or not, the tsar's government set the agenda and circularized the powers. A provision for arms limitation was conspicuously absent, a deliberate omission in view of Russia's presumed need to restore its military and naval strength. Izvolsky remained a cynical observer in St. Petersburg, recalling that he had termed the disarmament issue at the first conference an idea of "Socialists, Jews, and hysterical old maids" and had not since changed his mind. He expressed his concern that the new conference would be "one of discord," not "one of peace," and regretted that Lamzdorf had not yielded to Roosevelt's desire to serve as host.[15]

The Russian ambassador to France, Aleksandr Nelidov, was chosen to preside at the conference. The proceedings became extraordinarily complicated because most of the practical work was accomplished by an elaborate array of commissions, subcommissions, and special committees. Banquets, festivities, and excursions provided a lavish social life that threatened to overwhelm the minutiae of daily business. In addition to the delegates, numerous lobbyists gathered—pacifists, radicals, patriots, and others with political axes to grind—hoping to air their views. Because of the surprise attack on Port Arthur in 1904, Russia, with French support, pursued the issue of prohibiting warfare without a formal declaration. A suitable formula was accepted despite some equivocation and the embarrassing comment of a Chinese delegate that undeclared war had often been waged against his country under the guise of an "expedition." The prolonged labor of the delegates was not wholly in vain, for there were useful agreements, chiefly on the rules of war and arbitration procedure. Optimism prevailed, backed by an appropriate resolution, that a third conference would be held in the future. Yet the verdict of the *Times* of London that the conference had been a "fiasco" and a "sham" was difficult to refute. The important issues of war and peace had of necessity been virtually ignored, and the future carnage of 1914–1918 offered irrefutable proof that the attempts at pacification made at The Hague in 1899 and 1907, while sincerely intended, were feeble and only marginally relevant to the realities of global politics.

The Anglo-Russian convention achieved a rapprochement, not an entente. But within another year events both planned and unforeseen transformed "a negative arrangement applicable only to Asia into a positive understanding applicable mainly to Europe."[16] King Edward's visit to Russia, though it could hardly qualify as impromptu, forged a significant link in the chain of friendship. When a meeting between the two sovereigns had proved untimely in 1906, the British suggested that a naval squadron come instead. Nicholas promptly squashed the idea in a message to the king: "To have to receive foreign guests when one's country is in a state of acute unrest is more than painful and inappropriate. You know how happy I should have been to receive the English fleet in normal times, but now I can only beg of you to postpone the squadron visit till another year."[17]

The successful accord of 1907 revived the project of a royal visit, and Nicholas, now less concerned with the stability of his throne, gladly accepted the role of gracious host. All shades of Russian opinion welcomed the king's gesture of good will. British Leftists, however, were upset, and Ramsay MacDonald of the Labour Party objected to the head of a democratic state "hobnobbing with a bloodstained creature" such as the tsar. In late May of 1908 the two rulers met at Revel on the Baltic Sea. Nicholas, in a formal greeting, spoke of the recent agreements, which despite their limited scope could not but "help to spread among our two countries feelings of mutual good will and confidence." The king conferred with Izvolsky and Stolypin ("a grave, splendid-looking man with a long beard") while confining his conversation with Nicholas to family affairs. He pleased his royal cousin by appointing him an admiral in the British navy (technically an unconstitutional act), and Nicholas returned the compliment by conferring the same honor on the king on behalf "of our young and growing navy."[18] The scene was an ironic commentary on the vagaries of international relations, for the two fleets had verged on hostilities less than four years before.

The success of the Revel meeting lent encouragement to Izvolsky's expectation of British support should Russia have the opportunity to raise the Straits question. Always alert to the possibility of a diplomatic breakthrough, he perceived that a bargain might be struck with Austria-Hungary. Under its new foreign minister, Baron Alois Aehrenthal, the Dual Monarchy had demonstrated growing dissatisfaction with the status quo in the Balkans. It considered the disposition of Bosnia and Herzegovina basic to any solution to its internal problem of Slavic nationalism and of rivalry with Serbia. Since 1878 these two Turkish provinces had been administered by Austria, a frustrating ambiguity that Aehrenthal was determined to end by annexation.

The stage was thus set for a mutually agreeable exchange—or "friendly reciprocity," as Izvolsky put it in a memorandum to Vienna on June 19. Aehrenthal responded favorably, and Izvolsky, disregarding the tsar's admonition to take no initiative about a meeting, accepted an invitation to confer with him at the castle of Buchlau in Moravia. On September 3/16, 1908, the two foreign ministers were closeted for approximately six hours in what became in retrospect one of the most notorious and controversial meetings in the annals of diplomacy. No record of the conversations was kept, not even a document summarizing the decisions that had been reached. Izvolsky, according to his version, received assurances that the major agreement—Bosnia and Herzegovina in exchange for Russian access to the Straits—would be subject to the tsar's approval and that final determination would be made at a conference of the European powers.

Confident that he had achieved a diplomatic feat comparable to his successes of the previous year, Izvolsky enjoyed a brief vacation near Munich and then set out for Italy, France, and England to gain the assent of their governments for his Balkan project. A rude shock awaited him in Paris. A message from Aehrenthal informed him that the annexation was imminent, and in fact it occurred only two days later on September 23/October 6. Although the enormity of the foreign minister's blunder was not yet apparent to the Russian public, Austria's behavior called forth a groundswell of popular indignation. Stolypin's reaction upon learning of the Buchlau agreement was one of suppressed anger, and he protested to the tsar, threatening to resign. Nicholas, who had been kept reasonably well informed of Izvolsky's policy, feigned ignorance and roundly condemned the annexation. Privately he referred to Aehrenthal's conduct as "positively ignominious" and to the man himself as a "scoundrel" who had made Izvolsky his "dupe." He was chagrined to learn from the foreign ministry archives that on three previous occasions prior to his reign Russia had promised not to oppose the seizure. "You will understand," he wrote his mother, "what an unpleasant surprise this is and what an embarrassing position we are in."[19]

Izvolsky gained sympathy in Paris and London but only token satisfaction regarding a European conference. As to a revision of the Straits convention, he received no tangible support. In Berlin he was politely told that Germany would stand by its ally even though the kaiser, who ostentatiously avoided politics in his conversation with Izvolsky, professed to be vastly annoyed by Austria's action and regretted Aehrenthal's "fearful stupidity."[20] He returned to St. Petersburg on October 16 thoroughly depressed, his reputation badly tarnished. He talked of resignation but retained the tsar's confidence—or at least his indulgence. Nicholas wrote Emperor Franz

Joseph that the Austrian move had made a "painful impression" and that he deeply deplored the "unilateral act" in violation of an international treaty. Stolypin's displeasure with Izvolsky had scarcely diminished, and at the next session of the Council of Ministers he asked the errant diplomat to explain the Buchlau episode. Izvolsky refused, citing the tsar's explicit instructions against discussing foreign policy within the Council. "Stolypin reddened but said nothing."[21] But the foreign minister had merely delayed the inevitable, for on October 25 he was obliged to defend himself at a formal meeting of his colleagues, who found his conduct negligent at best. The session represented a modest victory for Stolypin's conception of a unified cabinet whose members would be responsible to their chairman as well as to the tsar. By declining to intervene in the matter Nicholas appears to have given his tacit consent to the principle, at any rate in the realm of foreign policy.

Austria and Germany, recognizing Russia's military weakness, were content to let the Bosnian crisis blow over. Yet the threat of war lingered, sustained by Serbia's sense of outrage and the refusal of Nicholas and his government to recognize the annexation or to abandon the cause of Slavic nationalism. Turkey was also among the aggrieved powers but accepted a handsome indemnity from Austria for the loss of the two provinces. Nicholas denounced Aehrenthal in another letter to Franz Joseph on December 17. He went on to express his "deep regret" at having to write in such a vein and his "acute sense of apprehension" about the future. Referring to military measures that threatened Austria's southern neighbors, he warned that if a conflict arose it would result in a "great effervescence, not only in the Balkan peninsula, but also in Russia, and you will understand the particularly difficult situation in which I should find myself. God guard us against such an eventuality which would end all possibility of good relations between Russia and Austria-Hungary and might lead Europe into a general war."[22] Nicholas' well-chosen words clearly anticipated the greater crisis of 1914.

Russia desired peace, and in December Nicholas again appealed to the kaiser, in the name of "an old friendship," to intercede with Vienna for an appropriate settlement. William replied somewhat testily that neither the agreement with England nor the meeting at Revel "produced any uneasiness or disappointment" but that in the past two years Russia had backed away from Germany, seemingly to form an entente with France and England.[23] Serbia continued to demand territorial compensation, and military posturing in both Vienna and Belgrade kept tensions high. Under pressure from France and Britain, Izvolsky's resolve to support Serbia wavered. A special "war council" held at Tsarskoe Selo on March 1, 1909, concluding that Russia remained unprepared to contest the issue by force of arms, underscored his decision. The tsar telegraphed the kaiser on March 9 seeking anew his "powerful help" in persuading Aehrenthal to moderate his "adventurous policy." "I am as strongly convinced as you," he declared, "that Russia and Germany must be as closely united as possible and form a strong bond for the maintenance of peace and monarchical institutions. God help us both to bring the present crisis to a rapid and peaceful solution."[24]

The plea came too late to alter Berlin's determination, in the guise of mediation, to wring a forthright response from Izvolsky. On March 8/21 Bülow instructed the German ambassador in St. Petersburg to request Russia's acceptance or rejection of the Bosnian annexation: "Your Excellency will make clear to Mr. Izvolsky that we expect an unequivocal answer—yes or no. Any evasive, conditional, or ambiguous reply would have to be regarded by us as a refusal. In that event we shall withdraw and allow events to take their course. The responsibility for all that follows will rest exclusively with Mr. Izvolsky." The language, though peremptory, fell short of an ultimatum since no threat of force was specifically mentioned. A unanimous cabinet decision, approved by the tsar, accepted the German terms in the belief that Russia was preventing, at the very least, an Austro-Serbian war. Privately Nicholas concluded that there had been "nothing for it but to swallow one's pride, give in and agree." He grumbled about the "patriots" who were "prepared to sacrifice Serbia, whom we could not help at all in the case of an Austrian attack." But the bitter aftertaste of national dishonor could not be ignored, and he complained that the "form and the method of Germany's action—I mean towards us—has simply been brutal and we won't forget it. I think they were again trying to separate us from France and England—but once again they have undoubtedly failed. Such methods tend to bring about the opposite result."[25]

Nicholas expressed himself with clarity and prescience. But judged by immediate results, the Central Powers had achieved a diplomatic triumph. More than one Russian newspaper referred to a "diplomatic Tsushima." Yet in the long run, as future events were to demonstrate, Aehrenthal and Bülow had badly miscalculated. Serbia, deprived of its "legitimate" route of expansion, became a hotbed of subversion and agitation in which Austria emerged as the evil oppressor of its South Slav population. Germany, too, by loyally supporting its ally, proved overly addicted to "blank check" diplomacy. Russia, if not wholly traumatized by the episode, suffered a deep sense of humiliation. The spirit of revenge festered in military and bureaucratic circles, though Nicholas appeared to be less vindictive than many in his entourage. Izvolsky considered his usefulness at an end but received a second dispensation from the tsar, who stubbornly clung to his discredited foreign minister to avoid giving additional satisfaction to Russia's adversary. Izvolsky, profoundly embittered, devoted the remainder of his diplomatic career to vindicating himself and his country's honor by any means that would discredit the Triple Alliance and nourish the Triple Entente.

Europe's return to something approaching great-power normality following the crisis atmosphere of early 1909 allowed Nicholas to proceed with a series of foreign visits. He met the kaiser in June off the Finnish coast while cruising in his largest yacht, the elegant *Shtandart*. In July he called at the French port of Cherbourg to meet President Armand Fallières and witness a naval review. For security reasons—rumors of assassination plots abounded—the imperial family avoided Paris. London was likewise off limits, and arrangements were made for Nicholas to return King Edward's Revel visit at Cowes on the Isle of Wight. Three British warships escorted *Shtandart* from Cherbourg, and Nicholas reviewed the powerful British fleet and renewed his friendship with the king. Izvolsky, who accompanied the official party, had opportunities to discuss diplomatic business, and "after his invariable exordium of abuse of Aehrenthal" expressed his concern that Austria's success with Serbia might lead to a similar domination of Bulgaria. Nicholas appeared "very cheerful and pleasant," Alexandra "nervous and sad." The meeting was considered eminently successful and further evidence of a growing Anglo-Russian friendship.[26]

Nicholas' visit to King Victor Emmanuel III of Italy in October was the most politically rewarding of his journeys abroad in 1909. The imperial party avoided crossing Austrian territory, an ostentatious display of resentment that received wide publicity. The two monarchs met at the castle of Racconigi near Turin, and Izvolsky presented the Italian foreign minister, Tommaso Tittoni, with a draft proposal concerning the Near East. After the details had been ironed out, an agreement was reached on October 11/24 in the form of letters exchanged between the two ministers that were to be kept secret except for the tsar and king. The two powers ritualistically agreed to preserve the status quo in the Balkans; to support the principle of nationality and to consult with each other in case of foreign interference among the Balkan states; and to "view with good will" each other's special interests—Italy in Libya and Russia in the Straits. In substance, the agreement involved an anti-Austrian maneuver on Izvolsky's part, a recognition of Russia's renewed Balkan ambitions, and an attempt to lure Italy from the Triple Alliance.[27]

In part through German and Italian mediation, efforts were made to repair the breach between Russia and Austria early in 1910. Normal relations were restored in March, according to declarations made in St. Petersburg and Vienna, but Izvolsky, always seeking revenge against Aehrenthal, took it upon himself to send copies of the negotiation documents to the other European capitals. The "rapprochement" thus failed to generate any degree of cordiality. By this time Izvolsky's residue of good will with the tsar had nearly dissipated. During the summer friction arose because Izvolsky disagreed with Stolypin's nationalist policy toward Finland; he submitted hs resignation, which was formally accepted in September.

The illness and subsequent death of Aleksandr Nelidov allowed Izvolsky to exit gracefully by taking over the Parisian embassy, and he was permitted (with Stolypin's benevolent acquiescence) to designate his successor at the foreign ministry. The choice fell upon Sergei Sazonov,[28] a diplomat of modest experience and ability whom Izvolsky had carefully groomed during the past year as assistant foreign minister. He was also Stolypin's brother-in-law; thus, as contemporaries saw it, the appointment reeked of nepotism. Since both accepted the mentor-disciple relationship, no major policy change was anticipated. They were, however, profoundly different in character and temperament. A colleague described Sazonov as having almost none of his predecessor's faults, "but, alas, almost none of his virtues. Simple, modest, affable, upright, absolutely disinterested, with a highly developed moral sense and deeply religious, very Orthodox and very Russian . . . he would have made an excellent candidate for the post of procurator general of the Holy Synod or even a leading prelate of the Russian church. It was not for nothing that a very persistent rumor credited him in his youth with the intention of becoming a monk."[29] His rectitude and lack of vanity, a welcome contrast to Izvolsky's boundless ego, remained unrewarded in the higher councils of government. If he was not quite the "weak and uninfluential man in his own country" that Nicolson perceived,[30] he nevertheless dutifully accepted the sovereign's will and, briefly as it turned out, the leadership of Stolypin.

Nicholas sensed that the time had come because of Izvolsky's departure to refurbish the tarnished relations between St. Petersburg and Berlin. During the late summer of 1910 he and his family enjoyed some ten weeks' vacation at Friedberg Castle in Hesse, Alexandra's native land. The opportunity for a meeting with the kaiser seemed propitious, and Nicholas hinted as much through the good offices of the local Prussian envoy. William responded to the indirect invitation with a sour marginal comment: "Neither the tone nor the desire are of any use now—after the Triple Entente and six new Russian army corps."[31] Nicholas persisted in his efforts and called Sazonov to Berlin for talks with the new German chancellor, Theobald von Bethmann-Hallweg. When these preliminary negotiations showed promise, the emperors met at Potsdam on October 22–23.

The result restored some measure of harmony between the two countries. Russia promised not to support any anti-German policy on Britain's part, and Germany made a similar pledge to discourage possible Austrian expansion in the Balkans. Both powers agreed to work for peace among the Balkan states and indicated (if with less precision) their desire to cooperate on problems concerning Turkey and Persia. Since no written record of the discussions was made, the Germans requested that a formal document be drawn up and submitted a draft convention. Sazonov, with the tsar's authority, maintained that the verbal agreements of the two monarchs were sufficient. In any case, he objected because the Russian commitment toward

England was far-reaching, while Germany's obligation was confined to the Balkans. Nor did he wish to arouse British suspicions that his government had acted in bad faith. The Russian attitude dampened the prospects for a more enduring détente, but negotiations continued for a written understanding on Persian "railway politics," a document that was duly signed in the summer of 1911. As Sazonov had foreseen, reports of the alleged "Potsdam agreement" disturbed London and Paris, casting a shadow over the efficacy of the Triple Entente.[32]

The Agadir crisis of 1911 and its resolution offered assurance, feeble though it was, that Russia remained faithful to its Western partners. A French protectorate over turbulent Morocco seemed a foregone conclusion when Germany intervened with an unexpected display of gunboat diplomacy: the warship *Panther* anchored at the port of Agadir on June 19/July 1 under the pretext of protecting German citizens. Berlin in reality sought bargaining leverage to gain territorial concessions from France, preferably in the Congo. Great Britain gave the French strong support, while Russia maintained a lukewarm attitude not unlike the Anglo-French response during the Bosnian crisis. Izvolsky, with the tsar's permission, attempted to moderate the bellicose mood in official and semi-official Parisian circles, intimating that his country would not countenance a colonial war and pointing out that its military preparations were incomplete. A compromise was found—the subjugation of Morocco by France in return for a small but strategic portion of the French Congo—but the affair marked a dangerous trend in international relations. Chauvinist sentiment, fanned in great part by an irresponsible press, had been aroused to such a pitch that in future confrontations public opinion seemed likely to impede if not overwhelm diplomatic solutions.

Italy's attack on the Turkish province of Tripoli in the fall of 1911 promptly afforded a case study in the "new nationalism." Having conceded Libya—that is, Tripoli and Cyrenaica—to Italy at Racconigi, Russia directed its diplomacy less toward mediation than to expanding its own opportunities in Turkey and the Balkans. The perennial Straits question received new emphasis, with the tsar's blessing. Nikolai Charykov, the ambassador at Constantinople, approached the Turks with ambitious proposals that might lead to a rapprochement. Inflexible, opinionated, and with a penchant for immersing himself in diplomatic trivia, he was lampooned by a colleague as one who "loves to administer enemas to flies."[33] The "Charykov kite" never got off the ground because the Porte (as the Ottoman government was known) resorted to delaying tactics, and London and Paris demonstrated a distinct lack of enthusiasm. Sazonov, who had been on an extended sick leave, returned to duty in November and formally withdrew the project.[34] To emphasize the government's repudiation of such "personal" diplomacy, the luckless envoy was recalled several months later.

As the war over Libya dragged on, Turkey's Balkan domain became increasingly vulnerable to internal disruption and external attack. Russia could not fail to take heed as the traditional "big brother" of the Balkan Slavs. Yet neither the tsar nor his foreign minister had any intention of becoming embroiled in a military conflict. Nicholas had impressed that upon Anatoly Neklyudov, his minister to Bulgaria, before the latter departed for his post in Sofia in 1911: "Do not for one instant lose sight of the fact that we cannot go to war. . . . I shall do all in my power to preserve for my people the benefits of peace. But at this moment, of all moments, everything which might lead to war must be avoided. It would be out of the question for us to face a war for five or six years, in fact till 1917."[35] Neklyudov did not ignore this stern admonition, but he and his counterpart in Serbia, Nikolai Hartwig, pursued a course that scarcely improved the prospects for peace in the Balkans.

Sazonov, while fully aware of the difficulties that beset the Ottoman government, failed to monitor the activities of his two energetic ministers with the proper degree of vigilance. He was, however, kept informed of the negotiations between Serbia and Bulgaria for an alliance, ostensibly of a defensive nature, and greeted the prospect with delight: "Well, but this is perfect! If only it could come off! Bulgaria closely allied to Serbia in the political and economic sphere; five hundred thousand bayonets to guard the Balkans—but this would bar the road for ever to German penetration, Austrian invasion!"[36] The alliance became a reality in late February of 1912, followed by a military convention. A similar pact between Bulgaria and Greece was signed later in the year, and Montenegro also joined the developing coalition, known as the Balkan League, that prepared for war with Turkey. Russia looked on with nervous benevolence, reluctant to believe that its authority might be flagrantly disregarded. Not only Sazonov, who had foreseen in some measure the "dangerous proclivities" in Sofia and Belgrade, but also Kokovtsov and the sovereign himself viewed the Balkan powder keg with undue complacency. Of the three, Nicholas was apparently the most skeptical about Russia's ability to hold its Balkan disciples in check. "We shall do all we can to preserve peace," he told the French ambassador in June 1912, "but it will probably be a waste of breath. For the Balkan populations the chance will be too tempting."[37]

During the late summer of 1912, as the situation worsened, the great powers finally bestirred themselves. Austria took the lead, suggesting a program of internal reform in Turkey and delivering a sharp reprimand to the Balkan governments. The formula lacked precision and expired for lack of international support. Russia proved disinclined to assume the initiative, but Sazonov did discuss the problem in conjunction with French Premier Raymond Poincaré's visit to St. Petersburg in August. Presented for the first time with the full text of the Serbo-Bulgarian treaty, Poincaré immediately perceived its bellicose intention ("But it's an agreement for war!") and expressed indignation that his ally had withheld such a provocative document. He explained to Sazonov that French opinion would not sustain a war to salvage Russia's Balkan aims unless Germany intervened. Returning to Paris, he proposed that Russia and Britain agree on a plan to restrain the Balkan states and present it to Germany and Austria. The necessary arrangements, though acceptable to the five powers, took time, and when a joint Russo-Austrian warning arrived in the Balkan capitals on September 25/October 8 it was already too late. On the same day Montenegro declared war on Turkey, and Bulgaria, Greece, and Serbia soon followed. Chauvinist fervor had triumphed over realpolitik.

The Balkan allies quickly mounted an offensive and with astonishing ease all but drove the Turks from Europe. The powers sought to localize the conflict. The Russian government—that is, the tsar and Sazonov—heartily concurred. But the foreign minister's task was complicated by newspaper editorials and other manifestations of public sentiment demonstrating passionate support for the Balkan Slavs. Demands for his resignation were openly voiced, and in an effort, at least in part, to appease his critics, he concluded that it had become "necessary to find new formulas corresponding to the new situation."[38] Nicholas wrote his mother from Spala on October 21, "I am watching the war between the Christians and the Turks very carefully, and I rejoice at their brilliant successes against the common enemy." He foresaw difficulty in the peacemaking process because of the "egotistical schemes of the great powers," and he singled out England for backing Greece's territorial demands at Turkish expense. His own country, he implied, had no imperial ambitions. "In Russia, thank goodness, no decent person wants a war for the sake of the Slavs"; only the "wretched Jewish newspapers," with Guchkov at their head, "write that public opinion in Russia is stirred—it is a lie and a calumny."[39]

Nicholas appears to have been singularly ill informed as to the state of Russian opinion. But his conviction that zealotry on behalf of the Slavs was somehow a cause sponsored by Jews and "liberals" of the Guchkov stripe probably reinforced his preference for a pacific solution to the war. His desire for peace extended only reluctantly, however, to curbing his "patriotic" war minister, Sukhomlinov, who called for mobilization on the Austrian frontier. The order was rescinded at the eleventh hour when Nicholas summoned a special conference at Tsarskoe Selo on November 10 which unanimously agreed that a military disposition of such magnitude was too risky to pursue. Kokovtsov made a particularly impassioned plea, and Nicholas admitted that Russia's armed forces were unprepared for hostilities. He conceded that his minister was "perfectly correct in terming the very thought of a war as folly," but he went on to say that the problem was "a simple measure of precaution, consisting of . . . moving up the troops now removed too far in the rear somewhat closer [to Austria]." Kokovtsov had to remind him that Germany's attitude could not be considered a separate issue, nor could Russia ignore its obligation to France for consultation on a matter as serious as mobilization. Nicholas accepted the alternate suggestion that the term of military service be extended by six months and expressed his gratitude to Kokovtsov despite the latter's "violence" and "sharp thrusts" at the war minister. Sazonov also denounced Sukhomlinov, but in private: "Don't you understand even yet where you very nearly pushed Russia? Are you not ashamed to make such a game of the fate of the tsar and your country?"[40]

Seeking to avert a crisis with Austria, Sazonov withdrew his support for the Serbian demand that it be granted a port on the Adriatic Sea. Nicholas received the Austrian ambassador in an endeavor to reassure him on this point, yet nationalist and anti-Serb feeling gripped Vienna. If war came, the Serbs, bereft of Russian assistance, had little choice other than to capitulate. Hoping to avoid public humiliation, they chose to await the decision of the great powers: a "European" solution was obviously more honorable than submitting to an Austrian ultimatum.

The defeated Turks had requested an armistice and outside mediation early in November 1912. A month later an ambassadorial conference of the major powers in London began the arduous task of achieving a peace settlement. Representatives of the belligerents also met in London in separate negotiations. In January 1913 a faction of the Young Turk movement seized power in Constantinople, providing an opportunity for the Balkan allies to denounce the truce and resume the offensive. As Bulgarian troops with Serbian help laid siege to the Turkish fortress of Adrianople, Emperor Franz Joseph sent a personal emissary to the tsar in an attempt to reduce Russo-Austrian tension. The two rulers exchanged friendly letters, but no immediate results were evident. In March, when the fall of Adrianople prompted pro-Slav demonstrations in the streets of the capital, Rodzyanko, an unabashed imperialist, pleaded with Nicholas to intervene: "Your Majesty, there is still time. We must take advantage of the popular enthusiasm. The Straits must become ours. A war will be joyfully welcomed, and will raise the Government's prestige." "The Emperor," Rodzyanko recorded, "maintained a stony silence."[41]

Nicholas, to his credit, held firm against the "war party." He expressed his approval of Sazonov's policy "so unambiguously that it at once silenced the hostile chorus of my opponents and of the lovers of intrigue and scandal among the ranks of our self-styled patriots."[42] His sovereign's backing allowed Sazonov the leeway to restrain Serbian ambitions while the ambassadorial conference resumed the search for peace. In May 1913 the Treaty of London ended hostilities. Except for a buffer zone adjacent to Constantinople, the Turks were shorn of their European possessions. Among their losses was Albania, a newly created state whose size and political complexion awaited the disposition of the powers.

A durable peace in the Balkans proved illusory. Sazonov failed to develop a firm and consistent policy toward Russia's Slavic "clients," thus contributing to the belligerent mood of the allies as they quarreled over territorial spoils attending the Turkish defeat. He did, however, persuade the tsar to intercede with the Serbian and Bulgarian monarchs in a personal appeal for peace. "If they refuse to listen to me," Nicholas declared, "the instigators of the trouble will bear the punishment. I shall have done my duty and my conscience will be at rest."[43] Identical telegrams, drafted by Sazonov, were sent to Belgrade and Sofia enlisting royal support against "a criminal war" that would betray the cause of "Slavdom." The replies, though ostensibly favorable to Russian mediation, were not without equivocation. On the strength of this "success" Sazonov invited the Balkan prime ministers to attend a conference in St. Petersburg. On June 17/30, 1913, before the Russian initiative could be realized, Bulgaria attacked Serbian and Greek forces in Macedonia, and a fresh round of hostilities witnessed a common front against the aggressor. Romania joined Serbia and Greece, while Turkey seized the opportunity to regain lost territory. Once more Russia's prestige suffered through its inability to manage—still less to dictate—a peace settlement. The tsar labeled the war an "abomination" in which "Bulgaria's greed has brought God's chastisement on her." "We warned them many times," he scolded, but they "refused to listen, and have now got themselves into a dreadful mess."[44]

Bulgaria's effrontery was swiftly punished. On July 28/August 10 Sofia accepted the severe terms of the Treaty of Bucharest. The tsar had stoutly resisted his own "patriots" and preserved his country's neutrality, yet Russia's position in the Balkans, seemingly so dominant in 1912, had fallen into disarray. Serbia and Montenegro remained loyal, for they lacked an alternative. But an alienated Bulgaria and an ungrateful Romania sought diplomatic ties with Vienna, while Greece pursued its own course.

If, as Sazonov put it, the "Peace of Bucharest was but a plaster upon the unhealed Balkan wounds," at least a general European war had been averted. The powers were gratified that another crisis had safely passed, although the arms race continued unabated and statesmen, diplomats, and soldiers contemplated with growing uneasiness the prospect of war. Paradoxically, the fatalistic Russian emperor, always prepared to accept God's will, remained more optimistic than the German emperor. In May 1913 the two rulers met for what proved the last time when Nicholas attended the wedding of the kaiser's daughter in Berlin. Taking advantage of the convivial atmosphere, Nicholas expressed his desire to improve the state of Russo-German relations. He offered to retreat on the Straits question, allowing Turkey to remain the "doorkeeper," if William would curb Austrian ambitions in the Balkans. William's lack of enthusiasm for this proposal was conditioned by his private view that war with Russia had become inevitable: "The fight between Slavs and Germans is no longer avoidable. It is bound to come. When? We shall soon see."[45]

During the festivities in Berlin, William mentioned to his guest that at

Turkey's request he had sanctioned a military mission to Constantinople under General Otto Liman von Sanders. Nicholas duly relayed the information to Sazonov upon his return to Russia. The news made no particular impression on the foreign minister, for German officers had served in Turkey for many years as military advisers. But in October 1913, relying upon a report of the Russian ambassador in Constantinople, he grew alarmed at the scope and authority of the mission, which placed the general in command of Turkish troops in the capital. He had a "stormy" interview with the German ambassador and resolved that Russia should take a firm stand against the military collaboration of the two countries. To yield, he told the tsar in December, "would be equivalent to a political defeat and might have altogether disastrous consequences."[46] He recognized Russia's weakness, however, and did not relish the prospect of war. Germany found a compromise solution at the close of the year when Liman von Sanders was promoted to field marshal and appointed inspector-general of the Turkish army. His removal from a command post in Constantinople mollified Sazonov, yet the affair embittered Russo-German relations and led to rancorous press exchanges in February–March 1914.

Wary and apprehensive, the European powers nevertheless avoided a fresh crisis during the winter and spring of 1914. Rumors flourished in Germany of a "war party" that supposedly lurked at the tsar's court. No such faction existed, though the dowager empress and the tsar's cousin, Grand Duke Nikolai Nikolayevich, had never concealed their anti-German views. Nicholas himself, if not precisely hostile toward Germany and Austria, had become more critical of their conduct and less inclined to back away from a confrontation. At the same time his old antipathy toward England had been replaced by an amiability that might have led to closer diplomatic ties had the British demonstrated a serious interest in an Anglo-Russian naval accord. But his—and Sazonov's—objective of converting the Triple Entente into a triple alliance remained only a fanciful vision.

During the spring of 1914 Nicholas and his family spent some two months at Livadia. The welfare of the Tsarevich Alexis, whose health seemed to improve in the more beneficent climate of the Black Sea, was a principal reason for the prolonged sojourn so far from the capital. Yet the business of government, though inconvenienced by the tsar's absence, was not seriously impaired. Ministers were summoned if necessary, and Sazonov was present in May when a Turkish mission, dispatched by the sultan as a token of respect, reached the Crimea. The chief emissaries, Minister of the Interior Talaat Bey and General Izzet Pasha, conveyed their greetings at a formal reception. Nicholas allowed himself an allusion to the Liman von Sanders affair amid the platitudes of the occasion. Sazonov, who held separate talks with the two envoys, was far more blunt. He warned that Turkey's national interest had become endangered and that "a position bordering on vassalage to Germany" was entirely possible.[47] Whether moved or not by this lurid depiction of the German menace, Talaat did venture on the eve of his departure to suggest to the astonished Sazonov a Russo-Turkish alliance. Perhaps launched as a trial balloon, the proposal languished amid the signs of an impending European conflict. The Germans "got an ally they had not wanted, and Turkey a war which, by her weakness and vacillations, she had helped to precipitate."[48]

On June 1 Nicholas undertook a more active diplomatic role by attempting to draw Romania from the tentacles of the Triple Alliance. At Sazonov's prompting he and his family, conveyed by the *Shtandart*, called on King Carol at the Romanian port of Constanza. There a full day of ceremonies enhanced the personal friendship of the two sovereigns, but Sazonov's project of a political marriage between the Romanian crown prince and the tsar's eldest daughter, the Grand Duchess Olga, did not prosper. The Russian foreign minister boldly crossed the border into the Hungarian province of Transylvania, a reminder of Romanian irredentism that vastly irritated opinion in Budapest and Vienna. His prediction to Nicholas that "Romania will attempt to go with the side that turns out to be the stronger and can offer her the biggest gain" proved entirely accurate.[49]

The assassination in Bosnia on June 15/28 of the Archduke Franz Ferdinand, the heir to the Austrian throne, though a shocking act of political fanaticism, did not at first appear to threaten the peace of Europe. Nicholas promptly offered his condolences to Emperor Franz Joseph, but in the absence of an immediate diplomatic crisis other matters of state claimed his attention. Among them was the impending visit of President Poincaré of France. He arrived at Kronstadt on July 7 just as a major strike in St. Petersburg erupted into full-scale rioting. The Grand Duke Nikolai Nikolayevich naively confided to Poincaré his belief that Germany had somehow fomented the violence to mar the serenity of the occasion. Nicholas accorded his guest deferential and lavish hospitality, including a diplomatic reception at the Winter Palace. The French ambassador, Maurice Paleologue, noted the enthusiastic welcome along Poincaré's route: "The police had arranged it all. At every street corner a group of poor wretches cheered loudly under the eye of a policeman."[50] Tsar and president had an opportunity to review the full range of political and diplomatic questions, among them the growing dispute between Austria and Serbia. Nicholas is said to have minimized the danger: "Notwithstanding appearances the Emperor William is too cautious to launch his country on some wild adventure, and the Emperor Francis Joseph's only wish is to die in peace."[51] Poincaré's departure on July 10 coincided with an Austrian ultimatum to Serbia containing demands that, as Belgrade complained to the Russian government, were obviously incompatible with the dignity of a sovereign nation.

Austria's bellicose attitude rested upon the conviction that the archduke's assassin had been part of a conspiracy involving Serbian officials and that Germany would again furnish the proverbial "blank check" for whatever measures were deemed necessary to punish Serbia. Later evidence, if it did not wholly confirm Austria's suspicions, lent credence to the view that the authorities in Belgrade had been criminally negligent in dealing with a nest of political terrorists known in the West as the Black Hand. Regardless of Serbian complicity, however, military aggression amounted in the best of circumstances to a dangerous gamble. Such a course assumed that Russia, having absorbed the humiliation of 1908, would again bow to the threat of superior force. The error of this calculation—the realization came so late that the conflict could not be localized—was the key to the tragedy that followed.

Sazonov, when informed of the Austrian ultimatum, recognized the danger at once: "C'est la guerre européenne." Nicholas contented himself with the more pedestrian "This is disturbing."[52] The Council of Ministers met in the afternoon of July 11 and accepted Sazonov's formula of mobilizing four military districts as a bargaining chip against Austria. The decision was confirmed the next morning when Nicholas presided over a special ministerial conference. But a technical distinction was drawn between partial mobilization and the measures known by statute as the "period preparatory to war." Unfortunately for Sazonov's diplomatic strategy, Russia's military leaders failed to explain at the outset that partial mobilization had not been foreseen in their war plans and that halfway measures might actually jeopardize the progress of general mobilization.

To Prince Alexander of Serbia's plea for help Nicholas responded on July 14 with "heart-felt good will towards the Serbian people" and declared his determination to explore every possibility that might avert "the horrors of a fresh war while upholding the dignity of Serbia." "Should we be unsuccessful in this, in spite of our most sincere desire," he concluded, "Your Highness may rest assured that Russia will in no case remain indifferent to the fate of Serbia." The message was received in Belgrade with profound gratitude just as Austria declared war on Serbia; Sazonov circularized the Russian ambassadors with the announcement that his "mediatory explanations" had been "rendered purposeless." He also emphasized in a separate telegram that Germany should be informed that Russia had no "aggressive intentions" toward it.[53]

Berlin's attitude was crucial to a peaceful resolution of the crisis. The kaiser's impulsive reaction to the assassination had been brazenly provocative: "Now or never. . . . The Serbs must be disposed of, *and* that right *soon*!"[54] His position later moderated, in language if not entirely in substance. News of the Austrian ultimatum reached him as he was cruising in Norwegian waters, and he returned to Potsdam to find the conciliatory Serbian reply encouraging. But neither he nor his officials pressured Vienna to restrain its belligerence while a negotiated settlement remained possible. William approached the tsar instead, calling upon their monarchical solidarity to punish the "outrageous crime" at Sarajevo and promising in the name of their "hearty tender friendship" to do his utmost "to induce the Austrians to deal straightly to arrive at a satisfactory understanding with you." Nicholas grasped at the straw of past fellowship and responded on July 16 with his own plea for cooperation: "An ignoble war has been declared on a weak country. The indignation in Russia, shared fully by me, is enormous. I foresee that very soon I shall be overwhelmed by the pressure brought upon me and forced to take extreme measures which will lead to war. To try to avoid such a calamity . . . I beg you in the name of our old friendship to do what you can to stop your allies from going too far."[55]

Indeed, Nicholas was already under siege by his foreign minister and the military chiefs. Officially Russia had not mobilized a single reservist, yet the "period preparatory to war" placed the nation on a state of alert, and these "secret" measures did not go unnoticed in Berlin. On the evening of the 16th Nicholas sent a second message to the kaiser asking him to explain the discrepancy between his "conciliatory and friendly" telegram and the "very different tone" of the German ambassador. He also proposed to submit the Austro-Serbian dispute to the Hague Tribunal. A little over an hour later he receive an answer to his earlier telegram. William justified Austria's conduct and suggested that Russia ought to "remain a spectator" in the conflict with Serbia. He again insisted that Germany was "continuing its exertions" to promote peace but that Russian military measures threatening to Austria "would precipitate a calamity we both wish to avoid, and jeopardize my position as mediator."[56]

Early in the morning of July 17/30 Nicholas dispatched a third telegram to the kaiser. He stated that he was sending his personal military representative to Berlin with instructions, and he defended Russia's military preparations "decided five days ago" as necessary to offset Austria's mobilization. "I hope with all my heart," he concluded, "that these measures won't in any way interfere with your part as mediator, which I greatly value. We need your strong pressure on Austria to come to an understanding with us." Again the evidence of pressure on Austria, strong or otherwise, was lacking, but Nicholas' indiscreet admission that his army had been placed in a state of readiness—to use no more compromising a term—could not have impressed William with Russia's peaceful intentions. On the strength of this personal diplomacy between the two monarchs, however, Nicholas revoked an order for general mobilization that he had made just a few hours before. Partial mobilization remained in force, affecting the four military districts closest to Austria as well as the Baltic and Black Sea fleets.

On the afternoon of July 17 Sazonov, Sukhomlinov and the chief of the general staff, General Nikolai Yanushkevich, renewed their assault on the vacillating emperor. Rodzyanko and Minister of Agriculture Krivoshein also played secondary but not insignificant roles in the campaign for full mobilization. Nicholas dreaded the prospect of a "monstrous slaughter," and Sazonov, who served in effect as spokesman for the military "lobby," saw his assignment as a "painful duty" but one that he had no right to shirk because he believed that war was inevitable and that further delay endangered national security. Nicholas was not easily convinced. Sazonov described him as pale and agitated, his expression betraying "a terrible inner struggle." "This [mobilization] would mean sending hundreds of thousands of Russian people to their death," Nicholas declared. "How can one help hesitating to take such a step?" Seemingly the specter of revolution, which, along with military weakness, had inhibited Russian diplomacy since 1905, played no part in his thinking. At last the painful decision was extracted: "You are right," he conceded. "There is nothing left us but to get ready for an attack upon us. Give then the Chief of the General Staff my order for mobilization."[57] Sazonov promptly relayed the order by telephone to Yanushkevich. At approximately the same time the kaiser sent a new message warning that his function as mediator would be "endangered if not ruined" by Russian mobilization, and placing on Nicholas the onus of "the responsibility for peace or war."

Nicholas was slow to grasp that his order had made further negotiations virtually meaningless. He doggedly continued the telegraphic duet by admitting to William on the 18th that it was "technically impossible" to stop Russia's military preparations but promising that his troops would not take "any provocative actions" as long as negotiations continued. "I put all my trust into God's mercy," he concluded in a characteristic declaration of fatalistic piety, "and hope in your successful mediation in Vienna for the welfare of our countries and for the peace of Europe." The message crossed another from William, who denied any imputation of wrongdoing: "The responsibility for the disaster which is now threatening the whole civilized world will not be laid at my door." Peace might still be maintained "if Russia will agree to stop the military measures which must threaten Germany and Austria-Hungary."[58]

Nicholas refused to back down, and with Germany's mobilization on July 19/August 1 he renewed his plea to William, asking for the "same guarantee from you as I gave you." He insisted that military measures "*do not* mean war" and offered the now-forlorn hope "that we shall continue negotiating for the benefit of our countries and universal peace dear to all our hearts." William's reply—the final item in their lengthy correspondence—demanded Russian demobilization as the "only way to avoid endless misery." Nicholas noted on the margin of the telegram: "Received after [Germany's] declaration of war."[59] According to Ambassador Paleologue's recollection, Nicholas retained a full measure of bitterness toward his royal cousin: "He was never sincere; not for a moment! In the end he was hopelessly entangled in the net of his own perfidy and lies." Furthermore, William had "dealt a terrible blow to the monarchical principle."[60]

By its premature mobilization the Russian government—in essence,

Nicholas and his foreign minister—acquired a generous share of the "war guilt" that historians have sought to apportion among the belligerent powers. France, too, because of its uncritical support of Russia, cannot be exculpated. Yet the Central Powers, if they may be excused of deliberately provoking a European war, demonstrated a relentless determination to punish Serbia by military aggression. Berlin, not Vienna, held the whip hand as the crisis escalated, and in the last analysis the German government must therefore be charged with the major responsibility for the outbreak of war in 1914.

12

The Politics of Armageddon

Violence—or at least the emotions that produce it—is probably rooted in human nature. Its sudden reappearance in the form of organized warfare after a century of relative tranquility in European affairs was not unwelcome to millions of normally peaceful citizens. The exhilaration of unbridled patriotism momentarily eclipsed private anxieties, providing moral and material sustenance to beleaguered governments determined to pursue their national interest. Judged by outward appearances, the Russian public proved no less susceptible to chauvinist fervor. The strike movement quickly disintegrated; crowds gathered in the streets to demonstrate their devotion to the cause; a mob sacked the German embassy; and the soldiers, largely of peasant origin, maintained their traditional loyalty to the fatherland in times of external peril. Yet the initial enthusiasm that stirred the urban masses echoed more faintly in the countryside, where passivity if not indifference soon came to exemplify the prevailing mood. The Empress Alexandra's observation in September 1914 that the carnage had "lifted up spirits, cleansed the many stagnant minds, brought unity in feelings and is a 'healthy war' in the moral sense,"[1] provided a grotesque commentary on the kind of complacency and political idiocy that had already gone far to estrange the population from the ruling dynasty.

On July 20 Nicholas presided over an impressive spectacle at the Winter Palace. Over five thousand dignitaries assembled to witness the proclamation of Russia's official entry into the war. Following the customary religious observances, the court chaplain read an imperial manifesto justifying the government's course of action and expressing confidence in the union of tsar and people that would allow Russia to "repel the insolent assault of the enemy." Nicholas then mounted the altar and declared with regal solemnity: "Officers of my guard, here present, I greet in you my whole army and give it my blessing. I solemnly swear that I will never make peace so long as one of the enemy is on the soil of the fatherland." The oath, based on that taken by Alexander I in 1812, invoked a wild outburst of cheering. When Nicholas made an appearance on the balcony, an enormous crowd in the palace square carrying flags, banners, icons, and portraits of the tsar knelt and sang the national anthem. This emotional scene, blending personal and patriotic devotion, renewed Nicholas' faith that he was but an instrument of God's will and destined to lead his country to ultimate victory.

He remained head of the armed forces even after the constitutional provisions of 1906. But his impulse to assume direct military command in the manner of Alexander I met strong opposition from his ministers. "If your Majesty would graciously read the memoirs and correspondence of that period," Sazonov is said to have argued, "you would see how your august ancestor was criticized and blamed for taking command of the operations in person. You would also see how many evils might have been avoided if he had remained in his capital to control affairs from the head."[2] Nicholas deferred to such advice and appointed the Grand Duke Nikolai Nikolayevich commander in chief, much to the chagrin of General Sukhomlinov. The grand duke, a veteran cavalryman, was hardly an inspiring choice, though he was conscientious, personally courageous, and popular with the army's rank and file. The French ambassador was impressed with his "fierce energy" and "gigantic stature" but taken aback by his "military and mystic grandiloquence" when he proclaimed that "God and Joan of Arc are with us! We shall win!"[3]

The deputies of the State Duma, eager to demonstrate their support of the war effort, met in a special one-day session on July 26. Nicholas received them cordially at the Winter Palace, the first such occasion since the inaugural assembly of 1906. Rodzyanko, Goremykin, and Sazonov all spoke in the name of national unity. Even that notorious "radical," Milyukov, wrote a patriotic statement on behalf of the Kadets: "We are united in this struggle; we set no conditions and we demand nothing. On the scales of war, we simply place our firm will for victory."[4] The sincerity of Milyukov and his colleagues cannot be doubted, but all the same they shared unspoken and questionable assumptions—namely, that the wartime experience in partnership with democratic allies would mellow the regime and produce a truly liberal monarchy. The Duma's socialists, however, abstained from voting war credits, walking out of the assembly hall. Yet they too proposed to defend the homeland against foreign invasion. Only the five Bolshevik deputies, under the lash of Lenin's promptings from abroad, were prepared, though with extreme reluctance, to take a defeatist stand and oppose the "imperialist war" altogether.

The vaunted "sacred union" forged between the government and the people's representatives proved short-lived. Had Minister of the Interior Maklakov been allowed a free hand the Duma would not have reconvened until the fall of 1915. The senior deputies protested that such a policy was not only insulting but illegal, for the Duma, according to the Fundamental Laws, should meet at least annually to approve the state budget. Goremykin ignored the complaints, and the leadership turned to Minister of Agriculture Krivoshein, still an effective "power broker" whose prestige and influence at the court overshadowed that of his nominal superior. Krivoshein took up the Duma's cause so vigorously that the "reactionaries" in the Council of Ministers, if not precisely routed, were obliged to retreat. A compromise envisaged a new session no later than February 1, 1915; Nicholas endorsed the arrangement without otherwise compromising himself as to the Duma's future role. Unofficially the Duma continued to meet in the form of a committee, chaired by Rodzyanko and including deputies residing in the capital, that ostensibly concerned itself with war relief. But its evolution into a quasi-political agency was hastened by military reverses and bureaucratic ineptitude.

The government's nonpolitical measures were more consistent with the trend of "educated" public opinion than its gingerly treatment of the Duma. Nicholas accepted but presumably did not initiate a symbolic gesture of Germanophobia: the name "St. Petersburg," with its distinctly Teutonic ring, was replaced by Petrograd, its Slavic equivalent. He made a more significant contribution to the war effort by prohibiting the sale of alcoholic beverages throughout the empire. Moral scruples thus combined with patriotic endeavor, but at an excessive cost to the state treasury. The cause of temperance achieved only a temporary victory since human ingenuity contrived the usual remedies for the shortage of vodka and lesser stimulants. Nonetheless, alcohol consumption did decline during the war years.

In another exercise in wartime pageantry, Nicholas and the imperial family repaired to Moscow and its historic Kremlin. There on August 3 an eloquent and popular reaffirmation of official Russian patriotism took place, with the British and French ambassadors as honored guests. Religious services predominated amid the jeweled splendor of mitres and chasubles and the priceless relics of the Orthodox faith, including, it was claimed, a crucifix containing a portion of the True Cross. Paleologue speculated fancifully on the Kremlin's "incoherent jumble of sacred and secular buildings . . . this blend of advanced civilization and archaic barbarism, this violent contrast of the crudest materialism and the most lofty spirituality." Are they not, he asked rhetorically, the "epic of the Russia nation, the whole inward drama of the Russian soul?"[5] The thoughts of his British colleague, Sir George Buchanan, were more pragmatic: "I could not help wondering how long this national enthusiasm would last, and what would be the feeling of the people for their 'Little Father' were the war to be unduly prolonged."[6]

Indeed, contrived displays of piety and public zeal were no substitute for victories on the battlefield. Nicholas himself exuded resolution and confidence, though he apparently foresaw a difficult and perhaps lengthy campaign. "I shall fight this war to the bitter end," he is reported to have said. "To wear down Germany I shall exhaust all my resources; I'll retreat to the Volga if necessary."[7] He took great pride in his army while consistently overlooking its glaring deficiencies. Although far from the "steamroller" touted in Western lore, it did have manpower reserves unmatched by any of the belligerents. But numerical superiority no longer sufficed in the dawning age of total war, and Russia's political and military elite remained woefully unprepared to face the might of the German army and the industrial base upon which it rested. Very early in the fighting, shortages of rifles, artillery, munitions, and supplies placed Russia at great disadvantage that belied the conventional dictum that the war would be a short one.

The strategy of the high command called for a vigorous offensive against Austria-Hungary, not only to protect Serbia from occupation but also because Austria was obviously a less formidable opponent than Germany. An attack on Austrian Galicia in August succeeded beyond expectations. Russian troops seized the capital, Lemberg (Lvov), laid siege to the key fortress of Przemysl, and took over 100,000 prisoners. This impressive victory was overshadowed by a more spectacular defeat. In deference to the French alliance and in response to the rapidity of the German advance on the western front, which threatened to envelope Paris, Generals Pavel Rennenkampf and Aleksandr Samsonov launched an invasion of East Prussia. Though hastily planned and without proper logistical support, the offensive forced the outnumbered defenders to retreat. But an unexpected German counterattack routed Samsonov's army in mid-August near Tannenberg. Rennenkampf, who had failed to aid his fellow officer in timely fashion, suffered a similar defeat in late August in the battle of the Masurian Lakes. The combined disaster in East Prussia, costing over 250,000 casualties, exposed the incompetence of a command structure ridden by seniority and nepotism. It also cast serious doubt on Russia's ability to compete in the technology of modern warfare.

As the first winter of the war approached German troops occupied a deep salient in Russian Poland, but Warsaw had been spared, and ethnic Russia appeared safe from the enemy as long as the bulk of Germany's strength remained concentrated on the western front. Secrecy, censorship, and "patriotism" helped to conceal or to minimize the flagrant military blunders, especially the severe losses on the battlefield and the chronic shortage of war matériel. Even so, the euphoric mood of July had been gradually supplanted by one of pessimism and war-weariness.

The tsar continued to play a ceremonial rather than an inspirational role in the war effort. As in peacetime, neither he nor his advisers understood— or appreciated—the power of public opinion. Content to issue proclamations and make numerous tours of inspection, he never doubted the loyalty and devotion of his subjects, taking for granted that ultimate victory was in itself a sufficient reward for their patriotic sacrifice. A wartime leader of stature and experience was desperately needed to fill the political void, preferably another Witte or Stolypin. But only mediocrities seemed to rise to the surface; abler functionaries may have been stifled within the rigid pecking order of government service. Goremykin, the highest-ranking official, was unfitted to lead the Council of Ministers, still less to undertake the forbidding task of overhauling the bureaucracy, correcting the army's appalling supply problem, and generating public confidence. The Grand Duke Nikolai, another potential candidate, had authority, prestige, and charismatic appeal but possessed no more self-confidence or political instinct than the emperor himself.

Whatever his leadership deficiencies, Nicholas was not insensible to the military crisis. In November he had already taken note of the "insufficiency of munitions," necessitating "economy and discretion during action." Infantry losses had become "colossal"; some army corps "have become divisions; the brigades have shrunk into regiments, and so forth." Furthermore, half the reinforcements "have no rifles," and there was "nobody to collect them on the battlefields." Yet his optimism remained unruffled by disagreeable facts, and he wrote to his wife shortly thereafter of his "delightful" impressions: "What the country is achieving and will go on achieving till the end of the war is wonderful and immense."[8] Just what these achievements were he neglected to specify. He retained his confidence in the war minister, and in December he is reported to have stated, "Here everybody is falling upon General Sukhomlinov, but look and see how brilliantly things are going under him."[9]

The extent of Nicholas' gullibility is debatable. That he was credulous and susceptible to self-delusion seems well established. Nor was he immune to flattery, at least of the more subtle variety. And like most rulers, monarchs in particular, he was sheltered from the consequences of his own mistakes and the seamier aspects of governmental policy. There is additional evidence, however, that his isolation from reality, especially during the war years, was deliberately promoted by his ministers and other officials who took it upon themselves to withhold vital information of an unpleasant nature.[10]

On January 1, 1915, Nicholas received the diplomatic corps at Tsarskoe Selo. "As usual," the French ambassador commented, the proceedings were marked "by the full display of pageantry, luxury of setting and that inimitable exhibition of pomp and power in which the Russian court has no rival." Nicholas assured Paleologue that the army was "animated by splendid ardour and enthusiasm" despite the lack of munitions, a situation that called for patience. "At the earliest possible moment," he maintained, "my army will resume the offensive and the struggle will be continued until our enemies sue for peace. My recent journey all over Russia [visits to the Austrian front, the Black Sea naval base at Sevastopol, and Caucasian troops near the Turkish frontier] has shown me that I and my people are one on this point." He then spoke bitterly of rumors that had come to his attention, spread by "vile creatures, German agents," claiming that "I am discouraged, that I see no possibility of crushing Germany and am even thinking of making peace. . . . But all their intrigues and inventions are beneath contempt. It is my will alone that counts and you may be sure that I shall not change." Paleologue reflected later on Nicholas' "splendid moral resolution" and exalted sense of duty "perpetually nourished, vitalized and illuminated by his religion." But he concluded that in the "practical use of power he is patently not equal to his task."[11]

On January 11 Nicholas, upon the advice of the Council of Ministers, consented to a brief session of the Duma. Goremykin insisted on limiting the agenda to a consideration of the state budget, a matter that had already been under review in committee. Privately many of the deputies grumbled about the government's feeble conduct of the war, with special reference to Sukhomlinov and to internal problems under Maklakov's jurisdiction. In the more public atmosphere of the Duma proceedings, however, harmony and decorum still prevailed in the name of the "sacred union." The budget passed unanimously since the Bolhevik deputies had been arrested and the remaining dissenters chose to abstain. On January 29, the third day of the session, Rodzyanko received official word that the assembly had been prorogued until November. Long before the allotted time the honeymoon atmosphere between government and Duma dissipated in mutual distrust and recrimination.

The winter lull on the eastern front ended abruptly in late January of 1915 when a German attack, launched from East Prussia in a blinding snowstorm, caught the Russians by surprise and inflicted a fresh disaster, the second battle of the Masurian Lakes. But a giant pincer movement that sought to envelop Russian Poland failed dismally when Austrian troops, with German reinforcements, were defeated in a harrowing campaign through the Carpathians. The fortress of Przemysl, besieged for six months, fell in March. Austria-Hungary seemed on the point of military collapse, and Russia prepared to deliver a knockout blow.

Encouraged by the prospect of adding Galicia to his empire, Nicholas toured the province during the second week in April. Russian officials, bolstered by a sizable contingent of Orthodox priests, had already fallen upon the largely Ukrainian population with less than benign intent. (Grand

Duke Nikolai was said to have complained, "I'm expecting trainloads of ammunition. They send me trainloads of priests!")[12] Count G. A. Bobrinsky, the governor-general, coordinated a noxious policy of Russification. The most outrageous example of persecution involved the Uniate Church (Orthodox in ritual but loyal to the papacy), whose leaders were arrested and exiled to Russia. Nicholas spoke in Lemberg of an "indivisible Russia" stretching to the Carpathians, an imperialist scenario that was rudely shattered when on April 18 a massive Austro-German offensive began on the eastern front. Galicia, the immediate target, had to be evacuated by early summer, and the enemy pressed on against Russian Poland and the Baltic provinces.

With the Russian army in headlong retreat, civilians were obliged to share the ordeal by forced evacuation. The rationale of a "scorched earth" policy, appropriate in 1812, scarcely applied to a front of some nine hundred miles. Of the million or more refugees created in the name of military necessity, many thousands perished of malnutrition, exposure, and disease. Jews, already a popular scapegoat for wartime failures, constituted a high proportion of the dispossessed, and many were further victimized by acts of violence, looting, and arson. Krivoshein assailed the army's policy before his fellow ministers: "Curses, sickness, misery, and poverty are spreading over all Russia. The naked and the hungry spread panic everywhere, dampening the last remnants of the enthusiasm which existed in the first months of the war. They come in a solid phalanx, trampling down the crops, ruining the meadows, the forests. Behind them is left a virtual desert, as if the locusts or the army of Tamerlane had come through."[13] Nicholas, poorly informed about the refugee problem, blamed the victims: "It is quite impossible to restrain these poor people from abandoning their homes in face of the attacking enemy." But he noted with compassion that with cold weather approaching, "this pilgrimage is beginning to be terribly distressing; the children suffer very acutely, and many of them, unfortunately, die on the way."[14]

The crisis at the front, though it had no immediate political repercussions, generated a sense of public alarm that the government could not long ignore. Convinced that it was his patriotic duty, Nicholas returned to Stavka (army headquarters), located at the rail junction of Baranovichi in Russian Poland, to observe the situation at first hand. He found troop morale "admirable, as it has always been; the only thing which causes anxiety, as in the past, is the shortage of munitions." Grand Duke Nikolai "wept in my private room, and even asked me whether I thought of replacing him by a more capable man." Nicholas kept busy, without interfering in military decisions. Aside from church services "nearly every day," government documents to be read, and "endless conversations," he toured the countryside by automobile. "For the last few days," he reported, "the weather has been magnificent, the woods smell so delightfully and the birds sing so loudly. It is a veritable rustic idyll—if only it were not for the war!"[15]

After nine days at Stavka, Nicholas left for Petrograd on May 13. His attitude was one of moderate concern—not, as it should have been, one of grave anxiety. He nevertheless accepted Rodzyanko's plea for a special council on war supplies that would include industrialists, financiers, public men, legislators, and representatives from the war ministry. When reports of the project reached Sukhomlinov, he sought to block it as illegal and a serious infringement of his authority. But his initial support in the Council of Ministers dwindled as the emperor's will became known. Goremykin bluntly told his colleagues, "I think that this is not an occasion for prolonged debate: we have but to conform to the will of our gracious Sovereign."[16] Only Maklakov dared to record a negative vote. Rodzyanko's idea, brought to fruition by official favor, spawned a series of special councils to improve economic efficiency. Almost inevitably they proved "extremely unwieldly," but they were at the same time "like fresh water pouring into the stagnant pond of the bureaucracy."[17] Their work, supplemented by a host of unofficial organizations, provided some hope that the most egregious examples of governmental bungling might be overcome.

Having in his view won a signal victory over the forces of sloth and ineptitude, Rodzyanko tested his mettle anew in a more direct confrontation with imperial authority. He sought to rid the cabinet of those ministers which progressive public opinion had long condemned as die-hard reactionaries and symbols of a losing war effort. The ultimate goal was to create, as the newly coined Kadet slogan put it, "a ministry of public confidence." His task was nearly sabotaged from the outset by the Duma's bête noir, Maklakov, who persuaded Nicholas that Rodzyanko was prepared to submit extraordinary demands verging on an ultimatum and that he was attempting to enhance his own power at the expense of the monarchy. Maklakov also revived the notion of transforming the Duma into a consultative institution. Nicholas responded with naive eagerness: "It is indeed high time to reduce the powers of the Imperial Duma. It will be interesting to see how Messrs. Rodzianko & Co. will take it."[18]

Rodzyanko requested an imperial audience, and Nicholas received him, after considerable delay, on May 30. The emperor's "very pale and upset" appearance brought involuntarily to the president's mind the stories he had heard about Maklakov's intrigues. He assured Nicholas that he had not come to discuss the Duma but "to speak on general matters, to confess to you as a son to his father, to tell you the whole truth, as I know it." Granted formal permission to proceed, he delivered an impassioned indictment that lasted for over an hour. Nicholas refrained from smoking a single cigarette—with him "always a sign of attention." Rodzyanko reviewed "all the painful and harassing details of the past weeks." He stressed the inadequacy of war matériel—"of the troops, dying heroically at the front and

betrayed in the rear by those who managed the supplies." He also denounced Maklakov, Sukhomlinov, and Shcheglovitov and asked for the
resignation of the Grand Duke Sergei Mikhailovich, the tsar's cousin, for
his incompetent supervision of the Artillery Department. Nicholas, "visibly
affected," thanked him for his "straightforward, frank and courageous report."[19]

Rodzyanko underscored his rhetoric with a letter to the tsar urging the
removal of Sukhomlinov and an expeditious meeting of the Duma. "I did
not conceal that the debates would be tempestuous and the criticism of the
Government scathing," he recalled, "but it would be better for this to take
place within the walls of the Duma than out in the streets." His initiative
may have been the catalyst in the ensuing "purge" of the Council of Ministers. Goremykin, the most egregious misfit, was said to have "broken
down under the strain of age and the course of events" and became the
first to request that he be allowed to resign. He received an evasive reply
and remarked to a friend, "The Emperor can't see that the candles have
already been lit round my coffin and that the only thing required to complete the ceremony is myself!"[20]

Resignations—the term "dismissal" seldom found favor in official ter-
minology—were soon forthcoming. Maklakov stepped down on June 6;
Prince Nikolai Shcherbatov reluctantly took over the interior ministry, in
large measure upon the recommendation of Grand Duke Nikolai. Shcherbatov, a well-meaning moderate, had gained his administrative experience
as director of the state stud farms, and the appointment proved less than
auspicious. The by-now-notorious Sukhomlinov accepted the inevitable on
June 12. Nicholas let him go with genuine regret, for the war minister had
undeniably become a scapegoat to appease public fury—his later indictment on charges of embezzlement and treason was politically motivated.
His replacement, General Aleksei Polivanov, had served as assistant war
minister, and his clash with Sukhomlinov at that time now became almost
an endorsement. On the other hand, he was also regarded as a liberal in
Duma circles and had formed a friendship with Guchkov, a circumstance
that seemed guaranteed to alienate imperial favor. Nicholas, however, interviewed the candidate at length and chose to overlook his indiscretion.

Additional cabinet changes were in the offing when Nicholas returned to
Stavka on June 11. Three days later he presided over a ministerial conference, including the two recent appointees, which Grand Duke Nikolai and
his staff also attended. An imperial rescript addressed to Goremykin attempted to rally the country with the assurance of a "radiant future" and
the "full and final triumph of the Russian armies." The major government
concession involved the impending recall of the legislature. Nicholas remained at headquarters with sufficient leisure to play dominoes, visit an
animal preserve, and compose his daily missive to Alexandra, but the

"damnable question of the shortage of artillery ammunition and rifles" continued to bother him.[21]

Back in the capital at the end of the month, Nicholas put the finishing touches on his ministerial shakeup. Shcheglovitov at Justice and Vladimir Sabler of the Holy Synod, widely perceived as arch-reactionaries, were formally ousted on July 5–6. Aleksandr Khvostov, a Goremykin protégé but with an excellent reputation, became minister of justice; Aleksandr Samarin, a conservative Slavophile who enjoyed a "halo of integrity," assumed responsibility for religious affairs. Cabinet "liberals" chafed at Goremykin's immunity despite the loss of his chief supporters; Sazonov, for one, still considered him "dangerous" because of his "hopeless laziness and cynical indifference."[22]

Nicholas' willingness to compromise won public good will at a time when his image had become tarnished by military defeats for which he bore no direct responsibility. His early recall of the Duma—it met on July 19—was also accepted as a positive gesture. But expectations were aroused that Nicholas had no intention of fulfilling. He assumed, as always, that the government remained *his* government, not the creature of the Duma or of some broader constituency. This misunderstanding was not immediately apparent. The political symbolism of the "sacred union," though seriously impaired, had not yet been drained of its patriotic mystique. But in the long run "society" began demanding more concessions from the government than Nicholas was prepared to bestow.

The tractable Duma of the past two sessions disappeared as the accumulated grievances of the losing war effort found an open forum. Goremykin's hackneyed speech announcing the government's "program of victory" received a chilly reception. Polivanov, in declaring his intention to work with the Duma, aroused lively applause, but the enthusiasm was in large part an expression of satisfaction that a competent replacement had been found for the infamous Sukhomlinov. With this major exception, the government and its spokesmen were placed on the defensive. Paleologue noted a "constant and implacable diatribe against the conduct of the war" in which "all the faults of the bureaucracy are being denounced and all the vices of Tsarism forced into the limelight." Nicholas, as usual, remained above the battle and exempt from direct public criticism. Privately, however, a cacophany of complaints were voiced. Alexandra bore the brunt of them because of her German origin and her continued association with Rasputin. Gradually, in reaction to further setbacks at the front, the fanciful notion arose that "dark forces"—in effect, a pro-German cabal—constituted the chief barrier to a successful prosecution of the war. The politically knowledgeable could scoff at such tales as mere rumor and gossip, but even as loyal a servant of the monarch as Sazonov lamented the isolation of the royal couple: "It's perfectly deplorable! They've gradually created a void about themselves; no one goes near them now. . . . Apart

from the Emperor's official relations with his ministers, no voice from outside ever reaches [him]." Perhaps such criticism penetrated the imperial
entourage. At any rate, Sazonov began to notice in Nicholas "a certain
reserve which prevented me from speaking to him with perfect frankness
as I had done, with his consent, from the very first day of assuming office."[23]

Sazonov's reproach about the seclusion of the sovereign and his consort
was not wholly accurate. Their lifestyle had always been reclusive except
when state occasions dictated otherwise. Their preference for the privacy
of Tsarskoe Selo in contrast to the urban exposure of the Winter Palace
was well known. But if Nicholas was scarcely more accessible to the general
public during the war years, he traveled more frequently and extensively
than ever before. Aside from patriotic motives, he sincerely believed that
his efforts boosted the morale of soldiers and civilians alike. Opinions differed as to his effectiveness. General Aleksei Brusilov considered his Galician visit "worse than untimely," observing that "the Tsar displayed his
habitual indecision" and in greeting the troops "could not find the words
which would have raised their spirits and won their regard."[24] Paleologue,
on the other hand, found his ceremonial performance at the launching of
a new battle cruiser in June 1915 "quite impressive." Nicholas toured the
shipyards afterward for nearly an hour, "often stopping for a chat, with
that calm, confident and dignified ease which is his superlative merit in
approaching those of low estate. Enthusiastic cheers, cheers which seemed
to come from every throat, accompanied him during the whole of his visit."
Upon being congratulated, his "eyes lit up with a melancholy smile," and
he replied, "I like nothing better than to feel myself in touch with my
people. I needed it to-day."[25]

Nicholas could flatter himself that he kept in spiritual if not physical
contact with "his" people. For Alexandra, such self-deception was beside
the point. She sought no personal popularity and was content to bask in
her husband's reflected glory, never doubting the strength and stability of
the monarchial system. Shy and ill at ease except within the family circle
or among female intimates, she acquired a reputation for aloof haughtiness.
Even among her own kind—that is, the court aristocracy—she achieved
little more than polite constraint. Her health and appearance had deteriorated under the burden of her son's hemophilia, still a family secret. Neurasthenic and reportedly suffering from a heart condition, she recuperated
sufficiently under the stimulus of the war emergency to devote herself
(along with her daughters) to nursing the wounded at her own hospital in
Tsarskoe Selo.

The news from the front, if not always accurate as to the extent of the
German advance, continued to be gloomy. General Polivanov shocked his
colleagues on July 16, 1915, with a brutally frank appraisal of the military

situation: "I consider it my duty as a citizen and an official to announce to the Council of Ministers that our country is in danger." He went on to paint a frightful picture of conditions in the army. The soldiers were "becoming steadily demoralized," and the rate of "desertion and surrender are assuming tremendous proportions. The Germans are pursuing us with artillery alone; their infantry takes no part in the action; we are powerless to withstand their gunfire, deprived as we are of ammunition. Moreover, the Germans are suffering no losses, while we are losing men by the thousands." Although the enemy's firepower was not quite as overwhelming nor his immunity from casualties as absolute as Polivanov maintained, the report greatly aggravated the sense of frustration and alarm in the cabinet. The ministers were virtually leaderless, for Nicholas declined to exert moral suasion or to provide political guidance, while Goremykin strove only to protect the sovereign "from all excitement and unpleasantness."[26]

Nicholas, though sheltered at Tsarskoe Selo from public opinion and its reverberations in the Duma and the Council of Ministers, could not ignore the state of the army and the failing war effort. Deterred from asserting direct military control at the beginning of the war, he began to think seriously of supplanting Grand Duke Nikolai. His chief motivation was one of patriotism, however misguided. "You have no idea how depressing it is to be away from the front," he explained in a rare moment of self-revelation to a member of the household staff. "It seems as if everything here saps energy and enfeebles resolution. The most pessimistic rumours and the most ridiculous stories are accepted. . . . Out at the front men fight and die for their country. . . . All else is forgotten, and, in spite of our losses and our reverses, everyone remains confident. Any man fit to bear arms should be in the army. Speaking for myself, I can never be in too much of a hurry to be with my troops."[27] Nicholas was also accustomed to justifying major decisions as countenanced, if not inspired, by supernatural intervention. "I remember so well," he wrote Alexandra, "that when I stood opposite the large ikon of Our Savior, up above the large church [at Tsarskoe Selo], some inner voice seemed to persuade me to come to a definite decision and to write to Nic. [Nikolai Nikolayevich] immediately about my resolve, independently of what our Friend [Rasputin] said to me."[28] His determination was further bolstered by long hours of prayer at Petrograd's most famous cathedrals, those of Kazan and of Peter and Paul.

The emperor's intention was first disclosed to his war minister on August 6, though Goremykin had received preliminary intimations. But Polivanov, certainly the appropriate official to confide in, was not the soul of discretion. He expected an "irreparable [military] catastrophe momentarily," for the army "is no longer retreating—it is simply running away." Only two days before he had informed his colleagues, with calculated irony, "I rely on impassable spaces, on impenetrable mud, and on the mercy of St. Nicholas, the patron of Holy Russia." Despite the breakdown at the front, he perceived "a far more horrible event which threatens Russia." Deliberately violating the secrecy of the imperial audience chamber, he startled the other ministers by revealing the sovereign's determination to take over the role of commander in chief. When the cacophony of voices speaking at cross-purposes died down, Polivanov described the fateful meeting in some detail. "Knowing the Emperor's suspiciousness and his stubbornness about all decisions of a personal nature," he went on, "I tried, with the greatest caution, to dissuade him. . . . I allowed myself to emphasize how dangerous it was for the Head of the State to assume command at a time when the army was demoralized and depressed in consequence of continued misfortune and a long-lasting retreat." But his eloquent arguments—he ventured to suggest that even Petrograd and Moscow might have to be evacuated in the emperor's name—were in vain: "His Majesty listened to me attentively and replied that he had weighed everything, and was conscious of the difficulties of the moment and that, nevertheless, his decision was final."[29]

Only Goremykin, while agreeing that the tsar was taking "a very risky step which can have grave consequences," dissented from the ministerial consensus that some form of collective protest was necessary. He warned that attempts to dissuade the emperor would be useless: "His conviction was formed a long time ago. He has told me, more than once, that he will never forgive himself for not leading the army at the front during the Japanese war. According to his own words, the duty of the Tsar, his function, dictates that the Monarch . . . be with his troops in moments of danger, sharing both their joy and their sorrow." Disregarding Goremykin's opinion, the Council members parted with the understanding that Polivanov would renew his remonstrances in their name and that such imperial confidants as General Vladimir Voyeikov, the palace commandant, would be approached in the same cause.[30]

Nicholas' old-fashioned sense of duty and honor did him credit on a personal level, but his obstinate resolve to identify with the army as supreme commander was both foolhardy and perilous. As Goremykin had predicted, he resisted all efforts to reverse his decision. Rodzyanko reinforced the ministerial appeals in an audience at Tsarskoe Selo. To his argument about the danger to the throne, Nicholas declared firmly, "I know; I may perish, but I will save Russia."[31] By this time rumors were flying as to the tsar's intention; the most popular version assumed that Alexandra, with Rasputin's connivance, had fomented the "plot" because she detested the Grand Duke Nikolai. She did indeed suspect him of political ambition, if not more sinister designs on the throne, but Nicholas did not take her views seriously. Paleologue, ever alert to the latest gossip, ascribed the emperor's policy to the "machinations" of General Sukhomlinov, who "secretly saved his credit with the sovereigns, notwithstanding his scandalous failures."[32] Nicholas, though he remained sympathetic to his former minister, could hardly have been swayed from this quarter.

To soften the blow to the grand duke Nicholas sent a personal letter recognizing his "invincible courage" and expressing "profound gratitude" for his services, a letter that Polivanov conveyed to Stavka, now situated at Mogilyov because the German advance threatened Baranovichi. The war minister later recalled that the supreme commander, who had already been alerted to his impending dismissal, received him most cordially with no question of "any resistance or disobedience." Nikolai accepted his new assignment as viceroy of the Caucasus and commander of the Russian front against Turkey as an honorable solution to his personal dilemma. Polivanov also observed that the grand duke's nerves were "shot" and that he was "completely worn out." After reporting on his mission to Nicholas at Tsarskoe Selo, he told the Council of Ministers on August 12 that in his opinion the tsar's "interest in personal leadership of the armies was considerably weakened during my absence."[33]

Polivanov's words revived hope that Nicholas might yet change his mind. But Sazonov warned that it would be imprudent to pursue "arguments and petitions." "It is dangerous to evoke stubbornness," he reminded his associates. "We know what this has led to sometimes. It is better, for the moment, to use the tactic of silence, acting indirectly, by roundabout ways." On August 20 the cabinet seized another opportunity to confront Nicholas when he presided over a conference at Tsarskoe Selo. The stalemate continued, however, and the ministers carried on their debate among themselves. Samarin, accounting himself a loyal servant of the emperor, nevertheless argued that the monarch needed "thinking men, not a slavish execution of orders." The truth must be told: "We could never forgive ourselves our silence at a time when the fate of our motherland is at stake." Goremykin, still a minority of one, noted that the discussion had acquired "a hopeless character." He equated the "will of the Tsar" with the "will of Russia" and once more stated his willingness to resign: "Plead with the Emperor to throw me out."[34]

As a final measure of their desperation the ministers assembled at Sazonov's private quarters at the foreign ministry on August 21 and composed a collective appeal. The ministers of war and naval affairs, though wholly sympathetic, declined to participate because of their special status with the armed forces. The adamant Goremykin was not even asked for his support, and of those present only Aleksandr Khvostov refused to sign. Samarin drafted the letter, and though it was addressed to their "most gracious sovereign" and humbly phrased, it forthrightly pointed out that the decision "threatens with serious consequences Russia, your dynasty and your person." The concluding sentence amounted to an offer to resign as a body: "Under such conditions we do not believe we can be of real service to Your Majesty and to our country."[35] Such a document was unprecedented in the tsar's experience, and he expressed his profound displeasure, comparing the ministerial action to a strike. As Nicholas left for Mogilyov on August 22 the rumor mills ground out the report that Krivoshein, Polivanov, and Sazonov were the leading candidates for the chairmanship of the Council of Ministers.

Nicholas gratefully turned his back on the political intrigues and "poisoned air" of the capital for the fresh challenge at the front. He announced his new status in a brief order of the day, again confirming his faith in God's help and his "unshakable confidence in final victory." His military expertise scarcely ventured beyond the parade ground, and he recognized his deficiency by allowing his chief of staff, General Mikhail Alekseyev, a free hand in planning overall strategy. A talented officer, Alekseyev was unfortunately an inexperienced courtier and not always capable of guiding his royal superior in a direction beneficial to the military tasks at hand. Described as "a charmless effigy of the virtues his predecessors ought to have displayed," he succeeded in removing Stavka's "aristocratic furniture," the sole exception being Count Kapnist, "skilled at devising pompous missives." But Nicholas' restraint did not extend to military personnel, and his propensity for selecting mediocre if not incompetent senior officers rivaled his ineptitude at choosing political appointees.[36]

Nicholas reported to Alexandra the calm and uneventful manner in which the transfer of authority at Stavka took place. He ignored the potential consequences of his act—"casting his crown into the arena," in the words of one observer.[37] Nicholas claimed to be at peace with himself, much as he felt after partaking of Holy Communion: "A new clean page begins, and only God Almighty knows what will be written on it!" He asked for his wife's assistance and expressed gratitude for her "untiring importunity" in exhorting him "to be firm and to stick to my own opinions." In his only reference to politics, he asked that she convey a message to Goremykin: "Please tell him . . . that as soon as the Council of State and the Duma finish their work they must be adjourned."[38]

An embarrassing anachronism to most of his colleagues and a symbol of reactionary incompetence to the lower legislative chamber, Goremykin clung to his post with the dogged loyalty of a faithful retainer. He followed with growing concern the development of the Progressive Bloc in the Duma, a coalition of moderates that excluded the extremes of Left and Right. His complaint that "a great deal of nonsense is being chattered there" was overshadowed by the possibility that the deputies might defy an order of dismissal. He professed confidence that "if separate little groups of intriguers begin to make mischief, there are enough police for them"; as for the danger of riots, he considered that eventuality to have been exaggerated by Milyukov "and the rest of that crowd for the purpose of instilling fear."[39]

Unable to exert his will on the Council of Ministers, Goremykin enjoyed compensatory solace from the empress at Tsarskoe Selo. Alexandra had already compiled her own political blacklist based on her conception of the tsar's "enemies." The Grand Duke Nikolai, who had topped the list, was no longer a danger, but Rodzyanko, Milyukov, and Guchkov remained. New names were added, essentially supplied by "the old man," as the empress affectionately called Goremykin: Sazonov, Krivoshein, Shcherbatov, and Samarin. Indeed, the "enemies" constituted almost a full roster of cabinet members—in effect those who disagreed with Goremykin and supported the reforms proposed by the Progressive Bloc. Alexandra became so incensed that she described the hapless ministers as "fiends" and "worse than [the] Duma" in a letter to Nicholas.[40]

Krivoshein neatly summed up majority opinion in the Ministerial Council on August 28: "We, old servants of the Tsar, take upon ourselves the unpleasant duty of adjourning the Duma, and, at the same time, firmly state to His Imperial Majesty that the general internal situation of the country requires a change of Cabinet and of the political course. His Majesty's decision on the basic question, in one or another way, will also decide the personal composition of the future government." Goremykin left for Stavka the next day, promising to convey in detail the sometimes heated arguments of his associates. He expressed regret that he had to "vex the Emperor with the tale of our disagreement and the weak nerves of the Council of Ministers." His task, as he saw it, was "to exonerate the Tsar from all reproaches and discontent." Adopting the stance of a martyr, he defied his critics: "Let them accuse me and curse me—I'm already old and I will not live long. But while I'm alive, I will fight for the inviolability of the Tsar's power. The whole strength of Russia lies only in the monarchy. Otherwise there will be such a mess that everything will be lost."[41]

Goremykin returned from his mission on September 1 with an imperial order to prorogue the Duma and to maintain the status quo in the Council of Ministers. Military affairs permitting, the emperor would summon the ministers and make necessary decisions later. Despite badgering by Polivanov and Sazonov as to what had been reported on the state of ministerial opinion, Goremykin refused to elaborate. The meeting concluded with frayed nerves and hot tempers. Sazonov, "virtually hysterical," called Goremykin a "madman"; Polivanov was "boiling over with bile, and looked ready to bite"; and Krivoshein "looked hopelessly sad and anxious."[42]

The apprehension expressed in the cabinet that a suspension of the Duma would lead to public disorder proved ill founded. The plodding Goremykin, at least in the short run, turned out to be a better prophet than his fractious colleagues. He notified Rodzyanko of the impending adjournment, arousing indignation and astonishment among the deputies. The senior leaders convened early on September 3, and some of the speeches bordered on revolutionary agitation, including demands that the Duma proclaim itself a constituent assembly. With help from Milyukov and Ivan Dmitryukov, Rodzyanko pacified the "hotheads" so as "not to ruin the Duma and the country by playing into Goremykin's hands." The regular session opened later in a state of excitement as if "a huge hive . . . had been disturbed." After the decree of dissolution had been read, the deputies gave their customary cheer for the emperor and slowly dispersed without so much as a peep of protest. In Rodzyanko's opinion the deputies had responded to the government's "provocation" with "statesmanship and wisdom."[43] Other interpretations were possible. Chief among them was the militant view that the "conciliationists," having betrayed the cause of the Progressive Bloc, snatched defeat from the jaws of victory. Cowardice—or at least timidity— not only disrupted the Duma's newfound sense of unity and purpose but effectively blocked a promising alliance with the Council of Ministers. Against all the odds, Nicholas and Goremykin had carried the day for autocracy.

That impression was reinforced by events in Moscow, where representatives of the Union of Zemstvos and the Union of Towns (Zemgor, in the Russian acronym) convened from September 7 to the 9th. As Shcherbatov warned his fellow ministers, "The whole flower of the opposition intelligentsia is gathered there, and is demanding power to direct the war to victory. The workers, and the population as a whole, are gripped by some sort of madness and are like gunpowder. An outburst of disorders is possible at any moment."[44] The prospect of "revolution and anarchy," as Guchkov put it, restrained the government's critics. The Zemgor debates were fiery, the result trivial. At Stavka, Nicholas correctly assumed that he had no more to fear from Zemgor than he had from the Duma. When General Alekseyev inquired if he intended to send a greeting to the conferees, he replied testily, "Is it worth it? All this work is a systematic attempt to undermine my rule. I understand these things very well. They should all be arrested, not thanked." Alekseyev started to object but was interrupted: "Well, all right, all right. Send them a greeting. The time will come when I will reckon with them."[45] A six-man Zemgor delegation requested an audience with Nicholas but was not received. Rodzyanko met a similar rebuff.

Frustrated and deeply resentful, the ministerial "liberals" who had courageously protested the tsar's decision to assume military command boldly renewed their dispute with Goremykin. They petitioned Nicholas to replace the chairman or to accept their resignation. Angered by this second cabinet "strike," he summoned them to Stavka for a conference. He had become convinced that the ministers, "always living in town, know terribly little of what is happening in the country as a whole. Here *I can judge* correctly the real *mood* among the various classes of the people."[46] His determination to put these upstart servitors in their place was bolstered by Alexandra's daily missives, which contained nagging reminders to prove himself a worthy autocrat, "the Lord & Master of Russia." "Clean out all," she advised, "give *Goremykin* new ministers to work with & God will bless you & their work." She also prompted her husband "several times to comb yr. hair with His [Rasputin's] comb before the sitting of the ministers."[47]

The meeting took place on September 16, and Nicholas proudly reported to his wife, "I told them my opinion sternly to their faces."[48] "You prophesied an ill omen if I assumed command of the army," he scolded his ministers, "but only good came of it. You believed that there would be a revolution if the Duma was prorogued, but nothing of the sort happened. How can I believe you after such a mistaken understanding of the present moment?"[49] His peremptory stand was not received in docile silence. Krivoshein pointed out the danger of disregarding public opinion, for cooperation between government and people was essential in wartime: "Goremykin has not only adopted the directly opposite point of view but is even ready to oppose persistently the desires of the people and thus systematically irritate them. Under these conditions, naturally, he is not acceptable to them." Samarin spoke eloquently of his desire to serve the tsar not in fear but in sincerity, and he declared that he could not reconcile his collaboration with Goremykin with the dictates of his conscience. Shcherbatov, speaking in a more conciliatory vein, maintained that the ministers had the greatest personal esteem for Goremykin but could not work with him.[50]

Nicholas remained unbending, and the anti-Goremykin faction retained its cohesion, refusing to retreat in the face of royal displeasure. There could be only one solution to such an impasse. The principled Shcherbatov was the first to go. In late September he was replaced by Aleksei Khvostov (not to be confused with his uncle, the minister of justice), a Duma representative of the extreme Right whose candidacy was vigorously championed by the empress. In 1911 he had been seriously considered for the interior ministry but lost out to Makarov. Obese but not phlegmatic, he was an ambitious and energetic demagogue who launched an ostentatious campaign against the high cost of living, raised the level of popular xenophobia by denouncing the alleged threat of "German domination," and blamed the Jews for inflation and food shortages. Rumored to be an admirer of Rasputin, presumably to please the empress, he represented himself to Rodzyanko as just the opposite. His bizarre schemes encompassed the notion of insinuating a monk named Mardary into the court at Tsarskoe Selo, and an "intoxication fund," to which he supposedly contributed five thousand rubles, for the purpose of rendering the imperial favorite harmless.[51]

Samarin was also forced out in late September, having served less than three months at the Holy Synod. An intrigue involving Bishop Varnava of Tobolsk, a Rasputin protégé, provided the occasion. He had defied Samarin's authority in a dispute over the canonization of an eighteenth-century archbishop, Alexandra portraying Varnava as the innocent party in letters to her husband. In October the relatively obscure Aleksandr Volzhin, reputed to be Khvostov's choice and "one of Rasputin's cronies," was appointed to the vacant post. Varnava had his way, but Volzhin proved too independent for the empress, and he too had a short tenure in office.[52]

Krivoshein, "the most eminent representative of monarchical liberalism,"[53] foresaw the inevitability of his "retirement" and asked to be relieved of his duties as minister of agriculture. Nicholas accepted his resignation toward the end of October and replaced him with Aleksandr Naumov, a political moderate with creditable zemstvo experience. Naumov at first declined the honor, but at Khvostov's prompting the tsar overrode his objections. Although Nicholas refrained from more sweeping action against the cabinet "troublemakers," Sazonov and Polivanov remained vulnerable. Their precarious status was tempered, however, by their importance to the war effort—the one seemingly indispensable because of his thorough acquaintance with the minutiae of Russian diplomacy, the other for his proficiency in the vital work of military procurement.

After a respite at Tsarskoe Selo during the last week of September, Nicholas returned to duty at Mogilyov. Despite the painful separation from his family, service at the front invigorated him and provided the illusion that he had patriotically sacrificed his personal comfort and civilian status to share with millions of his subjects the rigors of a soldier's life. Petrograd, on the other hand, symbolized gossip, rumor, and duplicity. "What a shame! What a disgrace!" he exclaimed to Paleologue. "How *can* men be so devoid of conscience, patriotism and faith!"[54] Alexis accompanied him back to headquarters, much to the distress of Alexandra. Nicholas was content to play a largely ceremonial role, reviewing troops, visiting hospitals, factories, and military installations, and dispensing the Cross of St. George, Russia's highest military decoration, with profligate generosity. Alexis, attired in a private's uniform, usually accompanied his father on these tours of inspection and aroused much curiosity, but as a stimulus to morale his presence seemed to have limited effect.

Tsar and heir shared adjoining camp beds in the governor's mansion, located high on a bluff overlooking the Dnieper River. The daily routine at Mogilyov varied only sightly. Every morning about 9:30 Alekseyev briefed Nicholas on the military situation, using a large map with miniature flags to show the disposition of the opposing forces. Later in the morning the emperor received ambassadors, military attaches, army officers, and an assortment of officials and dignitaries. In the early afternoon lunch was served to thirty or more guests, normally including Alekseyev and his staff, the imperial suite, and Allied officers. Then, after an hour or so of work in his study or receiving more visitors, Nicholas would generally undertake an automobile excursion, stopping on occasion for walks in the countryside. Dinner came at seven, followed by several hours of leisure in which reading, music, and dominoes were favorite pastimes. In many ways it was an idyllic existence, insulated for the most part from the cares of government and the necessity of making troublesome decisions. He deliberately avoided reading newspapers and deeply resented any reference to political questions among his officers. He could truly claim, with heartfelt satisfaction, "The life I lead at the head of my army is so healthy and comforting!"[55]

Russia's military fortunes were at their nadir when Nicholas took over the supreme command. But the army, though ravaged by heavy losses, had retreated in good order and deprived the Germans of spectacular gains on the scale of Tannenberg. The acute shortage of war matériel began to ease under the direction of Polivanov and the help of public-spirited volunteers, of whom Guchkov was the most active. On the western front static trench warfare prevented any major breakthroughs, and Russian opinion became increasingly exasperated by the seeming disparity of sacrifice against the common foe. One general's waspish complaint that "history would despise England and France for having 'sat still like rabbits' month after month in the Western theatre, leaving the whole burden of the war to be borne by Russia," expressed widespread public resentment.[56]

Nor were the Entente powers without grievances. Paradoxically, the most persistent and vexatious was the least substantial: it arose from Russia's domestic turmoil and the erroneous belief that the war effort was being hindered if not sabotaged by a pro-German "court camarilla" centered around the tsaritsa and Rasputin. The fantasy gained renewed vigor with Nicholas' prolonged absences from the capital and Alexandra's self-appointed role as her husband's political surrogate. Paleologue was tempted to bribe Rasputin, if only as an experiment, but admitted that it would be "futile, compromising, and also dangerous."[57] The British ambassador, while conceding that Rasputin was not in German pay and had no communication with Berlin, claimed unconvincingly that "he was largely financed by certain Jewish bankers, who were, to all intents and purposes, German agents."[58]

A related specter that proved illusory involved a separate peace between Russia and Germany. "Reactionaries" at the court and elsewhere supposedly favored the idea, and indeed there were low-level efforts in Stockholm, Copenhagen, and other neutral sites to initiate something more serious than rumor and idle talk. London and Paris monitored these attempts with uneasiness and some anxiety. At a higher level, the king of Denmark ventured a peace "feeler," as did the grand duke of Hesse, Alexandra's brother. Count Philip von Eulenburg, an intimate of the kaiser, wrote to Count Frederiks in November 1915 suggesting a rapprochement leading to a peace settlement. Nicholas commissioned Sazonov to draft an answer but decided to ignore the letter, for a reply of any kind might be construed as a desire to enter negotiations. A few weeks later an even more ambitious scheme invoked the services of Maria Vasilchikova, a Russian citizen and former confidante of the empress who had been interned at a villa in Austria at the outbreak of war. After receiving no response to a series of letters to the tsar and other dignitaries, she was authorized by the Grand Duke of Hesse to undertake a peace mission to Petrograd bearing a message for Sazonov and a letter each for the royal couple. According to Paleologue, Nicholas reacted angrily to Sazonov's report: "To accept such a commission from an enemy sovereign! This woman is either wicked or a fool. How could she fail to realize that in carrying these letters she ran the risk of seriously compromising the Empress and myself?" He supposedly ordered Vasilchikova's banishment to a convent in Chernigov (or to her sister's estate, according to another version).[59]

These minor irritants to Allied-Russian relations were overridden by military necessity. Unity, if not essential to success on a given battlefield, was basic to the strategy of coalition warfare. Diplomacy followed the dictates of political expediency, and the Allied governments, acting prematurely on the venerable principle that to the victor belongs the spoils, secretly parceled out the territorial assets of the enemy with lavish abandon. Russia's prospective share promised to gratify its most ardent imperialists, but the immediate objective, once war had begun, was to preserve the existing empire. Poland and the Ukraine were especially vulnerable to unrest because of ethnic kinship with the Slavs under Austro-Hungarian rule. Technically an internal matter, the problem touched on Sazonov's domain, and he enlisted the emperor in the cause of Polish autonomy. Nicholas was reluctant to lend his name to so "radical" a concept, however politic, and a proclamation issued on August 3, 1914, was signed instead by the Grand Duke Nikolai. The document, a nostalgic appeal to Polish nationalism, offered "resurrection" under "the scepter of the Russian Tsar": Poland would be "free in faith, in language, and in self-government." But a declamatory promise did not amount to a considered policy. On August 11 another proclamation sought to arouse the Ukrainians in Galicia to "cast off the [Austrian] yoke" and "hoist the banner of great undivided Russia." The fortunes of war rendered both pronouncements obsolete, though the question of Poland remained open despite its occupation by German troops.

Turkish belligerence permitted Russia to revive its traditional goal of acquiring Constantinople and the Straits. Britain and France readily acquiesced in return for a partition of Asiatic Turkey in their favor. Nicholas also laid claim to Armenia, with annexation a distinct possibility. "I shall only do so if the Armenians expressly ask me to," he informed Paleologue in November 1914. "Otherwise I shall establish an autonomous regime for them." As for Austria-Hungary, he contemplated radical surgery: "reduced to her ancient hereditary states, German Tyrol and the district of Salzburg. . . . Galicia and the western half of Bukovina will enable Russia to obtain her natural frontier, the Carpathians"; Bohemia would be independent or autonomous, while Hungary would lose Transylvania to Romania. He was equally generous with the other Balkan states. Serbia should be allowed to annex Bosnia, Herzegovina, Dalmatia, and northern Albania; Greece ought to obtain southern Albania, except for a province to be assigned to Italy. "If Bulgaria behaves properly," he declared, "she should receive compensation in Macedonia from Serbia."

The German empire was also scheduled for dismemberment. "Posen and possibily a portion of Silesia," the tsar maintained, "will be indispensable for the reconstruction of Poland." Aside from a "rectification" of the Russian frontier with East Prussia, Belgium would receive territorial compensation, Denmark would regain Schleswig, France would reannex Alsace-Lorraine (and perhaps the Rhine provinces), and the German colonies would be taken over by France and England. Even Hanover might be revived. "By setting up a small independent state between Prussia and Holland," Nicholas asserted, "we should do much towards putting the future peace on a solid basis." In February 1915, in a still more exuberant mood, he told Paleologue that he wanted France to emerge from the war as great and strong as possible: "I agree beforehand to everything your Government wishes. Take the left bank of the Rhine; take Coblentz; go even further if you think it wise."[60]

Russia's military prospects, if not wholly contradictory to the tsar's grandiose designs, left few grounds for optimism. Admittedly neither the Austrians nor the Turks were capable of a serious threat to Russia's security. But Germany's striking power was convincingly demonstrated once more in September 1915 when its troops, with Austrian assistance, routed the Serbian army and took Belgrade. Bulgaria, spurred by the promise of acquiring Macedonia, joined the Central Powers and participated in the continuing offensive against Serbia. This "fratricidal" act aroused deep resentment in Russia, and Nicholas issued a doleful manifesto on October 5 denouncing Bulgaria's perfidy: Russia "draws its sword" with a "bleeding heart," leaving "the fate of these traitors to the Slav cause to the just chastisement of God." The episode greatly troubled Nicholas, and his confessor, Father Aleksandr Vassilyov, commented to Sazonov that "our beloved Tsar is overwhelmed with grief—and almost remorse—at the misfortunes of Serbia."[61] In private Nicholas remarked, "If anyone had told me that I should one day sign a declaration of war on Bulgaria I should have called him a lunatic. Yet that day has come."[62]

The tsar as supreme commander resumed his tours of inspection in mid-October and eventually covered almost the whole front from the Baltic to the Black Sea. His visits supposedly aroused "immense enthusiasm" among both soldiers and civilians, fortifying Nicholas' confidence in his own popularity and the patriotism of the common people. He found little time for his duties at Mogilyov, perfunctory though they were. A journey to the Galician frontier in early December was interrupted by another illness of the tsarevich, and Nicholas hastily escorted his son back to Tsarskoe Selo.

Alexis soon recovered, and Alexandra gave the credit to Rasputin's prayers.[63]

The fighting on the eastern front subsided in late autumn, corresponding to a relatively peaceful interlude in domestic politics. In the Duma's absence the Progressive Bloc fell prey to internal dissension over political tactics, and Milyukov observed with dismay that the Kadet party, too, had split into factions. The government accordingly held the whip hand and declined to honor its promise to reconvene the Duma in November. Rodzyanko, for one, refused to be encouraged by outward tokens of stability and contended that the country was "going from bad to worse." "Profiteering, bribery and other abuses were flourishing on an unprecedented scale," he charged. "In the towns prices were soaring up owing to the disorganization of transport," and strikes "began to occur at the munitions factories." By early December he was persuaded that public feeling in Moscow had taken "a distinctly revolutionary turn" and that the "most well-intentioned people" spoke openly of governmental corruption "and did not scruple to lay all the blame on the Emperor and Empress."[64]

Rodzyanko deemed the time propitious to renew the assault on Goremykin, who was held responsible by the educated public for the "general confusion" and who invariably replied to questions relating to the war, "The war does not concern me. It is the War Minister's business." Since complaints to the tsar had no effect, Rodzyanko wrote personally to Goremykin, his letter being approved beforehand by selected members of the Duma. He foresaw the country "heading for ruin" because of governmental apathy and lack of initiative. "If the Council of Ministers fails to take such steps as may yet save our country from disgrace and humiliation, the entire responsibility will rest upon you." He pleaded with the ministerial chairman: "If you . . . feel that you lack strength to bear this heavy burden," muster the courage to admit it and "make way for younger and more energetic men." Goremykin read the letter to the cabinet and, though resentful of its "harsh tone," promised to inform the emperor of its contents. Rodzyanko himself submitted a copy to Nicholas at an audience late in December in which he urged the immediate convocation of the Duma.[65]

The tsar remained at army headquarters during most of January 1916 and kept his political intentions to himself. But he had come to recognize Goremykin's unpopularity if not his incompetence—even Alexandra now admitted his unsuitability—and thought "incessantly about a successor for the old man." He consulted "fat Khv[ostov]," asking his opinion of Boris Stürmer, the ultra-conservative member of the State Council who had been seriously considered as mayor of Moscow in 1913. Khvostov praised him but considered him too old (at sixty-seven) and commented that "his head is not as clear as formerly." His German name had a "noxious ring," as Rodzyanko put it, and Stürmer proposed to overcome that difficulty by changing it to Panin, his mother's maiden name; Nicholas refused permission without the consent of the surviving members of the Panin family. Stürmer was widely regarded as Alexandra's and Rasputin's candidate, and they did indeed support him. Nicholas, however, appeared to make his choice independently and with deliberation. He resisted Alexandra's suggestion to invite Stürmer to Mogilyov, declaring it "inconvenient." "I receive here exclusively people who have some connection or other with the war," he explained. "His arrival, therefore, would only serve as an occasion for various rumours and suppositions. I desire that his appointment, if it does take place, should come like a clap of thunder."[66]

Nicholas achieved the "thunderclap" on January 20 with a rescript praising Goremykin but announcing his retirement for reasons of health and his replacement by Stürmer. Tall, white-haired, and well groomed, the new minister made an impressive appearance. He attempted to curry public favor by declaring the government's benevolence toward the Duma and its imminent recall. The fragmented Progressive Bloc greeted Goremykin's departure with relief, and most of the deputies looked forward to working more closely with his successor. But the initial spirit of good will faded rapidly as Stürmer's deficiencies became too glaring to ignore. His reputation as a puppet of Rasputin, though based on scanty evidence, was sufficiently damning in itself. Paleologue's opinion, probably relying on the wisdom of hindsight, spoke for the politically sophisticated: "worse than a mediocrity—third-rate intellect, mean spirit, low character, doubtful honesty, no experience, and no idea of State business. The most that can be said is that he has a rather pretty talent for cunning and flattery."[67] Milyukov complained that Stürmer was "totally ignorant of everything he undertook; he was unable to connect two words to express any kind of serious thought. . . . In serious questions he preferred to maintain a mysterious silence, as if to hide his decision. On the other hand, he knew very well how to preserve his own interests in all appointments."[68]

To allay popular discontent and to sustain national morale, Rodzyanko considered it "absolutely necessary" that the emperor be persuaded to pay his respects to the Duma at its impending session. He used an intermediary for the purpose, "an old patriot and idealist" for whom Nicholas retained an affectionate regard. Alexandra and Rasputin, among others, also favored the idea, and presumably this combined intercession achieved its aim—an unprecedented royal visit to the Tauride Palace at the reopening of the Duma on February 9. Nicholas, "deadly pale," with his hands "trembling with agitation," attended a moving *Te Deum* in the presence of the deputies, Allied ambassadors, and government dignitaries. The impressive spectacle appeared to quiet his nerves, and the "strained look on his face gave way to one of calm satisfaction." He addressed the members of the Duma briefly, in a "colorless but well disposed" effort, and shook hands with most of the senior leaders. Rodzyanko urged him to seize the "joyous occasion" and proclaim a responsible ministry on the spot; "By doing so you will write a page of gold in the history of your reign." Nicholas, apparently taken aback by this bold suggestion, ventured a noncommittal reply: "I will think it over." He departed to "thundering cheers" after thanking Rodzyanko: "This has all been very pleasant. This is a day I shall never forget."[69]

Once again Nicholas had aroused vain expectations of compromise and reconciliation. He had paid his respects to the people's "chosen representatives," as he obligingly called them, but he reserved the right to form his own cabinet without consulting the Duma. He returned to duty at Stavka the next day seemingly content that his ceremonial appearance had calmed the political waters. Stürmer meanwhile read a statement to the Duma replete with "longwinded and incoherent phrases," further obfuscating to the government's policy. By mid-February Nicholas was back in Tsarskoe Selo for an extended visit, and Rodzyanko renewed his importunities in an audience on the 24th that lasted an hour and a half. Speaking with "complete frankness," the Duma president recited a veritable litany of grievances that included ministerial intrigues, the continued drift in government leadership, "widespread abuse and contempt of public opinion," and inevitably, the Rasputin scandal. He cited the "orgies and debauchery" of the royal favorite, his influence on affairs of state ("the despair of all honest men"), and his role as a German agent that was "no longer open to doubt." "No one tries to open your eyes with regard to the part played by this disreputable *starets*," Rodzyanko declared. "His presence in the Imperial Court undermines the nation's confidence in the Crown; it may have fatal consequences for the fate of the dynasty, and turn the hearts of your subjects against their Sovereign." Nicholas listened to "these unpleasant home truths" affably and in silence except for an occasional interjection of surprise. Presumably the report was taken seriously, for an order was issued three days later for Rasputin's deportation to the Siberian city of Tobolsk. Alexandra intervened, however, and the order was quickly rescinded.[70]

Rodzyanko, although wholly sincere in his fulminations about Rasputin, confused legend with reality. The wily charlatan had indeed succumbed to weaknesses of the flesh and even harbored pretensions of a quasi-political nature. But he never sought to become the power behind the throne, nor was he the depraved monster of popular imagination. The "German agent" charge was sheer fantasy, another accretion of wartime hysteria. The public had acquired a taste for scapegoats, and in time, with the stresses induced by military defeat, its appetite became insatiable. As the symbol of a decadent monarchy Rasputin achieved unparalleled notoriety, and if his political impact was negligible by normal standards, he proved one of the most durable and controversial personalities in the history and folklore of modern Russia.

13

The Collapse of the Monarchy

Because the nature of Alexis' illness remained a well-kept secret, Alexandra's protracted association with Rasputin appeared to the public as both sinister and bizarre. The scandal ballooned into almost obscene proportions when it became common gossip that their relationship involved sexual intimacy. Such a scenario was preposterous. It would not have occurred to Alexandra, and Rasputin, despite his lecherous habits, knew his place. In the royal presence he managed a delicate balance between respectful deference and the familiarity permitted to a "man of God."

Before the war Rasputin's political pretensions, if they existed at all, were modest indeed. He apparently exercised a pernicious influence in church affairs but demonstrated little interest in matters of statecraft and high politics. Nor did access to the royal family confer special advantages, other than to create the kind of notoriety that eventually attracted petitioners, opportunists, and favor-seekers who imagined that he enjoyed immense power and its attendant privileges. But in 1912–1913, except for discreet visits to the capital, he avoided publicity by residing in his native Siberia.

By coincidence, on the very day that the Archduke Franz Ferdinand was assassinated in 1914, Rasputin barely escaped a similar fate. He was stabbed and severely wounded by a former lover, recovering in a Tyumen hospital. He opposed Russia's involvement in the war and pleaded with Nicholas by letter and telegram to avoid the impending disaster: "You are the Tsar, the Father of the People; don't allow the madmen to triumph and destroy themselves and the People. . . . The destruction is terrible, the grief without end." Another message called for the dismissal of "Nikolashka" as commander in chief and warned that "if you declare war . . . evil will befall you and the Tsarevich."[1] Nicholas did not take kindly to such importunate meddling in affairs of state, and for the balance of the year Rasputin remained in imperial disfavor, though Alexandra's faith in him was seemingly unshaken. During Nicholas' increasingly prolonged absences at army headquarters, she saw the *starets* frequently at Tsarskoe Selo and had no inhibitions about relaying "our Friend's" remarks to her husband. This second-hand advice, sometimes garbled in Alexandra's imperfect English, was not bereft of insight into public issues but hardly constituted a guide to governmental policy.

That the empress had become a pawn of Rasputin by 1916, if not before, is an assumption that rests upon dubious evidence. A shrewd if idiosyncratic observer of human frailty, he soon learned to read the cues that she provided, and as a general rule he simply told her what she wanted to hear. She valued his advice as "wisdom endowed by God" but at the same time learned to overcome her timidity and take an active and independent role in political affairs. "I am no longer the slightest bit shy or affraid [*sic*] of the ministers," she confided to her husband, "& speak like a waterfall in Russia[n]!!! And they kindly don't laugh at my faults." For his part Nicholas did not invariably yield to his wife's remonstrances, though he was deferential and grateful for her opinion. At one point he urged her to be his "eyes and ears there in the capital. . . . It rests with you to keep peace and harmony among the Ministers—thereby you do a great service to me and to our country. . . . I am so happy to think that you have found at last a worthy occupation! Now I shall naturally be calm, and at least not worry over internal affairs." But his momentary burst of enthusiasm waned with practical experience of Alexandra's newfound interest in politics. His delegation of authority, so spontaneously invoked, never became a reality, and his "worries" mounted under the constant pressure of domestic events. Nor was Nicholas oblivious to Rasputin's influence and erratic judgment: "Our Friend's opinions are sometimes very strange, as you know yourself."[2] He patiently tolerated his wife's obsession while as unobtrusively as possible setting his own course.

The Stürmer era lasted until November 1916. In retrospect, it constituted a grace period for the monarchy, a final desperate chance for the regime to put its house in order. Preoccupied with his military and ceremonial role, Nicholas attempted to delegate to Stürmer burdens that even a Witte or a Stolypin would have found insupportable. His designated "strong man," though probably not the craven bungler that his critics have maintained, presided over the climactic phase of the "ministerial leapfrog" that did so much to discredit the tsar and his government.

Minister of Interior Aleksei Khvostov became the first casualty under the new dispensation. Involved in a foolhardy plot to assassinate Rasputin

(Nicholas pronounced the affair "a damnable story!"), he was dismissed on March 3, 1916, despite his protestations of devotion to the monarch.[3] The interior ministry was added to Stürmer's duties. Nicholas thereby broke one of his own "rules" in effect since Stolypin's death—that is, combining the cabinet chairmanship with a ministerial portfolio. But it amounted to a rousing vote of confidence in Stürmer.

The next victim was General Polivanov, whose performance as war minister in the provisioning and training of the army had been exemplary. His close ties with the War Industry Committees—doubly suspect since they were headed by Guchkov—aroused the sovereign's displeasure, and Alexandra harped incessantly on the need to remove him. Nicholas received him cordially at Stavka but shortly thereafter, on March 15, abruptly dismissed him without the customary gestures of appreciation. "Society" received the news with "profound consternation," in Rodzyanko's words. Nicholas rejected his wife's candidate and selected General Dmitri Shuvayev as the new war minister ("honest, absolutely loyal, is not at all afraid of the Duma, and knows all the faults and shortcoming of these committees"). Whatever his merit, Shuvayev doubted his own ability to undertake such a demanding assignment, and subsequent experience demonstrated that his self-estimate was correct.[4]

With mounting inflation, growing food shortages in the cities, labor unrest, and increasing disenchantment with the war, the situation demanded effective leadership. Nicholas experienced no sense of alarm, if indeed he ever became fully aware of the severity of such problems. He seemed to feel that his cabinet reorganization, especially the elevation of Stürmer, demonstrated his capacity to rule with firm and decisive authority. But Stürmer had quickly lost his credibility with the Duma and with public opinion generally. In theory the Progressive Bloc was presented with a splendid opportunity to fill the power vacuum during an unusually long session of the Duma from February 9 to June 20 (interrupted only by a month's recess). Its leadership continued to regress, however, and Milyukov, the key figure in holding together a moderate coalition, chose to join a deputation of legislators on a good will mission to western Europe. A new low in the Duma's fortunes came as a self-inflicted blow: a quorum could not always be obtained for voting purposes. As summer arrived the only cheerful note in an otherwise gloomy outlook came from an unexpected quarter—the battlefield. Under General Aleksei Brusilov an offensive on the southwestern front broke through the Austrian lines, forcing the enemy to suspend its campaign in northern Italy and providing some relief from the German onslaught on the French fortress of Verdun.

With the Duma prorogued until November, Rodzyanko journeyed to Mogilyov for an imperial audience. Nicholas, whose courtesy seldom flagged despite his private view that the Duma president "talked a lot of nonsense," listened to the "unpleasant news of disorder in the rear without murmur or contradiction." Rodzyanko came to the realization that his detailed and candid report had miscarried and that "a kind of indifference or weariness was noticeable in the Emperor's attitude towards everything that was taking place."[5] Among the topics discussed was a proposal by General Alekseyev to establish a "dictatorship" to direct and coordinate the nation's domestic life, with emphasis on the war effort.[6] Although Nicholas brushed aside the idea in conversing with Rodzyanko, the scheme remained very much alive. On June 28 a ministerial conference took place at Stavka, ostensibly to examine the merits of the project but in reality to accept the royal mandate. Stürmer became the nominee, much to his initial dismay. He protested his inability to hold three posts simultaneously, and Nicholas obligingly shifted Aleksandr Khvostov from the ministry of justice to Interior. Stürmer's "dictatorship" became official on July 1, but his authority, even had he possessed the necessary aptitude and determination, remained purely nominal, in part because control of the interior ministry was vital to the exercise of effective power.

Having provided a bureaucratic "solution" to the country's internal problems, Nicholas supplemented his handiwork by a major personnel change in external affairs. Sazonov, the one "liberal" of note to have survived previous cabinet purges, was abruptly terminated as foreign minister on July 10. His downfall, long rumored, was ascribed by Sazonov himself to the empress: "She's never forgiven me for begging the Emperor not to assume command of his armies. She brought such pressure to bear to secure my dismissal that the Emperor ultimately gave way." His allegation was not mistaken, but the immediate circumstances were more complex than Sazonov acknowledged. A firm advocate of autonomy for Poland, he submitted a draft constitution for the tsar's consideration and received the latter's assurance of support in a personal meeting at Mogilyov. Delighted, his face beaming with "joy and pride," Sazonov related his triumph to the two Allied ambassadors: "The Emperor has entirely adopted my views—all my views—though I can assure you we had a pretty warm debate! It's all over now! I won all along the line. You should have seen Stürmer and Khvostov storm!" He left for Finland to take a working vacation and soon discovered that his declaration of victory had been decidedly premature. Stürmer, as a spokesman for Russian nationalism, and Alexandra, indisposed to relinquish her son's patrimony, intervened to convince Nicholas that action on Poland's status could be delayed indefinitely at no great political cost. The rescript dismissing Sazonov praised his "tireless zeal" and "devoted service," maintaining the pretense that he had resigned because of ill health.[7]

Stürmer added the foreign ministry to his impressive array of duties, convinced that it would enhance his prestige while requiring no significant expenditure of time and effort. Wholly lacking in diplomatic experience, he concealed his incompetence by inactivity. "Many," wrote Milyukov with witty contempt, "began recalling out loud the story of how the Roman Emperor Caligula made his favorite horse a senator."[8] Too late, the Allied ambassadors tried in vain to intercede with the tsar on Sazonov's behalf. Profoundly distrustful of Stürmer, they were inclined to accept the unfounded rumors that linked him with the supposed pro-German machinations of the "dark forces," at least to the extent of his favoring a separate peace with Germany. But Stürmer, except on the Polish question, was content to follow Sazonov's lead and sought to reassure the Allies of Russia's fidelity to the common cause. Nor did he ordinarily intervene in the routine business of the foreign ministry, relying heavily on the expertise of an able deputy, Anatoly Neratov. As for the Poles, their aspirations were left to dangle. Nicholas preferred to postpone action until Russian forces reached the Polish boundary. But since the Central Powers eventually granted "independence," he reluctantly conceded autonomy in a manifesto released on December 13, 1916. The document, more than two years overdue, failed to inspire Poland's leaders with sentiments of gratitude.

Imperial confidence in Stürmer reached its zenith in the spring of 1916 but declined precipitously during the fall. As early as June 11 Nicholas began to entertain doubts about his chief minister. "He is an excellent, honest man," he wrote Alexandra, "only, it seems to me, he cannot make up his mind to do what is necessary." The "necessities" included dealing with a fuel crisis, deficient railway transportation, and a shortage of iron and copper for the production of munitions. Such problems amounted to a "regular curse" and a source of "constant anxiety." "I cannot make out where the truth lies. But it is imperative to act energetically and to take firm measures, in order to settle these questions once for all."[9] The "questions" persisted nonetheless, and Stürmer, though by no means indolent, provided few if any answers. Most of his ministerial colleagues lost respect for him, and the ambitious minister of communications, Aleksandr Trepov, strove to organize an anti-Stürmer faction. Minister of Interior Aleksandr Khvostov was also hostile and ordered the arrest on extortion charges of Ivan Manasevich-Manuilov, a shady character who served as confidential aide to Stürmer and as contact man with Rasputin. Stürmer gained revenge, with the assistance of the tsaritsa, when Khvostov was forced to resign on September 16 under the pretext of poor health.[10]

Alexandra and Rasputin had already selected a candidate to replace Khvostov, but Nicholas complained of the rapid turnover of ministers: "All these changes make my head go round. In my opinion, they are too frequent. In any case, they are not good for the internal situation of the country, as each new man brings with him alterations in the administration."[11] Nevertheless, he suspended his own judgment, disregarded Stürmer's recommendations, and accepted his wife's choice, Aleksandr Protopopov, as acting minister of the interior. The appointment was unconventional in that Protopopov, as vice president of the Duma, an Octobrist, and a nominal member of the Progressive Bloc, represented a royal gesture of conciliation toward "society"—or to be more precise, the moderates of the Duma opposition. Unhappily for Nicholas' benign intentions, the new minister became a public relations disaster. He possessed no governmental experience and few obvious qualifications for office apart from an ingratiating manner and a façade of dapper elegance. Perhaps to compensate for his parvenu status, he conceived grandiose schemes of reform, not simply of the administrative structure but of Russian society as a whole. Rodzyanko thought his personal behavior "very peculiar," and others noted mental aberrations that suggested an advanced case of syphilis.

Initially Protopopov received substantial backing from Duma sympathizers, in part because he was free of bureaucratic contamination. To many patriots, however, he had committed the unforgivable sin: as chairman of the parliamentary delegation that journeyed abroad earlier in the year, he conferred with a German diplomat in Stockholm. The rumor spread that a separate peace had been discussed, thus providing further "proof" of a pro-German conspiracy, conveniently linking Alexandra, Rasputin, Stürmer, and of course Protopopov himself. The parting of the ways between the new interior minister and his former colleagues of the Duma apparently came on October 19 at a private meeting at Rodzyanko's apartment. Milyukov led the charge, accusing Protopopov of abandoning his "liberalism" for the expediency of holding office: "A man who serves with Stürmer, a man who has freed Sukhomlinov, who is considered a traitor by the entire country, a man who persecutes the press and social-welfare organizations cannot be our comrade. And furthermore, they say that Rasputin is behind your appointment." Protopopov turned aside most of the accusations, pleading lack of confidentiality of their discussion. But he refused to back down and boldly proclaimed his monarchist principles: "Now I know the tsar personally and have come to love him. And I don't know why, but he loves me also." As the meeting ended, Milyukov delivered a parting sally: "You are leading Russia to destruction."[12]

Although Nicholas found welcome relief at Mogilyov from the political cares and intrigues of the capital, he could hardly avoid them altogether. Alexandra provided a steady stream of gossip, information, and advice, much of it prompted by Rasputin's "wonderful, God sent wisdom." Stürmer sent frequent reports and was received on occasion, as were other ministers and officials. The twin specters of inflation and food shortages were brought to Nicholas' attention in September. "Old St.[ürmer] cannot overcome these difficulties," he wrote his wife. "It is the most damnable problem I have ever come across! I never was a business man, and simply do not understand anything in these questions of supplying and provisioning." Alexandra tried to reassure him: "Our Friend begs you not to too much worry over this question of *food supply*, . . . says things will arrange themselves & the new Minister [Protopopov] has already set to work at once." Nicholas conferred with Protopopov for two hours on September 28 and expressed his sincere hope "that he will prove suitable and will justify our expectations; he is, it seems, inspired by the best intentions, and has an excellent knowledge of internal affairs."[13] Protopopov did indeed grapple with the looming crisis of urban famine; his solution involved transferring the procurement of civilian food supplies from the ministry of agriculture to his own jurisdiction at Interior. Nicholas endorsed the proposal, but Protopopov declined to act, fearful of a public backlash on the eve of the Duma's autumn session.

Late in October, Nicholas, accompanied by Alexis, visited Kiev to see his mother, who had moved from Petrograd, presumably to avoid proximity to Alexandra and Rasputin. Nicholas recalled a previous visit in 1911: "The death of the unhappy Stolypin came back to me so vividly." His sister Olga, also at the family reunion, was shocked to see him "so pale, thin, and tired," and his mother expressed concern at his "excessive quiet." Alexis' tutor also noticed the change: "He had never seemed to me so worried before. He was usually very self-controlled, but on this occasion he showed himself nervous and irritable, and once or twice he spoke roughly to Alexis." Nicholas had long talks with his mother and was more impressed with her warnings about Stürmer than her strictures against Rasputin.[14]

Back at army headquarters Nicholas received his cousin, the Grand Duke Nikolai Mikhailovich, a respected historian and virtually the only Romanov with intellectual pretensions. They conversed for some time, and Nikolai presented a letter upon his departure that stated frankly what he hesitated to say in person. "You trust Alexandra Fyodorovna," he wrote, "which is easy to understand. But what she tells you is not the truth; she is only repeating what has been cleverly suggested to her. If you are unable to remove these influences from her, at least protect yourself from these constant and systematic maneuvers by those who act through your beloved wife." He went on to recommend a government of public confidence and warned of new disturbances, even of attempts at assassination. "Believe me," he concluded, "that in trying to loosen you from the chains that bind you, I do it from no motives of personal interest . . . but in the hope and in the expectation of saving you, your throne, and our dear country from irreparable consequences."[15] With its unmistakable reference to Rasputin, the letter could not fail to offend Alexandra, however tactfully phrased. Nicholas sent it on to her—unread, so he claimed—and she reacted with unrestrained fury. "He is the incarnation of all that's evil," she wrote, and his "loathsome" action was "next to high treason." Nicholas apologized for upsetting her but pointed out that Nikolai had not mentioned her in their conversation. "Had he said anything about you, you do not really doubt that your dear hubby would have taken your part?"[16]

On November 7 the deposed supreme commander, Nikolai Nikolayev-

ich, arrived in Mogilyov to intercede with his cousin. He came to the point
with caustic frankness: "I wanted to get a rise out of him," but Nicholas
"just sat silently and shrugged his shoulders. I told him directly: 'I would
be more pleased if you swore at me, struck me, kicked me out than at your
silence. Can't you see that you are losing your crown? . . . Grant a responsible ministry. . . . You just procrastinate. For the moment there is still time,
but soon it will be too late.' " Nicholas remained unmoved. Only too familiar with Alexandra's strident hostility toward her "enemies," he prudently declined to discuss the latest confrontation with her and simply
stated that "so far all conversations have passed off well."[17]

Noting the tsar's mood of fatalistic lethargy, Ambassador Paleologue
consulted three of the grand dukes and concluded that "despondency, apathy and resignation can be seen in his actions, appearance, attitude and
all the manifestations of the inner man." He also maintained that in recent
months Nicholas "frequently suffered from nervous maladies which betray
themselves in unhealthy excitement, anxiety, loss of appetite, depression
and insomnia." Constipation could have been added to the list. Alexandra
allegedly consulted Badmayev, the Buryat "quack" who had been administering to Protopopov. "The charlatan soon discovered in his pharmacopoeia the remedy appropriate to the case of his august patient: it is an elixir
compounded of 'Tibetan herbs' according to a magic formula and has to
be prescribed very strictly." The drug is said to have performed therapeutic
wonders, "the baneful symptoms . . . vanished in a twinkling. He has not
only recovered sleep and appetite, but experienced a general feeling of well-
being, a delightful sense of increased vigour and a curious euphoria."
"Judging by its effects," Paleologue concluded, "the elixir must be a mix-
ture of henbane and hashish, and the Emperor should be careful not to
take too much."[18]

Always eager to embellish a good story, whether based on hard evidence
or high-level gossip, the ambassador was probably more accurate than not
in depicting Nicholas' physical and emotional distress. But the implication
that Nicholas found more than temporary relief in Badmayev's concoction,
if in fact he used it at all, is mistaken, for the state of his health continued
to deteriorate. Count Pavel Benkendorf, a loyal servitor, noted the tsar's
indisposition and confided to the court physician, "His Majesty is a
changed man. . . . He is no longer seriously interested in anything. Of late,
he has become quite apathetic. He goes through his daily routine like an
automaton, paying more attention to the hour set for his meals or his walk
in the garden than to affairs of state. One can't rule an empire and command an army in the field in this manner."[19]

The Duma reconvened on November 1, 1916, with the Progressive Bloc
in continued disarray. The moderates, faced with a massive shift in the
public mood that placed the monarchy in imminent peril, were hardly pre-

pared to lead or even to join a revolutionary crusade. Yet they were bitterly critical of a government that could dismiss the Duma at any time and deprive the deputies of a national forum. A series of private meetings only compounded the dilemma. Milyukov garnered some support in favor of a political tightrope act that would condemn Stürmer and the "dark forces" while avoiding direct criticism of the tsar. "But certain things will have to be said from the tribune," he told Paleologue. "Otherwise we should lose all our influence with our constituents and they would go over to the extremists."[20]

The session opened to packed galleries and an atmosphere of sullen irascibility among the deputies. Forewarned of trouble ahead, Stürmer and the other cabinet ministers departed following Rodzyanko's inaugural address. Sergei Shidlovsky, the Octobrist leader, read a declaration of the Progressive Bloc, and Aleksandr Kerensky, a prominent lawyer of the Trudovik faction, denounced the government with such vehemence that Rodzyanko declared him out of order. Milyukov then mounted the rostrum to deliver what was to become the most famous speech in the annals of the Duma. He ranged broadly over the breakdown of the war effort, with particular attention to the scandals involving Sukhomlinov and Manasevich-Manuilov, while reserving his choice barbs for Stürmer. And he broke precedent by referring to the sinister influence of the empress. The most sensational aspect of his remarks involved a sequence of accusations against Stürmer in which he repeatedly intoned the rhetorical query, "Is this stupidity, or is this treason?" Clearly he preferred the latter alternative at the time, but upon later reflection he declared unconvincingly that he had intended the former.[21]

Milyukov likened the impact of his speech to a "pus-filled sack [that] had burst."[22] It provided a simplistic explanation for complicated events that found resonance in the national psyche, and it transformed the Kadet leader into an instant celebrity. Many, including Milyukov himself, saw it in retrospect as the opening salvo of the revolutionary struggle. Censorship deprived the public of the text, but illegal versions, often more inflammatory than the original, circulated in countless numbers. The government's counterattack proved surprisingly feeble, chiefly because the Council of Ministers rejected an effort to prosecute Milyukov; Stürmer instead pursued a charge of slander, which was to be nullified by the fall of the monarchy. Ironically, he had a sound case if one may divorce political posturing and unabashed hyperbole from the rules of evidence: Milyukov had known then (and certainly did later) that he had no proof of Stürmer's "treason" or indeed any manifestations of treachery on the part of the "court camarilla." None was ever to appear.[23]

Nicholas' confidence in Stürmer had gradually weakened under the badgering of his relatives and pressure from General Alekseyev, and it collapsed with the firestorm in the Duma. Alexandra, too, was half-prepared to jettison the besieged minister. Sympathetic ("Poor old man may die fr. the vile way his spoken to & of at the *Duma*"), she acknowledged that since he had become "the red flag for that madhause" it would be better for him to "disappear a bitt & then in Dec. when they will have been cleared out return again." Nicholas agreed that Stürmer "acts as a red flag, not only to the Duma, but to the whole country, alas!. . . . It is much worse than it was with Goremykin last year. I reproach him for his excessive prudence and his incapacity for taking upon himself the responsibility of making them all work as they should do. . . . I do not understand how it is, but nobody has confidence in him!"[24]

Nicholas told Stürmer in person of his dismissal on November 9, informing Alexandra that the "poor old man was calm and touching." He also decided to replace Protopopov—"a good, honest man, but he jumps from one idea to another and cannot make up his mind on anything. . . . It is risky to leave the Ministry of Internal Affairs in the hands of such a man in these times!" He alluded to reports that Protopopov had been "not quite normal" several years ago "after a certain illness" (presumably syphilis) and had sought Badmayev's advice. Recognizing his wife's aggressive role in recent ministerial appointments, he tried to sidestep the "Rasputin factor." "I beg you," he wrote, "do not drag our Friend into this. The responsibility is with me, and therefore I wish to be free in my choice."[25] Minister of Transport Trepov, an energetic conservative, assumed the chairmanship of the Ministerial Council on the understanding that further cabinet changes would take place, notably the removal of Protopopov. After some delay, Nikolai Pokrovsky, whose chief experience had been in financial matters, filled the foreign ministry vacancy.

Whether Alexandra consulted Rasputin about the appointments is uncertain, but she showed no hesitation in expressing her views. "I have no very good opinion of *Trepov*," she wrote, because of his "disagreeable character" and his "wishing to clear out people devoted to me." Aside from Rasputin, her chief "devotee" was Protopopov, and she regarded his retention as a test case between tsar and Duma. "Forgive my again writing," she pleaded, "but I am fighting for your reign & Baby's future. God will help, be firm don't listen to men, who are not from God but cowards."[26]

Alexandra departed for Mogilyov on November 13 on a prearranged visit. Her will prevailed over that of Trepov, and Protopopov kept his post. But Nicholas managed to overrule her regarding the ministry of agriculture, where the reputable Aleksandr Rittikh replaced the incompetent Aleksei Bobrinsky. Nor did Alexandra succeed in undermining Trepov, though he mortgaged his future by attempting to bribe Rasputin. The scheme amounted to a dangerous gamble, likely to end up badly for all concerned, But Trepov plunged ahead: "If it must it must. I will risk it. In any case I am quite prepared to go. The tsar will say nothing to me about Rasputin, but he will find a pretext that will do to get rid of me. I am putting all my stakes on this one card. So long as Protopopov is Minister of the Interior it will be impossible for me to carry on the Government." The proposal was transmitted by General Aleksandr Mosolov, the head of the Court Chancellery and Trepov's brother-in-law, who offered Rasputin a payment of 200,000 rubles, a house in Petrograd, and other perquisites if he would refrain from meddling in government appointments and confine his influence to church affairs. The *starets* refused after a lengthy meeting at which Madeira wine flowed freely. Mosolov had the unpleasant duty of reporting the "fiasco" to Trepov, who "realized that he was done for."[27]

Alexandra's sojourn and Nicholas' return visit to Tsarskoe Selo in late November dashed the serenity of their normal relationship. He referred to their "difficult" days together and asked for forgiveness for being "moody or unrestrained—sometimes one's temper must come out!" "I firmly believe," he wrote, "that the most painful is behind us and that it will not be as hard as it was before. And henceforth I intend to become sharp and bitter [toward the political opposition]." Alexandra was less apologetic and, though as devoted as always, stressed Nicholas' autocratic duty: "Show to all, that you are the Master & your will shall be obeyed—the time of great indulgence & gentleness is over. . . . Obedience they must be taught, they do not know the meaning of that word, you have spoilt them by yr. kindness & all forgivingness."[28]

Trepov, aware of the hazards that lay ahead in pleasing so fickle a royal master, made a good-faith effort to work with the Duma. Yet in succeeding Stürmer he himself became the symbol of governmental mismanagement; the deputies of the Left regarded him with emotions ranging from distrust to open hostility. Those of the socialist persuasion jeered him at his first appearance at the reconvened Duma on November 19. A number were forcibly expelled, finally allowing Trepov to speak, but his conciliatory remarks found little favor despite his revelation that Russia had signed an agreement with its allies on the Straits question. Vladimir Purishkevich, a firebrand of the extreme Right, provided the sensation of the day by excoriating Rasputin and the "dark forces" in language that resembled Milyukov's.[29] That sinister phrase, once the shibboleth of the Progressive Bloc, had now become a political war cry irresistible to monarchists and to revolutionaries alike. A veritable orgy of recrimination ensued. The Duma passed a resolution denouncing the pernicious "dark forces" on November 22, and the State Council, once a bastion of the status quo, followed suit. Even the Congress of the United Nobility joined the stampede, although its resolution specified that a ministry enjoying the "confidence of the country" should be "responsible to the monarch alone."

Few bothered to question or to contradict the new orthodoxy. The French ambassador, no dissenter himself, did speculate on the program and leadership of the empress' "camarilla." He reasoned that she was "too impulsive, wrong-headed and unbalanced to imagine a political system and carry it out logically" and that therefore she was acting as the "omnipotent political tool of the conspiracy." But who were the "conspirators"? Paleologue provided a list, headed of course by Rasputin. Others included Stürmer and Protopopov; Anna Vyrubova, a confidante of both Alexandra and Rasputin; General Voyeikov, the palace commandant; and Prince Mikhail Andronnikov, a notorious homosexual, influence peddler, and political opportunist. Paleologue surmised, however, that they were "only subordinates . . . servile plotters or marionettes." Then who, he wondered, controlled these servitors? Questioning those who seemed most likely to satisfy his curiosity, he received only "vague or contradictory replies, hypotheses and suppositions." "But if I *had* to come to some conclusion," he declared, "I should say that the evil course for which the Empress and her coterie will be responsible to History is inspired by four individuals." He named Shcheglovitov, the former minister of justice and a leader of the far Right in the State Council; Metropolitan Pitirim of Petrograd, a Rasputin protégé; Stepan Beletsky, a former assistant minister of the interior in charge of police affairs; and Ignace Manus, a Jewish banker rumored to have suspicious contacts with Germany. The latter was assigned the role of archconspirator: "It is he who keeps it [the conspiracy] in touch with Berlin, and through him that Germany plans and fosters her intrigues among Russian society. He is the distributor of the German subsidies."[30] Paleologue displayed no little ingenuity and a large dose of imagination in populating his rogue's gallery. Though in many respects an unsavory lot, they hardly constituted the seditious cabal that he so boldly nominated.

Nicholas regarded these renewed insinuations as deeply offensive. He had already made numerous concessions to the Duma, as he saw it, and did not propose to retreat before an onslaught of demagogy. Nor did he take kindly to the notion of a "ministry of confidence," a slogan of the Progressive Bloc that reverberated throughout the country. Even the "conservative" grand dukes became alarmed, and at a family gathering in late November, Pavel Aleksandrovich, the doyen and Nicholas' only surviving uncle, was authorized to recommend political reform. He pleaded with Nicholas, only to be curtly rebuffed: "What you ask is impossible. The day of my coronation I took my oath to the Absolute Power. I must leave the oath intact to my son."[31] For all his stubborn insistence on his autocratic rights, Nicholas did not succumb to his wife's intractable stance against the enemies of the throne as she perceived them, an almost paranoid reaction that induced her to recommend sending "revolutionaries" such as Milyukov, Guchkov, and Polivanov to exile in Siberia. Of the genuine revolutionaries, the activists and theoreticians of the variant strands of socialism, she, like her husband, remained almost wholly uninformed.

Alexandra's dislike of "that horrible *Trepov*" intensified when word of the abortive offer to Rasputin reached her. Nicholas came to share her opinion, and under her prodding he resolved to be "sharp, firm and ungracious" and to "know what to answer" when consulting his first minister. After fortifying himself by praying before a favorite icon, he received Trepov at Mogilyov on December 10; later he reported him to have been "quiet and submissive and [that he] did not touch upon the name of Protopopov. Probably my face was ungracious and hard, as he wriggled in his chair." Among other topics, they spoke of adjourning the Duma until January 19, and then if "they begin blundering and making trouble he is prepared to hurl thunders at them . . . and close the Duma finally." "It is unpleasant," Nicholas confided with cynical disdain, "to speak to a man one does not like and does not trust, such as Trepov. But first of all it is necessary to find a substitute for him, and then kick him out—after he has done the dirty work. I mean to make him resign after he has closed the Duma. Let all the responsibility and all the difficulties fall upon his shoulders, and upon the shoulders of his successor."[32]

In mid-December Nicholas concluded several of his letters to Alexandra with the phrase, "Your 'poor weak-willed little hubby,' " a self-mocking acknowledgment that his wife was the stronger of the two. "Russia loves to feel [the] whip," she contended. "Its their nature—tender love and then the iron hand to punish & guide. How I wish I could pour my will into your veins. . . . I suffer over you as over a tender, softhearted child." The next day (December 14) she renewed her exhortation: "Be Peter the Great, Ivan the Terrible, Emperor Paul—crush them all under you." She did have the grace to apologize for her "impertinent letters" but justified them on the grounds of her "deepest love."[33] Unfortunately for Nicholas, her well-meant advice was not only wholly inappropriate as a guide to political conduct but also encouraged his own stubborn and half-hearted attempts to be "firm" and "autocratic." With the public now thoroughly disenchanted by a regime perceived to be hopelessly inept, the dry rot of self-doubt undermined the convictions even of staunch monarchists.

A stunning example of monarchist illusions gone berserk occurred in the capital on the night of December 16–17. A band of aristocrats, persuaded that they were rescuing the throne from its own defilement, succeeded in murdering the chief polluter himself. Rasputin, having barely escaped with his life in 1914 and the object of several other assaults and attempted assassinations, succumbed to these singularly inefficient killers. The foremost plotter, Prince Feliks Yusupov, was related to the tsar by marriage and among the wealthiest men in Russia. He persuaded Purishkevich, whose Duma speech had greatly impressed him, to join the conspiracy, and they recruited the Grand Duke Dmitri Pavlovich, said to be Nicholas' favorite cousin. Rasputin's licentious reputation had not been based on idle gossip, and he was supposedly lured to the Yusupov mansion on the pretext of meeting the prince's beautiful wife. Once there he indulged in refreshments heavily laced with cyanide. When the poison failed to finish him off, he was shot three times and his comatose body was then dropped through a hole in the ice of a canal near the Neva River. The rugged "holy man" apparently drowned, though the autopsy report was not conclusive.

The crime and its perpetrators could not be long concealed. Alexandra received an early report of Rasputin's disappearance that left her in "utter anguish." "I cannot & won't believe He has been killed," she wrote Nicholas. "God have mercy." When his death had been confirmed she bore her "inconsolable grief" with quiet dignity, but her "agonized features" betrayed her intense suffering. Nicholas telegraphed Alexandra that he was "horrified and shaken" by the news and returned to Tsarskoe Selo. His unruffled demeanor, which struck some observers as almost serene, led to speculation that he was secretly relieved by the murder—that it extricated the monarchy from an intolerable burden.[34] Whatever his true feelings, he gave first priority to comforting his wife. Outside the court entourage, especially among urban dwellers, open rejoicing greeted Rasputin's demise. But in rural areas, where his alleged misdeeds were only vague rumors, many peasants identified with him as one of their own, a martyred hero who had perished at the hands of their aristocratic oppressors. Within weeks the tale of one of Rasputin's prophecies, repeated to their majesties on numerous occasions, became common gossip: "If I die or you desert me, you will lose your son and your crown within six months."[35]

Rasputin received a quiet funeral at Tsarskoe Selo in the presence of the royal family. Nicholas noted the "sad scene" in his diary, "the burial of the unforgettable Grigory, assassinated by monsters at the home of Yusupov."[36] His anger derived less from the deed itself than from the culpability of his relatives. "Before all Russia," he reportedly exclaimed, "I am filled with shame that the hands of my kinsmen are stained with the blood of a simple peasant."[37] His sense of outrage was tempered by the realization that criminal proceedings would only sensationalize the affair, to the embarrassment of Alexandra and the detriment of the throne. The punishments he meted out were therefore of the token variety: Yusupov was exiled to one of his country estates, and Dmitri was obliged to serve with the Russian army in Persia. Purishkevich, who hastily left Petrograd for the front, enjoyed celebrity status as well as limited immunity from arrest as a member of the Duma. Nicholas prudently declined to press charges. Dmitri's relatives rallied around to request leniency, but Nicholas rejected their plea: "No one is allowed to indulge in murder. I know that the consciences of many [who signed the petition] are disturbed. I am surprised at your approach to me."[38]

The killing of Rasputin aroused concern in court circles that Nicholas and his consort, if not in imminent danger of assassination, might be overthrown in a palace revolution. Rumors and idle talk of "conspiracies," mostly imaginary, drifted through the capital at an accelerating pace during the winter months. According to Paleologue, the Moscow public was "furious" with the "German Woman," as Alexandra was called, and advocated that she be "put away as a lunatic." As for Nicholas, "men do not stop at remarking that he would do well to reflect on the fate of Paul I" (murdered in 1801, the last emperor to be deposed).[39] Various indiscretions by his relatives, even the possibility of a grand ducal conspiracy, induced Nicholas to strike back, though with penalties more annoying than punitive. Chastisement usually came in the form of house arrest or banishment from the capital, but two of the grand dukes were dispatched on "inspection tours." The political climate reminded historian Nikolai Mikhailovich of the "vulgar Florentine nobles in the epoch of the Borgias and the Medicis."[40]

Several high-level intrigues reached a more ambitious stage than wishful thinking. One was engineered by Prince Georgi Lvov, president of the Union of Zemstvos. Increasingly troubled by the malignant influence of Rasputin, he had approached General Alekseyev in November 1916 to sound him out on the prospect of arresting the empress and compelling the emperor to grant a responsible ministry under Lvov's chairmanship. Alekseyev at first refused but reconsidered and supposedly expressed his willingness to cooperate. After illness caused him to take convalescent leave in the Crimea, he finally rejected the scheme as likely to get out of hand by forcing Nicholas' removal. Lvov also tried without success to enlist the Grand Duke Nikolai Nikolayevich in a similar plot.[41]

Guchkov, as ringleader of another group, proposed to seize the imperial train on one of Nicholas' trips between Mogilyov and Petrograd and to demand his abdication. Various delays prevented the execution of the plan before the February Revolution intervened. Since neither plot attracted effective military support and confidentiality was shockingly lax, allowing police agents to exercise loose surveillance, the prospects for a successful coup were limited. Nicholas, aware of the potential threat, suggested arresting Guchkov, but Protopopov persuaded him that such action would be premature and overly provocative.[42] Guchkov, Lvov, and other "palace revolutionaries" were not unlike Rasputin's assassins in their desire to "purify" the monarchy. Their methods were radically different, but they shared in common, along with Milyukov and the Progressive Bloc, a fear of "real" revolution arising from a groundswell of mass discontent. "Patriotism," meaning the government's sacred duty to defeat the enemy, served as their political rationale for what Nicholas could properly regard as subversive behavior.

Nicholas decided to remain at Tsarskoe Selo indefinitely. His protracted absence from the front made a sham even of his figurehead status as supreme commander. Isolated, dispirited, and insensible to the drumfire of advice recommending a government that would command popular support, he clung tenaciously to his autocratic role. Protopopov, who absorbed much of the invective previously directed toward Rasputin, was promoted to full minister on December 20. Now restored to imperial favor, he became the linchpin shoring up the monarchy during the semi-retirement of the monarch. He was also rumored to conjure up Rasputin's spirit for the edification of the empress. But the interior minister, though an accomplished courtier, was no mere time-server. Unlike most conservative royalists, who took for granted the loyalty of the masses, he had a lively appreciation of radicalism from below and the agitators who would presumably incite it. He (or his assistant for police affairs, Pavel Kurlov) accordingly tightened security measures in the capital, cracked down on clandestine revolutionary groups, and arrested the labor representatives of the War Industries Committees.

Toward the close of the year, before immersing himself in self-imposed isolation, Nicholas undertook the last round of "ministerial leapfrogging." Trepov, who had more than once asked for his release, was succeeded as chairman of the Council of Ministers by Prince Nikolai Golitsyn. The shocked Golitsyn, as head of a committee to aid Russian war prisoners, had become friendly with the empress. He tried to beg off on the grounds of old age, poor health, and lack of experience but reluctantly bowed to the sovereign's command.[43] Three other ministers were allowed to resign: the respected Count Pavel Ignatyov at Education, Aleksandr Makarov at Justice, and General Shuvayev at War. The new appointees, chosen for their loyalty to the throne rather than their competence, were virtually unknown to the public. Nicholas rounded out his final cabinet "purge" by dismissing sixteen members of the State Council and appointing eighteen new ones, all adherents of the Right. The infamous Ivan Shcheglovitov, the former minister of justice, became chairman.

The Allied ambassadors, thoroughly alarmed by a looming domestic crisis that would surely disrupt the wartime coalition, sought audiences with Nicholas. Paleologue was received on December 25 and noted the emperor's "tired look," his "anxious and absorbed expression," and his "dead, dull voice, which I had never heard before." When the ambassador ventured to discuss internal affairs, referring to the "symptoms," the "horrible doubts," and the "anxiety" that he had observed, Nicholas refused to be drawn into a political discussion, commenting only, "I know that there is great excitement in the Petrograd drawing-rooms." The two parted with a show of affection, and Paleologue reflected on his disappointing reception as the imperial train conveyed him from Tsarskoe Selo to the capital in a blinding snowstorm. "The Emperor's words," he wrote (probably with more than a touch of hindsight), "his silences and reticences, his grave, drawn features and furtive, distant gaze, the impenetrability of his thoughts and the thoroughly vague and enigmatical quality of his personality, confirm me in a notion which has been haunting me for months, the notion that Nicholas II feels himself overwhelmed and dominated by events, that he has lost all faith in his mission or his work, that he has so to speak abdicated inwardly and is now resigned to disaster and ready for the sacrificial altar."[44]

Sir George Buchanan had no better results in the course of his audience five days later, though he was much less reticent than his colleague. By this time the litany of complaints must have been all too familiar to Nicholas: German intrigue, Protopopov's harmful influence, the food shortage, and the revolutionary danger. The one safe course, the ambassador insisted, was "to break down the barrier that separates you from your people and to regain their confidence." With haughty dignity, for the remark touched a raw nerve, Nicholas responded: "Do you mean that I am to regain the confidence of my people or that they are to regain *my* confidence?" The ambassador's tactful, "Both, sir," helped to smooth over the incident, and the sincerity of his closing plea to choose the path leading to "victory and a glorious peace" over "revolution and disaster," elicited from Nicholas a friendly goodbye: "I thank you, Sir George."[45]

By the year's end only apostles of the extreme Right, among whom Nicholas could properly qualify, expressed confidence in the regime's continued stability. With the Duma again in recess over the holidays, there was little trace of "legal" opposition to the government's suicidal course. The Council of Ministers, riddled with dissension, functioned haphazardly, and Protopopov ceased to attend its meetings with any regularity. Minister of Finance Bark, who had been on sick leave, unsuccessfully attempted to resign. Foreign Minister Pokrovsky also tried to submit his resignation, at the same time warning Nicholas of Protopopov's false counsel and of "imminent catastrophe." Prince Golitsyn conveyed an even more lurid message early in January 1917, claiming that the sovereigns' lives were endangered and that regiments in Moscow talked openly of proclaiming another tsar. Nicholas reacted with "placid indifference," allegedly remarking: "The Empress and I know that we are in God's hands. His will be done!"[46]

Rodzyanko, distrusted by Nicholas and anathema to Alexandra, joined the procession of notables to Tsarskoe Selo. His first request for an audience denied, he renewed it, and on January 7, 1917, he delivered a hair-raising report of "chaos" throughout the country, of "no Government and no system," of "monstrous" rumors of "treason and espionage." He charged that "not a single honest or reliable man [is] left in your entourage; all the best have either been eliminated or resigned, and only those who have bad reputations have remained." Nor did he spare the empress: "She is looked upon as Germany's champion." Nicholas, as well he might, interjected, "Give me facts, there are no facts to confirm your statements." Rodzyanko admitted that there were no "facts," only a "whole trend of policy." He pleaded with the emperor not to "compel the people to choose between you and the good of the country. So far, the ideas of tsar and Motherland were indivisible, but lately they have begun to be separated." Nicholas appeared shaken. "Is it possible," he asked, "that for twenty-two years I tried to act for the best, and that for twenty-two years it was all a mistake?" Rodzyanko could have equivocated, but instead he answered with unflinching candor: "Yes, your Majesty for twenty-two years you followed a wrong course." Despite the harsh words, Nicholas bade his usual polite farewell with no display of resentment.[47] If self-doubt had momentarily entered his mind, there was no reflection of it in the days that followed.

Despite his virtual retirement, allowing more time for his family and other leisure pursuits than on any occasion since the outbreak of war, Nicholas was a profoundly troubled man. His physical condition and emotional stability had progressively worsened. Count Kokovtsov, who had not seen him in a year, obtained an audience on January 19. He found the emperor almost unrecognizable: "His face had become very thin and hollow and covered with small wrinkles. His eyes, usually of a velvety dark brown, had become quite faded, and wandered aimlessly from object to object instead of looking steadily at his interlocutor. The whites were of a decidedly yellow tinge, and the dark retinas had become colorless, gray, and lifeless." Shocked and alarmed, Kokovtsov could not refrain from inquiring about his health. Nicholas "bore an expression of helplessness" and a "forced, mirthless smile was fixed upon his lips" as he answered, repeating himself several times, "I am perfectly well and sound, but I spend too much time without exercise, and I am used to much activity." Later in their conversation, the "sickly smile" returned and Nicholas "literally lost all self-possession." "For a long time," Kokovtsov commented, "he looked at me in silence as if trying to collect his thoughts or to recall what had escaped his memory." The meeting left Kokovtsov distraught and in tears, convinced that the tsar suffered from a serious illness "of a nervous character."[48] His testimony, confirmed by Paleologue, raises the question of possible drug addiction. Both Nicholas and Alexandra employed opium and cocaine for minor ailments, but the evidence will not sustain the rumors then current that Nicholas' health suffered major impairment from the excessive use of drugs.[49]

Whatever the state of his health, Nicholas conscientiously performed his ceremonial duties when the Inter-Allied Conference, a lavish gathering of officials, diplomats, and generals, convened in Petrograd to discuss strategic, political, and supply problems relating to the war. He presided at a reception at Tsarskoe Selo on January 18 to honor the visitors and proved adept at small talk ("Have you had a pleasant journey? I hope you are not too tired? Is this your first visit to Russia?") but woefully inadequate—or simply apathetic—when it came to more substantive matters. Although he confined himself to similar innocuities at a state banquet three days later, he did receive the civilian head of each delegation. The only business of note transacted in private conversation involved an agreement with France, represented by Minister of Colonies Gaston Doumergue, for the annexation of Alsace-Lorraine and a free hand to determine its Rhine frontier with Germany. In return, Russia received assurances, with Pokrovsky in charge of the negotiations, that it would have a similar right to revise its border with Germany and Austria-Hungary.[50] Aside from the frontier agreement, an assessment of the Russian army's requirements, and an exchange of views on a wide variety of topics, the conferees had nothing to show for three weeks of labor and intermitant social rituals. The British vice-consul in Moscow summed up the experience aptly enough: "Rarely in the history of great wars can so many important ministers and generals have left their respective countries on so useless an errand."[51]

Nicholas' estrangement from his normal routine continued well into February. But he was by no means incommunicado. A number of his male relatives were not prepared to abandon the struggle to enlighten him, and his brother Mikhail, hitherto aloof, joined the effort. Sandro (the Grand Duke Aleksandr Mikhailovich), Nicholas' brother-in-law and boyhood companion, had already written many letters of advice and was received by the royal couple on February 10. Nicholas sat passively smoking cigarettes, and Sandro directed his arguments to Alexandra. She sneered at his plea for a government acceptable to the Duma: "All this talk of yours is ridiculous. Nicky is an autocrat. How could he share his divine rights with a parliament?" Sandro reminded her that Nicholas had ceased to be an autocrat on October 17, 1905, and the discussion soon escalated into a shouting match. "For thirty months," he yelled at her, "I never said as much as a word to you about the disgraceful goings-on in our government, better to say in *your* government! I realize that you are willing to perish and that your husband feels the same way, but what about us? Must we all suffer for your blind stubbornness? No, Alix, you have no right to drag your relatives with you down a precipice!"[52]

Nicholas also granted an audience to Rodzyanko on February 10. Absentminded and obviously impatient with the length of the report, he took exception to Rodzyanko's Cassandra-like cries about the prospect of revolution. "My information," he declared, "is directly contrary to yours," and he threatened to dissolve the Duma, still in recess, should its members indulge in the "harsh utterances" of its previous session. Rodzyanko concluded with a final warning: "I consider it my duty, Sire, to express to you my profound foreboding and my conviction that this will be my last report to you." He went on in answer to the sovereign's laconic interrogative, "Because the Duma will be dissolved, and the course the Government is taking bodes no good. There is still time; it is still possible to change everything and grant a responsible Ministry. . . . You, your Majesty, disagree with me, and everything will remain as it is. The consequence of this, in my opinion, will be revolution and a state of anarchy which no one will be able to control." Nicholas remained silent except to bid the Duma president a curt farewell.[53]

The Duma reopened quietly on February 14. The absence of incendiary rhetoric or popular disturbances reassured Nicholas that his political instinct had proved more reliable than that of his panicky critics. But the "leading role," as Milyukov admitted, no longer belonged to the Duma. Nor did it reside in the so-called public organizations involved in the war effort, although the arrest of the workers' delegates to the War Industries Committees did provoke strikes and demonstrations. "The bony hand of hunger," a metaphor that became notorious later in the year, had already made an appearance. The Okhrana's agents knew better than the tsar about the state of public opinion. "With each passing day," read one police report, "the food question becomes more aggravated and forces the average citizen to curse everyone having anything at all to do with food, and to curse them in the most uncensored expressions." Another report stressed that children were "starving in the most literal sense of the word" and predicted that if revolution came it would be "spontaneous, quite likely a hunger riot."[54]

If not entirely oblivious to the rising tide of revolt, Nicholas appeared confident of Protopopov's ability to contain it. Irritated rather than enlightened by the numerous warnings he had received, he resented any allusion to the danger of revolution. When on February 14 one of his courtiers implied that the monarchy might be in need of public support, he reacted with unaccustomed asperity. "Are you too going to tell me of the peril that menaces the dynasty? People are continually harping on this supposed peril. Why, you have been with me and have seen how I was received by the troops and the people! Are you too, even you, panicking?"[55]

For some time Nicholas remained irresolute about the Duma, debating whether to dissolve it or to appear before it to grant a responsible ministry. Prince Golitsyn was overjoyed when the latter prospect appeared imminent, but his hopes were dashed when Nicholas recalled him on February 22 to announce his departure for Mogilyov that evening. According to Golitsyn, the decision was based on the sovereign's wish to avoid more reports, conferences, and deliberations.[56]

Nicholas caught a mild cold on his return journey and telegraphed at a stopover that he felt "lonely and sad." Alexandra resumed her letters, reminding him once again of his royal obligation to be firm and masterful. Nicholas readily agreed: "Be assured that I do not forget." But he gently rebuked her, pointing out that "it is not necessary to snap at people right and left every minute. A quiet, caustic remark or answer is often quite sufficient to show a person his place." On February 23 serious disorders erupted in the capital, but he wrote on the 24th with a sense of contentment, "My brain is resting here—no Ministers, no troublesome questions demanding thought. . . . I hate this separation, especially at such a time! [Alexis and his sisters had been stricken with measles.] I shall not be away long—direct things as best I can here, and then my duty will be fulfilled."

Meanwhile Alexandra dismissed the turbulent demonstrations as a "hooligan movement" and recommended that strikers be sent to the front.[57]

Although Golitsyn and Protopopov refused to be alarmed by crowds milling in the streets, the "bread riots" of February 23–24 quickly escalated into full-scale insurrection. Nor did Nicholas, informed of these events only on the 25th, appreciate the gravity of the situation. He did, however, telegraph General Sergei Khabalov, commander of the Petrograd Military District, to suppress the disturbances, "inadmissible during this difficult time of war." That evening he attended church services and experienced "an excruciating pain in the chest" for some fifteen minutes. "I could hardly stand the service out," he informed Alexandra, "and my forehead was covered with drops of perspiration. I cannot understand what it could have been, because I had no palpitation of the heart; but later it disappeared, vanishing suddenly when I knelt before the image of the Holy Virgin."[58] Most likely the episode reflected a psychosomatic reaction to stress, but it furnished another indication that Nicholas' health had suffered in recent months.

By February 26, when troops and police had regained temporary control of the streets, Rodzyanko apprised Nicholas by telegraph of the "anarchy" prevailing in the capital. "The Government," he claimed, "is paralyzed; the transport service is broken down; the food and fuel supplies are completely disorganized. . . . There is wild shooting on the streets; troops are firing at each other. It is urgent that some one enjoying the confidence of the country be entrusted with the formation of a new Government. There must be no delay. Hesitation is fatal. I pray God that at this hour the responsibility may not fall upon the monarch."[59] Ironically, Rodzyanko's vivid summation of the crisis in Petrograd proved accurate in the long run but exaggerated in the short run. Nicholas, whose information was more reliable if unduly optimistic, could justifiably ignore the drastic warning. "Again this fat Rodzyanko," he remarked to Count Frederiks, "has written me all sorts of nonsense to which I won't even reply."[60] The Duma president had succumbed to the temptation of forcing the pace of events, confident that he had become the logical choice to head a new government.

The precarious balance between containment and further attrition shifted inalterably during the course of the next day, February 27, when key units of the Petrograd garrison mutinied and joined the rebellion. A second telegram from Rodzyanko to the tsar, sent that morning, this time did not overstate the case: "The situation is growing worse. Measures should be taken immediately, as tomorrow will be too late. The last hour has struck, when the fate of the country and dynasty is being decided."[61] General Khabalov's message to General Alekseyev at Stavka was less dramatic but more ominous, for it contradicted previous reports of a reassuring nature: "I implore you to report to his imperial majesty that I could not fulfill the command to restore order in the capital." Rebels had seized portions of the city.[62] The Council of Ministers met three times during the day and made tentative decisions that were rapidly overtaken by events. Protopopov, under pressure from his colleagues, resigned because of "illness" and found temporary sanctuary at the state controller's building. Golitsyn, granted what little authority remained to the government, submitted the cabinet's resignation to the tsar and suggested that he establish a dictatorship in Petrograd under the regency of the Grand Duke Mikhail Aleksandrovich.[63] Even desperate measures were now too late to stave off revolution in the capital. But Russia was not Petrograd, and Nicholas believed, not without reason, that loyal troops would rally to his cause.

The flow of information to Stavka and to Nicholas never ceased. Yet it was often distorted and filtered though the lenses of wishful thinking and the desire to please the sovereign. Without grasping the full implications of the news from Petrograd, Nicholas resolved to send troops to suppress the insurrection. On the 27th he appointed General Nikolai Ivanov commander of a punitive expedition. A competent soldier popular with his men, Ivanov entertained no doubts about his success, "judging by the instructions he gave to his adjutant, to buy turkeys and other delicacies for his friends in Petrograd, as though he were going there on a pleasant holiday."[64] Nicholas wrote Alexandra of the "many frightened faces here" but found that Alekseyev had retained his composure and "thinks it necessary to appoint a very energetic man, so as to compel the Ministers to work out the solution of the problems—supplies, railways, coal, etc."[65]

Nicholas was also determined to return to Tsarskoe Selo, less for political reasons than to be with his family at a time of crisis. His departure, originally scheduled for the afternoon of the 28th, was hastened by ever more disturbing reports. Even though it was now too late for political compromise, he resisted every attempt to provide a peaceful solution. Aside from Rodzyanko, his brother Mikhail tried to intercede by telegraph. He also spurned Golitsyn's advice and refused to accept the wholesale resignation of the Council of Ministers. Alekseyev twice rose from a sickbed to plead for a positive answer to Golitsyn's telegram, but Nicholas stood by his "definitive and unalterable decision," insisting that "it would be utterly useless to report anything more to me on the subject."[66]

Nicholas left Mogilyov at 5:00 A.M. on February 28. The imperial train followed a circuitous route because the direct line was reserved for Ivanov's forces. It proceeded without difficulty until arriving at Malaya Vishera, about one hundred miles from Petrograd, where mutinous troops were reported to be in the vicinity. General Voyeikov decided, with the sovereign's assent, to return along the same line to Bologoe and then head west for Pskov, the headquarters of the northern front. Nicholas and his entourage arrived at Pskov about 7:30 P.M. on March 1, and there he discovered that the prospects for his continued rule had seriously eroded during his journey of nearly two days. An amorphous government had already emerged in the capital, and the possibility of locating troops willing to contest a popular revolution was remote indeed.

Nicholas had prorogued the Duma on February 26, and its members, unwilling to defy an imperial decree, moved to another chamber of the Tauride Palace. There they became, technically speaking, simply an assembly of concerned citizens. A Provisional Committee was elected by the senior deputies; its initial objectives centered on restoring order in the city and securing a constitutional monarchy. The committee's self-imposed mandate was soon challenged by a rival body. As Vasily Shulgin, a conservative deputy, put it, "If we don't take power, others will, those who have already elected some scoundrels in the factories."[67] The "scoundrels," joined by representatives of the armed forces, constituted the Soviet of Workers' and Soldiers' Deputies, a revival of the St. Petersburg Soviet of 1905. The Soviet, without assuming power in any formal sense, became a formidable pressure group that forestalled attempts by the proponents of monarchy to preserve the dynasty.

Relying on his credentials as the president of the Duma, Rodzyanko took it upon himself to arbitrate the political crisis. Always officious—Nicholas, among others, would have said pompous—he had long been thwarted in his ambition to become chairman of the Council of Ministers. After his two telegrams to the emperor had been ignored, he sought to enlist the three senior grand dukes in another attempt to persuade Nicholas to accept a constitutional order. A draft manifesto, which the empress pronounced "idiotic," was drawn up to that effect, but it was never presented to the tsar because by March 1 majority opinion in the Provisional Committee favored abdication.[68] A reaction against Rodzyanko's pretentious meddling set in, and his critics accused him of seeking to become "the dictator of the Russian revolution."[69] In the negotiations to select the new Provisional Government, a task dominated by Milyukov and the Kadets, the Duma president was unceremoniously dropped from consideration.

Nicholas, marooned in Pskov, could only wait on events. Together with his retinue, he assumed that the rebellion had been confined to Petrograd and that Ivanov, if not Khabalov, would take the necessary measures to suppress it. But Alekseyev, better informed, called off Ivanov's operation, and Nicholas was eventually obliged to acquiesce. General Nikolai Ruzsky, the commander of the northern front, braced himself to confront the sovereign with distasteful political realities. Kept waiting in a corridor of the imperial salon car for an hour, he was finally received about 10:00 P.M. on March 1. Ruzsky, whose own information was obsolete, boldly insisted that Nicholas grant a responsible ministry. The old refrain failed to budge the Tsar: "I am responsible before God and Russia for everything that has happened and will happen." He explained that his desire to retain power was not simply personal ambition but a matter of conscience.[70] His attitude was no mere posturing, for he truly regarded his role as a sacred trust, divinely sanctioned and endorsed by centuries of tradition.

The heated discussion was interrupted about 11:00 P.M. by the arrival of a telegram from Alekseyev. It supported Ruszky's arguments: the two generals had apparently agreed to a joint appeal in a telegraphic conversation earlier that evening. Alekseyev recommended that Rodzyanko head a new ministry and that Nicholas announce the governmental reorganization in a manifesto drafted at Stavka. That his chief of staff had now joined the parliamentary "lobby" was the final straw in breaking Nicholas' resolve to uphold his autocratic rights. He recognized that to resist Alekseyev would mean a radical restructuring of the army's high command, at best a dangerous gamble in time of war. He consented to send a telegram to Rodzyanko requesting him to organize a cabinet, with the exception of the ministers of war and foreign affairs. In reading a draft copy, Ruzsky was astonished to discover that no mention had been made of a ministry responsible to the Duma. Despite the late hour he felt obligated to seek a second audience, and this time Nicholas signed a revised message to Rodzyanko and the proposed manifesto without further equivocation.[71]

Exhausted, Ruzsky sought some rest but was called again about 3:30 A.M. on March 2 to converse by telegraph with Rodzyanko. Ruzsky briefed him on the tsar's decision and received the shocking reply that the situation in Petrograd had gone too far for concessions: "I consider it necessary to tell you that what you have proposed is not sufficient; the problem of the dynasty has been put point blank." "Power is slipping from my hands," Rodzyanko went on. "Anarchy has reached such a degree that I am compelled tonight to announce the formation of the Provisional Government. Unfortunately, the manifesto was too late." His alarming message, however, was hedged with ambiguity in that he conveyed the false impression that despite the "anarchy" in Petrograd he remained the key political figure in any future government.[72]

Later that morning the text of the Ruzsky-Rodzyanko exchange was transmitted to Stavka, and Nicholas was also informed. Alekseyev concluded that abdication was a virtual necessity, but he sought the moral support of the commanding generals and admirals. His circular telegram posed the question in such patriotic terms that a flat refusal would have seemed almost an act of military sabotage. The war, he asserted, could be "continued to a victorious end only if requests for the Emperor's abdication in his son's favor, with Mikhail Aleksandrovich acting as regent, are satisfied. . . . The army in the field must be saved from disintegration. We must carry on the struggle with the external enemy; we must safeguard Russia's independence and the future of the dynasty." As expected, the commanders unanimously sustained Alekseyev's recommendations, though not without protestations of loyalty to the throne and, in one case, denunciation of the "criminal designs" of that "gang of bandits called the State Duma."[73] By the time their replies reached Pskov in the early afternoon Nicholas had decided to abdicate. His stubbornness the day before in resisting the role of constitutional monarch had given way to a passive acceptance of a far graver act. His reasoning, while eccentric by the standards of orthodox political behavior, conformed to his private code of honor. As a patriot, he would abandon the throne "for the salvation of Russia and the preservation of the army at the front."[74] But in his self-image of an absolute monarch he had already disgraced his heritage, and the final irrevocable step had become a moral duty to appease his conscience.

Nicholas made his decision formally known at a meeting with Ruzsky in the mid-afternoon of March 2. Two other generals and Count Frederiks were also present. After reviewing the telegrams that had arrived during the day and listening to the three officers, all of whom agreed with Alekseyev, Nicholas lapsed into a painful silence. "His face, ordinarily impassive, twitched in spite of himself," and he "pressed his lips together" in a rare sign of agitation. Finally he spoke in a firm tone: "My mind is made up. I have decided to abdicate in favor of my son Alexis." He crossed himself solemnly and said, "Let me thank you for your gallant and loyal service. I trust that it will continue under my son's reign." He embraced Ruzsky, shook hands all around, and went back to his private car.[75] There he composed telegrams notifying Alekseyev and Rodzyanko of his decision. When Ruzsky discovered, however, that the Provisional Committee had despatched a delegation to Pskov, he withheld the message to Rodzyanko.

The members of the imperial suite, angered and dismayed by the prospect of abdication, considered Ruzsky the chief culprit in engineering a "plot" against the tsar. Admiral Konstantin Nilov even threatened to arrest the general and execute him on the spot. But tempers cooled and tears were shed as the inevitability of the historic occasion appeared certain. At Stavka, General Nikolai Bazily, who headed the office of Diplomatic Chancery, was assigned the task of drafting an abdication manifesto. In an hour's time he produced a document, redolent of patriotism and ending on a note of piety, that met Alekseyev's expectations. With a few minor changes, the text was transmitted to Pskov that evening for Nicholas' approval.[76]

The delegates sent from Petrograd were Guchkov, the tsar's old enemy, and Shulgin, who hoped to preserve the monarchy as a safeguard against "the revolutionary rabble in Petrograd."[77] Their train, delayed by enthusiastic crowds en route, arrived about 10:00 P.M. Although tired and unkempt, they were escorted immediately to the imperial salon car. Nicholas arrived in a few minutes and greeted them with a handshake. Frederiks was present, as was General Kirill Naryshkin, who took notes on the meeting. Guchkov served as spokesman and presented a stark eyewitness account of the situation in Petrograd that confirmed telegraphic reports. Nicholas was particularly shocked by the news that his personal guard at Tsarskoe Selo had defected to the revolutionary cause. Ruzsky joined the group later. Since the two emissaries had not been briefed on the tsar's intention to abdicate, they approached the subject hesitantly, expecting strenuous opposition. Ruzsky interrupted Guchkov to reveal that the decision had already been made. Nicholas had been listening somewhat absentmindedly and, ignoring Ruzsky, spoke for himself. He explained that because of the illness of his son—Alexis' physician had been consulted in the afternoon—he had changed his mind and would abdicate in favor of his brother Mikhail. "I hope," he added, "you understand the feelings of a father."[78] His declaration astonished Guchkov and Shulgin, and the former could only blurt out an inane comment. A brief recess enabled them to compose their thoughts. They had doubts about the legality of Mikhail succeeding to the throne, but lacking expert advice, they acceded to the tsar's wishes. Shulgin presented an abdication manifesto that he had composed on the train. Nicholas countered with the Bazily draft, a far more elegant document, and Shulgin quickly withdrew his version. A few changes were made, notably the transfer of royal authority from Alexis to Mikhail. Nicholas signed two copies of the manifesto about 11:40 P.M., though the time was written as 3:00 P.M. to reflect that he had renounced the throne voluntarily, not at the behest of the Duma emissaries. At Guchkov's request he also signed two decrees, one designating Prince Lvov prime minister, the other reappointing Grand Duke Nikolai commander in chief. The decrees were scarcely relevant, for Lvov had already been named to head the new Provisional Government, and the grand duke, though he returned to Mogilyov to resume command, resigned under pressure and retired to one of his estates in the Crimea. They were embarrassing nonetheless to the new regime in their implication that it had received its credentials from the former monarch.

As befitted his character and training, Nicholas faced the ordeal of abdication with outward composure. But he deeply resented the politicians and generals who had deserted him, and his bitterness, otherwise concealed, welled up in a single sentence of his diary entry for March 2: "Treachery, cowardice, and deceit all around!"[79]

Indeed, the theme of "betrayal" was taken up by apologists for the monarchy in later years. Few in number but not without influence—or at least with firm opinions—they portrayed Nicholas as a maligned hero. His "most awesome achievement," one historian has written, was his "magnificent struggle against impossible odds in leading Russia to the threshold of victory. His enemies, however, prevented Russia from crossing that threshold."[80] That Nicholas was patriotic and devoted to his country can hardly be denied. But his "victory," even had it been achieved (and without reckoning the cost in human lives), would have been a hollow one. Nor were his "enemies" responsible for the blundering incompetence of his leadership, which continually flouted public opinion, if not arrogantly at least with paternalistic indifference.

Another historian, aside from questioning the "spontaneity" of the February Revolution, has credited Nicholas' prompt abdication with avoiding civil war.[81] Such a view is highly implausible, ignoring as it does the tsar's profound unpopularity, especially as an object of mass anger and frustration with the unending war, and the spiritual defection of large sections of the ruling elite even before the rebellion in Petrograd. A determined ruler with greater intestinal fortitude than Nicholas might have rallied a number of loyal generals as well as select military units to his cause. That they could have succeeded in the face of wholesale mutiny and civil disaffection strains credulity. Had Nicholas attempted to cling to power by armed force, he would more likely have signed his own death warrant than fanned a civil war.

Surprisingly, for the time being Nicholas remained a free man. Since neither Guckhov nor Shulgin raised an objection, his train left Pskov for Mogilyov at 1:00 A.M. in the morning of March 3.

14

The Tragic Odyssey of Citizen Romanov

Concerned about the welfare of his family in Tsarskoe Selo, Nicholas nevertheless felt duty-bound to bid farewell to his staff at headquarters. To keep him informed of the latest events, Alekseyev sent General Bazily to meet the imperial train at Orsha. About 6:00 A.M. on March 3 Nicholas received him in the same gray uniform of a Caucasian infantry regiment that he had worn at Pskov. "His face and his small beard were as carefully groomed as ever," Bazily reported. "His expression was absolutely calm, and betrayed no trace of emotion. The look in his fine blue eyes was affable as always." The general told him that the situation in the capital was "desperate" and that since the Grand Duke Mikhail had been prevented by public opinion from accepting the throne—technically he renounced it—the dynasty "was in danger of falling." Nicholas listened impassively, registering no surprise and repeating the phrase, "But yes, naturally," at each new piece of information. "I was stupefied by the calm of his replies, by his extraordinary self-possession." In conclusion Bazily ventured to express regrets that Nicholas had not abdicated in favor of his son; the reply was simply, "You know that my son is ill. I could not separate myself from him."[1]

Bazily joined Nicholas and his suite for the remainder of the journey. At dinner he noted that while Nicholas' face revealed no emotion, "violent contractions shook the muscles of his throat from time to time, betraying the moral suffering that he otherwise succeeded so well in hiding." Taciturn at first, the former emperor gradually became more talkative and inquired about the names and background of the recently appointed ministers of the

Provisional Government. He reached Mogilyov that evening, where Alekseyev and his staff greeted him. Silently he shook hands with the officers
and civilians assembled at the station platform. "All were greatly moved,"
according to Bazily, "and stifled sobs could be heard." Nicholas retained
his composure, but a "few tears formed in the corners of his eyes and he
brushed them away with a gesture of his hand."[2]

The next day Nicholas sent Alexandra two telegrams with no reference
to politics except for the laconic statement, "Despair is passing away." His
mother arrived from Kiev to comfort him, though their reunion—destined
to be their last—was marred by her bitter tears and the reproaches she
directed toward Alexandra. Protocol was maintained, along with a full
retinue of courtiers and servants, and Alekseyev continued to deliver his
daily report. Nicholas bore no apparent ill will toward the general, who
above all others fit his indictment of "treachery, cowardice, and deceit."
Insofar as he expressed irritation toward anyone, it was his brother, the
inoffensive Grand Duke Mikhail, a hapless victim of revolutionary turmoil
and anti-monarchist fervor. "Misha should not have done a thing like that
[forsaken the throne]," he naively remarked to his brother-in-law. "I wonder who could have given him such strange advice." The comment left
Sandro "speechless," coming as it did "from a man who had surrendered
one-sixth of the earth's surface to a mob of drunken reservists and rioting
workers."[3]

In a moving ceremony, Nicholas took formal leave of the general staff
and headquarters personnel. He also devoted much effort to composing a
farewell message to the army. Florid and patriotic, with several references
to the Almighty, it exhorted his "gallant troops" to defend the homeland
from the "evil foe," to "obey the Provisional Government," and to "listen
to your commanders." Thoroughly innocuous, the text was nonetheless
banned from publication, though it received a modest private circulation.[4]
Relatively few, however, regarded Nicholas as a danger to the revolution.
Aleksandr Kerensky, the new minister of justice, pronounced him "quite
harmless" and contended that as a former monarch "he seemed to have
been suddenly and completely deleted from the nation's thoughts."[5]
Whether as an individual or as monarch, such was hardly the case, for
animosity against the deposed "tyrant" now fueled a minor political storm.
The Petrograd Soviet's Executive Committee voted to arrest him, a decision
at odds with the Provisional Government's plan to allow his emigration to
England. Through Alekseyev, Nicholas asked for a safe passage to Tsarskoe
Selo and time with his family until the children had recovered from measles.
He was then to be allowed, presumably with his wife and children, to leave
Russia via Romanov-on-the-Murman (later Murmansk) and return after
the war to his residence in Livadia. Alekseyev approved all but the last
request.

On March 7, with the problem seemingly unresolved, the Soviet Executive Committee received a declaration, signed by over a hundred deputies, calling for the detention of "Nicholas II the Bloody" and "all members of the House of Romanov in a single designated place under the reliable guard of the peoples' revolutionary army."[6] Anticipating unilateral action by the Soviet, the Provisional Government, in a move reminiscent of the Guchkov-Shulgin mission, had already authorized four little-known deputies of the Fourth Duma to escort Nicholas to Tsarskoe Selo. They arrived at three o'clock in the afternoon of the 7th and declined an opportunity to meet him or to place him under formal arrest, permitting Alekseyev to relay the news of his altered status. They did banish Admiral Nilov from the "official" retinue—his belligerent attitude at Pskov had apparently become known—and Nicholas, heeding Alekseyev's request, excluded Frederiks and Voyeikov, who had become expendable scapegoats to appease popular revulsion against the monarchy. As the imperial train prepared to leave in the late afternoon, Nicholas' self-control broke down, and he wept while parting from his mother. The four deputies and a guard of ten occupied the rear car. Alekseyev, on the platform with other ranking officers, saluted Nicholas but made a deep bow to the deputies as the train departed. Townspeople had also gathered, few of whom demonstrated either approval of or hostility toward their former ruler.

Kerensky noted that only a week before Nicholas had embarked upon the same journey: "He was *going* then; but now he was being *taken*."[7] The train reached Tsarskoe Selo in the late morning of March 9. The garrison commander, the stationmaster, and other officials were waiting on the platform. The Duma representatives, their mission accomplished, returned to Petrograd, while Nicholas was driven by car to the Alexander Palace. No overt attempt was made to restrict his freedom. The members of his entourage, unsure of their fate, were allowed to go their own way; only a few chose to join the Romanov family under house arrest. Alexandra had been in despair, refusing at first to believe reports of her husband's abdication. Pale, thin, and looking much older, she had regained her composure and greeted Nicholas joyfully with a kiss and an embrace. They saw the children and, finally alone, "gave way to their feelings, and wept quietly for a long time." Nicholas had not survived the ordeal unscathed: "[He] was deathly pale, his face was covered with innumerable wrinkles, his hair was quite grey at the temples, and blue shadows encircled his eyes. He looked like an old man."[8]

An uncensored press, free to indulge in scandal and rumor as well as more serious fare, was quick to expose the misdeeds of the old regime, whether real or imagined. The more sensational newspapers pandered to public opinion by excoriating the people's oppressor, and agitators demanded Nicholas' imprisonment in the Peter and Paul Fortress or at Kronstadt, where mutinous sailors had shown little mercy toward their officers. To extremists on the Left a trial and execution seemed almost a foregone conclusion. Salacious tales about Rasputin, many involving Alexandra, were also featured in the press. Nor was his corpse allowed to repose undisturbed; about midnight on the same day that Nicholas returned to Tsarskoe Selo, a group of soldiers desecrated his grave and made off with the body. At a site near Petrograd the remains were cremated on a funeral pyre of logs saturated with gasoline, and the ashes were buried under the snow. Romantics could now claim that the *starets* had prophesied his ultimate fate. "The fools don't understand who I am," he supposedly told a journalist in 1916. "A sorcerer? A sorcerer may be. They burn sorcerers, and so let them burn me too. But there is one thing they do not understand: if they do burn me Russia is finished. . . . They will bury us together."[9]

The Provisional Government had no intention of satisfying the popular desire for vengeance against the fallen monarch. Kerensky boldly proclaimed that he would "never be the Marat of the Russian Revolution." But the gnawing suspicion that the "Rasputin clique" had committed treasonable acts induced the government to conduct a thorough and impartial investigation. Kerensky appointed a commission of inquiry that, in effect, exonerated the royal couple, although, paradoxically, they were not called upon to testify. The inquiry also elicited firsthand information from the elite of tsarist officialdom, among other witnesses, that proved of great value to future historians.[10] Unfortunately, both Nicholas and Alexandra burned many private papers and documents, but they spared most of their own correspondence as well as Nicholas' diary.

Reports that Nicholas would be sent abroad aroused an angry response from the Petrograd Soviet. Railroad workers were alerted to prevent an escape by train. During the evening of March 9 an infantry detachment, bolstered by a machine gun company, arrived in Tsarskoe Selo to check on the security arrangements. The commanding officer, Sergei Mstislavsky, a prominent Socialist Revolutionary, demanded that he be allowed to "inspect" the exalted prisoner. After a tense jurisdictional dispute, the palace guard gave way and arranged through intermediaries for Nicholas to be observed walking down a corridor in his private quarters. Mstislavsky's description, though tinged with animosity, may have been accurate: "His face was puffy and red, his swollen eyelids forming a heavy frame for his dull, bloodshot eyes. . . . The still yellow gaze of the Emperor, so like that of a tired, hunted wolf, suddenly flickered with a flame which broke to the surface of its leaden indifference. It was a spark of deadly malice. . . . Nicholas paused, shifted from foot to foot, and sharply turned around, walking rapidly away, twitching his shoulders, and limping."[11] According to Kerensky's somewhat inaccurate version of the incident, the "senseless midnight trip" had been privately organized, but the Petrograd Soviet justified it after the fact as a security measure and necessary "to forestall any secret moves" that the Provisional Government might undertake on Nicholas' behalf.[12]

The restrictions initially placed on the Romanov family were lenient for a state of formal arrest. Several officers of the palace guard were indulgent, even sympathetic, toward their prisoners; the soldiers, while more likely to be hostile, had few opportunities for harassment. Confined to the palace area, Nicholas frequently walked in the park and could be seen by the curious, some of whom jeered and whistled. They gazed at him "as if he were some rare animal in a cage" and spoke of him "as though he were a beast unable to hear or understand them."[13] Aside from these and other forms of petty humiliation, life inside the palace was not unpleasant and proceeded in the traditional manner. The etiquette appropriate to royalty was strictly observed, and a reduced complement of servants attended to their normal duties. The number of courtiers also shrank. A retired officer in the Horse Guards, Count Pavel Benkendorf, served as marshal of the court, with his stepson, Prince Vasily Dolgorukov, as deputy.

On March 21 Kerensky paid the first of a number of visits to Nicholas and Alexandra. He inspected the palace, including security procedures, and harangued the guards and servants on their revolutionary duty to report anything suspicious. Benkendorf remembered him as "abrupt and nervous," a description that tallies with Kerensky's own recollection that he was "anything but calm." Finally, with regal ceremony, the visitor was permitted to enter the family's personal quarters as Benkendorf intoned, "His Majesty bids you welcome." Prepared to be brusque and "meticulously correct," Kerensky "underwent a lightning change." He observed a "huddled, perplexed little group," and from this "cluster of frightened humanity there stepped out, somewhat hesitantly, a man of medium height in military kit, who walked forward to meet me with a slight, peculiar smile. It was the Emperor." Nicholas, unsure of himself, was put at ease by the minister's direct manner and firm handshake. Recovering from his momentary confusion and smiling once more, he led Kerensky to his family. The children were "burning with curiosity," but Alexandra remained aloof, "proud, domineering and irreconcilable."[14]

Kerensky assured Nicholas of the Provisional Government's benign intentions and of his own good will. "Anything I begin," he declared, "I always carry through to the bitter end, with all my might. I wanted to see everything myself, to verify everything so as to be able to report at Petrograd, and it will be better for you." During his later visits he sought to "decipher the human being behind the Emperor." He found him to be an "extremely reserved, reticent man, with much mistrust and infinite contempt for others. Not very intelligent, poorly educated and lacking vitality to a remarkable degree, he nevertheless had something of an instinctive knowledge of life and men." Kerensky was struck by his "utter indifference to the world around him" and by how his face seemed to mask his emotions: "Behind that smile, behind those bewitching eyes, one saw something lifeless, icy, deadening—abysmal loneliness, utter desolation." He observed in Nicholas the traits of a mystic, "passionately seeking communion with heaven," bored with the exercise of power, relieved that a "heavy burden had been taken off his shoulders." It should have occasioned no surprise that he "calmly laid aside his scepter to take up a gardener's spade."[15]

The government's attempt to provide a haven abroad for the Romanovs foundered meanwhile on the harsh realities of Russian and British politics. When informed of the tsar's abdication, King George V expressed his personal regrets. "My thoughts are constantly with you," he telegraphed Nicholas, "and I shall always remain your friend, as you know I have been in the past." Sent to Mogilyov, the message never reached the former emperor. The British ambassador's request to Milyukov, the newly appointed foreign minister, that it be forwarded was rebuffed because the telegram "might be misinterpreted" and used as an argument for Nicholas' detention. Milyukov was eager, however, to safeguard the Romanovs from possible violence and inquired if the British government would grant asylum. The prime minister, David Lloyd George, conferred with several colleagues and agreed to receive Nicholas, a decision that the king questioned "on general grounds of expediency." Unfortunately for the negotiations, the offer became public knowledge and aroused indignation among the many critics of tsarist Russia in England.

The reaction in Russia was far less restrained and effectively prevented the Provisional Government from proceeding with its plans for asylum. The king, mistakenly accused of originating the proposal, received many abusive letters. He suggested that the offer be withdrawn in view of public disapproval, and Lloyd George turned to France as an alternative place of refuge. The foreign secretary, Arthur Balfour, politely rebuffed the monarch by pointing out that his ministers did not believe that it was "now possible to withdraw the invitation which has been sent." At first willing to acquiesce, the king returned to the subject with some vehemence through his private secretary: "[Ambassador] Buchanan ought to be instructed to tell Milyukov that the opposition to the Emperor and Empress coming here is so strong that we must be allowed to withdraw from the consent previously given."

Lloyd George and Balfour were susceptible to the king's argument, for they recognized that his popularity—indeed, the monarchy itself—might be seriously impaired. But they were also concerned with the military alliance with Russia and the necessity of maintaining good relations with its new government. Inevitably the personal fate of Nicholas and his family became subordinate to affairs of state. On March 31/April 13 Buchanan received a telegram from Balfour that virtually withdrew the invitation without employing the wounding language of a blunt refusal (the government "does not insist on its former offer of hospitality to the Imperial family"). Subsequent inquiries from the Provisional Government met only "bland immobility." The king's role in the whole affair reflected poorly upon his personal integrity, even though it seems hardly likely that the Romanovs could have been rescued in any case. His involvement remained a well-kept secret in which the principal "collaborators," Lloyd George and Balfour, joined without enthusiasm in a conspiracy of silence. Eventually the king's biographers, with access to official papers, revealed the embarrassing circumstances.[16]

Kerensky, who took no part in the negotiations with the British government, visited Tsarskoe Selo a second time on March 27. Although his attitude toward the royal couple had mellowed, he was keenly aware that their situation remained precarious and that benevolence on his part would lead to criticism and perhaps more ominous signs of dissatisfaction. Still under the impression that Alexandra had been involved in pro-German machinations, he determined to conduct his own investigation. She was to be isolated from her family during the period of interrogation, but Kerensky relented in the face of strenuous protests—not all of her children had recovered from the measles—and sequestered Nicholas instead. Husband and wife were to be reunited only during meals and at religious services, conditional on the promise that they would converse only in Russian. Their separation, such as it was, lasted only sixteen days and apparently had a favorable effect on Nicholas: "He became livelier, happier, more confident." Kerensky questioned them both but elicited little information of political significance. He did satisfy himself, however, as to the falsity of the "treason" charges against Alexandra and was impressed by "the clarity, the energy and the frankness of her words." She in turn acquired a grudging respect for Kerensky after previously denouncing him as "mean" and "despicable." Nicholas, too, expressed his confidence: "He is a man who loves Russia, and I wish I could have known him earlier because he could have been useful to me."[17] His attitude toward others involved in his downfall embraced a range of emotions from animosity to admiration. In his conversations with Kerensky he intimated that he "still hated Guchkov, that he considered Rodzyanko superficial, that he could not imagine what Milyukov was like, that he held Alekseyev in great esteem, and respected Prince Lvov."[18]

Despite continued agitation for more drastic treatment of the former monarch, including prison confinement, the Petrograd Soviet took no action. Indeed, its leaders appeared to reject the demagogic extremism of the rank and file. On May 21 the official Soviet newspaper *Izvestia* published a refutation of charges that the Romanovs were receiving special privileges. The statement, signed by the palace commandant and the commander of the Tsarskoe Selo garrison, asserted that "the proper high standard of surveillance over the arrested Nicholas Romanov and his wife is being maintained and will continue." A week later *Izvestia* commented editorially that the revolution had deprived of freedom only those enemies who discredited themselves by their crimes: "They will be tried by the people at a free and public trial. But a trial is not a revenge. The revolution has no intention of making martyrs out of its enemies, and least of all do its plans include making a martyr out of the former Tsar Nicholas Romanov."[19]

The warmer spring weather allowed the prisoners more outdoor activity. Nicholas, with the assistance of the children, courtiers, and those servants who volunteered, worked several hours daily to plant a vegetable garden. He also helped to cut up dead trees for firewood, anticipating another winter under house arrest. In the evening he often read aloud to the family and took a renewed interest in the Russian literary classics. He also read popular foreign works, including Bram Stoker's *Dracula*, Conan Doyle's Sherlock Holmes stories, and Alexander Dumas' *The Count of Monte Cristo*. Never power-hungry, he shed the cares of state with obvious relief. "How glad I am," he commented, "that I need no longer attend to those tiresome audiences and sign those everlasting documents! I shall read, walk, and spend my time with the children."[20]

Nicholas was not always well informed of events outside Tsarskoe Selo, but his patriotic fervor never flagged, and he expressed chagrin that Russia had assumed a defensive posture toward Germany. "I can't believe that our army at the front is as bad as they say," he declared; "it can't have fallen to this extent in two months."[21] Reflecting the profound war-weariness of the populace, the armed forces had "fallen" more precipitously than Nicholas could bring himself to admit. The Provisional Government remained faithful to its allies, but Milyukov's indiscreet support of the secret treaties signed by the tsarist regime proved politically embarrassing. In response to serious demonstrations in Petrograd that raised "the frightful specter of civil war and anarchy," as Prince Lvov put it, the two forthright "imperialists" in the cabinet, Milyukov and Guchkov, were forced to resign during the last week in April. Kerensky shifted from Justice to take Guchkov's portfolio as minister of war, maintaining his role as benefactor of the ex-royal family.

By early summer the political situation had stabilized, and the fate of the Romanovs was no longer a pressing issue. To Kerensky and his colleagues the time seemed propitious to revive the plan for sanctuary in England. Through a neutral source the German government promised a safe passage via Murmansk. But a renewed query to the British government brought a negative response unmistakable in its finality. "With tears in his eyes, scarcely able to control his emotions," Buchanan personally conveyed the message to the new Russian foreign minister, Mikhail Tereshchenko.[22] Similar appeals to the French government received no encouragement.[23]

Russia's stability proved more apparent than real. Under Lenin's astute guidance the Bolsheviks acquired a mass following, based less upon the attractions of Marxism than upon growing dissatisfaction with the "bourgeois" Provisional Government. Their cause was strengthened when Kerensky, bent upon reviving the government's prestige and demonstrating Russia's fidelity to its allies, launched an ill-timed military offensive against

Austria on June 18. A "radiant" Nicholas welcomed the initial Russian advance—a "pseudo-victory" in Benkendorf's phase—by ordering a *Te Deum*, only to be bitterly disappointed when a German counterattack brought disaster. The aftershock found a political outlet in Petrograd, where riots and mass protests by soldiers and workers threatened to topple the government. Order was finally restored, but the July Days, for which the Bolsheviks took the blame, led to another cabinet crisis which elevated Kerensky to the prime ministership in place of the hapless Lvov.

Nicholas was encouraged by the transfer of authority, noting in his diary, "This man is certainly in his right place at the present moment. The more power he gets, the better it will be."[24] He hoped to be sent to the Crimea, where the dowager empress, among other relatives, had found a reasonably secure refuge. But a journey by rail would involve passing through industrial centers with militant workers and rural areas where rebellious peasants were solving the land question to their own satisfaction. Kerensky was determined, however, to find a safe haven for the family. He feared a resurgence of Bolshevik propaganda, which had already penetrated the palace garrison, and at the other extreme he became aware of "amateur monarchist plotters" who had begun to send Alexandra "mysterious little notes and to hint at prompt liberation." After much indecision he chose Tobolsk in western Siberia, a provincial backwater lacking rail transportation and without an industrial working class that might prove obstreperous. His knowledge of the city was "curiously accidental" since it was based on childhood memories involving friends of his parents who had relocated there. Two government representatives, Pavel Makarov and V. M. Vershinin, were sent to investigate its suitability, returning in mid-July with a favorable report. Despite the cabinet turnover, Kerensky and his subordinates made all the necessary arrangements in secrecy. Only after the transfer had been accomplished was the public informed.[25]

Kerensky personally supervised the final preparations at Tsarskoe Selo. He lectured the soldiers who were to serve as guards on proper behavior: "Remember that he is a former Emperor and that neither he nor his family must suffer any hardships." Nicholas was permitted a farewell visit with his brother Mikhail, and though both were deeply moved, "they plunged into that fragmentary, irrelevant small-talk which is so characteristic of such short meetings." Departure was delayed many hours by enormous piles of luggage and personal effects to be transported to the train and by the reluctance of the railway workers to cooperate, for rumors had circulated about the impending move. At last all was in readiness, and the long journey began on August 1 about 6:00 A.M. A retinue of thirty-nine, including servants, accompanied the Romanovs, with Makarov and Vershinin in charge and Dolgorukov as Benkendorf's successor. The troop detachment was commanded by Colonel Yevgeny Kobylinsky, "whose life was subsequently rendered unbearable" by zealous monarchists who accused him of being the tsar's jailer and "Kerensky's henchman." But Nicholas would remember him as "my last friend."[26]

The destination, apparently no secret to the prisoners, was revealed in due course. The accommodations were agreeable, and the trip proceeded without incident. Nicholas and his party were allowed a daily respite when the train halted for half an hour to allow a walk in the fresh air. The passengers reached Tyumen in the late evening of the 4th and transferred to a river steamboat for the remainder of the journey. The voyage was uneventful except that at one point the family had a clear view from the deck of Rasputin's home in his native village of Pokrovskoe. In Tobolsk the governor's house had been designated the family's place of confinement, but Makarov and Dolgorukov found it to be without furnishings and in need of renovation. While the necessary alterations were completed, the Romanovs resided on shipboard for another week. The house was spacious and comfortable, though the grounds were too small for much exercise. The daily regimen fell into a pattern resembling that at Tsarskoe Selo. The townspeople were friendly, and gifts of food came from peasants, merchants, and nuns of a local convent. Kobylinsky was solicitous and helpful, an attitude that rubbed off on some of the soldiers of the guard; others were aloof and hostile.

In mid-September two emissaries sent by Kerensky, Vasily Pankratov and Aleksandr Nikolsky, arrived to take charge of the prisoners, although Kobylinsky remained military commander. Both were Socialist Revolutionaries who had suffered years of imprisonment and exile under the tsarist regime. But Pankratov, the senior leader, sought no personal vengeance and treated Nicholas with tact and consideration. Nikolsky, on the other hand, was rude and arrogant, intent upon enforcing to the letter every petty regulation.[27]

Despite his confinement Nicholas suffered no privations or indignities. As winter approached, his chief complaint centered on the paucity of news. Unlike Tsarskoe Selo, where he had regular access to the press, at Tobolsk the mail was erratic and information of a political nature difficult to obtain. The only newspaper available was a "nasty local rag printed on packing paper," which provided "telegrams several days old and generally distorted and cut down." But Nicholas eagerly followed events as best he could. He was briefly encouraged by General Lavr Kornilov's attempt to seize power in late August, and he was sorely disappointed when the coup failed. He feared imminent catastrophe, for the first time speaking of his abdication with regret. His decision had been made to avoid civil war in the face of the enemy, he explained to his son's French tutor, Pierre Gilliard. But "had not his departure been almost immediately followed by the appearance of Lenin and his acolytes, the paid agents of Germany, whose criminal propaganda had destroyed the army and corrupted the government?" His renunciation of the throne he now considered to have been in vain: in reality he had done his country a disservice. The idea haunted him and finally "gave rise to grave moral anxiety."[28]

If his isolation made it difficult to grasp what was happening in Russia, Gilliard wrote, "the rest of Europe was almost a closed book." The Bolshevik insurrection in late October which overthrew the Provisional Government had worldwide reverberations but only a distant echo in Tobolsk; the news arrived only after a week's delay. The alarming implications of a new regime based on doctrinaire Marxist principles could not be ignored by the exiles. The Bolsheviks, however, had more pressing business than the fate of the ex-tsar and his family, and there were no immediate repercussions. Within a month, however, a soldiers' committee among the guards, emboldened by events in Petrograd, became a formidable rival to Kobylinsky's authority and placed increasingly onerous restrictions on their captives. In January 1918, for example, Nicholas submitted to a prohibition against epaulets on military uniforms. A few weeks later the committee forced the resignation of Pankratov and Nikolsky, followed shortly by the removal of guard units sympathetic to the Romanovs and their replacement by a "pack of blackguardedly-looking young men." On March 1 (the Russian and Western calendars now coincided) due to a Bolshevik decree the whole family was put on soldiers' rations. Their expenses, formerly paid by the state, had to come from personal income. A monthly limit of six hundred rubles—severely depreciated by inflation—was set for each individual. In order to economize ten servants were dismissed, leaving a number of them virtually destitute. Kobylinsky raised a loan of twenty thousand rubles from a sympathetic merchant, and Count Benkendorf, who had returned to Petrograd, received many contributions from monarchist supporters. A sum of 200,000 rubles was collected in Moscow and sent to Tobolsk but apparently confiscated by local Bolsheviks.[29]

The Treaty of Brest-Litovsk, signed by the Bolshevik government on March 3, at last achieved the peace with Germany and Austria that Russia so desperately needed. Nicholas reacted with anger and frustration: "To think that *they* called Her Majesty a traitress! . . . Who is the real traitor?"[30] He commented to Gilliard, "It is such a disgrace for Russia and amounts to suicide. I should never have thought the Emperor William and the German Government could stoop to shake hands with these miserable traitors. But I'm sure they will get no good from it; it won't save them from ruin!" (Although Germany's "ruin" was in fact not far off, Russia's "suicide" came near to reality due to civil war, not from peace with the Central Powers.) Nicholas was also offended by a rumor that a clause in the treaty demanded the release of the Romanovs to Germany unharmed: "This is either a maneuver to discredit me or an insult."[31]

The rumor was false, but the prospect of escape helped to sustain the family's morale during the frigid months of the Siberian winter. They rejected any notion of German assistance, believing that "loyal friends" might contrive their rescue since the Bolsheviks had so far sent neither troops nor a representative. With Kobylinsky's complicity, it seemed to Gilliard "easy to trick the insolent but careless vigilance of our guards." But the prospect was greatly complicated by Nicholas' insistence that the family not only stay together but also remain on Russian soil. Gilliard counted on "a few bold spirits outside," and there were indeed individuals prepared to sacrifice their personal safety to effect a rescue. But the necessary organization, leadership, and logistical arrangements never materialized. Seemingly the most daring of these self-appointed knights-errant was Boris Solovyov, whose colorful career had included study at an Indian seminary founded by the famous theosophist, Madam Helena Blavatsky, and marriage to one of Rasputin's daughters. He maintained close relations with several monarchist groups, from which he accepted money, and resided briefly in Tobolsk, where he contacted Alexandra through one of her parlor maids. He established "headquarters" in Tyumen for an imaginary Brotherhood of St. John of Tobolsk, claiming to have numerous supporters among the soldiers of the region. Alexandra, with full confidence in Solovyov, repeatedly stated her belief that there were three hundred faithful officers willing to lend assistance at the proper time.[32]

In late March a detachment of over a hundred Red Guards drove into Tobolsk "at breakneck speed in smart troikas festively adorned with little bells." They came from Omsk, traditionally the administrative center of western Siberia, but they possessed no credentials from Moscow, where the Bolshevik government had relocated the capital. A potential jurisdictional conflict was averted by Kobylinsky's deferential attitude. On April 13, to complicate the situation, another detachment of troops arrived from the Ural city of Yekaterinburg, a hotbed of Bolshevism with a long tradition of anti-tsarist sentiment. Their leader, Sergei Zaslavsky, announced that he had been sent to prevent Nicholas' escape, citing in particular Solovyov's activities. He suggested that the captives be confined to a regular prison, where guarding them would be an easier task. Kobylinsky managed to abort the plan, but Zaslavsky launched a campaign within the garrison to undermine the colonel's authority. The atmosphere of intrigue was heightened when one of the commanders of the Omsk contingent proposed an alliance with Kobylinsky to drive out the Yekaterinburg intruders.

On April 22 the arrival in Tobolsk of Vasily Yakovlev, a commissar sent by the Soviet government along with 150 Red troops, intimidated the contending factions. Described as "tall and thin with jet-black hair," he dressed like a sailor but appeared to be an educated man accustomed to authority. The enigmatic Yakovlev was actually a veteran Bolshevik of considerable prominence.[33] His papers described his mission as one of special importance and stated that he was empowered to shoot out of hand anyone who disobeyed his orders. "Everyone is restless and distraught," Gilliard noted in his diary. Yakovlev's presence "is felt to be an evil portent, vague but real."

The new emissary, always "scrupulously polite," inspected the prisoners' residence. Accompanied by an army physician, he observed firsthand that Alexis, who had injured himself again, was indeed seriously ill. "We are all," Gilliard reported, "in a state of mental anguish." On the 25th Yakovlev informed Nicholas that he had strict instructions to escort him from Tobolsk—no destination was stated—and that in view of his son's condition he might have to go alone. Nicholas responded with surprising spirit: "I shall not go, and that's that!" Yakovlev tactfully pointed out that his orders were explicit and that he would either have to resort to force or give up his mission; a replacement might be less considerate. "You need not entertain any fears for your safety. I answer for your life with my head."[34]

Nicholas speculated about Yakovlev's motives and came to a wildly erroneous conclusion: "They want to make me sign the Treaty of Brest-Litovsk. But I'll see my right hand cut off before I do it." Alexandra agreed and, having learned little or nothing from her misfortunes, vented her spleen on Guchkov and Rodzyanko for persuading her husband to abdicate. On the more practical matter at hand, she spent the next few hours in a state of nervous agitation trying to choose between departing with Nicholas or remaining with Alexis. Loyalty to her husband prevailed, and it was decided, with Yakovlev's permission, that her daughter Marie, Dolgorukov, Dr. Yevgeny Botkin, the household physician, and three servants would accompany them. Nicholas and Alexandra received the members of their entourage in the evening, but the atmosphere was "mournful and depressing." "There was not much talking and no pretense to gaiety," recorded one participant. "It was solemn, tragic, a fit prelude to inescapable catastrophe."[35]

About 4:00 A.M. the following morning the journey began. Because melting river ice prevented the use of a steamboat, crude peasant carts were provided, along with a small cavalry escort. Yakovlev directed the procession toward the nearest railhead at Tyumen, nearly two hundred miles away, without revealing that the ultimate destination was Moscow. The roads were rough and treacherous, clogged with semi-frozen mud, and carriage wheels had to be repaired several times. But the chief hazard lay in crossing the ice-choked rivers. The horses crossed the Irtysh with water up to the axles, and a dangerous passage across the Tobol had to be negotiated on foot. Alexandra recorded the ordeal in her diary: "Road perfectly atrocious, frozen ground . . . water up to the horses' stomachs, fearfully shaken, pain all over."[36] At Pokrovskoe a change of horses took place, by coincidence next to Rasputin's house. Alexandra noted the incident matter-of-factly: "Stood long before our Friend's house, saw his family & friends looking out the window."[37] Some fourteen miles before reaching Tyumen a squadron of Red cavalry reinforced the escort. Alexandra gazed at them in the naive hope that they might be the "good Russian men" she had been led to believe would attempt a rescue. But Solovyov had no such intentions.

Whether for financial gain or some less obvious motive, he apparently served the Bolsheviks as an agent provocateur while continuing his pro-monarchist charade.

Arriving at Tyumen on the evening of April 27, the prisoners were placed aboard a special train while Yakovlev telegraphed Moscow, conversing with Yakov Sverdlov, a top party leader and the titular head of state.[38] The Ural Soviet, based at Yekaterinburg, had made no secret of its desire to seize the Romanovs, and Yakovlev, with Sverdlov's permission, directed the train eastward toward Omsk in order to reach Moscow by an alternate route. This unexpected reversal of direction struck the Yekaterinburg authorities as highly suspicious, indeed a betrayal of the revolutionary cause. They alerted their counterparts in Omsk, and the train was halted before reaching its interim destination. Yakovlev renewed his telegraphic contact with Sverdlov, who faced an awkward dilemma: he was morally obliged to support the government's official emissary, yet the Ural Bolsheviks, whose loyalty to Moscow was tenuous, had superior armed strength. Expediency won the day, and Nicholas was sent to Yekaterinburg. He recognized the danger: "I would go anywhere at all but the Urals. . . . Judging from the papers, the Urals are harshly against me."[39] Yakovlev, whose own safety was temporarily in jeopardy, returned to Moscow. His later defection to the anti-Bolshevik forces, known as the Whites, during the civil war prompted accusations that he had harbored monarchist views all along and had been plotting to liberate the Romanovs. It has also been suggested that he was a British agent;[40] another scenario maintained that he was acting in Germany's interest.[41] Such conspiracy theories are unwarranted. An alternate explanation is more likely, that he tried to carry out his assignment conscientiously but failed because of circumstances beyond his control.

One of Sverdlov's motives in trying to transfer Nicholas from Tobolsk to Moscow was probably security. Exaggerated reports of monarchist schemes reached the Kremlin at a time when Siberia appeared vulnerable to anti-Bolshevik movements. Perhaps the underlying reason, however, lay in the perceived need to legitimize the new regime by a violent assault on the old: what better means of redressing the iniquities of the past than a well-publicized trial of the chief malefactor himself? The execution of "Nicholas the Bloody" would have been almost a foregone conclusion. Trotsky volunteered his services as chief prosecutor and later upheld "summary justice" for the Romanov's as "not only expedient but necessary." The Bolsheviks had to show the world that they "could continue to fight on mercilessly, stopping at nothing." Execution would not only "frighten, horrify, and dishearten the enemy but also . . . shake up our own ranks, to show them that there was no turning back, that ahead lay either complete victory or complete ruin."[42]

Lenin seems to have favored a trial for Nicholas, at least initially, but he never went on public record about the desirability of such a spectacle. There can be no doubt, however, that in principle he favored regicide and even mass destruction of the Romanov clan. As early as 1911 he justified execution as essential to a successful revolution. "If in a civilized country such as England," he wrote, "a country which has never known anything like the Mongol yoke, bureaucratic oppression, or the tyranny of a military clique, it was necessary to behead one crowned brigand in order to teach kings to be 'constitutional' monarchs, in a country like Russia it is necessary to behead at least a hundred Romanovs to teach their successors not to organize Black-Hundred murders and Jewish pogroms."[43] Indeed, the revolutions of seventeenth-century England and eighteenth-century France had not flinched from spilling royal blood: Charles I and Louis XVI became the inevitable scapegoats, not so much for political malpractice as for an accumulation of grievances that demanded a kind of civic catharsis through execution. In the Russian case, the exigencies of civil war foreclosed the possibility of judicial formalities to legitimize the death penalty.

On April 30 Nicholas, Alexandra, and Marie were incarcerated at Ipatyev House, the spacious residence of a wealthy Yekaterinburg merchant and retired army engineer who had been evicted only the day before. The new arrangements, though not devoid of amenities, were more rigorous than those of Tobolsk. Resentful that the family possessions had been thoroughly searched, Nicholas vigorously protested: "I abruptly expressed my opinion to the commissar."[44] The commandant of the "House of Special Purpose," as the mansion was now ominously designated, was a Bolshevik named Aleksandr Avdeyev. If lacking the tactful sophistication of a Yakovlev, he was no monster of depravity. He could even be considered a fair-minded jailer under the circumstances, as Nicholas himself virtually conceded later on. But he felt duty-bound to enforce the harsh restrictions authorized by the Ural Regional Soviet. Gilliard, who had been left in Tobolsk, may have overstated the case when he described Avdeyev as an "inveterate drunkard" who "gave rein to his coarse instincts," and who with the help of subordinates "showed great ingenuity in daily inflicting fresh humiliations upon those in his charge." "There was no alternative," he wrote, "but to accept the privations, submit to the vexations, yield to the exactions and caprices of these low, vulgar scoundrels."[45]

On May 23 a joyful family reunion took place when Alexis and his three sisters arrived in Yekaterinburg. Conditions now became more crowded, with twelve people, including four servants, occupying five rooms on the second floor. Dolgorukov had been arrested, and Kobylinsky, who remained in Tobolsk, was dismissed and his troops disbanded. Dr. Botkin ministered to Alexis, who was still feeble, and acted as an intermediary between the prisoners and their guards. Other members of the retinue who had accompanied Nicholas from Tsarskoe Selo to Tobolsk, Gilliard among them, were allowed to go free. Although their confinement was depressing and their daily routine monotonous, the Romanovs were not physically abused, and their treatment was much superior to that once endured by political offenders in tsarist prisons. Some of the guards indulged in petty harassment, even following the girls to the toilet, where obscene drawings of Alexandra and Rasputin had been scrawled.[46] But others were friendly and respectful, so much so that Avdeyev's superiors began to suspect that laxity had undermined the austere regimen originally imposed.

By June of 1918 the once-faint stirrings of counterrevolution had escalated into civil war. The catalyst for both internal strife and foreign intervention was provided by the Czechoslovak Legion, a corps of some thirty-five thousand former war prisoners and deserters from the Austrian army. Arrangements had been made to evacuate the Czechs by rail to Vladivostok, where Allied ships would transport them to France for combat duty on the western front. The agreement broke down, however, and the rebellious legionnaires asserted control over most of the cities on the Trans-Siberian Railroad. Yekaterinburg and much of the Urals remained in Red hands, but the likelihood that White forces in conjunction with the Czechs would occupy the area was worrisome to Moscow. Because Nicholas could be exploited as a live banner around which monarchists could rally, greater precautions were ordered.

On June 21 a team of six officials conducted a thorough investigation of the Ipatyev House and reported to the Soviet government on security measures and the condition of the Romanovs. Everything appeared to be in order, although the chairman of the Yekaterinburg Soviet, Pavel Bykov, was constantly alert to sinister plots. From the first days, he later complained, "there began to flock in monarchists in great number, beginning with half-crazy ladies, countesses and baronesses of every caliber and ending with nuns, clergy, and representatives of foreign Powers." Supposedly they established contact with the Romanov family through Dr. Vladimir Derevenko, Alexis' longtime physician, who was allowed a private practice in Yekaterinburg. According to Bykov, notes were intercepted inside loaves of bread, and one was discovered in the cork of a milk bottle. A typical message read, "The hour of liberation is approaching and the days of the usurpers are numbered."[47]

That such machinations flourished with relative impunity, whatever the degree of Derevenko's involvement, is highly unlikely. Yet there were royalist supporters committed in theory to a rescue attempt and, if their performance never matched their good intentions, it is conceivable that they could have somehow offered Nicholas sporadic encouragement. But his diary entry for June 27 recorded only disappointment: "Spent an anxious night and kept vigil fully dressed. All this because a few days ago we received two letters . . . in which we were told to prepare to be rescued by some dedicated people! The days have passed and nothing has happened, and the waiting and uncertainty have been very painful."[48] More recent evidence demonstrates that the letters to which Nicholas referred (and others) were provocations instigated by the local authorities.[49] Monarchist conspiracies to rescue the family would help to justify the massacre to come.

On July 4 Aleksandr Beloborodov, chairman of the Ural Soviet, and several other officials appeared at the Ipatyev House to reveal that Avdeyev had been dismissed. His negligence, among other deficiencies, had contributed to his removal, but his successor, Yakov Yurovsky, better personified the ruthless efficiency that Moscow preferred. Yurovsky headed the local Cheka, or secret police, and became commandant of a new detachment of guards referred to as "Letts." The term was loosely applied to Communists of non-Russian extraction; of the ten replacements, five were allegedly Hungarian prisoners of war. Nicholas regretted Avdeyev's departure, as well he might, for Yurovsky, while more courteous than his predecessor, conveyed an unmistakable aura of quiet menace. Almost compulsive about security matters, he ordered the installation of an iron grating over one of the windows. Nicholas commented, "We like this type less and less!"[50]

Meanwhile Filip Goloshchekin, the military commissar of the Ural Soviet (and to his detractors "a homicidal sadist"), had gone to Moscow to confer with Sverdlov. Circumstantial evidence indicates that the fate of the Romanovs was the principal item of discussion and that Lenin himself participated in the decisions that were made. The consensus favored a public trial for Nicholas in late July, but when Goloshchekin returned to Yekaterinburg on July 12 the military situation had deteriorated so rapidly that the city seemed likely to fall to the Whites within a few days. Lenin and Sverdlov then, in effect, signed a death warrant for the family by telegraphing the Ural Soviet to arrange for their execution. Yurovsky was placed in charge of the procedural details.[51]

Nicholas made his last diary entry on July 13. He reported the weather to be "warm and pleasant," and in a reference to would-be rescuers commented, "We have no news from the outside." On the afternoon of the 16th he and his daughters took their customary walk in the garden. By this time Yurovsky's preparations for the forthcoming massacre were well advanced; they had been carried out methodically and with cool deliberation. Early in the evening he collected from the sentries twelve revolvers that were to be the weapons of execution. The family had retired for the night when about 1:30 A.M. they were awakened on the pretext that danger threatened and that they were to be moved to the lower floor. Nicholas carried Alexis downstairs in his arms, and the others followed, including Dr. Botkin, the cook, the maid, and the valet. They were escorted to a semi-basement room, where several chairs were brought at Nicholas' request. Whether the prisoners were lulled into a false sense of security is not clear. One witness reported that they were "calm in appearance and did not seem to be conscious of danger." Another stated his impression that they had "guessed their fate, but not a single word was uttered."[52]

Yurovsky soon appeared with four of his colleagues, including Golosh-chekin, and a squad of seven Chekists. He confronted Nicholas and, with words that have been variously rendered, declared that a decision had been made to shoot him and his family. Nicholas interjected a startled "What? What?" Yurovsky repeated his words and ordered the detachment to prepare. Nicholas turned to face his family, some incoherent cries were heard, and the shooting began. Yurovsky dispatched Nicholas at close range, as the other executioners began firing at their assigned victims. Alexandra had time to make the sign of the cross before she lay dead. Alexis, only wounded in the initial salvo, was finished off by Yurovsky's revolver. Anna Demidova, the maid, may have survived the longest; she carried a pillow concealing a box of jewelry that probably deflected some of the bullets. Screaming, she tried to flee and was cut down by bayonets.[53]

The odyssey of "Citizen Romanov" (and that of his loved ones) thus ended in an orgy of bloodshed, a gruesome preview of the atrocities that both Reds and Whites would perpetrate in the months to come.

Nicholas II and the Fate of Imperial Russia

Yurovsky and his accomplices disposed of their victims with the grim determination that had characterized the execution. After a hasty search for valuables—Alexandra and her daughters had sewn jewels in their clothing—the bodies were wrapped in bedsheets and taken by truck to a rural wooded area that had been previously selected about ten miles from Yekaterinburg. After a reexamination of the clothing for precious stones, the corpses were stripped and dismembered with axes and saws near an abandoned mine. According to Yurovsky, "Each of the girls turned out to be wearing a picture of Rasputin around her neck with text of his prayer sewn into an amulet."[1] The remains, soaked in gasoline and burned on wooden pyres, were lowered into the mine shaft with ropes. Hand grenades were thrown in to help cover the site.

Later investigators were puzzled by their failure to find bones or other body parts, giving rise to speculation that the Romanovs had been spared after all. But Yurovsky's testimony, finally published in 1989, revealed a second burial site. The original mine was deemed too shallow for concealment, and during the night of July 18–19 the remains were disinterred for disposal in a deeper mine shaft in the region. The mission was aborted, however, when the truck conveying its grisly cargo bogged down in the mud. Yurovsky decided upon an impromptu reburial nearby. Sulphuric acid was poured on the corpses—or what remained of them—as they lay in a grave about six feet deep. Planks were placed on top, then covered with dirt.[2]

In Yekaterinburg, meanwhile, the guard detachment attempted to wash away the blood from the murder room and the courtyard. Some of the guards looted the personal belongings of the Romanovs, stealing cash and jewelry. But most items of value were confiscated as state property, including Nicholas' diary and letters, and conveyed to Moscow by Goloshchekin. Sverdlov had been promptly informed by telegraph of the execution and announced it to his colleagues at a meeting of the Council of People's Commissars. The official proclamation of the Soviet government appeared in the press on July 19. It referred to Czech troops threatening Yekaterinburg and to a "new plot of counterrevolutionaries" to rescue the "royal hangman." "In view of this," the statement continued, "the presidium of the Ural Regional Soviet decided to shoot Nicholas Romanov, which was done on July 16. . . . [His] wife and son . . . were sent to a safe place."[3] Lenin and Sverdlov thus avoided direct responsibility for the deed and deliberately concealed the murder of Alexandra and the children as too bloodthirsty for public consumption.

Although the Soviet regime refused to admit officially that the entire family had perished, it eventually authorized a more credible version, which was translated and published abroad in several languages.[4] Yet in a bizarre but little-publicized attempt to shift the blame for the killings, a "revolutionary tribunal" in the Ural city of Perm tried twenty-eight Socialist Revolutionaries in September 1919. The supposed ringleader of the executioners confessed and received a death sentence, while four others were found guilty of robbing the corpses. All five were apparently executed.[5] One may surmise that the Soviet authorities had rigged a "kangaroo court" to settle a score with their political enemies.

Czech and White forces occupied Yekaterinburg without opposition on July 25, 1918. The military leaders established a commission to conduct an investigation. Ostensibly a unified effort to sift the evidence, the inquiry was handicapped by jurisdictional disputes, lack of experience, and other difficulties. In time, freelance "detectives" arrived to supplement the ranks of the "official" investigators. The first major lead to the original burial site came from local peasants, who reported suspicious activity and the discovery of burned clothing, pieces of jewelry, and other items. More systematic inspection of the area by the Yekaterinburg authorities turned up other objects that could be identified as possessions of the Romanovs. This evidence, together with clues furnished by a search of the Ipatyev House, pointed to the conclusion that the whole family had been killed.

On August 7 the inquiry was turned over to a local judge, Ivan Sergeyev, who had a reputation for fair-mindedness and had no political ax to grind. Water in the mine shaft was pumped out, and a more thorough search of the area was conducted, but little progress was made toward unraveling the mystery. Sergeyev was criticized as incompetent, and General Mikhail Diterikhs, a White commander, later directed an anti-Semitic slur at him: "The investigation was in the hands of a member of the murderers' race—a

Jew."[6] Since Sverdlov and Yurovsky were Jews, as well as other prominent Bolsheviks, many ultra-royalists (and others on the extreme Right) embraced the notion of a Jewish conspiracy to explain the rise of Communism in general and the murder of the Romanovs in particular.

On January 23, 1919, Sergeyev was abruptly dismissed on the initiative of General Diterikhs, who served the anti-Bolshevik regime of Admiral Aleksandr Kolchak based in Omsk. On February 7 Nikolai Sokolov, a convinced monarchist but also an experienced and conscientious investigator, was appointed to Sergeyev's post. He spent most of the next five months in or near Yekaterinburg in an even more thorough examination of the murder scene and the locale of the mine shaft. His work had to be abandoned when Soviet troops reoccupied Yekaterinburg in July 1919, but he later conducted many interviews with Russian émigrés, including such notables as Kerensky, Milyukov, Guchkov, and Yusupov. The massive dossier on the case and the relics he had collected eventually reached Europe in the custody of General Maurice Janin, chief of the French military mission in Siberia. The ultimate fate of the originals of these records is uncertain. The dowager empress, who resided in Denmark, declined to receive them but contributed $5,000 to the cause, which purportedly "saved" the investigation. When Sokolov visited Berlin, apparently in 1920, seven volumes of his journal dealing with the inquiry were allegedly seized in an armed raid by Russian and German Communists. According to the local police, the material was "sent on to Moscow via Prague."[7] But a copy of the dossier had been entrusted to a British journalist, Robert Wilton, and at his death it was sold at auction. Eventually Bayard Kilgour, a wealthy American businessman, purchased the collection and in 1964 donated it to Harvard University, where it remains in the custody of the Houghton Library.[8]

Sokolov based his conclusion that the Romanovs were shot in Yekaterinburg on convincing evidence, and it was accepted by scholars with virtual unanimity, whatever their political persuasion. But many die-hard monarchists were offended: "Sokolov, as the bearer of bad tidings, was shunned."[9] His findings proved a classic example of the messenger being blamed for the message. They were not summarized in book form until a French-language edition appeared in 1924, followed by a slightly revised Russian translation published in Berlin in 1925.[10]

Given the nature of the investigation, Sokolov could not provide definitive answers to every possible question. He maintained that he had accomplished as much as could be expected under the circumstances: "I do not for a moment pretend that I have established all the facts concerning the fate of the Imperial family. It may be that I have overlooked some details. But I myself feel rather certain that I have established and interpreted the main facts correctly."[11] Inevitably dissenters appeared who detected flaws in his presentation. John F. O'Conor, a retired American lawyer, expressed his criticism in a work entitled *The Sokolov Investigation* (New York, 1971). Without impugning Sokolov's integrity, he argued that the evidence adduced was susceptible to other interpretations. He suggested the possibility that the Romanovs had survived the alleged massacre but offered only speculation as to how it might have occurred.

Two British journalists, Anthony Summers and Tom Mangold, offered a broader panorama and a more daring thesis in *The File on the Tsar* (New York, 1978). They claimed that Sokolov concealed pertinent data, at least in his published account, and that the "Romanov case is redolent of conspiracy and cover-up."[12] Their reconstruction of events was based to a large extent on conjecture; they concluded that Alexandra and her daughters did not die at Yekaterinburg but were sent to Perm, where they were presumably killed in the fall of 1918.

Other scenarios have appeared with even more improbable assumptions.[13] Disagreement with the "orthodox" canon of Sokolov was understandable, but the theory that some or all of the Romanovs contrived to escape was not only highly improbable but stumbled over the inconvenient obstacle that none of them was ever seen alive by reliable witnesses after the July massacre. For a time "sightings" took place with monotonous regularity, and imposters flourished in the atmosphere of mystery that followed the family's disappearance. The notorious Solovyov, operating from Vladivostok, was said to have organized "a regular business of exporting Grand Duchesses," with local courtesans, presumably well paid for their trouble, assuming the role.[14] With a single exception, however, the impostors were quickly exposed. The one claimant who caught the popular imagination was "Anastasia."[15] Known to the public during most of her remarkable career as Anna Anderson, she married an American historian and genealogist late in life and died of natural causes in Charlottesville, Virginia, in 1984. Her modest renown was based to some extent on the Hollywood movie *Anastasia* (1956), which won an Academy Award for its star, Ingrid Bergman, and somewhat less so upon the television production of the same name (but a different script) originally broadcast in 1986. In 1970 a West German court, after years of litigation, declined to render a verdict as to the authenticity of "Anastasia's" claims. Historians were more skeptical, preferring the standard version of the "real" Anastasia's demise.

Unhappily for Anastasia buffs and other proponents of Romanov survival, the traditional view of the execution was finally borne out in recent times. The grave apparently lay undisturbed for over sixty years. In 1979 three geologists from Sverdlovsk (as Yekaterinburg was known during the Soviet era) and a writer from Moscow, relying on directions left by Yurovsky, unearthed the skeletons. Recognizing the political implications of their discovery, they prudently restored the grave site and maintained the secret for another dozen years. In 1991, with the Soviet Union collapsing and the danger of reprisal negligible, the original "conspirators" reopened the grave and disinterred the remains. Nine skulls and an assortment of bones were recovered, along with "fragments from the containers for the sulphuric acid that was supposed to disfigure the bodies beyond the point of recognition, and pieces from the rope used to raise the bodies out of the first mine shaft."[16] There had been eleven victims; two remained unaccounted for. Eventually a government commission that included forensic medical specialists, anthropologists, and molecular scientists examined the bones. British and American experts were also consulted. In a preliminary report released in Moscow on September 6, 1994, the commission revealed that the remains were indeed those of the royal family and that the two missing skeletons were those of Alexis and Marie.[17] The leading American expert, however, maintained that Alexis and Anastasia were the missing siblings.

Shortly thereafter the results of two independent investigations, using DNA analysis, established that Anna Anderson could not have been the "lost" Anastasia. With the failure to retrieve the corpses of Alexis and Marie (or Anastasia), a new generation of pretenders began to flourish. They claimed to be Romanov descendants, and several received a measure of publicity as well as support from Russian monarchist groups.

Nicholas II's posthumous image has for the most part been decidedly negative. For some seventy years Soviet historians, journalists, and Communist Party spokesmen, when not demonizing him as a bloody or at least mean-spirited tyrant, were content to minimize his influence or to ignore him altogether. In more recent times, under the relatively benign leadership of Mikhail Gorbachev and Boris Yelstin, and stimulated by popular nostalgia for the fancied merits of a bygone era, his reputation has been upgraded. A Romanov "cult" formed around the martyred family. The vacant site where the Ipatyev House once stood—it was destroyed in accordance with a Politburo decision in 1977—became something of a shrine to the tsar's memory. Ironically it was Yeltsin, the former party secretary in Sverdlovsk, who had been obliged to carry out the demolition order. He later expressed his profound regret: "Sooner or later we will be ashamed of this piece of barbarism. Ashamed we may be, but we can never rectify it."[18] Nicholas' admirers erected a cross and held rallies, sometimes invoking the anti-Semitism that flourished among monarchists following the 1918 massacre. A church to be constructed on the site may eventually become a more tangible shrine for pilgrimages. In 1990 the Palace of Youth in Moscow opened a popular exhibit on the "Last Days of the Romanovs" featuring photographs and family documents."[19]

In the West, where scholarship has seldom been the handmaiden of political or ideological constraints, Nicholas, with a few exceptions, has fared only marginally better than in his homeland (in the Soviet era). He was rarely excoriated as a brutal despot, but his glaring deficiencies and gross incompetence have been thoroughly documented in a host of memoirs, biographies, and scholarly monographs. In monarchist émigré circles, however, his image as the kindly and benevolent tsar remained untarnished. In 1981, in an extreme example of his apotheosis, he and the members of his family were canonized in New York City by the Russian Orthodox Church Outside Russia, a bitterly anti-Communist organization that claimed 270,000 adherents, including 150,000 in the United States.

Despite the annihilation of the immediate family, the House of Romanov survived abroad, at least in the opinion of Russian monarchists. The matriarch herself, the Dowager Empress Marie, found temporary safety in the Crimea. When in April 1919 Red troops threatened to occupy the region, she departed on a British warship. After residing in England for a time, she returned to her native Denmark, where she died in 1928 at the age of eighty-one. Refusing to concede the demise of her son and his family, she nevertheless rebuffed any contact with "Anastasia" and other impostors. Her daughters both died in 1980, Olga in Canada and Xenia in England.

Grand Duke Nikolai Nikolayevich escaped from the Crimea with the dowager empress and died in southern France in 1929. The logical pretender to the vacated throne, he avoided monarchist politics, and the role of presumptive heir was assumed by Grand Duke Kirill Vladimirovich, a first cousin and the senior survivor among Nicholas' closer relatives. He presided over a "court" in the French coastal village of St. Briac, becoming a "conscientious mail-order sovereign" whose correspondents "offered information, asked for advice, and sought favors."[20] But his following, even among monarchists émigrés, was limited, in part because he had been the only Romanov of consequence to greet the February Revolution with open approval. Nor did his sympathetic attitude toward fascism aid his cause, except among anti-Communists who embraced the politics of the extreme Right. He died in Paris at the age of sixty-two in 1938, and his son Vladimir succeeded him as pretender. Vladimir, who resided chiefly in Madrid, lived long enough to observe (from afar) the collapse of Communism in Russia but died in Miami, Florida, at the age of seventy-four in 1992. In what would have seemed unimaginable a few years before, he was accorded a lavish funeral in St. Petersburg. His daughter Marie, a grand duchess according to the Romanov tradition, assumed the role of pretender.

Less fortunate relatives joined Nicholas in martyrdom. His brother Mikhail was shot by a Red "death squad" on June 12, 1918, near Perm in the Urals. The following July 17 six prominent Romanovs, including Alexandra's sister, were executed in a particularly gruesome fashion near the town of Alapayevsk in the northern Urals. Local Bolsheviks, perhaps with Moscow's authorization, murdered five of the victims, allegedly pushing them alive down a mine shaft, where several may have died of starvation, exposure, and injuries. On January 29, 1919, four grand dukes, including the historian Nikolai Mikhailovich, were shot in Petrograd after incarceration in the fortress of St. Peter and Paul.[21]

The political legacy that Nicholas bequeathed aroused no following of consequence. The White commanders, if vaguely sympathetic to the principle of monarchy, deliberately ignored the prospect of a Romanov restoration as suicidal to their cause. The dynasty perished as a Russian institution, just as the House of Hohenzollern in Germany and that of Habsburg in Austria collapsed, under less dramatic circumstances, in 1918. But the death agony of dynastic absolutism prepared the way for more radical solutions to Europe's disarray. The Communism of Joseph Stalin and the National Socialism of Adolf Hitler proved so destructive of human life that the oppressive regimes of tsar and kaiser seemed in comparison almost models of enlightened statecraft. Nor did Nicholas succumb to mental derangement; the megalomania of a Hitler or the paranoia of a Stalin did not debase his reign. In retrospect, therefore, the "tyranny" of absolute or semi-absolute monarchy, so outrageous to radicals and repulsive to liberals, had much to recommend it in the light of the brutal dictatorships that the twentieth century later spawned.

The bumbling inadequacies of Nicholas II have been chronicled in detail. Yet it would be unjust and historically inaccurate to allow negative stereotypes and half-truths about his personal qualities to stand without modification. Although sorely deficient in educational background, political judgment, and the gift of leadership, he was by no means devoid of natural intelligence, a fair measure of common sense, and some of the attractive features of an aristocratic heritage. Despite a severely limited intellectual range—he appeared ignorant of and indifferent to the world of ideas—he readily absorbed ministerial reports and the contents of government documents. His legendary indecisiveness and absence of willpower were not always in evidence, and he could act with stubborn determination when the mood seized him and the occasion seemed to demand it. Unfortunately for his reputation, such instances all too frequently involved real or fancied assaults on royal authority. Partly for that reason his record in the making and unmaking of ministers, if not invariably deplorable, was haphazard and capricious. If one accepts these acts of temperamental indulgence, he possessed almost none of the personal attributes or political instincts of a true autocrat. On the other hand, his self-discipline and devotion to duty, his "bourgeois" virtues as a devoted husband and father, and his gentle demeanor and tactful courtesy were traits admirably suited to constitutional monarchy.

Tragically, Nicholas' immersion in the mystique of dynastic absolutism prevented him from fulfilling his "natural" role. Nor did his earnest piety and fatalistic brand of Christianity blend smoothly with the growing secularization of urban society. As befitted an unsophisticated neo-Slavophile, he was a throwback to an earlier age. That his favorite tsar was the benign and devout Alexis (1645–1676), for whom he named his son, was not fortuitous. Neither was it happenstance that his least favorite tsar was Peter the Great. He acknowledged his "ancestor's great merits" but complained that Peter "had too much admiration for European 'culture.' . . . He stamped out Russian habits, the good customs of his sires, the usages bequeathed by the nation."[22]

The failings and shortcomings of the monarch, though they should not be minimized, do not in themselves explain the collapse of the monarchy. War was obviously the catalyst of revolution. Given a generous interval of peace accompanied by political concessions, domestic stability, growing affluence, and upward social mobility, especially for the educated elite, the regime might have survived for some years the perils and obstacles embedded in the fabric of Russian society. But war, if not inevitable, was an integral part of the European state system, and the great powers (excluding Austria and Italy) were far more capable of withstanding the heavy sacrifices demanded by armed conflict than tsarist Russia.

Less obvious answers as to why Russia succumbed to a profound revolutionary upheaval are almost as varied as the commentators who have ventured opinions. But if nothing akin to a consensus has emerged, there is general recognition among critics of the old regime that its problems were many and the remedies few. In early 1917 there were gloomy forecasts and much foreboding, but virtually no one, including avowed revolutionaries, predicted the imminent downfall of the monarchy. Hindsight, it is well to be reminded, can do wonders to clarify complex historical phenomena. From the perspective of the late twentieth century and with the evidence compiled by decades of scholarly investigation, a tentative theory of revolutionary causation is possible.

A logical beginning would be the people themselves. Overwhelmingly, the tsar's subjects were peasants. Poor by Western standards but not necessarily impoverished, they constituted a massive if normally latent protest movement against the status quo. Had they been mobilized in a revolutionary crusade, their power would have been irresistible. Instead, their resentment and sense of alienation were directed toward the landowning nobility. The monarchy represented a remote abstraction that had no practical bearing on village life. In Marxist terms, their aspirations were "petty bourgeois" because the acquisition of landed property eclipsed any political goal or ideological motivation. The peasantry nevertheless formed a huge and volatile force for disorder, not only in times of crisis but in the "disguise" of workers and soldiers.

Soldiers, the proverbial "peasants in uniform," played a key revolutionary role, as was amply demonstrated in the failed "dress rehearsal" of 1905 and the successful Petrograd mutiny of 1917. But it was the new industrial working class, recruited for the most part from the countryside, that furnished the cutting edge for the war of attrition against the autocracy. Numerically insignificant, perhaps three million by 1914, they were exploited in the classic manner of other industrializing societies. Unlike their counterparts in the West, who were weaned from revolutionary activism by rising wages, trade unionism, and the growth of parliamentary democracy, Russian workers were often radicalized by their urban environment. Labor unions and strikes were forbidden before 1905, and the government's readiness to suppress worker grievances (and their public manifestations) with armed force tended to merge the economic struggle with the larger movement of political protest. The unusual concentration of workers in St. Petersburg and Moscow and their relatively high rate of literacy provides additional insight into the militance of a crucial segment of the population.

The rise of industrial capitalism inevitably expanded the ranks of the business elite. Bankers, entrepreneurs, and managers joined the older merchant class as arbiters of the urban economy. Since most capitalists supported the autocracy, their near-exclusion from the levers of political power aroused less animosity. In sharp contrast to such complacency, the professionals (teachers, lawyers, zemstvo workers, etc.) who shared the "bourgeois" label were generally resentful of the old regime and its restrictions on civil liberties.

By 1914 the nobility seemed the only sizable group that gave more than token support to the tsarist regime. Although there were numerous defectors, even a few radicals, the nobility could be vaguely identified as the "ruling class." Other than top officials, however, few of its members played any significant role in the political life of the country. Increasingly the government bureaucracy replenished its ranks from the talented and educated, paying less attention to aristocratic pedigrees.

As opinion-molders, the intelligentsia constituted the most powerful "class" of all. A small and ill-defined group in any society, its members should, ideally, possess an inquiring mind, formal education, and a thirst for knowledge, supplemented with the affluence and leisure to avoid or postpone the struggle for economic survival. Above all, they should aspire to an objectivity that transcends their own self-interest. They normally share a critical, sometimes contemptuous, attitude toward the existing order, and an active minority seeks political influence commensurate with its intellectual pretensions. In Russia professional revolutionaries formed the radical wing of the intelligentsia; moderates, more numerous, pursued a less dangerous existence in a variety of respectable occupations not necessarily involving intellectual pursuits. But from terrorists on the extreme Left to liberals closer to the center of the political spectrum, the intelligentsia achieved remarkable unanimity in condemning the tsarist "establishment." Although much of the doctrine of protest trickled down to the masses in a distorted or demagogic form, the basic message permeated all sectors of the population, with special resonance in the urban centers. By 1917 only the royal family and the palace "camarilla" turned a deaf ear to the public mood of sullen resentment.

Finally, there were the national minorities, whose expectations often coincided with those of ethnic Russians, depending upon class alignments and a host of geographical and historical circumstances. Nationalism matured and even prospered under the lash of Russification, and politically conscious Finns, Poles, Caucasians, and Central Asian Muslims clamored for autonomy or independence (the Jews were a special case). These minorities played no direct part in the overthrow of the monarchy, but they contributed conspicuously to the disruption of the social order in the last years of the empire.

If poverty and oppression are fundamental causes of revolution, most of mankind would remain in a perpetual state of rebellion. Yet economic hardship, at least in its more extreme manifestations, produces hunger, malnutrition, and listlessness, not the spirit of revolt. As for oppression, tyrannical and authoritarian regimes have flourished throughout history with relative impunity from either political disaffection or mass insurrection. In the Russian case, the people had for centuries been quiescent in the face of economic and political deprivation, except for occasional and unsuccessful peasant uprisings. How had conditions changed by the reign of Nicholas II? The altered state of public opinion has been noted. Much of the growing alienation between government and people derived from structural changes that few could articulate at the time. For lack of a more suitable expression, scholars coined the term "modernization" to describe the process that Russia (and other countries) was undergoing in the twentieth century as it evolved from an agrarian to an industrial society. The tsarist regime was not "progressive," but even Nicholas gave lip service—and sometimes more tangible assistance—to industrial development, land reform, civil liberties, education, and the peaceful resolution of international disputes. As a patriot devoted to his country, he took pride in its achievements; and though his perception was often skewed by the demands of a risky foreign policy—Russia could ill afford to lag behind as it did in military preparedness and industrial technology—he was persuaded that domestic reform within the tradition of autocracy was desirable.

Alexis de Tocqueville, the great historian and political theorist, was the first to conclude, in his analysis of the French Revolution, that mass discontent and rebellion are more likely to occur when the times are increasingly prosperous and the population is encouraged to hope for a better future. This "revolution of rising expectations," as the phenomena came to be called, can be applied to Russia with some credibility. Yet as a historically "backward" country, perpetually striving to catch up with the West in industrial production, living standards, and civic and cultural amenities, Russia remained a country of paradox. It shared in part the disabilities of other undeveloped societies in Asia, Africa, and Latin America, but its size, population, resources, and military potential entitled it to great-power status within the European community.

Leon Trotsky, though extravagantly pretentious in citing the "laws" of history in his comments on revolutionary causation, singled out the phenomena of "unevenness" and "combined development" to explain Russia's backwardness in conjunction with its rapid progress toward "modernization." His argument, if suggestive, was excessively brief and schematic. It did, nonetheless, highlight the growth of industry, the political immaturity of the bourgeoisie, and the radicalism of the proletariat. The "indubitable and irrefutable belatedness of Russia's development under [the] influence and pressure of the higher culture from the West," he maintained, "results not in a simple repetition of the West European historic process, but in the creation of profound *peculiarities* demanding independent study."[23] Unfortunately, such studies are in short supply, insofar as it is possible to make valid comparisons between Russian and Western civilization. It seems clear, nevertheless, that Russia's "uneven" and "combined" development fostered conditions that led to revolution instead of democracy and political stability under the aegis of a large and prosperous middle class.

The spontaneity and popularity of the February Revolution emphasized the isolation and abject capitulation of the old order. The intellectual and moral juices of the ruling elite, normally available to uphold and to justify the regime in power, were sapped long before 1917. Except for the tsar's entourage, the Council of Ministers, and the nobility in higher bureaucratic, ecclesiastical, and military service, there were few in positions of authority who did not entertain serious doubts about the legitimacy of the government and their own responsibility in supporting it. The war years had eroded the morale and loyalty even of its generals and ministers, leaving only the court aristocracy to defend its privileges.

The humiliating collapse of the old regime was not, in retrospect, as startling an event as it appeared at the time. Far more shocking, at least to Western sensibilities, was the Bolshevik "succession" of October 1917. But the particularities of the Bolshevik Revolution, while undeniably linked to the deep malaise of tsarism, lie beyond the scope of the present study. The ultimate failure of Communism and the disintegration of the Soviet regime do, however, invite historical analogies to imperial Russia. At least one obvious conclusion may be drawn: neither the autocratic monarchy of Nicholas II nor the Communist dictatorship of Lenin and his heirs was able to preside over a political and social order that fulfilled the aspirations of the Russian people.

Abbreviations

Alexandra, *Letters*	Sir Bernard Pares (introd.), *Letters of the Tsaritsa to the Tsar, 1914–1916* (London, 1923)
BD	G. P. Gooch and Harold Temperley (eds.), *British Documents on the Origins of the War, 1898–1914* (11 vols. in 13; London, 1926–38)
GARF	Gosudarstvenny Arkhiv Rossiiskoi Federatsii (State Archive of the Russian Federation), Moscow
GD	*Gosudarstvennaya Duma: Stenograficheskie otchety* (126 vols.; St. Petersburg, 1906–17)
GP	Germany. Foreign Office. *Die Grosse Politik der europäischen Kabinette, 1871–1914* (40 vols.; Berlin, 1922–27)
KA	*Krasny Arkhiv* (106 vols.; Moscow, 1922–41)
MERSH	*Modern Encyclopedia of Russian and Soviet History* (55 vols.; Gulf Breeze, Fla., 1976–93)
Nicholas II, *Letters*	C. H. Vulliamy (ed.), *The Letters of the Tsar to the Tsaritsa, 1914–1917* (London, 1929)
Padenie	P. E. Shchegolev (ed.), *Padenie tsarskogo rezhima* (7 vols.; Moscow, 1924–27)
SEER	*Slavonic and East European Review* (London)

Witte 1   Abraham Yarmolinsky (ed. and trans.), *The Memoirs of Count Witte* (Garden City, N.Y., 1921)

Witte 2   Sidney Harcave (ed. and trans.), *The Memoirs of Count Witte* (Armonk, N.Y., 1990)

Notes

CHAPTER 1

1. Grand Duke Alexander of Russia, *Once a Grand Duke* (New York, 1932), p. 59.

2. *Ibid.*, p. 62.

3. E. J. Dillon, *The Eclipse of Russia* (London, 1918), pp. 77–78. See also Peter A. Zaionchkovsky, *The Russian Autocracy in Crisis, 1878–1882* (Gulf Breeze, Fla., 1979), p. 348, n. 3.

4. Peter A. Zaionchkovsky, *The Russian Autocracy under Alexander III* (Gulf Breeze, Fla., 1976), pp. 16, 269, n. 9. For the background see I. Michael Aronson, *Troubled Waters: The Origins of the 1881 Anti-Jewish Pogroms in Russia* (Pittsburgh, 1990); Stephen M. Berk, *Year of Crisis, Year of Hope: Russian Jewry and the Pogroms of 1881–1882* (Westport, Conn., 1985); and John D. Klier and Shlomo Lambroza (eds.), *Pogroms: Anti-Jewish Violence in Modern Russian History* (Cambridge, Eng., 1992).

5. See Robert D. Warth, "Pobedonostsev, Konstantin Petrovich," MERSH, 28 (1982), pp. 139–42. The authoritative biography is Robert F. Byrnes, *Pobedonostsev: His Life and Work* (Bloomington, Ind., 1968).

6. Mohammed Essad-Bey, *Nicholas II: Prisoner of the Purple* (New York, 1937), p. 11.

7. Alexander Kerensky, *The Crucifixion of Liberty* (New York, 1934), p. 165; Kerensky, *Russia and History's Turning Point* (New York, 1965), p. 157.

8. Nikolai II, *Dnevnik Imperatora Nikolaya II, 1890–1906 gg.* (Berlin, 1923). Also French and German editions. The bound volumes of the original diary (not yet published in full) may be found in GARF, fond 601, opis 1, delo 217 ff. (hereafter abbreviated).

9. Constantin de Grunwald, *Le Tsar Nicolas II* (Paris, 1965), p. 2. See also Ilya Surguchev, *Detstvo imperatora Nicolaya II* (Paris, 1953).

10. A. A. Mossolov, *At the Court of the Last Tsar* (London, 1935), p. 6.

11. Alexander Iswolsky, *Memoirs* (Gulf Breeze, Fla., 1974), pp. 248–49.

12. *Times* (London), May 19, 1884; A. A. Polovtsov, *Dnevnik* (Moscow, 1966), I, pp. 215–16.

13. Edward J. Bing (ed.), *The Secret Letters of the Last Tsar* (New York, 1938), pp. 33, 36.

14. [V. P. Obninsky], *Posledny samoderzhets* (Berlin, 1912), p. 36.

15. Witte 2, pp. 93–95, 97–98; *Times* (London), November 1, 1888; Ian Vorres, *The Last Grand-Duchess* (London, 1964), pp. 29–31.

16. GARF, f. 601, op. 1, d. 227.

17. Grunwald, p. 9.

18. Nikolai II, *Dnevnik*, pp. 28–30, 32; Princess Romanovsky-Krassinsky, *Dancing in Petersburg* (London, 1960), pp. 32–35, 37–40.

19. See Robert D. Warth, "Ukhtomskii, Esper Esperovich," MERSH, 40 (1985), pp. 161–62.

20. Unless otherwise indicated the details of the journey are based on Prince E. Ookhtomsky, *Travels in the East of Nicholas II, Emperor of Russia When Cesarewitch* (2 vols.; London, 1896).

21. *Journal intime de Nicolas II* (Paris, 1925), p. 32.

22. See Robert D. Warth, "Wallace, Donald Mackenzie," MERSH, 43 (1986), pp. 137–38.

23. Nikolai II, *Dnevnik*, p. 40.

24. Bing, p. 42.

25. Grand Duke Alexander, p. 167.

26. Ookhtomsky, II, pp. 451–53; *Times* (London), June 13, 1891; Prince Nicholas of Greece, *My Fifty Years* (London, 1926), p. 103; Charles Lowe, *Alexander III of Russia* (New York, 1895), pp. 347–49; George Alexander Lensen, "The Attempt on the Life of Nicholas II in Japan," *Russian Review*, 20 (July 1961), pp. 232–53.

27. Iswolsky, p. 251.

28. Bing, pp. 52, 54.

29. Lensen, "The Attempt," pp. 248–52.

30. Harmon Tupper, *To the Great Ocean: Siberia and the Trans-Siberian Railway* (Boston, 1965), p. 82.

31. S. Yu. Vitte, *Vospominania* (Moscow, 1960), I, pp. 434–35.

32. D. N. Lyubimov, "Russkaya smuta nachala devyatisotykh godov, 1902–1906," pp. 83–84, Bakhmeteff Archive, Columbia University.

33. Andrew Dickson White, *Autobiography* (New York, 1905–6), II, p. 10.

34. Lyubimov, p. 81.

35. V. N. Lamzdorf, *Dnevnik, 1891–1892* (Moscow, 1934), p. 259.

36. GP, VII, Nos. 1526, 1527; William L. Langer, *The Franco-Russian Alliance* (Cambridge, Mass., 1929), pp. 302–4.

37. Bing, p. 59; George Earle Buckle (ed.), *The Letters of Queen Victoria* (3rd series; London, 1930–32), II, p. 269.

38. Lowe, p. 355.

39. Grand Duke Alexander, p. 169.
40. Witte 2, p. 213.

CHAPTER 2

1. Lowe, pp. 356–57.
2. F. Rodichev, "The Liberal Movement in Russia (1891–1905)," *Slavonic Review*, 2 (1923–24), pp. 250–51; V. I. Gurko, *Features and Figures of the Past* (Stanford, Calif., 1939), pp. 19, 602, n. 23.
3. *Polnoe sobranie rechei Imperator Nikolaya II* (St. Petersburg, 1906), p. 7.
4. Princess Catherine Radziwill, *Nicholas II: The Last of the Tsars* (London, 1931), pp. 102–3.
5. See Robert D. Warth, "Struve, Petr Berngardovich," MERSH, 37 (1984), pp. 229–34. Richard Pipes, *Struve* (2 vols.; Cambridge, Mass., 1970–80), is a comprehensive biography.
6. Text in Peter Struve, "My Contacts with Rodichev," *Slavonic Review*, 12 (1933–34), pp. 353–54.
7. L. G. Deich (ed.), *Gruppa "Osvobozhdenie Truda"* (Moscow, 1923–28), II, p. 333.
8. Theodore H. Von Laue, *Sergei Witte and the Industrialization of Russia* (New York, 1963), p. 126.
9. S. S. Oldenburg, *Last Tsar: Nicholas II, His Reign & His Russia* (Gulf Breeze, Fla., 1975–78), I, p. 44.
10. Gurko, p. 75.
11. N. V. Tcharykow, "Reminiscence of Nicolas II," *Contemporary Review*, 134 (October 1928), p. 447.
12. Grand Duke Alexander, p. 173.
13. V. N. Lamzdorf, *Dnevnik, 1894–1896* (Moscow, 1991), p. 404.
14. Gleb Botkin, *The Real Romanovs* (New York, 1931), p. 45.
15. Grand Duke Alexander, pp. 156–57; Vorres, pp. 94–96.
16. Bing, pp. 88–89.
17. Field-Marshal Lord Grenfell, *Memoirs* (London, 1925), p. 136.
18. Iswolsky, pp. 262–63.
19. See Robert D. Warth, "The Khodynka Catastrophe of 1896," MERSH, 16 (1980), pp. 157–59. In addition to the sources listed there, see Grenfell, p. 142; Vorres, pp. 77–79; *Times* (London), June 1, 1896; Clifton R. Breckinridge to Richard C. Olney, No. 332 (June 22, 1896), Department of State Record Group 59, Roll 49, National Archives, Washington, D.C.; Vl. Fon-Shtein, "Khodynskaya katastrofa 1896 goda," *Istoricbesky vestnik*, 118 (1909), pp. 473–506. More recent secondary accounts include Harrison E. Salisbury, *Black Night, White Snow* (Garden City, N.Y., 1978), pp. 52–58, 63–64, and W. Bruce Lincoln, *The Romanovs* (New York, 1981), pp. 624–27.
20. KA, 17 (1926), p. 220.
21. See Robert D. Warth, "Nizhnii Novgorod Exposition of 1876 [1896]," MERSH, 25 (1981), pp. 26–28. Also Witte 2, pp. 244–45.
22. N. F. Grant (ed.), *The Kaiser's Letters to the Tsar* (London, 1920), p. 22.
23. Buckle, *Letters*, III, p. 82.

24. Margaret M. Jefferson, "Lord Salisbury and the Eastern Question, 1890–1898," SEER, 39 (December 1960), pp. 44–60, and the same author's "Lord Salisbury's Conversations with the Tsar at Balmoral, 27 and 29 September 1896," *ibid.*, pp. 216–22; J. A. S. Grenville, *Lord Salisbury and Foreign Policy* (London, 1964), pp. 78–83.

25. Giles St. Aubyn, *Edward VII* (New York, 1979), p. 300.

CHAPTER 3

1. KA, 3 (1923), p. 99.
2. Von Laue, p. 37.
3. Dillon, p. 113.
4. KA, 46 (1931), p. 116 (January 6, 1897).
5. Von Laue, p. 145; Witte 2, pp. 246–49.
6. Iswolsky, p. 118.
7. I. F. Gindin, quoted in Von Laue, p. 184.
8. Theodore H. Von Laue (ed.), "A Secret Memorandum on the Industrialization of Imperial Russia," *Journal of Modern History*, 26 (March 1954), pp. 60–74.
9. A. S. Suvorin, *Dnevnik* (Moscow, 1923), p. 224.
10. See Robert D. Warth, "Sipiagin, Dmitrii Sergevich," MERSH, 35 (1983), pp. 147–49.
11. Gurko, pp. 85–88; Edward H. Judge, *Plehve* (Syracuse, N.Y., 1983), pp. 220–22.
12. Witte 2, pp. 771–72, n. 4.
13. Witte 1, p. 250; Witte 2, pp. 222, 224, 369, 461; Gurko, pp. 108, 111; Lowe, p. 63.
14. Maurice Bompard, *Mon ambassade en Russie, 1903–1914* (Paris, 1937), p. 66.
15. KA, 3 (1923), p. 114 (Polovtsov's diary, January 26, 1902).
16. D. N. Shipov, *Vospominania i dumy o perezhitom* (Moscow, 1918), pp. 169–71.
17. Gurko, p. 228.
18. *Ibid.*, pp. 217–18.
19. *Ibid.*, p. 237.
20. KA, 3 (1923), p. 161 (September 22, 1902).
21. See Chapter 4.
22. See Chapter 9.
23. Dillon, pp. 117–18.
24. Gurko, p. 225.
25. Witte 2, pp. 314–15; Prince von Bülow, *Memoirs* (Boston, 1931), II, p. 50; KA, 2 (1922), p. 60 (Aleksei Kuropatkin's diary, August 19, 1903); Count Kokovtsov, *Out of My Past* (Stanford, Calif., 1935), pp. 6–7.
26. Witte 2, pp. 316, 774–75 (n. 6), 783 (n. 20).
27. D. M. Wallace, "The Career and Fall of M. Witte, Russian Minister of Finance, December 1903," *Times* (London) Archives.
28. Norman Davies, *God's Playground: A History of Poland* (New York, 1982), II, p. 109.

29. Edward C. Thaden (ed.), *Russification in the Baltic Provinces and Finland, 1855–1914* (Princeton, N.J., 1961), p. 420.

30. *Ibid.*, pp. 435–36.

31. Bing, pp. 157–62.

32. Thaden, p. 443.

33. See Leonard Schapiro, "The Role of the Jews in the Russian Revolutionary Movement," SEER, 40 (December 1961), pp. 148–67.

34. The literature on Kishinev is extensive. Primary sources include Michael Davitt, *Within the Pale* (New York, 1903), Part 2; Gurko, pp. 246–49; and Prince Serge Dmitriyevich Urussov, *Memoirs of a Russian Governor* (New York, 1908), pp. 77–85. Brief secondary accounts include W. Bruce Lincoln, *In War's Dark Shadow* (New York, 1983), pp. 219–22; Taylor Stults, "Kishinev Pogrom of 1903," MERSH, 17 (1980), pp. 45–48; and Klier and Lambroza, pp. 198–207. Edward H. Judge, *Easter in Kishinev: Anatomy of a Pogrom* (New York, 1992), is comprehensive.

35. The standard biography is Boris Nikolajewsky, *Aseff the Spy* (Garden City, N.Y., 1934). See also Richard E. Rubenstein, *Comrade Valentine: The True Story of Azeff the Spy* (New York, 1994).

36. Judge, *Plehve*, p. 233.

37. Boris Savinkov, *Memoirs of a Terrorist* (New York, 1931), p. 60.

38. Nikolai II, *Dnevnik*, p. 161.

CHAPTER 4

1. Eugene de Schelking, *Recollections of a Russian Diplomat* (New York, 1918), p. 154.

2. Witte 2, pp. 250–51.

3. *Ibid.*, pp. 251–52; KA, 1 (1922), pp. 152–62; KA, 47–48 (1931), pp. 50–70. See also Vladimir Khostov's articles on the Bosphorus episode in *Istorik marksist*, 13 (1929), pp. 19–54, and 20 (1930), pp. 100–129.

4. Bing, pp. 118–19.

5. KA, 8 (1925), p. 3.

6. Bing, p. 121.

7. Bülow, I, pp. 160–62.

8. Buckle, *Letters*, III, pp. 439, 461.

9. KA, 63 (1934), pp. 124–26.

10. Bing, p. 135.

11. Sir Sidney Lee, *King Edward VII* (New York, 1927), II, pp. 73–76.

12. KA, 18 (1926), pp. 4–18.

13. Henry H. Howarth, "Some Plain Words about the Tsar's New Gospel of Peace," *Nineteenth Century*, 45 (February 1899), p. 203.

14. Calvin De Armand Davis, *The United States and the First Hague Peace Conference* (Ithaca, N.Y., 1962), p. 43.

15. Dillon, p. 275. Dillon was among the first to minimize Nicholas II's role. This viewpoint is expressed in Thomas K. Ford, "The Genesis of the First Hague Peace Conference," *Political Science Quarterly*, 51 (1936), pp. 354–82, and in Barbara W. Tuchman, *The Proud Tower* (New York, 1966), especially pp. 236–37.

16. For a "revisionist" view see Dan L. Morrill, "Nicholas II and the Call for the First Hague Conference," *Journal of Modern History*, 46 (June 1974), pp. 296–313.

17. KA, 54–55 (1932), p. 56.

18. KA, 50–51 (1932), p. 75.

19. *Budushaya voina* (6 vols.; St. Petersburg, 1898). Only the final volume appeared in an English translation: Jean De Bloch, *The Future of War . . .* (Boston, 1902; reprint ed., New York, 1971).

20. Donald Mackenzie Wallace, "Rough Notes on the Foreign Policy of Russia during the Reign of Nicholas II" (December 5, 1903), *Times* (London) Archives. See also W. T. Stead, *The United States of Europe* (London, 1899), p. 133; Bertha von Suttner, *Memoirs* (New York, 1972), II, pp. 183, 252; Andrew D. White, *The First Hague Conference* (Boston, 1912), p. 15.

21. KA, 50–51 (1932), p. 67.

22. GP, XV, No. 4222.

23. Philip Magnus, *King Edward the Seventh* (New York, 1964), p. 249; Tuchman, p. 239.

24. Christopher Andrew, *Théophile Delcassé and the Making of the Entente Cordiale* (New York, 1968), p. 134.

25. GP, XV, No. 4320.

26. Grant, pp. 10–11.

27. B. A. Romanov, *Russia in Manchuria (1892–1906)* (Ann Arbor, Mich., 1952), p. 68.

28. See Robert D. Warth, "Russian–Chinese Bank," MERSH, 32 (1983), pp. 82–85; Rosemary Quested, *The Russo-Chinese Bank* (Birmingham, Eng., 1977).

29. Baron Rosen, *Forty Years of Diplomacy* (New York, 1922), I, p. 198.

30. Romanov, p. 71.

31. KA, 52 (1932), p. 94.

32. Dillon, p. 261.

33. Romanov, pp. 84–85, 402–3, n. 74.

34. Marcella Bounds, "The Sino-Russian Secret Treaty of 1896," *Papers on China* (Harvard University seminar), 23 (July 1970), pp. 109–25.

35. See Roger F. Hackett, *Yamagata Aritomo in the Rise of Modern Japan, 1838–1922* (Cambridge, Mass., 1971).

36. Rosen, I, pp. 125–26.

37. GP, XIV, No. 3689.

38. KA, 52 (1932), pp. 103–8.

39. GP, XIV, No. 3739.

40. On the bribery arrangements see KA, 2 (1922), pp. 287–93.

41. Witte 2, pp. 276–77. See also Howard R. Spendelow, "Russia's Lease of Port Arthur and Talien," *Papers on China*, 24 (December 1971), pp. 146–69.

42. Rosen, I, p. 159.

43. KA, 14 (1926), p. 31, n. 1.

44. Schelking, p. 165.

45. Rosen, I, pp. 174–75.

46. Witte 2, p. 769, n. 3.

47. Bing, p. 138.

48. Witte 1, p. 114.

49. Andrew Malozemoff, *Russian Far Eastern Policy, 1881–1904* (Berkeley, Calif., 1958), pp. 161–62.

50. Witte 2, p. 281.

51. See Robert D. Warth, "Vonliarliarskii, Vladimir Mikhailovich," MERSH, 43 (1986), pp. 29–30.

52. Romanov, pp. 273–74.

53. KA, 18 (1926), p. 45.

54. B. B. Glinsky (ed.), *Prolog russkoi-yaponskoi voiny: Materialy iz arkhiva grofa S. Yu. Vitte* (Petrograd, 1916), pp. 253–59.

55. Gurko, p. 276.

56. KA, 17 (1926), p. 79.

57. Ian Nish, *The Origins of the Russo-Japanese War* (New York, 1985), pp. 189–90.

58. KA, 2 (1922), p. 80 (Kuropatkin's diary, October 28, 1903).

59. *Ibid.*, p. 95 (December 15, 1903).

60. *Ibid.*, p. 106 (January 25, 1904).

CHAPTER 5

1. Urussov, p. 177.

2. Bing, p. 172.

3. See Chapter 9.

4. *Contemporary Review*, 86 (August 1904), p. 290; Witte 2, p. 386.

5. Nikolai II, *Dnevnik*, p. 141.

6. *Ibid.*, p. 163; Denis and Peggy Warner, *The Tide at Sunrise* (New York, 1974), pp. 358–59.

7. David Walder, *The Short Victorious War: The Russo-Japanese Conflict, 1904–5* (London, 1973), p. 158.

8. GARF, f. 601, op. 1, d. 1200.

9. Nikolai II, *Dnevnik*, p. 188.

10. J. N. Westwood (ed.), *Witnesses of Tsushima* (Tokyo, 1970), pp. 82–83.

11. Nikolai II, *Dnevnik*, p. 175.

12. GARF, f. 601, op. 1, d. 248, 1131; Bing, pp. 174–75.

13. Richard Hough, *The Fleet That Had to Die* (New York, 1958), p. 58.

14. A. Novikoff-Priboy, *Tsushima* (London, 1936), p. 155.

15. Nikolai II, *Dnevnik*, p. 201; Bing, p. 175; Grand Duke Alexander, p. 223.

16. Elting E. Morison (ed.), *The Letters of Theodore Roosevelt* (Cambridge, Mass., 1951–54), IV, p. 1158.

17. M. A. DeWolfe Howe, *George von Lengerke Meyer* (New York, 1920), p. 161; KA, 28 (1928), pp. 191–204.

18. Morison, *Letters*, IV, pp. 1230, 1258.

19. J. J. Korostovetz, *Diary* (London, 1920), p. 12.

20. Kokovtsov, p. 53.

21. Witte 2, pp. 423–25.

22. Mossolov, p. 203; Witte 1, p. 412.

23. Grant, *Letters*, p. 139.

24. GP, XIX, No. 6220.

25. *Ibid.*, Nos. 6247, 6248.

26. *Ibid.*, No. 6146.

27. Vitte, *Vospominania*, II, p. 395.

28. *Ibid.*, p. 415; Korostovetz, p. 9; Witte 2, p. 426.

29. Joseph Bucklin Bishop, *Theodore Roosevelt and His Times* (New York, 1920), I, p. 418; Sir Cecil Spring-Rice, *Letters and Friendships* (Boston, 1929), II, p. 9.

30. Korostovetz, p. 31; Witte 1, p. 166; Count Sergius Witte, "My Meetings with Roosevelt and Morgan," *World's Work*, 41 (April 1921), p. 587.

31. Witte 1, p. 155.

32. Howe, pp. 197–202.

33. *Sbornik diplomatichesky dokumentov* (St. Petersburg, 1906), No. 180; Korostovetz, p. 105.

34. Nikolai II, *Dnevnik*, p. 214.

35. Dillon, p. 311.

36. Witte 2, p. 440; Raymond A. Esthus, *Double Eagle and Rising Sun: The Russians and Japanese at Portsmouth in 1905* (Durham, N.C., 1988), p. 183.

37. Nikolai II, *Dnevnik*, p. 215.

38. Witte 2, p. 441; Witte 1, p. 165.

39. Witte 2, p. 448.

40. *Ibid.*, p. 450.

41. *Ibid.*, pp. 460–61.

42. Bing, p. 175.

43. Witte 2, pp. 447, 704; John Lewis Gaddis, *Russia, the Soviet Union, and the United States* (2nd ed., New York, 1990), pp. 44–46.

CHAPTER 6

1. Gurko, p. 294.

2. Kokovtsov, p. 31.

3. Ye. A. Svyatopolk-Mirskaya, "Dnevnik," *Istoricheskie zapiski*, 77 (1965), p. 240.

4. Gurko, pp. 299–300.

5. Shipov, p. 265.

6. Oldenburg, II, p. 99.

7. Svyatopolk-Mirskaya, "Dnevnik," pp. 257–59.

8. Text in GARF, f. 601, op. 1, d. 872.

9. Gurko, pp. 302–3.

10. Svyatopolk-Mirskaya, "Dnevnik," p. 261.

11. Gurko, p. 304.

12. Witte 2, p. 399.

13. Text in Sidney Harcave, *The Russian Revolution of 1905* (London, 1970), pp. 282–85.

14. Witte 2, p. 400; Gurko, pp. 339–42.

15. See Jeremiah Schneiderman, *Sergei Zubatov and Revolutionary Marxism* (Ithaca, N.Y., 1976), and Dimitry Pospielovsky, *Russian Police Trade Unionism* (London, 1971).

16. See Walter Sablinsky, *The Road to Bloody Sunday: Father Gapon and the St. Petersburg Massacre of 1905* (Princeton, N.J., 1976).

17. Dillon, p. 157.

18. Father George Gapon, *The Story of My Life* (New York, 1906), p. 125.

19. Sablinsky, p. 168.

20. A. V. Bogdanovich, *Tri poslednikh samoderzhtsa* (Moscow, 1924), p. 331; Gapon, pp. 165–67.

21. Text in Sablinsky, pp. 344–49, and in Gapon, pp. 257–61.

22. Nikolai II, *Dnevnik*, p. 194.

23. Gapon, pp. 159–60.

24. *Ibid.*, p. 211.

25. Nikolai II, *Dnevnik*, p. 194.

26. Kokovtsov, p. 39.

27. Original text in KA, 20 (1927), pp. 241–42; Solomon M. Schwarz, *The Russian Revolution of 1905* (Chicago, 1967), p. 81.

28. Abraham Ascher, *The Revolution of 1905* (Stanford, Calif., 1988–92), I, p. 102.

29. Svyatopolk-Mirskaya, "Dnevnik," p. 266.

30. Witte 2, p. 405.

31. Gurko, pp. 355–56; Witte 2, pp. 405–6.

32. Grand Duke Alexander, p. 139.

33. E. M. Almedingen, *An Unbroken Unity: A Memoir of Grand-Duchess Serge of Russia 1864–1918* (London, 1964), p. 52; Savinkov, pp. 106–8.

34. Prince Felix Youssoupoff, *Lost Splendour* (London, 1953), p. 122.

35. *Pravitelstvenny vestnik*, February 18, 1905.

36. *Ibid.*, June 8, 1905; Martha Bohachevsky-Chomiak, *Sergei N. Trubetskoi* (Belmont, Mass., 1976), pp. 154–55.

37. Ascher, I, p. 119.

38. See Robert D. Warth, "*Potemkin* Mutiny of 1905," MERSH, 29 (1982), pp. 128–33; Nikolai II, *Dnevnik*, pp. 204–5.

39. See *Petergofskoe soveshchanie o proekte gosudarstvennoi dumy pod lychnym yego Imperatorskogo Velichestva predsedatelstvom: sekretnie protokoly* (Berlin, n.d.).

40. Gurko, pp. 394–95; Witte 1, p. 327.

41. Text in KA, 11–12 (1925), pp. 51–61.

42. Witte 2, p. 480.

43. Vitte, *Vospominania*, III, p. 12.

44. Mossolov, p. 90; Vitte, *Vospominania*, III, p. 41.

45. Bing, p. 184.

46. See Robert D. Warth, "October Manifesto," MERSH, 25 (1981), pp. 178–79.

47. Nikolai II, *Dnevnik*, p. 222.

48. Bing, p. 185.

49. Letter of D. M. Wallace (January 3, 1908) reporting his interview with Nicholas II on December 24, 1907, Wallace Papers, *Times* (London) Archives.

50. Witte 2, p. 492.

51. Bing, p. 188.

52. Editorial comment in Witte 2, p. 802, n. 4.

53. Leon Trotsky, *1905* (New York, 1971), p. 124.

54. Bing, p. 193.

55. *Ibid.*, p. 192.

56. *Ibid.*, pp. 187–88.

57. Jacob Frumkin *et al.* (eds.), *Russian Jewry (1860–1917)* (New York, 1966), p. 43. Witte 1, pp. 331–33.

58. See Robert D. Warth, "The Union of the Russian People," MERSH, 41 (1986), pp. 31–34.

59. Walter Laqueur, *Black Hundred: The Rise of the Extreme Right in Russia* (New York, 1993), p. 23.

60. Oldenburg, II, p. 178; Sovremennik, *Nikolai II razoblachenia* (Berlin, 1914), p. 309.

61. Alexander B. Tager, *The Decay of Czarism* (Philadelphia, 1935), pp. 11–12.

62. Bing, pp. 194–95.

63. Gurko, pp. 443–44.

64. Bing, pp. 198–99.

65. *Ibid.*, pp. 203–4.

66. *Ibid.*, p. 205.

67. *Ibid.*, pp. 206, 210; O. O. Gruzenberg, *Yesterday: Memoirs of a Jewish Lawyer* (Berkeley, Calif., 1981), p. 98.

68. V. P. Semennikov (ed.), *Revolyutsia 1905 goda i samoderzhavie* (Moscow, 1928), p. 23.

69. KA, 11–12 (1925), p. 439.

70. Bing, p. 211.

71. *Pravitelstvenny vestnik*, December 2, 1905.

CHAPTER 7

1. Bing, p. 211.

2. Witte 1, p. 329; Witte 2, p. 518.

3. Witte 1, p. 318.

4. Gurko, pp. 403–6; Witte 2, pp. 507–9.

5. Bing, p. 211.

6. Paul Miliukov, *Political Memoirs, 1905–1917* (Ann Arbor, Mich., 1967), p. 65.

7. For the council protocol see *Byloe*, 3 (September 1917), pp. 235–65.

8. Bing, p. 199.

9. S. M. Sidelnikov, *Obrazovanie i deyatelnost pervoi gosudarstvennoi dumy* (Moscow, 1962), pp. 76–77.

10. Nikolai S. Tagantsev, *Perezhitoe: uchrezdenie gosudarstvennoe dumy v 1905–1906 gg.* (Petrograd, 1919), p. 144; Gurko, p. 23.

11. For the council protocol see *Byloe*, 5–6 (November–December 1917), pp. 289–318.

12. *Ibid.*, 4 (October 1917), pp. 188–245.

13. *Ibid.*, pp. 204–9.

14. Ascher, II, p. 55. See James William Long, "Russian Manipulation of the French Press, 1904–1906," *Slavic Review*, 31 (June 1972), pp. 343–54.

15. Witte 2, pp. 562, 571.

16. KA, 10 (1925), pp. 3–35; Witte 2, pp. 565, 570–72; Kokovtsov, Chapter 10.

17. Witte 2, pp. 598–601; Gurko, pp. 455–57.

18. Witte 2, pp. 601–2.

19. Bing, pp. 219–20; Witte 2, pp. 602–3, 624–27.

20. Gurko, p. 458; Nicholas II, *Letters*, p. 29; Maurice Paleologue, *An Ambassador's Memoirs* (London, 1923–25), I, p. 303.

21. Countess Witte, Preface to Witte 1, pp. ix–x.

22. Général Guerassimov, *Tsarisme et terrorisme* (Paris, 1934), p. 116.

23. Kokovtsov, p. 127.

24. See Robert D. Warth, "Stolypin, Petr Arkad'evich," MERSH, 37 (1984), pp. 152–56.

25. KA, 22 (1927), p. 204.

26. Witte 2, p. 649.

27. Iswolsky, pp. 91–92; S. E. Kryzhanovsky, *Vospominania* (Berlin, n.d.), p. 91; Schelking, p. 169.

28. Witte 1, p. 361.

29. Gurko, p. 470; Howe, pp. 278–81.

30. Iswolsky, pp. 85–86.

31. Mossolov, p. 139.

32. V. P. Obninsky, *Polgoda russkoi revolyutsii* (Moscow, 1906), p. 69.

33. GD, April 27, 1906, p. 3.

34. Gurko, pp. 471–72.

35. Kokovtsov, pp. 139–40.

36. GD, May 13, 1906, pp. 321–24.

37. Iswolsky, p. 170.

38. GD, May 13, 1906, pp. 324–26; Miliukov, p. 106; V. A. Maklakov, *The First State Duma* (Bloomington, Ind., 1964), p. 98; Kokovtsov, pp. 140–41.

39. GD, May 16, 1906, pp. 389–91; Maklakov, pp. 167–171.

40. GD, June 8, 1906, pp. 1125–32.

41. Maklakov, pp. 176–77; GD, June 19, 1906, pp. 1469–84.

42. Maklakov, p. 193; Iswolsky, pp. 212–13.

43. Miliukov, pp. 108–110; Robert L. Tuck, "Paul Miljukov and Negotiations for a Duma Ministry, 1906," *American Slavic and East European Review*, 10 (April 1951), pp. 120–21.

44. Kokovtsov, pp. 146–48.

45. Iswolsky, pp. 180–87.

46. *Ibid.*, pp. 187–91.

47. Miliukov, pp. 114–15; Sir Bernard Pares, *The Fall of the Russian Monarchy* (New York, 1939), p. 97.

48. Shipov, pp. 446–60 (English translation in Gurko, pp. 710–15).

49. Kokovtsov, p. 149.

50. *Pravitelstvenny vestnik*, June 20, 1906.

51. Kokovtsov, p. 153; Gurko, p. 485.

52. Gurko, p. 486; Kokovtsov, pp. 155–56; Witte 2, p. 653; P. N. Milyukov, *Vospominania* (New York, 1955), I, p. 402.

53. Bing, p. 212.

54. Iswolsky, pp. 204–6.

CHAPTER 8

1. Witte 2, p. 826, n. 4.
2. Shipov, pp. 461–71.
3. KA, 5 (1924), p. 102.
4. Bing, p. 212.
5. Gurko, pp. 498–99.
6. Nikolajewsky, p. 189.
7. KA, 5 (1924), pp. 103–4.
8. Gurko, p. 499.
9. KA, 11–12 (1925), p. 442.
10. Bing, pp. 216–19.
11. Pierre Polejaïeff, *Six années, la Russie de 1906 à 1912* (Paris, 1912), pp. 49–50.
12. Alfred Levin, *The Second Duma* (2nd ed.; Hamden, Conn., 1966), p. 262.
13. W. E. Mosse, "Stolypin's Villages," SEER, 43 (June 1965), p. 259.
14. V. I. Lenin, *Polnoe sobranie sochineny* (5th ed.; Moscow, 1958–65), XVI, pp. 424–25.
15. KA, 5 (1924), p. 105; Kokovtsov, pp. 166–68; Tager, pp. 14–15.
16. Ascher, II, p. 256, quoting German Foreign Office archives in Bonn.
17. Bing, pp. 222–23; KA, 5 (1924), p. 108.
18. GD, March 6, 1907, pp. 167–70.
19. KA, 5 (1924), pp. 108–10.
20. Bing, p. 228.
21. Kokovtsov, p. 181.
22. Bing, p. 228; Nikolajewsky, pp. 217–23; General Alexandre Spiridovitch, *Les Dernières années de la cour de Tzarskoïe-Selo* (Paris, 1928–29), I, Chapter 7.
23. KA, 19 (1926), pp. 122–24; testimony of Golovin, *Padenie*, V, pp. 365–69.
24. KA, 5 (1924), p. 113.
25. GARF, f. 601, op. 1, d. 1125.
26. *Russkaya znamya*, June 4, 1907.
27. Witte 2, p. 520; Vitte, *Vospominania*, II, p. 273.
28. Kryzhanovsky, pp. 112–13; Alfred Levin, "June 3, 1907: Action and Reaction," in Alan D. Ferguson and Levin (eds.), *Essays in Russian History* (Hamden, Conn., 1964), p. 251.
29. KA, 5 (1924), p. 115.
30. *Ibid.*, p. 118.
31. GD, May 27, 1908, pp. 1578–1599.
32. Quoted in Ben-Cion Pinchuk, *The Octobrists in the Third Duma 1907–1912* (Seattle, 1974), p. 69.
33. KA, 50–51 (1932), p. 188.
34. A. A. Polivanov, *Iz dnevnikov i vospominany po dolzhnosti voennogo ministra i yego pomoshchnika 1907–1916 g.* (Moscow, 1924), pp. 67, 69.
35. Kokovtsov, p. 178.
36. KA, 5 (1924), p. 120; Kokovtsov, pp. 222–23.
37. Kokovtsov, p. 224.
38. GD, November 16, 1907, p. 352.

39. Mary Schaeffer Conroy, *Peter Arkad'evich Stolypin* (Boulder, Colo., 1976), p. 125. For a broader discussion see Peter Waldron, "Stolypin and Finland," SEER, 63 (January 1985), pp. 41–55.

40. Alexander Zenkovsky, *Stolypin: Russia's Last Great Reformer* (Princeton, N.J., 1986), p. 81.

41. Maria Petrovna von Bock, *Reminiscences of My Father, Peter A. Stolypin* (Metuchen, N.J., 1970), pp. 263–64.

42. GARF, f. 601, op. 1, d. 1125 (March 9, 1911).

43. GD, April 27, 1911, pp. 2850–63, 3025.

44. V. N. Kokovtsov, *Iz moyego proshlago* (Paris, 1933), I, p. 458.

45. KA, 30 (1928), p. 86.

46. Zenkovsky, p. ix, with details in Chapters 3, 4, and 5. See also Conroy, pp. 73–75.

47. Bing, pp. 264–65.

48. Gurko, p. 515.

49. Bock, p. 280.

50. Kokovtsov, p. 341.

51. See A. Serebrennikov (comp.), *Ubiistvo Stolypin: Svidetelstva i dokumenty* (New York, 1986); George Tokmakoff, "Stolypin's Assassin," *Slavic Review*, 24 (June 1965), pp. 314–21; and Anna Geifman, *Thou Shalt Kill: Revolutionary Terrorism in Russia, 1894–1917* (Princeton, N.J., 1993). Soviet works include L. Bazylev, "Zagadka i sentyabrya 1911 goda," *Voprosy istorii*, 7 (July 1975), pp. 115–29, and A. Ya. Avrekh, *Stolypin i tretya duma* (Moscow, 1968), Chapter 8.

CHAPTER 9

1. Mikhail Iroshnikov et al., *The Sunset of the Romanov Dynasty* (Moscow, 1992), p. 148.

2. Witte 2, pp. 296–97.

3. Grand Duke Alexander, p. 186. Much of the remaining text and documentation for this chapter is drawn from Robert D. Warth, "Before Rasputin: Piety and the Occult at the Court of Nicholas II," *The Historian*, 48 (May 1985), pp. 323–37.

4. See Robert D. Warth, "Serafim of Sarov," MERSH, 34 (1983), pp. 23–24. See also Paleologue, I, pp. 207–9, and Robert L. Nichols, "The Friends of God: Nicholas II and Alexandra and the Canonization of Serafim of Sarov, July 1903," in Charles E. Timberlake (ed.), *Religious and Secular Forces in Late Tsarist Russia* (Seattle, 1992).

5. Witte 2, pp. 360–61.

6. Kerensky, *Crucifixion of Liberty*, p. 176.

7. Sergei Michailovich Trufanoff (Iliodor), *The Mad Monk of Russia, Iliodor* (New York, 1918), pp. 174–75.

8. Alexander Ular, *Russia from Within* (London, 1905), pp. 43–44. See also Witte 2, pp. 65–67.

9. René Fülöp-Miller, *Rasputin: The Holy Devil* (New York, 1928), pp. 120, 123–24.

10. Ferdinand Ossendowski, *The Shadow of the Gloomy East* (New York, 1925), pp. 80–81; Witte 2, p. 361.

11. Paleologue, I, p. 346; Fülöp-Miller, pp. 300–2; Trufanoff, pp. 167–77.

12. See Robert D. Warth, "Philippe, Nizier Anthelme," MERSH, 51 (1989), pp. 178–79.

13. Paleologue, I, p. 206.

14. Witte 2, pp. 359–60.

15. See Robert D. Warth, "Papus (Gérard Encausse)," MERSH, 26 (1982), pp. 241–42.

16. Paleologue, III, p. 174.

17. Henri Rollin, *L'Apocalypse de notre temps* (Paris, 1939), pp. 355–56.

18. James Webb, *The Occult Establishment* (Lasalle, Ill., 1976), pp. 253–56.

19. Paleologue, I, pp. 143–44.

20. For a brief biography see Robert D. Warth, "Rasputin, Gregory Efimovich," in George Jackson and Robert Devlin (eds.), *Dictionary of the Russian Revolution* (New York, 1989), pp. 474–77. For full-scale biographies see, among more recent works, Joseph T. Fuhrmann, *Rasputin: A Life* (New York, 1990), and Alex De Jonge, *The Life and Times of Grigorii Rasputin* (New York, 1982).

21. Grand Duke Alexander, pp. 183–84.

22. Igor Vinogradoff, "The Emperor Nicholas II, Stolypin, and Rasputin: A Letter of 16 October 1906," *Oxford Slavonic Papers*, 12 (1965), pp. 112–16.

23. M. V. Rodzianko, *The Reign of Rasputin* (Gulf Breeze, Fla., 1973), p. 24.

24. V. I. Gurko, *Tsar i tsaritsa* (Paris, 1927?), p. 90.

CHAPTER 10

1. Kokovtsov, p. 277.

2. See especially A. S. Tager, *The Decay of Czarism: The Beilis Trial* (Philadelphia, 1935); Maurice Samuel, *Blood Accusation: The Strange History of the Beilis Case* (New York, 1966); Hans Rogger, *Jewish Policies and Right-Wing Politics in Imperial Russia* (Berkeley, Calif., 1986), Chapter 3; and Robert S. Lindemann, *The Jew Accused* (Cambridge, Eng., 1991), Chapter 7.

3. V. L. Burtsev, *"Protokoly sionskikh mudretsov": dokazannia podlog* (Paris, 1938), pp. 105–6.

4. Spiridovitch, II, p. 447.

5. Gurko, p. 518.

6. Paleologue, I, p. 298.

7. Kokovtsov, pp. 282–83.

8. *Ibid.*, pp. 290–95.

9. *Ibid.*, pp. 295–98.

10. *Ibid.*, pp. 299–300, 326.

11. Rodzianko, pp. 40–47.

12. *Ibid.*, p. 59; Kokovtsov, p. 303; GD, March 9, 1912, p. 73.

13. Kokovtsov, pp. 307–8, 311. See also Kerensky, *Russia*, pp. 81–83; Richard Abraham, *Alexander Kerensky* (New York, 1987), pp. 54–56; and Michael Melancon, "The Ninth Circle: The Lena Goldfield Massacre of 4 April 1912," *Slavic Review*, 53 (Fall 1994), pp. 766–95.

14. Kokovtsov, p. 311.

15. Pares, p. 194.

16. Kokovtsov, p. 340.

17. Rodzianko, pp. 63–66; Kokovtsov, pp. 317–19.

18. Gurko, p. 522.

19. Oldenburg, III, p. 116.

20. Rodzianko, pp. 67–71.

21. Kokovtsov, pp. 326–27; Gurko, p. 521.

22. Anna Viroubova, *Memories of the Russian Court* (New York, 1923), pp. 90–94; Paleologue, I, p. 148.

23. Rodzianko, p. 11. For the Spala episode see also Bing, pp. 275–78; Mossolov, pp. 150–52; Spiridovitch, II, pp. 284–85, 288–90; and Pierre Gilliard, *Thirteen Years at the Russian Court* (New York, 1970), pp. 28–32. Massie, pp. 182–89, and Fuhrmann, pp. 94–98, provide detailed secondary accounts.

24. V. I. Mamantov, *Na gosudarevoi sluzhbe* (Tallin, 1926), p. 233.

25. Rodzianko, pp. 47, 75–77.

26. See Richard S. Wortman, " 'Invisible Threads': The Historical Legacy of the Romanov Tercentenary," *Russian History*, 16 (1989), pp. 389–406.

27. Kokovtsov, pp. 349–50.

28. *Ibid.*, pp. 350–52.

29. GD, May 27, 1913, pp. 65–66; Kokovtsov, pp. 339, 365–66; testimony of Volkonsky, *Padenie*, VI, pp. 133–34.

30. Kokovtsov, p. 379.

31. *Ibid.*, pp. 379–80.

32. V. P. Semennikov (ed.), *Monarkhia pered krusheniem* (Moscow, 1927), p. 92; testimony of Maklakov, *Padenie*, V, pp. 193–95.

33. For the background see Margaret Miller, *The Economic Development of Russia, 1905–1914* (London, 1967), pp. 245–49, and Boris M. Segal, *Russian Drinking: Use and Abuse of Alcohol in Pre-Revolutionary Russia* (New Brunswick, N.J., 1987).

34. Kokovtsov, pp. 407–10; Gurko, pp. 529–31.

35. Kokovtsov, pp. 411–12, 444.

36. Text, *ibid.*, pp. 418–19.

37. *Ibid.*, pp. 438–39; Gurko, p. 531.

38. Oldenburg, III, pp. 137–38.

39. Rodzianko, p. 102.

40. *Ibid.*, pp. 96–97.

41. Testimony of Shcheglovitov and Maklakov, *Padenie*, II, pp. 436–38, and III, pp. 133–34.

CHAPTER 11

1. Lee, II, pp. 283–89.

2. BD, IV, No. 208.

3. Harold Nicolson, *Sir Arthur Nicolson* (London, 1930), pp. 216–17.

4. G. P. Gooch, *Before the War: Studies in Diplomacy* (London, 1936–38), I, p. 292.

5. Nicolson, p. 239.

6. *Ibid.*, p. 222.

7. *Ibid.*, p. 243.

8. BD, IV, Nos. 483–84.

9. See Firuz Kazemzadeh, *Russia and Britain in Persia, 1864–1914* (New Haven, Conn., 1968).

10. BD, IV, No. 451.

11. Lee, I, p. 593.

12. The definitive text (in French): BD, IV, Appendix I (pp. 618–20). For a convenient summary in English see Nicolson, Appendix III, pp. 447–50.

13. For the text see Ernest Batson Price, *The Russo-Japanese Treaties of 1907–1916 Concerning Manchuria and Mongolia* (Baltimore, 1933), pp. 101–123. For the negotiations see Masato Matsui, "The Russo-Japanese Agreement of 1907," *Modern Asian Studies*, 6 (January, 1972), pp. 33–48.

14. Morison, *Letters*, V, p. 31.

15. Calvin De Armond Davis, *The United States and the Second Hague Peace Conference* (Durham, N.C., 1975), pp. 157–58, 217.

16. Nicolson, p. 261.

17. Lee, II, p. 565.

18. *Ibid.*, pp. 587, 590–94.

19. Bing, pp. 234–35; BD, V, No. 425.

20. GP, XXVI, Pt. 1, No. 8992.

21. Kokovtsov, p. 217.

22. *Österreich-Ungarns Aussenpolitik von der bosnischen Krise 1908 bis zum Kriegsausbruch 1914* (Vienna, 1930), I, No. 822.

23. GP, XXVI, Pt. 2, Nos. 9187–88.

24. *Ibid.*, No. 9465.

25. Bing, pp. 239–40.

26. Nicolson, p. 316; Lee, II, pp. 691–92.

27. Text in *Un livre noir* (Paris, 1928), I, pp. 357–58. For the background see Luigi Albertini, *The Origins of the War of 1914* (London, 1952–57), I, pp. 306–11.

28. See Robert D. Warth, "Sazonov, Sergei Dmitrievich," MERSH, 33 (1983), pp. 118–22.

29. Baron M. de Taube, *La Politique russe d'avant-guerre et la fin de l'empire des tsars* (Paris, 1928), pp. 248–49.

30. BD, IX, Pt. 2, No. 10.

31. Oldenburg, III, p. 68.

32. GP, XXVII, Pt. 2, Nos. 10155–59; *Un livre noir*, II, pp. 331–34.

33. Taube, p. 209.

34. See Edward C. Thaden, "Charykov and Russian Foreign Policy at Constantinople in 1911," *Journal of Central European Affairs*, 16 (April 1956), pp. 25–44.

35. A. Nekludoff, *Diplomatic Reminiscences* (New York, 1920), pp. 4–5.

36. *Ibid.*, p. 45.

37. *Documents diplomatiques francais*, Series 3, III, No. 151.

38. Serge Sazonov, *Fateful Years 1906–1916* (London, 1928), p. 71.

39. Bing, pp. 278–79.

40. Kokovtsov, pp. 344–48.

41. Rodzianko, p. 86.

42. Sazonov, p. 79.

43. *Ibid.*, p. 94.

44. Bing, p. 286.

45. Quoted in Michael Balfour, *The Kaiser and His Times* (New York, 1972), p. 339.

46. E. A. Adamov (ed.), *Konstantinopol i prolivy* (Moscow, 1925–26), I, p. 63.

47. Sazonov, p. 135.

48. H. S. W. Corrigan, "German-Turkish Relations and the Outbreak of War in 1914: A Reassessment," *Past and Present*, 36 (April 1967), p. 152.

49. *Mezhdunarodnie otnoshenia v epokhu imperializma* (Moscow, 1933), Third Series, III, No. 339.

50. Paleologue, I, 17.

51. *Ibid.*, p. 28.

52. [Baron M. F. Schilling], *How the War Began in 1914: Being the Diary of the Russian Foreign Office . . .* (London, 1925), pp. 28–29.

53. *Ibid.*, p. 44; Albertini, II, p. 355, n. 3; Sazonov, p. 178.

54. Immanuel Geiss (ed.), *July 1914* (London, 1967), pp. 64–65.

55. Schilling, pp. 45–47.

56. *Ibid.*, pp. 54–55.

57. Sazonov, pp. 204–5.

58. Schilling, pp. 72–74.

59. *Ibid.*, pp. 81–82; Geiss, p. 347.

60. Paleologue, I, p. 136.

CHAPTER 12

1. Alexandra, *Letters*, p. 9.

2. Paleologue, I, p. 56.

3. *Ibid.*, pp. 61–62.

4. Miliukov, p. 306.

5. Paleologue, I, p. 93.

6. Sir George Buchanan, *My Mission to Russia . . .* (London, 1923), I, p. 215.

7. Paleologue, I, p. 136.

8. Nicholas II, *Letters*, pp. 14, 18.

9. Miliukov, p. 307.

10. Testimony of Guchkov, *Padenie*, VI, pp. 256–58.

11. Paleologue, I, pp. 253–55.

12. *Ibid.*, p. 214.

13. Michael Cherniavsky (ed.), *Prologue to Revolution: Notes of A. N. Iakhontov on the Secret Meetings of the Council of Ministers, 1915* (Englewood Cliffs, N.J., 1967), p. 46. See also Paleologue, II, p. 41, and Daniel W. Graf, "Military Rule behind the Russian Front, 1914–1917," *Jahrbücher für Geschichte Ost europas*, 22 (1974), pp. 398–402.

14. Nicholas II, *Letters*, p. 73.

15. *Ibid.*, pp. 54–55.

16. Rodzianko, p. 134.

17. Lieutenant-General Nicholas N. Golovine, *The Russian Army in the World War* (New Haven, Conn., 1931), p. 155.

18. Rodzianko, p. 140.

19. *Ibid.*, pp. 137–39.

20. *Ibid.*, pp. 140–41; Paleologue, II, pp. 13–14.

21. Nicholas II, *Letters*, p. 66.

22. Sazonov, p. 290.

23. *Ibid.*, p. 284; Paleologue, II, p. 42.

24. General A. A. Brussilov, *A Soldier's Notebook, 1914–1918* (London, 1930), pp. 130, 133.

25. Paleologue, II, p. 19.

26. Gurko, pp. 556, 562.

27. Gilliard, p. 137.

28. Nicholas II, *Letters*, p. 241.

29. Cherniavsky, pp. 45, 76–77.

30. *Ibid.*, pp. 79, 82–83.

31. Rodzianko, p. 150.

32. Paleologue, II, p. 59.

33. Cherniavsky, pp. 106–7; Paleologue, II, pp. 70–71.

34. Cherniavsky, pp. 109, 162, 165.

35. Text in Sazonov, p. 294; Cherniavsky, p. 166.

36. Norman Stone, *The Eastern Front, 1914–1917* (New York, 1975), p. 192; Brussilov, pp. 29–30, 171.

37. Gilliard, p. 139.

38. Nicholas II, *Letters*, pp. 70–71.

39. Cherniavsky, pp. 176–78.

40. Alexandra, *Letters*, p. 127.

41. Cherniavsky, pp. 219, 226.

42. *Ibid.*, pp. 227, 235.

43. Rodzianko, pp. 154–55.

44. Cherniavsky, p. 236.

45. Mikh. Lemke, *250 dnei v tsarskoi stavke* (St. Petersburg, 1920), p. 631.

46. Nicholas II, *Letters*, p. 85.

47. Alexandra, *Letters*, pp. 150, 152, 166.

48. Nicholas II, *Letters*, p. 90.

49. Quoted in Ye. D. Chermensky, *IV gosudarstvennaya duma i sverzhenie tsarizma v Rossii* (Moscow, 1976), p. 131.

50. Gurko, pp. 579–81.

51. Rodzianko, p. 158.

52. Alexandra, *Letters*, pp. 128, 146, 150–51, 153–54, 159; Rodzianko, pp. 157–58; Paleologue, II, pp. 146–48; John Shelton Curtiss, *Church and State in Russia* (New York, 1940), pp. 389–92.

53. Paleologue, II, p. 101.

54. *Ibid.*, p. 91.

55. *Ibid.*, p. 90; Gilliard, pp. 148–50; General Basil Gourko, *War and Revolution in Russia, 1914–1917* (New York, 1919), pp. 186–88; A. Bubnov, *V tsarskoi stavka* (New York, 1955), pp. 179–84.

56. Major-General Sir Alfred Knox, *With the Russian Army, 1914–1917* (London, 1921), I, p. 352.

57. Paleologue, I, p. 343.

58. Buchanan, I, p. 245.

59. Paleologue, II, pp. 135–37, 138–40; Buchanan, I, pp. 251–52; Rodzianko, pp. 168–70; Frank Alfred Golder (ed.), *Documents of Russian History, 1914–1917* (New York, 1927), pp. 40–50; Robert D. Warth, *The Allies and the Russian Revolution* (Durham, N.C., 1954), pp. 12–13.

60. Paleologue, I, pp. 192–95, 297.

61. *Ibid.*, II, pp. 95–96, 105.

62. Gilliard, p. 151.

63. *Ibid.*, pp. 155–57; Paleologue, II, pp. 134–35.

64. Rodzianko, pp. 164, 166.

65. *Ibid.*, pp. 166–68.

66. Nicholas II, *Letters*, pp. 128, 133.

67. Paleologue, II, p. 166.

68. Miliukov, *Memoirs*, p. 334.

69. Rodzianko, pp. 174–77; testimony of Rodzyanko, *Padenie*, VII, pp. 129–30; Miliukov, *Memoirs*, p. 336; Paleologue, II, pp. 186–89.

70. Rodzianko, pp. 181–82.

CHAPTER 13

1. Fuhrmann, p. 109 (the translation has been slightly altered); Kerensky, *Russia*, pp. 164–65.

2. Alexandra, *Letters*, pp. 390, 409; Nicholas II, *Letters*, pp. 256, 269.

3. Nicholas II, *Letters*, p. 152.

4. Rodzianko, pp. 183–84; Knox, II, p. 416; Nicholas II, *Letters*, p. 157; testimony of Polivanov, *Padenie*, VII, pp. 82–87.

5. Rodzianko, pp. 196–98; Nicholas II, *Letters*, p. 219.

6. Semennikov, pp. 255–66.

7. *Ibid.*, pp. 172–97; Sazonov, pp. 304–5, 312–14; Paleologue, II, pp. 297–98, 310. On the Polish question see also Alexander Dallin, "The Future of Poland," in Dallin et al., *Russian Diplomacy and Eastern Europe, 1914–1917* (New York, 1963), pp. 1–77; C. Jay Smith, *The Russian Struggle for Power, 1914–1917* (New York, 1956), pp. 397–98, 400–404; and Edward Chmielewski, *The Polish Question in the Russian State Duma* (Knoxville, Tenn., 1970).

8. Paul N. Miliukov, *The Russian Revolution* (Gulf Breeze, Fla., 1978–87), I, p. 17.

9. Nicholas II, *Letters*, pp. 206–7.

10. Testimony of Khvostov, *Padenie*, V, pp. 454–57; Rodzianko, p. 211; Fuhrmann, pp. 125–26; Pares, pp. 347–48; E. H. Wilcox, *Russia's Ruin* (London, 1919), pp. 128–32.

11. Nicholas II, *Letters*, p. 257.

12. V. V. Shulgin, *The Years* (New York, 1984), pp. 270–77; Miliukov, *Memoirs*, pp. 359–60, 367–69.

13. Nicholas II, *Letters*, pp. 266, 274–75; Alexandra, *Letters*, pp. 408, 428.

14. Nicholas II, *Letters*, p. 285; Gilliard, p. 178; Vorres, p. 150.

15. *Lettres des Grand-Ducs à Nicolas II* (Paris, 1926), pp. 257–60; Golder, pp. 244–45.

16. Alexandra, *Letters*, p. 433; Nicholas II, *Letters*, p. 293.

17. Nicholas II, *Letters*, p. 296.

18. Paleologue, III, pp. 48, 96.

19. Gleb Botkin, *The Real Romanovs* (New York, 1931), p. 125.

20. *Ibid.*, pp. 88–89.

21. Golder, pp. 154–66 (incomplete text); Thomas Riha, *A Russian European: Paul Miliukov in Russian Politics* (Notre Dame, Ind., 1969), pp. 264–66; Miliukov, *Russian Revolution*, I, pp. 19–20.

22. Miliukov, *Memoirs*, p. 377.

23. S. P. Melgunov, *Legenda o separatnom mir* (Paris, 1957), Chapter 10, pursues the matter in detail.

24. Alexandra, *Letters*, pp. 433, 436; Nicholas II, *Letters*, pp. 295–96.

25. Nicholas II, *Letters*, pp. 297–98.

26. Alexandra, *Letters*, pp. 441–42.

27. Mossolov, pp. 168–73.

28. Nicholas II, *Letters*, p. 299; Alexandra, *Letters*, p. 442.

29. Golder, pp. 166–75; V. M. Purishkevich, *The Murder of Rasputin* (Ann Arbor, Mich., 1985), pp. 67–72.

30. Paleologue, III, pp. 114–15.

31. Princess Paley, *Memories of Russia* (London, 1924), p. 26.

32. Alexandra, *Letters*, p. 453; Nicholas II, *Letters*, pp. 302–3, 306–7.

33. Nicholas II, *Letters*, pp. 308–10; Alexandra, *Letters*, pp. 454–55, 457; KA, 4 (1923), pp. 174, 184, 187.

34. Alexandra, *Letters*, p. 462; Nicholas II, *Letters*, p. 312; Gilliard, p. 183; Voyeikov, p. 178; Paley, pp. 35–36.

35. Paleologue, III, p. 191.

36. Nicholas II, *Journal intime*, p. 73.

37. Viroubova, p. 183.

38. Paley, pp. 37–38; Marie, Grand Duchess of Russia, *Education of a Princess* (New York, 1931), p. 279.

39. Paleologue, III, p. 121.

40. Grand Duc Nicolas Mikhailovitch, *La fin du tsarisme: Lettres inédites à Frédéric Masson (1914–1918)* (Paris, 1968), pp. 137–38.

41. S. P. Melgunov, *Na putyak k dvortsovomu perevorotu* (Paris, 1931), pp. 97–102, 105–17; A. I. Denikin, *Ocherki russkoi smuty* (Berlin, 1921–26), I, pp. 37–39.

42. Testimony of Guchkov, *Padenie*, VI, pp. 277–79; Tsuyoshi Hasegawa, *The February Revolution: Petrograd, 1917* (Seattle, 1981), p. 189.

43. Testimony of Golitsyn, *Padenie*, II, pp. 250–51.

44. Paleologue, III, pp. 148–52.

45. Buchanan, II, pp. 42–49.

46. Paleologue, III, p. 168.

47. Rodzianko, pp. 251–54.

48. Kokovtsov, pp. 478–80.

49. Princess Cantacuzène, *Revolutionary Days* (Boston, 1919), pp. 92–93, 188–89; David Lloyd George, *War Memoirs* (Boston, 1933–37), V, p. 79. The evidence is assessed in W. Bruce Lincoln, *The Romanovs* (New York, 1981), pp. 712–13.

50. Paleologue, III, pp. 177–85, 187, 192–93, 196; Buchanan, II, pp. 52–54; Smith, pp. 460–66; Warth, *The Allies*, pp. 18–21.

51. R. H. Bruce Lockhart, *British Agent* (Garden City, N.Y., 1933), p. 159.

52. Grand Duke Alexander, pp. 282–84; *Arkhiv russkoi revolyutsii*, 5 (1922), pp. 333–36.

53. Rodzianko, pp. 259–61; testimony of Rodzyanko, *Padenie*, VII, pp. 163–65.

54. Miliukov, *Memoirs*, pp. 383, 386; Hasegawa, p. 201.

55. Mossolov, p. 131.

56. Rodzianko, p. 263.

57. Nicholas II, *Letters*, pp. 312, 314–15; KA, 4 (1923), p. 208.

58. Nicholas II, *Letters*, p. 316.

59. Golder, p. 278.

60. Testimony of Frederiks, *Padenie*, V, p. 38; N. Avdeyev (ed.), *Revolyutsia 1917 goda* (Moscow, 1923–30), I, p. 40.

61. Golder, p. 278.

62. KA, 21 (1927), pp. 15–16.

63. *Ibid.*, pp. 11–12; Hasegawa, pp. 303–4.

64. General Loukomsky, *Memoirs of the Russian Revolution* (London, 1922), p. 53.

65. Nicholas II, *Letters*, p. 317.

66. Loukomsky, p. 55.

67. Quoted in William Henry Chamberlin, *The Russian Revolution* (New York, 1965), I, p. 82.

68. Tsuyoshi Hasegawa, "Rodzianko and the Grand Dukes' Manifesto of 1 March 1917," *Canadian Slavonic Papers*, 18 (June 1976), pp. 154–67.

69. Miliukov, *Memoirs*, p. 396.

70. S. Vilchkovsky, "Prebyvanie Gosudar Imperator v Pskove . . . ," *Russkaya letopis*, 3 (1922), pp. 167–70.

71. *Ibid.*, p. 170; KA, 21 (1927), p. 53.

72. Text in *Russkaya letopis*, 3 (1922), pp. 127–33; KA, 21 (1927), pp. 55–59.

73. KA, 21 (1927), pp. 72–74; Robert Paul Browder and Alexander F. Kerensky (eds.), *The Russian Provisional Government, 1917* (Stanford, Calif., 1961), I, pp. 94–97.

74. KA, 20 (1927), p. 137.

75. General Goury Danilov, "How the Tsar Abdicated," *Living Age* 336 (April 1929), pp. 102–3; Hasegawa, pp. 504–5.

76. Text in Nicolas de Basily, *The Abdication of Emperor Nicholas II of Russia* (Princeton, N.J., 1984), pp. 131–32. See also Withold S. Sworakowski, "The Authorship of the Abdication Document of Nicholas II," *Russian Review*, 30 (July 1971), pp. 277–86.

77. V. V. Shulgin, *Days of the Russian Revolution* (Gulf Breeze, Fla., 1990), p. 186.

78. *Ibid.*, p. 185.

79. KA, 20 (1927), p. 137.

80. Oldenburg, IV, p. 159.

81. George Katkov, *Russia 1917: The February Revolution* (New York, 1967), pp. 344–45.

CHAPTER 14

1. Basily, pp. 142–44.

2. *Ibid.*, pp. 144–48.

3. Grand Duke Alexander, p. 288.

4. Browder and Kerensky, I, pp. 105–6; Basily, pp. 149–50.

5. Alexander Kerensky, "The Road to the Tragedy," in Kerensky and Captain Paul Bulygin, *The Murder of the Romanovs* (New York, 1935), p. 100.

6. KA, 81 (1937), pp. 122–23.

7. Kerensky, "The Road," p. 104.

8. Viroubova, p. 212; Paley, p. 84; Madam Lili Dehn, *The Real Tsaritsa* (Boston, 1922), pp. 188–91; Alexis Volkov, *Souvenirs* (Paris, 1928), p. 95; Kerensky, "The Road," p. 105.

9. N. A. Teffi, *Vospominania* (Paris, 1931), p. 299. See also Fuhrmann, pp. 214–15, and De Jonge, pp. 333–34.

10. P. E. Shchegolev (ed.), *Padenie tsarskogo rezhima* (7 vols.; Moscow, 1924–27).

11. Sergei Mstislavskii, *Five Days Which Transformed Russia* (Bloomington, Ind., 1988), p. 105.

12. Kerensky, "The Road," pp. 109–10. See also P. M. Bykov, *The Last Days of Tsardom* (London, 1934), pp. 33–35, and Count Paul Benckendorff, *Last Days at Tsarskoe Selo* (London, 1927), pp. 49–50.

13. Grand Duchess Marie, p. 308.

14. Kerensky, "The Road," pp. 121–23; Kerensky, *Russia*, pp. 328–29; Benckendorff, pp. 54–62.

15. Kerensky, "The Road," pp. 125–26; Gilliard, p. 223.

16. Harold Nicolson, *King George the Fifth* (London, 1952), pp. 299–302; Kenneth Rose, *King George V* (New York, 1984), pp. 209–18. See also Kerensky, "The Road," pp. 116–17; Buchanan, II, pp. 102–6; Meriel Buchanan, *The Dissolution of an Empire* (London, 1932), pp. 192–99; Lloyd George, III, pp. 508–16. Milyukov's articles on the subject are listed in Riha, p. 294, n. 28.

17. Kerensky, "The Road," p. 126; Benckendorff, pp. 77–78; Gilliard, p. 224; Bernard Pares, Introduction to Bulygin and Kerensky, *The Murder*, p. 15.

18. Kerensky, *Russia*, p. 333.

19. Browder and Kerensky, I, pp. 184–86.

20. Kerensky, *Russia*, p. 331.

21. Gilliard, p. 229.

22. Kerensky, "The Road," pp. 117–18.

23. N. Sokolov, *Ubiistvo tsarskoi semi* (Berlin, 1925), p. 269.

24. KA, 21 (1927), p. 91.

25. Kerensky, "The Road," pp. 118–21, 128.

26. *Ibid.*, pp. 128–30; Captain Paul Bulygin, "The Sorrowful Quest," in Bulygin and Kerensky, pp. 189–90; Benckendorff, pp. 104–12; Gilliard, pp. 234–35; George Gustav Telberg and Robert Wilton, *The Last Days of the Romanovs* (New York, 1920), pp. 82–84 (Kobylinsky deposition).

27. V. S. Pankratov, "S tsarem v Tobolske," *Byloe*, 25 (1924), pp. 195–220; Telberg and Wilton, pp. 92–94 (Kobylinsky).

28. Gilliard, pp. 243–44.

29. *Ibid.*, pp. 244, 246, 251–56; Benckendorff, pp. 129–30; Telberg and Wilton, pp. 101–2 (Kobylinsky); Bykov, p. 57; J. C. Trewin, *Tutor to the Tsarevich* (London, 1975), pp. 93–94.

30. Bulygin, p. 202.

31. Gilliard, p. 257.

32. *Ibid.*, p. 256; Bulygin, pp. 197–201; Bykov, pp. 50–51.

33. For his background see Edvard Radzinsky, *The Last Tsar* (New York, 1992), pp. 256–58.

34. Gilliard, pp. 259–60; Bulygin, pp. 206–8; Trewin, pp. 94–96; Bykov, pp. 65–66; Telberg and Wilton, pp. 26–27 (Gilliard), pp. 113–14 (Kobylinsky).

35. Trewin, p. 98; Bulygin, pp. 209, 222.

36. GARF, f. 640, op. 1, d. 326.

37. *Ibid.*

38. See Robert D. Warth, "Sverdlov, Yakov Mikhailovich," MERSH, 38 (1984), pp. 97–101.

39. Radzinsky, p. 278.

40. Victor Alexandrov, *The End of the Romanovs* (Boston, 1966), pp. 211–12.

41. Bulygin, pp. 222–26.

42. Leon Trotsky, *Trotsky's Diary in Exile* (Cambridge, Mass., 1958), p. 81.

43. Lenin, XXI, p. 17.

44. KA, 27 (1928), p. 126.

45. Gilliard, p. 282.

46. Trewin, pp. 106–7.

47. Bykov, pp. 76, 78; S. Melgunov, *Sudba Imperatora Nikolaya II posle otrechenia* (Paris, 1951), p. 578.

48. KA, 27 (1928) p. 136.

49. Edvard Radzinsky, "Rasstrel v Yekaterinburg," *Ogonyok*, 2 (1990), p. 27; Radzinsky, *Last Tsar*, pp. 320–24.

50. KA, 27 (1928), p. 137.

51. Trotsky, *Diary*, p. 81; *New York Times*, November 21, 1990; Bulygin, pp. 234–40; Melgunov, *Sudba*, pp. 400–407.

52. John F. O'Conor (comp.), *The Sokolov Investigation of the Alleged Murder of the Imperial Family* (New York, 1971), p. 208; Telberg and Wilton, p. 201 (Medvedeff).

53. Sokolov, especially Chapters 23–25; Bulygin, pp. 237–39; Telberg and Wilton, pp. 186–88 (Iakimoff), 199–202 (Medvedeff). See also the so-called Gutek file in Alexandrov, pp. 229–34. Interviews with Yurovsky may be found in Richard Halliburton, *Seven League Boots* (Indianapolis, 1935), Chapters 8, 10, 11, 12. Other sources include Francis McCullagh, *A Prisoner of the Reds* (London, 1922), Chapter 13, and *Russkaya letopis*, 1 (1921), pp. 150–55. Radzinsky, Chapter 15, provides additional information about the massacre.

CHAPTER 15

1. Radzinsky, p. 407.

2. *Ogonyok*, 21 (May 1989), pp. 31–32; Radzinsky, pp. 404–11.

3. *Izvestia*, July 19, 1918, quoted in Chamberlin, II, p. 92; *New York Times*, July 21, 1918.

4. P. M. Bykov, *The Last Days of Tsardom* (London, 1937).

5. Telberg and Wilton, pp. 328–31; Gilliard, p. 294; Botkin, p. 235.

6. M. K. Diterikhs, *Ubiistvo tsarskoi semi i chlenov doma Romanovykh na Ural* (Vladivostok, 1922), I, p. 146.

7. Bulygin, pp. 272–74.

8. Anthony Summers and Tom Mangold, *The File on the Tsar* (New York, 1976), pp. 62–63. See also Richard Pipes' review of this work in the *New York Times Book Review*, December 12, 1976. Selections from the Sokolov papers at Harvard University may be found in Nicholas Ross (ed.), *Gibel tsarskoi semi* (Frankfurt, 1987).

9. Bulygin, p. 272.

10. Nicolas Sokolov, *Enquête judiciaire sur l'assassinat de la famille imperiale russe* (Paris, 1924); N. Sokolov, *Ubiistvo tsarskoi semi* (Berlin, 1925). A new edition was published in Moscow in 1990. An English translation of Chapters 16–25 may be found in John F. O'Conor, *The Sokolov Investigation* (New York, 1971).

11. Botkin, pp. 234–35.

12. Summers and Mangold, p. 197.

13. Most notably Gary Hull, *The Conspirator Who Saved the Romanovs* (Englewood Cliffs, N.J., 1971), Michael Occlesaw, *The Romanov Conspiracies* (London, 1993), and three works by Guy Richards: *Imperial Agent: The Goleniewski-Romanov Case* (New York, 1966), *The Hunt for the Czar* (New York, 1971), and *The Rescue of the Romanovs* (Old Greenwich, Conn., 1975).

14. Botkin, p. 233.

15. See Peter Kurth, *Anastasia: The Riddle of Anna Anderson* (Boston, 1983), and James Blair Lovell, *Anastasia: The Lost Princess* (Washington, D.C., 1991).

16. Radzinsky, p. 436.

17. *New York Times*, September 7, 1994.

18. Boris Yeltsin, *Against the Grain* (New York, 1990), p. 82.

19. *New York Times*, November 21, 1990.

20. John J. Stephan, *The Russian Fascists* (New York, 1978), p. 13. See also Grand Duke Cyril, *My Life in Russia's Service* (London, 1939).

21. Sokolov, *Enquête*, pp. 256–67; Bulygin, pp. 254–56; Telberg and Wilton, Chapter 12; Serge Smirnoff, *Autour de l'assassinat des grands-ducs* (Paris, 1928).

22. Mossolov, p. 16.

23. Leon Trotsky, *The History of the Russian Revolution* (New York, 1936), I, pp. 5–15, and Appendix I (pp. 463–70). See also Louis Gottschalk, "Leon Trotsky and the Natural History of Revolutions," *American Journal of Sociology*, 44 (November 1938), especially pp. 345–47.

Bibliography

ARCHIVES

Gosudarstvenny Arkhiv Rossiskoi Federatsii (GARF), Moscow
    fond 543   Tsarsko-Selsky Dvorets
    fond 555   Guchkov, Aleksandr Ivanovich
    fond 568   Lamzdorf, Vladimir Nikolayevich
    fond 579   Milyukov, Pavel Nikolayevich
    fond 586   Plehve, Vyacheslav Konstantinovich
    fond 601   Nicholas II
    fond 605   Rodzyanko, Mikhail Petrovich
    fond 627   Stürmer, Boris Vladimirovich
    fond 640   Alexandra Fyodorovna
    fond 642   Marie Fyodorovna
    fond 1001   Mosolov, Aleksandr Aleksandrovich
National Archives, Washington, D.C.
    Record Group 59, General Records of the Department of State.
    Diplomatic Despatches, Russia. Microcopy Rolls 46–63
Public Record Office, Foreign Office correspondence, Kew and London
    Balfour, Arthur J.
    Bertie, Sir Francis
    Buchanan, Sir George
    Goschen, Edward
    Grey, Sir Edward
    Hardinge, Sir Charles
    Lansdowne, Lord
    Lascelles, Sir Frank

Nicolson, Sir Arthur
Spring-Rice, Sir Cecil
Cambridge University
    Papers of:
        Hardinge, Sir Charles
        Hoare, Sir Samuel
        Wallace, Sir Donald Mackenzie
Times Archives, London
    Donald Mackenzie Wallace Papers
Bakhmeteff Archive, Columbia University
    D. N. Lyubimov, "Russkaya smuta nachala devyatisotykh godov, 1902–1906"
    S. Yu. Witte Collection
Hoover Institution Archives, Stanford University
    Balk, General Aleksandr. "Poslednie pyat dnei tsarskago Petrograda 23–28 fev-
        ralia 1917 g.: Dnevnik . . ." (1929)
    Haliburton, Richard. "Massacre of the Romanoffs" (n.d.)
    Livingstead, Ivor M. V. Z. "The Downfall of a Dynasty" (n.d.)
    Nicholas II. Miscellaneous Papers
    Smolin, General I. S. "The Alapaevsk Tragedy: The Murder of the Russian
        Grand Dukes by the Bolsheviks" (n.d.)
    Verstraete, Maurice. "Sur les routes de mon passé" (1949)
    Volkonskii, Prince Vladimir Mikhailovich. "Canonization of Saint Seraphim of
        Sarov 1903" (1926)

DOCTORAL DISSERTATIONS

Allshouse, R. H. "Alexander Izvolskii and Russian Foreign Policy, 1910–1914."
    Case Western Reserve University, 1976.
Bohon, John William. "Reactionary Politics in Russia, 1905–1909." University of
    North Carolina, 1967.
Doctorow, Gilbert Steven. "The Introduction of Parliamentary Institutions in Rus-
    sia during the Revolution of 1905–1907." Columbia University, 1975.
Eddy, Eleanor Madeleine. "The Last President of the Duma: A Political Biography
    of M. V. Rodzianko." Kansas State University, 1975.
Feldman, Robert Stuart. "Between War and Revolution: The Russian General Staff,
    February–July 1917." Indiana University, 1967.
Glatfelter, Ralph Edward. "Russia in China: The Russian Reaction to the Boxer
    Rebellion." Indiana University, 1975.
Hamm, Michael F. "The Progressive Bloc of Russia's Fourth Duma." Indiana Uni-
    versity, 1971.
Kilcoyne, Martin. "The Political Influence of Rasputin." University of Washington,
    1961.
Kulikowski, Mark. "Rasputin and the Fall of the Romanovs." State University of
    New York, Binghamton, 1982.
McDonald, David MacLaren. "Autocracy, Bureaucracy, and Change in the For-
    mation of Russia's Foreign Policy, 1895–1914." Columbia University, 1988.
Rawson, Don C. "The Union of the Russian People, 1905–1907." University of
    Washington, 1971.

Santoni, Wayne D. "P. N. Durnovo as Minister of Internal Affairs in the Witte Cabinet." University of Kansas, 1968.

Shecket, Alexandra Deborah. "The Russian Imperial State Council and the Policies of P. A. Stolypin, 1906–1911." Columbia University, 1974.

Snow, George Edward. "Vladimir Nikolaevich Kokovtsov: Case Study of an Imperial Russian Bureaucrat, 1904–1906." Indiana University, 1970.

Thomson, Thomas John. "Boris Stürmer and the Imperial Russian Government, February 2–November 22, 1916." Duke University, 1971.

Wilfong, W. Thomas. "Rebuilding the Russian Army, 1905–14." Indiana University, 1977.

Yong-Shik Shin, Peter. "The Otsu Incident: Japan's Hidden History of the Attempted Assassination of Future Emperor Nicholas II in the Town of Otsu, Japan, May 11, 1891 and Its Implications for Historical Analysis." University of Pennsylvania, 1989.

BOOKS

Abraham, Richard. *Alexander Kerensky*. New York, 1987.

Abrikossow, Dmitrii I. *Revelations of a Russian Diplomat*. Seattle, 1964.

Ackerman, Carl. *Trailing the Bolsheviki*. New York, 1919.

Adamov, E. A. (ed.). *Konstantinopol i prolivy*. 2 vols. Moscow, 1925–26.

Albertini, Luigi. *The Origins of the War of 1914*. 3 vols. London, 1952–57.

Alekseyev, Venyamin. *Gibel Tsarskoe semi*. Yekaterinburg, 1994.

Alekseyeva, I. V. *Agonia serdechnogo soglasia: tsarizm, burzhuazia i ikh soyuzniki po Antante, 1914–1917*. Leningrad, 1990.

Alexander, Grand Duke of Russia. *Once a Grand Duke*. New York, 1932.

Alexandrov, Victor. *The End of the Romanovs*. Boston, 1967.

Alferev, E. E. *Imperator Nikolai II kak chelovek silnoi voli*. Jordanville, N.Y., 1983.

——— (ed.). *Pisma tsarskoi semi iz zatochenia*. Jordanville, N.Y., 1974.

Allshouse, Robert H. (ed.). *Photographs for the Tsar*. New York, 1980.

Almedingen, E. M. *An Unbroken Unity: A Memoir of Grand-Duchess Serge of Russia, 1864–1918*. London, 1964.

Ananich, B. V., et al. Krizis samoderzhavia v Rossii, 1895–1917. Leningrad, 1984.

Anderson, Eugene N. *The First Moroccan Crisis, 1904–1906*. Hamden, Conn., 1966.

Andrew, Christopher. *Théophile Delcassé and the Making of the Entente Cordiale (1898–1905)*. New York, 1968.

Aronson, Gregor, et al. *Russian Jewry* [1860–1967]. 2 vols. New York, 1966–69.

Aronson, Grigory. *Rossia nakanune revolyutsii*. New York, 1962.

Aronson, I. Michael. *Troubled Waters: The Origins of the 1881 Anti-Jewish Pogroms*. Pittsburg, 1990.

Ascher, Abraham. *The Revolution of 1905*. 2 vols. Stanford, Calif., 1988–92.

Atkinson, Dorothy. *The End of the Russian Land Commune, 1905–1930*. Stanford, Calif., 1983.

Avetyan, A. S. *Russko-germanskie diplomaticheskie otnoshenia nakanune pervoi mirovoi voiny, 1910–1914*. Moscow, 1985.

Avrekh, A. Ya. *P. A. Stolypin i sudby reform v Rossii.* Moscow, 1991.
————. *Raspad treteiyunskoi sistemy.* Moscow, 1985.
————. *Stolypin i tretya Duma.* Moscow, 1968.
————. *Tsarizm i treteiyunskaya sistema.* Moscow, 1966.
————. *Tsarizm i IV Duma, 1912–1914 gg.* Moscow, 1981.
————. *Tsarizm nakanune sverzhenia.* Moscow, 1989.
Badayev, A. *The Bolsheviks in the Tsarist Duma.* New York, 1929.
Balfour, Michael. *The Kaiser and His Times.* New York, 1972.
Bariatinsky, Princess Anatole Marie. *My Russian Life.* London, 1923.
Baron, Salo W. *The Russian Jew under Tsars and Soviets.* New York, 1964.
Basily, Nicholas de. *The Abdication of Emperor Nicholas II of Russia.* Princeton, N.J., 1984.
Beale, Howard K. *Theodore Roosevelt and the Rise of America to World Power.* Baltimore, 1956.
Becker, Seymour. *Nobility and Privilege in Late Imperial Russia.* De Kalb, Ill., 1985.
Benckendorff, Count Paul. *Last Days at Tsarskoe Selo.* London, 1927.
Berk, Stephen M. *Year of Crisis, Year of Hope: Russian Jewry and the Pogroms of 1881–1882.* Westport, Conn., 1985.
Bernstein, Herman. *The Truth about "The Protocols of Zion."* New York, 1971.
———— (ed.). *The Willy-Nicky Correspondence.* New York, 1918.
Bertholet, Dr. Ed. *La Réincarnation d'apres l'ensseignement d'un ami de Dieu: Le Maitre Philippe de Lyon.* Lausanne, n.d. [1959?].
Besthorn, R. O. *Alexandre III et Nicolas II.* Copenhagen, 1895.
Bestuzhev, I. V. *Borba v Rossii po voprosam vneshnei politiki, 1906–1910.* Moscow, 1961.
Bing, Edward J. (ed.). *The Secret Letters of the Last Tsar.* New York, 1938.
Bishop, Joseph Bucklin. *Theodore Roosevelt and His Times.* 2 vols. New York, 1920.
Black, Cyril E. (ed.). *The Transformation of Russian Society.* Cambridge, Mass., 1960.
Bloch, Jean de. *The Future of War . . .* New York, 1971.
Bock, Maria Petrovna von. *Reminiscences of My Father, Peter A. Stolypin.* Metuchen, N.J., 1970.
Bogdanovich, Générale A. V. *Journal.* Paris, 1926.
————. *Tri poslednikh samoderzhtsa.* Moscow, 1924.
Bogrov, V. *Dmitry Bogrov i ubiistvo Stolypina.* Berlin, 1931.
Bohachevsky-Chomiak, Martha. *Sergei N. Trubetskoi.* Belmont, Mass., 1976.
Bokhanov, A. N. *Smerki monarkhii.* Moscow, 1993.
Bokhanov, A. N., and D. E. Ismail-Zade (eds.). *Rossiisky imperatorsky dom: dnevniki, pisma, fotografii.* Moscow, 1992.
Bompard, Maurice. *Mon ambassade en Russie (1903–1908).* Paris, 1937.
Bonch-Bruyevich, M. *From Tsarist General to Red Army Commander.* Moscow, 1966.
Bonnell, Victoria E. *Roots of Rebellion: Workers' Politics and Organizations in St. Petersburg and Moscow, 1900–1914.* Berkeley, Calif., 1983.
Botkin, Gleb. *The Real Romanovs.* New York, 1931.

Bridge, F. R. *The Habsburg Monarchy among the Great Powers, 1815–1918.* New York, 1990.

Brinton, Crane. *The Anatomy of Revolution.* New York, 1965.

Browder, Robert Paul, and Alexander F. Kerensky (eds.). *The Russian Provisional Government, 1917.* 3 vols. Stanford, Calif., 1961.

Brussilov, General A. A. *A Soldier's Notebook, 1914–1918.* Westport, Conn., 1976.

Bubnov, A. *V tsarski stavke.* New York, 1955.

Buchanan, Meriel. *Ambassador's Daughter.* London, 1958.

———. *The Dissolution of an Empire.* London, 1932.

Buchanan, Sir George. *My Mission to Russia . . .* 2 vols. London, 1923.

Buckle, George Earle (ed.). *The Letters of Queen Victoria.* Third Series. 3 vols. London, 1930–32.

Bülow, Prince von. *Memoirs.* 4 vols. Boston, 1931–32.

Bulygin, Captain Paul, and Alexander Kerensky. *The Murder of the Romanovs.* New York, 1935.

Buranov, Yu., and V. Khrustalev. *Gibel imperatorskogo doma.* Moscow, 1992.

Burdzhalov, E. N. *Russia's Second Revolution: The February 1917 Uprising in Petrograd.* Bloomington, Ind., 1987.

Burtsev, V. L. *"Protokoly sionskikh mudretsov": dakazanny podlog.* Paris, 1938.

Busch, Briton Cooper. *Hardinge of Penshurst: A Study in the Old Diplomacy.* Hamden, Conn., 1980.

Bushnell, John. *Mutiny and Repression: Russian Soldiers in the Revolution of 1905–1906.* Bloomington, Ind., 1985.

Buxhoeveden, Baroness Sophie. *Before the Storm.* London, 1938.

———. *The Life and Tragedy of Alexandra Feodorovna.* London, 1928.

Bykov, P. M. *The Last Days of Tsardom.* London, 1937.

Byrnes, Robert F. *Pobedonostsev: His Life and Thought.* Bloomington, Ind., 1968.

Cantacuzène, Princess. *Revolutionary Days.* Boston, 1919.

Carlson, Maria. *"No Religion Higher Than Truth": A History of the Theosophical Movement in Russia, 1875–1922.* Princeton, N.J., 1993.

Carrère d'Encausse, Hélène. *Nicolas II, la transition interrompue.* Paris, 1996.

Chakirov, Nikita (introd.). *Palomnichestvo tsarya-muchenika.* New York, 1986.

Chamberlin, William Henry. *The Russian Revolution, 1917–1921.* 2 vols. New York, 1960.

Charques, Richard. *The Twilight of Imperial Russia.* London, 1965.

Chavchavadze, David. *The Grand Dukes.* New York, 1990.

Chen, Tien-fong. *A History of Sino-Russian Relations.* Washington, D.C., 1957.

Chermensky, E. D. *Burzhuazia i tsarizm v pervoi russkoi revolyutsii.* 2nd ed. Moscow, 1970.

———. *IV gosudarstvennaya duma i sverzhenie tsarizma v Rossii.* Moscow, 1976.

Cherniavsky, Michael (ed.). *Prologue to Revolution: Notes of A. N. Iakhontov on the Secret Meetings of the Council of Minsters, 1915.* Englewood Cliffs, N.J., 1967.

Chernov, Victor. *The Great Russian Revolution.* New Haven, Conn., 1936.

Chmielewski, Edward (ed.). *The Fall of the Russian Empire.* New York, 1973.

———. *The Polish Question in the Russian State Duma.* Knoxville, Tenn., 1970.

Churchill, Rogers Platt. *The Anglo-Russian Convention of 1907.* Cedar Rapids, Iowa, 1939.

Churchill, Winston S. *The Unknown War: The Eastern Front.* New York, 1932.

Clarke, William. *The Lost Fortune of the Tsars.* New York, 1995.

Clowes, Edith W., et al. (eds.). *Between Tsar and People: Educated Society and the Quest for Public Identity in Late Imperial Russia.* Princeton, N.J., 1991.

Clubb, O. Edmund. *China and Russia.* New York, 1971.

Cohn, Norman. *Warrant for Genocide: The Myth of the Jewish World-Conspiracy and the Protocols of the Elders of Zion.* New York, 1967.

Connaughton, R. M. *The War of the Rising Sun and the Tumbling Bear.* London, 1988.

Conroy, Hilary. *The Japanese Seizure of Korea, 1868–1910.* Philadelphia, 1960.

Conroy, Mary Schaeffer. *Peter Arkad'evich Stolypin.* Boulder, Colo., 1976.

Cooper, Sandi E. (introd.). *Arbitration or War? Contemporary Reactions to the Hague Peace Conference of 1899.* New York, 1972.

Cowles, Virginia. *The Last Tsar.* New York, 1977.

————. *The Russian Dagger: Cold War in the Days of the Czars.* New York, 1969.

Creighton, Mandell. *Historical Essays and Reviews.* London, 1902.

Crisp, Olga. *Studies in the Russian Economy before 1914.* London, 1976.

Crisp, Olga, and Linda Edmondson (eds.). *Civil Rights in Imperial Russia.* Oxford, 1989.

Cunningham, James W. *A Vanquished Hope: The Movement for Church Renewal in Russia, 1905–1906.* Crestwood, N.Y., 1981.

Curtiss, John Shelton. *Church and State in Russia: The Last Years of the Empire, 1900–1917.* New York, 1940.

————. (ed.). *Essays in Russian and Soviet History.* New York, 1963.

Cyril, Grand Duke. *My Life in Russia's Service.* London, 1939.

Dallin, Alexander, et al. *Russian Diplomacy and Eastern Europe, 1914–1917.* New York, 1963.

Dallin, David J. *The Rise of Russia in Asia.* New Haven, Conn., 1949.

Danilov, Youri. *La Russe dans la guerre mondiale.* Paris, 1927.

Danilov, Yu. N. *Veliky Knyaz Nikolai Nikolayevich.* Paris, 1930.

Davidovich, A. M. *Samoderzhavie v epokhu imperializma.* Moscow, 1975.

Davies, Norman. *God's Playground: A History of Poland.* 2 vols. New York, 1982.

Davis, Calvin De Armond. *The United States and the First Hague Peace Conference.* New York, 1962.

————. *The United States and the Second Hague Peace Conference.* Durham, N.C., 1975.

Davitt, Michael. *Within the Pale: The True Story of Anti-Semitic Persecutions in Russia.* New York, 1903.

Dehn, Madame Lili. *The Real Tsaritsa.* Boston, 1922.

Deich, L. G. (ed.). *Gruppa "Osvobozhdenie Truda."* 6 vols. Moscow, 1923–28.

De Jonge, Alex. *The Life and Times of Grigorii Rasputin.* New York, 1982.

Denikin, Anton I. *The Career of a Tsarist Officer.* Minneapolis, 1975.

————. *Ocherki russkoi smuty.* 5 vols. Berlin, 1921–26.

Denikin, General A. I. *The Russian Turmoil.* London, 1922.

Dennett, Tyler. *Roosevelt and the Russo-Japanese War.* Garden City, N.Y., 1925.

Deriabin, Peter. *Watchdogs of Terror: Russian Bodyguards from the Tsars to the Commissars.* 2nd ed. Frederick, Md., 1984.

Deutscher, Isaac. *The Prophet Armed: Trotsky, 1879–1921.* New York, 1954.

Dillon, E. J. *The Eclipse of Russia.* London, 1918.

Diterikhs, M. K. *Ubiistvo tsarskoi semi i chlenov doma romanovykh na Ural.* Vladivostok, 1922.

Drage, Geoffrey. *Russian Affairs.* New York, 1904.

Dubnow, S. M. *History of the Jews in Russia and Poland.* 3 vols. Philadelphia, 1916–20.

Dubrovsky, S. M. *Stolypinskaya zemelnaya reforma.* Moscow, 1963.

Duff, David. *Hessian Tapestry.* London, 1967.

Dyakin, V. S. *Russkaya burzhuazia i tsarizm v gody pervoi mirovoi voiny.* Leningrad, 1967.

———. *Samoderzhavie burzhuazia i dvoryanstvo v 1907–1911 gg.* Leningrad, 1978.

Dyakin, V. S., et al. *Krizis samoderzhavia v Rossi, 1895–1917.* Leningrad, 1984.

Edelman, Robert. *Gentry Politics on the Eve of the Russian Revolution.* New Brunswick, N.J., 1980.

Efremov, P. N. *Vneshnaya politika Rossii (1907–1914 gg.).* Moscow, 1961.

Elchaninov, Major-General A. *The Tsar and His People.* London, 1914.

Emets, V. A. *Ocherki vneshnei politiki Rossii v period pervoi mirovoi voiny.* Moscow, 1977.

Emmons, Terence. *The Formation of Political Parties and the First National Elections in Russia.* Cambridge, Mass., 1983.

Emmons, Terence, and Wayne S. Vucinich (eds.). *The Zemstvo in Russia.* Cambridge, Eng., 1982.

Encausse, Docteur Philippe. *Le Maitre Philippe, de Lyon.* 4th ed. Paris, 1955.

Encausse, Dr. Philippe. *Sciences occultes . . . Papus, sa vie, son oeuvre.* Paris, 1949.

Engelstein, Laura. *Moscow, 1905: Working-Class Organization and Political Conflict.* Stanford, Calif., 1982.

Essad-Bey, Mohammed [Leo Noussinbaum]. *Nicholas II: Prisoner of the Purple.* New York, 1937.

Esthus, Raymond A. *Double Eagle and Rising Sun: The Russians and Japanese at Portsmouth in 1905.* Durham, N.C., 1988.

———. *Theodore Roosevelt and Japan.* Seattle, 1966.

Fabritsky, S. S. *Iz proshlago: vospominania fligel-adyutanta gosudarya imperatora Nikolaya II.* Berlin, 1926.

Fay, Sidney Bradshaw. *The Origins of the World War.* 2nd ed.; 2 vols. in 1. New York, 1934.

Fenyvesi, Charles. *Splendor in Exile: The Ex-Majesties of Europe.* Washington, D.C., 1979.

Ferguson, Alan D., and Alfred Levin (eds.). *Essays in Russian History.* Hamden, Conn., 1964.

Ferro, Marc. *Nicholas II: The Last of the Tsars.* London, 1991.

———. *The Russian Revolution of February 1917.* Englewood Cliffs, N.J., 1972.

Fischer, George. *Russian Liberalism: From Gentry to Intelligentsia.* Cambridge, Mass., 1958.

Fleming, Peter. *The Siege at Peking.* London, 1959.

Florinsky, M. F. *Krizis gosudarstvennogo upravlenia v Rossii v gody pervoi mirovoi voiny (sovet ministrov v 1914–1917 gg.)*. Leningrad, 1988.

Florinsky, Michael T. *The End of the Russian Empire*. New York, 1961.

Footman, David. *The Alexander Conspiracy*. La Salle, Ill., 1974.

Frankel, Edith Rogovin, et al. *Revolution in Russia: Reassessments of 1917*. Cambridge, Eng., 1992.

Frankel, Jonathan. *Prophecy and Politics: Socialism, Nationalism, and the Russian Jews, 1862–1917*. Cambridge, Eng., 1981.

Frankland, Noble. *Imperial Tragedy*. New York, 1961.

Frölich, Klaus. *The Emergence of Russian Constitutionalism, 1900–1904*. The Hague, 1981.

Frumkin, Jacob, et al. (eds.). *Russian Jewry (1860–1917)*. New York, 1966.

Fuhrmann, Joseph T. *Rasputin: A Life*. New York, 1990.

Fuller, William C., Jr. *Civil-Military Conflict in Imperial Russia, 1881–1914*. Princeton, N.J., 1985.

———. *Strategy and Power in Russia, 1600–1914*. New York, 1992.

Fülöp-Miller, René. *Rasputin: The Holy Devil*. New York, 1928.

Gaddis, John Lewis. *Russia, the Soviet Union, and the United States*. 2nd ed. New York, 1990.

Galai, Shmuel. *The Liberation Movement in Russia, 1900–1905*. Cambridge, Eng., 1973.

Ganelin, R. Sh. *Rossiiskoe samoderzhavie v 1905 godu*. St. Petersburg, 1991.

Ganz, Hugo. *The Downfall of Russia*. London, 1904.

Gapon, Father George. *The Story of My Life*. New York, 1906.

Geifman, Anna. *Thou Shalt Kill: Revolutionary Terrorism in Russia, 1894–1917*. Princeton, N.J., 1993.

Geiss, Imanuel (ed.). *July 1914: The Outbreak of the First World War*. London, 1967.

Germany. Foreign Office. *Die Grosse Politik der europäischen Kabinette, 1871–1914*. 40 vols. Berlin, 1922–27.

Geyer, Dietrich. *Russian Imperialism: The Interaction of Domestic and Foreign Policy, 1860–1914*. New Haven, Conn., 1987.

———. *The Russian Revolution*. Leamington Spa, Eng., 1987.

Gillard, David. *The Struggle for Asia, 1828–1914: A Study in British and Russian Imperialism*. London, 1977.

Gilliard, Pierre. *Thirteen Years at the Russian Court*. New York, 1970.

Girault, René. *Emprunts russes et investissements francais en Russie, 1887–1914*. Paris, 1973.

Glenny, Michael, and Norman Stone. *The Other Russia*. New York, 1990.

Glinsky, B. B. (ed.). *Prolog russko-yapanskoi voiny: materialy iz arkhiva grafa S. Yu. Vitte*. Petrograd, 1916.

Golder, Frank Alfred (ed.). *Documents of Russian History, 1914–1917*. New York, 1927.

Golovine, Lieutenant-General Nicholas N. *The Russian Army in the World War*. New Haven, Conn., 1931.

Gooch, G. P. *Before the War: Studies in Diplomacy*. 2 vols. London, 1936–38.

Gooch, G. P., and Harold Temperley (eds). *British Documents on the Origins of the War, 1898–1914*. 11 vols. in 13. London, 1926–38.

Goremyka, Anton (ed.). *Nikolai II: yego lichnost, intimaya zhizn, i pravlenie.* London, 1905.

Gosudarstvennaya Duma: stenograficheskie otchet. 126 vols. St. Petersburg, 1906–1917.

Gourko, General Basil. *War and Revolution in Russia, 1914–1917.* New York, 1919.

Grabbe, Paul. *Windows on the River Neva.* New York, 1977.

Grabbe, Paul and Beatrice (eds.). *The Private World of the Last Tsar.* London, 1985.

Grant, N. F. (ed.). *The Kaiser's Letters to the Tsar.* London, 1920.

Greenburg, Louis. *The Jews in Russia.* 2 vols. New Haven, Conn., 1944–51.

Grenfell, Field-Marshal Lord. *Memoirs.* London, 1925.

Grenville, J. A. S. *Lord Salisbury and Foreign Policy.* London, 1964.

Grey, Marina. *Enquête sur le massacre des Romanov.* Paris, 1987.

Gronsky, Paul P., and Nicholas J. Astrov. *The War and the Russian Government.* New Haven, Conn., 1929.

Grunwald, Constantin de. *Le Tsar Nicolas II.* Paris, 1965.

Gruzenberg, O. O. *"Yesterday": Memoirs of a Russian-Jewish Lawyer.* Berkeley, Calif., 1981.

Guérassimov, Général [Aleksandr V.]. *Tsarisme et terrorisme.* Paris, 1934.

Gurko, V. I. *Features and Figures of the Past.* Stanford, Calif., 1939.

———. *Tsar i tsaritsa.* Paris, 1927.

Hackett, Roger F. *Yamagata Aritomo in the Rise of Modern Japan, 1838–1922.* Cambridge, Mass., 1971.

Hagen, Manfred. *Die Entfaltung politischer Öffentlichkeit in Russland, 1906–1914.* Wiesbaden, 1982.

Haimson, Leopold H. (ed.). *The Politics of Rural Russia, 1905–1914.* Bloomington, Ind., 1979.

Halliburton, Richard. *Seven League Boots.* Indianapolis, 1935.

Hamburg, G. M. *Politics of the Russian Nobility, 1881–1905.* New Brunswick, N.J., 1984.

Hanbury-Williams, Major General Sir John. *The Emperor Nicholas II As I Knew Him.* London, 1922.

Harcave, Sidney (ed. and trans.). *The Memoirs of Count Witte, see* Vitte and Witte.

Harcave, Sidney. *The Russian Revolution of 1905.* London, 1970.

———. *Years of the Golden Cockerel: The Last Romanov Tsars, 1814–1917.* New York, 1968.

Harper, Samuel N. *The New Electoral Law for the Russian Duma.* Chicago, 1908.

———. *The Russia I Believe In.* Chicago, 1945.

Hasegawa, Tsuyoshi. *The February Revolution: Petrograd, 1917.* Seattle, 1981.

Healy, Ann Erickson. *The Russian Autocracy in Crisis, 1905–1907.* Hamden, Conn., 1976.

Heenan, Louise Erwin. *Russian Democracy's Fatal Blunder: The Summer Offensive of 1917.* New York, 1987.

Helmreich, Ernst Christian. *The Diplomacy of the Balkan Wars, 1912–1913.* New York, 1969.

Hennessey, Richard. *The Agrarian Question in Russia, 1905–1907: The Inception of the Stolypin Reform.* Giessen, 1977.

Heresch, Elisabeth. *Nikolaus II*. Munich, 1992.

Hingley, Ronald. *The Russian Secret Police*. London, 1970.

Hinsley, F. H. (ed.). *British Foreign Policy under Sir Edward Grey*. Cambridge, Eng., 1977.

Hoare, Samuel. *The Fourth Seal*. London, 1930.

Hodgetts, E. A. Brayley. *The Court of Russia in the Nineteenth Century*. Vol. 2. London, 1908.

Holls, Frederick W. *The Peace Conference at the Hague*. New York, 1900.

Hosking, Geoffrey A. *The Russian Constitutional Experiment: Government and Duma, 1907–1914*. Cambridge, Eng., 1973.

Hough, Richard. *The Fleet That Had to Die*. New York, 1958.

Howard, Harry N. *The Partition of Turkey*. Norman, Okla., 1931.

Howe, M. A. DeWolfe. *George von Lengerke Meyer*. New York, 1920.

Hull, William I. *The Two Hague Conferences*. Boston, 1908.

Ienaga, Saburō (ed.). *Ōtsu jiken nisshi* [Journal of the Ōtsu Case]. Tokyo, 1971.

Ignatev, A. V. *Russko-angliiskie otnoshenia nakanune pervoi mirovoi voiny, 1908–1914 gg*. Moscow, 1962.

———. *Vneshnaya politiki Rossii v 1905–1907*. Moscow, 1986.

Ignatieff, Michael. *The Russian Album*. New York, 1987.

Ioffe, G. Z. *Krakh rossiiskoi monarkhicheskoi kontrrevolyutsii*. Moscow, 1977.

———. *Veliky oktyabr i epilog tsarizma*. Moscow, 1987.

Iroshnikov, Mikhail, et al. *The Sunset of the Romanov Dynasty*. Moscow, 1992.

Iswolsky, Alexandre. *Au service de la Russie: Correspondence diplomatique, 1906–1911*. 2 vols. Paris, 1937–39.

Iswolsky, Alexander. *Memoirs*. Gulf Breeze, Fla., 1974.

Ivanov, Georgy. *Kniga o poslednem tsarstvovanii*. Orange, Conn., 1990.

Janin, Général [Maurice]. *Ma mission en Sibérie, 1918–1920*. Paris, 1933.

Japan. Foreign Office. *Correspondence Regarding the Negotiations between Japan and Russia (1903–4)*. Washington, D.C., 1904?

Jarausch, Konrad H. *The Enigmatic Chancellor: Bethmann Hallweg and the Hubris of Imperial Germany*. New Haven, Conn., 1973.

Jelavich, Barbara. *Russia's Balkan Entanglements, 1806–1914*. New York, 1991.

———. *St. Petersburg and Moscow: Tsarist and Soviet Foreign Policy, 1814–1974*. Bloomington, Ind., 1974.

Joseph, Philip. *Foreign Diplomacy in China, 1894–1900*. New York, 1971.

Judge, Edward H., and James Y. Sims, Jr. *Modernization and Reform: Dilemmas of Progress in Late Imperial Russia*. New York, 1992.

Judge, Edward H. *Easter in Kishinev: Anatomy of a Pogrom*. New York, 1992.

———. *Plehve: Repression and Reform in Imperial Russia, 1902–1904*. Syracuse, N.Y., 1983.

Kaiser, David H. (ed.). *The Workers' Revolution in Russia, 1917*. Cambridge, Eng., 1987.

Kalmykow, Andrew D. *Memoirs of a Russian Diplomat*. New Haven, Conn., 1971.

Kassow, Samuel D. *Students, Professors, and the State in Tsarist Russia*. Berkeley, Calif., 1989.

Kasvinov, M. K. *Dvadtsat tri stupeni vniz*. Moscow, 1979.

Katkov, George. *Russia 1917: The February Revolution*. New York, 1967.

Kazemzadeh, Firuz. *Russia and Britain in Persia, 1864–1914*. New Haven, Conn., 1968.

Keep, J. L. H. *The Rise of Social Democracy in Russia*. Oxford, 1963.

Kennan, George F. *The Fateful Alliance: France, Russia, and the Coming of the First World War*. New York, 1984.

Kent, Marian (ed.). *The Great Powers and the End of the Ottoman Empire*. London, 1984.

Kerensky, Alexander. *The Catastrophe*. New York, 1971.

——. *The Crucifixion of Liberty*. New York, 1934.

——. *Russia and History's Turning Point*. New York, 1965.

King, Greg. *The Last Empress: The Life and Times of Alexandra Feodorovna, Tsarina of Russia*. New York, 1994.

Kizevetter, A. A. *Na rubezhde dvukh stolety*. Prague, 1929.

Klier, John D., and Shlomo Lambroza (eds.). *Pogroms: Anti-Jewish Violence in Modern Russian History*. Cambridge, Eng., 1992.

Knox, Major-General Sir Alfred. *With the Russian Army, 1914–1917*. 2 vols. London, 1921.

Kobylin, Viktor. *Imperator Nikolai II i general-adyutant M. V. Alekseyev*. New York, 1970.

Koch, H. W. (ed.). *The Origins of the First World War*. 2nd ed.; London, 1967.

Kochan, Lionel. *Russia in Revolution, 1890–1918*. London, 1967.

Kochan, Miriam. *The Last Days of Imperial Russia*. New York, 1976.

Koefoed, C. A. *My Share in the Stolypin Agrarian Reform*. Odense, 1985.

Kojima, Iken. *Ōtsu jiken nisshi*. Tokyo? 1971.

Kokovtsov, Count [Vladimir]. *Out of My Past*. Stanford, Calif., 1935.

Kokovtsov, Graf V. N. *Iz moyego proshlago*. 2 vols. Paris, 1933.

Korostovetz, J. J. *Pre-War Diplomacy: The Russo-Japanese Problem . . . Diary*. London, 1920.

Korostovetz, Vladimir. *Seed and Harvest*. London, 1931.

Krivoshein, K. A. *A. V. Krivoshein (1857–1921 g.)*. Paris, 1973.

Kryzhanovsky, S. E. *Vospominania*. Berlin, n.d.

Kucherov, Samuel. *Courts, Lawyers and Trials under the Last Three Tsars*. New York, 1953.

Kurlov, P. G. *Gibel Imperatorskoi Rossi*. Berlin, 1923.

Kuropatkin, General. *The Russian Army and the Japanese War*. 2 vols. London, 1909.

Kurth, Peter. *Anastasia: The Life of Anna Anderson*. London, 1983.

——. *Tsar: The Lost World of Nicholas and Alexandra*. Boston, 1995.

Kutakov, L. N. *Portsmutsky mirny dogovor*. Moscow, 1961.

Lamzdorf, V. N. *Dnevnik* [1886–1896]. 4 vols. Moscow, 1926–91.

Langer, William L. *The Diplomacy of Imperialism, 1890–1902*. New York, 1968.

——. *Explorations in Crisis*. Cambridge, Mass., 1969.

——. *The Franco-Russian Alliance, 1890–1894*. Cambridge, Mass., 1929.

Laporte, Maurice. *Histoire de l'Okhrana*. Paris, 1935.

Laqueur, Walter. *Black Hundred: The Rise of the Extreme Right in Russia*. New York, 1993.

——. *Russia and Germany*. London, 1965.

Lederer, Ivo J. (ed.). *Russian Foreign Policy*. New Haven, Conn., 1962.

Lee, Dwight E. *Europe's Crucial Years: The Diplomatic Background of World War I, 1902–1914.* Hanover, N. H., 1974.

Lee, Sir Sidney. *King Edward VII.* 2 vols. London, 1925–27.

Leggett, George. *The Cheka: Lenin's Political Police.* Oxford, 1981.

Lemke, Mik[hail]. *250 dnei v tsarskoe stavke.* St. Petersburg, 1920.

Lenin, V. I. *Polnoe sobranie sochineny.* 5th ed.; 55 vols. Moscow, 1958–65.

Lensen, George Alexander. *Balance of Intrigue: International Rivalry in Korea and Manchuria, 1884–1899.* 2 vols. Tallahassee, Fla., 1982.

——. *The Russo-Chinese War.* Tallahassee, Fla., 1967.

Lettres des Grand-Ducs à Nicolas II. Paris, 1926.

Leudet, Maurice. *Nicolas II intimé.* Paris, n.d.

Levin, Alfred. *The Second Duma.* 2nd ed. Hamden, Conn., 1966.

——. *The Third Duma: Election and Profile.* Hamden, Conn., 1973.

Levine, Isaac Don. *Eyewitness to History.* New York, 1973.

Un Libre noir: Diplomatie d'avant guerre d'apres les documents des archives russes. 3 vols. Paris, 1922–24.

Lieven, D. C. B. *Russia and the Origins of the First World War.* New York, 1984.

Lieven, Dominic (ed.). *British Documents on Foreign Affairs: Reports and Papers from the Foreign Office Confidential Print.* Series A; Russia, 1859–1914. Part I. 6 vols. Frederick, Md., 1983.

——. *Nicholas II.* New York, 1993.

——. *Russia's Rulers under the Old Regime.* New Haven, Conn., 1989.

Lincoln, W. Bruce. *In War's Dark Shadow.* New York, 1983.

——. *Passage through Armageddon: The Russians in War and Revolution, 1914–1918.* New York, 1986.

——. *Red Victory: A History of the Russian Civil War.* New York, 1991.

——. *The Romanovs.* New York, 1981.

Lindemann, Robert S. *The Jew Accused.* Cambridge, Eng., 1991.

Linke, Horst Gunther. *Das Zarische Russland und der Erste Weltkrieg: Diplomatie und Kriegsziele, 1914–1917.* Munich, 1982.

Lloyd George, David. *War Memoirs.* 6 vols. Boston, 1933–37.

Lockhart, R. H. Bruce. *British Agent.* Garden City, N.Y., 1933.

Louis, George. *Les Carnets.* 2 vols. Paris, 1926.

Logan, John A., Jr. *In Joyful Russia.* London, 1897.

Loukomsky, General [Aleksandr]. *Memoirs of the Russian Revolution.* Westport, Conn., 1975.

Lovell, James Blair. *Anastasia: The Lost Princess.* Washington, D.C., 1991.

Lowe, Charles. *Alexander III of Russia.* London, 1895.

Löwe, Heinz-Dietrich. *Antisemitismus und reaktionäre Utopie* [1890–1917]. Hamburg, 1978.

Lyons, Marvin. *Nicholas II.* London, 1974.

Macey, David A. J. *Government and Peasant in Russia, 1861–1906: The Prehistory of the Stolypin Reforms.* De Kalb, Ill, 1987.

Magnus, Philip. *King Edward the Seventh.* New York, 1964.

Maklakov, V. A. *The First State Duma.* Bloomington, Ind., 1964.

——. *Iz vospominany.* New York, 1954.

——. *Vlast i obshchestvennost na zakat staroi Rossii (vospominania).* Paris, 1939.

————. *Vtoraya gosudarstvennaya duma.* Paris, 1944.

Malozemoff, Andrew. *Russian Far Eastern Policy, 1881–1904.* Berkeley, Calif., 1958.

Mamantov, V. I. *Na gosudarevoi sluzhbe.* Tallin, 1926.

Manning, Roberta Thompson. *The Crisis of the Old Order in Russia: Gentry and Government.* Princeton, N.J., 1982.

Margolin, Arnold D. *The Jews of Eastern Europe.* New York, 1926.

Marie, Grand Duchess of Russia. *Education of a Princess.* New York, 1931.

Marinov, V. A. *Russia i Yaponia pered pervoi mirovoi voinoi.* Moscow, 1974.

Markov, S. *Pokinutaya tsarskaya semya.* Vienna, 1928.

Marks, Steven G. *Road to Power: The Trans-Siberian Railroad and the Colonization of Asian Russia, 1850–1917.* Ithaca, N.Y., 1991.

Massie, Robert K. *Nicholas and Alexandra.* New York, 1967.

————. (introd.). *The Romanov Family Album.* New York, 1982.

————. *The Romanovs: The Final Chapter.* New York, 1995.

Maylunas, Andrei (comp.). *Nicholas and Alexandra: The Family Albums.* London, 1992.

Maylunas, Andrei, and Sergei Mironenko (eds.). *A Lifelong Passion: Nicholas and Alexandra.* New York, 1997.

Mayre, George Thomas. *Nearing the End in Imperial Russia.* Philadelphia, 1929.

McCullagh, Francis. *A Prisoner of the Reds.* London, 1922.

McDaniel, Tim. *Autocracy, Modernization, and Revolution in Russia and Iran.* Princeton, N.J., 1991.

McDonald, David MacLaren. *United Government and Foreign Policy in Russia, 1900–1914.* Cambridge, Mass., 1992.

McKean, Robert B. (ed.). *New Perspectives in Modern Russian History.* London, 1992.

McKean, Robert B. *St. Petersburg between the Revolutions: Workers and Revolutionaries, June 1902–February 1917.* New Haven, Conn., 1990.

McKenzie, F. A. *The Tragedy of Korea.* London, 1908.

Medlin, Virgil D., and Steven L. Parsons. *V. D. Nabokov and the Russian Provisional Government, 1917.* New Haven, Conn., 1976.

Mehlinger, Howard D., and John M. Thompson. *Count Witte and the Tsarist Government in the 1905 Revolution.* Bloomington, Ind., 1972.

Melgunov, S. P. *Legenda o separatom mir.* Paris, 1957.

————. *Martovskie dni 1917 goda.* Paris, 1961.

————. *Na putyakh k dvortsovomu perevorotu.* Paris, 1931.

————. (ed.). *Nikolai II: Materialny dlya kharakteristiki lichnosti i tsarstvovania.* Moscow, 1917.

————. *Sudba Imperatora Nikolaya II posle otrechenia.* Paris, 1951.

Melnik, Tatyana. *Vospominania o tsarskoi semei eya zhizn do i posle revolyutsy.* Belgrade, 1921.

Menning, Bruce W. *Bayonets before Bullets: The Russian Imperial Army, 1861–1914.* Bloomington, Ind., 1992.

Meyendorf, Baron A. (ed.). *Correspondence diplomatique du M. de Staal.* 2 vols. Paris, 1929.

Michon, Georges. *The Franco-Russian Alliance, 1891–1917.* London, 1929.

Miliukov, Paul. *Political Memoirs, 1905–1917.* Ann Arbor, Mich., 1967.

————. *The Russian Revolution.* 3 vols. Gulf Breeze, Fla., 1978–87.

————. *Vospominania* [1859–1917]. 2 vols. New York, 1955.

Miller, Margaret. *The Economic Development of Russia, 1905–1914.* 2nd ed. London, 1967.

Ministerstvo inostrannykh del. *Mezhdunarodnie otnoshenie v epokhu imperialzma.* 14 vols. Moscow, 1931.

————. *Sbornik diplomaticheskikh dokumentov.* St. Petersburg, 1906.

Mitchell, Donald W. *A History of Russian and Soviet Sea Power.* New York, 1974.

Moishezon, B. *Sotvorenie mifa: zametski ob identifikatsii "Yurovskogo."* Jerusalem, 1990.

Monger, George. *The End of Isolation: British Foreign Policy, 1900–1907.* London, 1963.

Morison, Elting E. (ed.). *The Letters of Theodore Roosevelt,* see Roosevelt.

Mosse, W. E. *Perestroika under the Tsars.* London, 1992.

Mossolov, A. A. *At the Court of the Last Tsar.* London, 1935.

Moy, Carl Graf. *Als Diplomat am Zarenhof.* Munich, 1971.

Mstislavskii, Sergei. *Five Days Which Transformed Russia.* Bloomington, Ind., 1988.

Nabokoff, C. *The Ordeal of a Diplomat.* London, 1921.

Narishkin-Kurakin, Elizabeth. *Under Three Tsars.* New York, 1931.

Naumov, A. N. *Iz utselevshikh vospominanii, 1868–1917.* 2 vols. New York, 1954–55.

Neilson, Keith. *Strategy and Supply: The Anglo-Russian Alliance, 1914–17.* London, 1984.

Nekludoff, A. *Diplomatic Reminiscences (1911–1917).* New York, 1920.

Netchvolodow, A. *L'empereur Nicolas II et les Juifs.* Paris, 1924.

Nevsky, V. I. *Rabochee dvizhenie v yanvarskie dni 1905 goda.* Moscow, 1931.

Nicholas, Prince of Greece. *My Fifty Years.* London, 1927.

Nicolai II. *Journal intime.* Paris, 1926.

Nicolas Mikhailovitch, Grand-Duc. *La fin du tsarisme: Lettres inédites à Frédéric Masson (1914–1918).* Paris, 1968.

Nicolson, Harold. *King George the Fifth.* London, 1952.

————. *Sir Arthur Nicolson.* London, 1930.

Nikolai II. *Dnevnik Imperatora Nikolaya II, 1890–1906 gg.* Berlin, 1923.

————. *Dnevniki Imperatora Nikolaya II.* Moscow, 1991.

————. *Polnoe sobranie rechei Imperatora Nikolaya II, 1894–1906.* St. Petersburg, 1906.

Nikolai II: Materialy dla kharakteristiki lichnosti i tsarstvovania. Moscow, 1917.

Nikolai II Romanov: Yevo zhizn i deyatelnost. Petrograd, 1917.

Nikolajewsky, Boris. *Aseff the Spy.* Garden City, N.Y., 1934.

Nish, Ian. *The Origins of the Russo-Japanese War.* London, 1985.

Noskoff, Général A.-A. *Nicolas II inconnu.* Paris, 1920.

Notovich, Nicolas. *La Pacification de l'Europe et Nicolas II.* Paris, 1899.

Novikoff-Priboy, A. *Tsushima.* London, 1936.

Null, Gary. *The Conspirator Who Saved the Romanovs.* Englewood Cliffs, N.J., 1971.

Oberländer, Erwin (ed.). *Russia Enters the Twentieth Century, 1894–1917.* New York, 1971.

Obninsky, V. P. *Polgoda russkoi revolyutsii*. Moscow, 1906.

[————.] *Posledny samoderzhets*. Berlin, 1912.

Obolensky, Prince Dmitri D. (ed.). *Imperator Nikolai i yego tsarstvovanie (1894–1917)*. Nice, 1928.

Occleshaw, Michael. *The Romanov Conspiracies*. London, 1993.

O'Conor, John F. *The Sokolov Investigation of the Alleged Murder of the Russian Imperial Family*. New York, 1971.

Okamoto, Shumpei. *The Japanese Oligarchy and the Russo-Japanese War*. New York, 1970.

Oldenburg, S. S. *Last Tsar: Nicholas II: His Reign & His Russia*. 4 vols. Gulf Breeze, Fla., 1975–78.

Ookhtomsky, Prince E. *Travels in the East of Nicholas II Emperor of Russia When Cesarewitch, 1890–1891*. 2 vols. London, 1896.

Osatake, Takeshi. *Rokoku kōtaishi Ōtsu sōnan konan jiken [The Russian Crown Prince's Unfortunate Mishap at Ōtsu]*. Tokyo, 1951.

Ossendowski, Ferdinand. *The Shadow of the Gloomy East*. New York, 1925.

Ostaltseva, Alevtina. *Anglo-russkoe soglashenie 1907 goda*. Saratov, 1977.

Österreich-Ungarns Aussenpolitik von der bosnischen Krise 1908 bis zum Kriegsausbruch 1914. 8 vols. Vienna, 1930.

Ostrovsky, I. V. *P. A. Stolypin i yego vremya*. Novosibirsk, 1992.

Owen, Launcelot. *The Russian Peasant Movement, 1906–1917*. London, 1937.

Paganuzzi, Paul. *Pravda ob ubiistve tsarskoi semi*. Jordanville, N.Y., 1981.

Paléologue, Maurice. *An Ambassador's Memoirs*. 3 vols. London, 1923–25.

————. *Guillaume II et Nicolas II*. Paris, 1934.

Paley, Princess. *Memories of Russia, 1916–1919*. London, 1924.

Pankratov, V. S. *S tsarem v Tobolske*. Leningrad, 1990.

Pares, Sir Bernard. *The Fall of the Russian Monarchy*. New York, 1939.

————. (introd.). *Letters of the Tsaritsa to the Tsar, 1914–1916*. London, 1939.

————. *My Russian Memoirs*. London, 1931.

————. *Russia and Reform*. London, 1907.

————. *Russia between Reform and Revolution*. New York, 1962.

Pavlovsky, G. P. *Agricultural Russia on the Eve of the Revolution*. London, 1930.

Pearson, Raymond. *The Russian Moderates and the Crisis of Tsarism, 1914–1917*. New York, 1977.

Petergofskoe soveshchanie o proekte gosudarstvennoi dumy pod lichnym yego Imperatorskago Velichestva predsedatelstvom: sekretnie protokoly. Berlin, n.d.

Pinchuk, Ben-Cion. *The Octobrists in the Third Duma, 1907–1912*. Seattle, 1974.

Pinson, Koppel S. (ed.). *Essays on Antisemitism*. New York, 1942.

Pipes, Richard (ed.). *Revolutionary Russia*. Cambridge, Mass., 1968.

————. (ed.). *The Russian Intelligentsia*. New York, 1961.

————. *The Russian Revolution*. New York, 1990.

————. *Struve*. 2 vols. Cambridge, Mass., 1970–80.

Pisarev, Yu. A. *Velikie derzhavy i Balkany nakanune pervoi mirovoi voiny*. Moscow, 1985.

Platonov, Oleg. *Ubiistvo tsarskoi semi*. Moscow, 1991.

Poléjaïeff, Pierre. *Six années: La Russie de 1906 à 1912*. Paris, 1912.

Poliakoff, V. (Augur). *Mother Dear: The Empress Marie of Russia and Her Times*. New York, 1926.

Poliakov, Léon. *The History of Anti-Semitism.* 4 vols. New York, 1965–85.

Polivanov, A. A. *Iz dnevnikov i vospominany po dolzhnosti voennogo ministra i yego pomoshchnika, 1907–1916 g.* Moscow, 1924.

Polonsky, J. (trans.). *Documents diplomatiques secrets russes.* Paris, 1928.

Polovtsov, A. A. *Dnevnik gosudarstvennogo sekretarya Polovtsova.* 2 vols. Moscow, 1966.

Polvinen, Tuomo. *Imperial Borderland: Bobrikov and the Attempted Russification of Finland, 1898–1904.* Durham, N.C., 1995.

Pospielovsky, Dimitry. *Russian Police Trade Unionism: Experiment or Provocation?* London, 1971.

Pozdnyshev, S. *Raspni yego.* Paris, 1952.

Price, Ernest Batson. *The Russo-Japanese Treaties of 1907–1916 Concerning Manchuria and Mongolia.* Baltimore, 1933.

Pridham, Vice-Admiral Sir Francis. *Close of a Dynasty.* London, 1956.

Pronin, V. M. *Poslednie dni tsarskoi stavki.* Belgrade, 1929.

Purishkevich, V. M. *The Murder of Rasputin.* Ann Arbor, Mich., 1985.

Quested, R. K. I. *"Matey" Imperialists? The Tsarist Russians in Manchuria, 1895–1917.* Hong Kong, 1982.

Quested, Rosemary. *The Russo-Chinese Bank.* Birmingham, Eng., 1977.

Radzinsky, Edvard. *The Last Tsar: The Life and Death of Nicholas II.* New York, 1992.

Radziwill, Princess Catherine. *Nicholas II: The Last of the Tsars.* London, 1931.

Ragsdale, Hugh (ed.). *Imperial Russian Foreign Policy.* Washington, D.C., 1993.

Raleigh, Donald J. (ed.). *The Emperors and Empresses of Russia.* Armonk, N.Y., 1996.

Reinach, J.-P. *Le Traité de Bjoerkoë (1905).* Paris, 1935.

Rich, Norman. *Friedrich von Holstein.* 2 vols. Cambridge, Eng., 1965.

Richards, Guy. *The Hunt for the Czar.* New York, 1971.

———. *Imperial Agent: The Goleniewski-Romanov Case.* New York, 1966.

———. *The Rescue of the Romanovs.* Old Greenwich, Conn., 1975.

Riha, Thomas. *A Russian European: Paul Miliukov in Russian Politics.* Notre Dame, Ind., 1969.

Rivet, Charles. *The Last of the Romanovs.* London, 1918.

Robbins, Richard G., Jr. *Famine in Russia, 1891–1892.* New York, 1975.

Robinson, Geroid Tanquary. *Rural Russia under the Old Regime.* Berkeley, Calif., 1967.

Rodichev, Fedor Ismailovich. *Vospominaniia i ocherki o russkom liberalizme.* Newtonville, Mass., 1983.

Rodzianko, M. V. *The Reign of Rasputin.* Gulf Breeze, Fla., 1973.

Rogger, Hans. *Jewish Policies and Right-Wing Politics in Imperial Russia.* Berkeley, Calif., 1986.

———. *Russia in the Age of Modernisation and Revolution, 1881–1917.* London, 1983.

Rollin, Henri. *L'Apocalypse de notre temps.* Paris, 1939.

Romanov, B. A. *Ocherki diplomaticheskoi istorii russko-yaponskoi voiny, 1895–1907.* 2nd ed. Moscow, 1955.

———. *Russia in Manchuria (1892–1906)* Ann Arbor, Mich., 1952.

[Romanov], Veliky Knyaz Gavriil Konstantinovich. *V Mramornom dvortse.* New York, 1955.

Romanovsky-Krassinsky, Princess. *Dancing in Petersburg: The Memoirs of Kschessinska.* London, 1960.

Roosevelt, Theodore. *Letters.* 8 vols. Cambridge, Mass., 1951–54.

Rose, Kenneth. *King George V.* New York, 1984.

Rosen, Baron [Roman]. *Forty Years of Diplomacy.* 2 vols. New York, 1922.

Rosenberg, William G. *Liberals in the Russian Revolution: The Constitutional Democratic Party, 1917–1921.* Princeton, N.J., 1974.

Ross, Nikolai (ed.). *Gibel tsarskoi semi: Materialy sledstvia po dela ob ubiistve tsarskoi semi.* Frankfurt, 1987.

Rossos, Andrew. *Russia and the Balkans* [1908–1914]. Toronto, 1981.

Rostunov, I. I. (ed.). *Istoria russko-yaponskoi voiny.* Moscow, 1977.

———. *Russky front pervoi mirovoi voiny.* Moscow, 1976.

Rubenstein, Richard E. *Comrade Valentine: The True Story of Azef the Spy.* New York, 1994.

Rupen, Robert A. *Mongols of the Twentieth Century.* 2 vols. Bloomington, Ind., 1964.

Russian, A. (B. W.). *Russian Court Memoirs, 1914–16.* London, 1917.

Rutherford, Ward. *The Russian Army in World War I.* London, 1975.

Sablinsky, Walter. *The Road to Bloody Sunday: Father Gapon and the St. Petersburg Massacre of 1905.* Princeton, N.J., 1976.

St. Aubyn, Giles. *Edward VII.* New York, 1979.

Salisbury, Harrison E. *Black Night, White Snow: Russia's Revolutions, 1905–1917.* Garden City, N.Y., 1978.

Samuel, Maurice. *Blood Accusation: The Strange History of the Beiliss Case.* New York, 1966.

Savinkov, Boris. *Memoirs of a Terrorist.* New York, 1931.

Savinsky, A. *Recollections of a Russian Diplomat.* London, 1927.

Sazonov, Serge. *Fateful Years, 1909–1916.* New York, 1971.

Schapiro, Leonard. *The Communist Party of the Soviet Union.* 2nd ed. New York, 1971.

———. *Russian Studies.* New York, 1987.

Schelking, Eugene de. *Recollections of a Russian Diplomat.* New York, 1918.

Schilling, Baron M. F. (introd.). *How the War Began in 1914: Being the Diary of the Russian Foreign Office . . .* London, 1925.

Schmitt, Bernadotte E. *The Annexation of Bosnia, 1908–1909.* New York, 1970.

———. *The Coming of the War, 1914.* 2 vols. New York, 1930.

Schneiderman, Jeremiah. *Sergei Zubatov and Revolutionary Marxism.* Ithaca, N.Y., 1976.

Schwarz, Solomon M. *The Russian Revolution of 1905.* Chicago, 1967.

Segal, Boris M. *Russian Drinking: Use and Abuse of Alcohol in Pre-Revolutionary Russia.* New Brunswick, N.J., 1987.

Semennikov, V. P. (ed.), *Monarkhia pered krusheniem, 1914–1917.* Moscow, 1927.

———. *Nikolai II i velikie knyazya.* Leningrad, 1925.

———. *Politika Romanovykh nakanune revolyutsii.* Leningrad, 1925.

———. *Revolyutsia 1905 goda i samoderzhavie.* Moscow, 1928.

————. *Romanovy i germanskie vliyania vo vremya mirovoi voiny.* Leningrad, 1929.

————. *Za kulisami tsarizma: arkhiv tibetskogo vracha Badmayeva.* Leningrad, 1925.

Semenoff, E. *The Russian Government and the Massacres.* Westport, Conn., 1972.

Seraphim, Ernst. *Russische Porträts.* 2 vols. Zurich, 1943.

Serebrennikov, A. (comp.). *Ubiistvo Stolypina.* New York, 1986.

Service, Robert (ed.). *Society and Politics in the Russian Revolution.* New York, 1992.

Seton-Watson, Hugh. *The Decline of Imperial Russia, 1855–1914.* London, 1952.

————. *The Russian Empire, 1801–1917.* Oxford, 1967.

Shakhovskoi, Knyaz Vsevolod Nikolayevich. *"Sic transit gloria mundi" (1893–1917).* Paris, 1952.

Shanin, Teodor. *The Roots of Otherness: Russia's Turn of the Century.* 2 vols. New Haven, Conn., 1986.

Shavelsky, Georgi. *Vospominania proslednego protopresvitera russkoi armii i flota.* 2 vols. in 1. New York, 1954.

Shchegolev, P. Ye. (ed.). *Otrechenie Nikolaya II.* Leningrad, 1927.

————. (ed.). *Padenie tsarskogo rezhima.* 7 vols. Moscow, 1924–27.

————. *Posledny reis Nikolaya vtorogo.* Moscow, 1928.

Shidlovsky, S. I. *Vospominania.* 2 vols. Berlin, 1923.

Shipov, D. N. *Vospominania i dumy o perezhitom.* Moscow, 1918.

Showalter, Dennis E. *Tannenberg: Clash of Empires.* Hamden, Conn., 1991.

Shulgin, V. V. *Days of the Russian Revolution.* Gulf Breeze, Fla., 1990.

————. *The Years.* New York, 1984.

Sidelnikov, S. M. *Obrazovanie deyatelnost pervoi gosudarstvennoi dumy.* Moscow, 1962.

Siegelbaum, Lewis H. *The Politics of Industrial Mobilization in Russia, 1914–17.* New York, 1983.

Simanovich, Aron. *Rasputin i Yevrei.* Riga, n.d.

Simmons, Ernest J. (ed.). *Continuity and Change in Russian and Soviet Thought.* Cambridge, Mass., 1955.

Smirnoff, Serge. *Autor de l'assassinat des grands-ducs.* Paris, 1928.

Smith, C. Jay. *The Russian Struggle for Power.* New York, 1956.

Smolianoff, Madame Olga de. *Russia (The Old Regime), 1903–1919.* New York, 1935.

Sokolov, Nicholas. *Enquête judiciaire sur l'assissinat de la famille imperiale russe.* Paris, 1924.

Sokolov, N. *Ubiistvo tsarskoi semi.* Berlin, 1925.

Solovyov, Yu. B. *Samoderzhavie i dvoryanstvo v kontse XIX veka.* Moscow, 1973.

————. *Samoderzhavie i dvoryanstvo v 1902–1907 gg.* Leningrad, 1981.

————. *Samoderzhavie i dvoryanstvo v 1907–1914 gg.* Leningrad, 1990.

Sovremennik. *Nikolai II razoblachenia.* Berlin, 1914.

Spence, Richard B. *Boris Savinkov: Renegade on the Left.* New York, 1991.

Spiridovitch, General Alexandre. *Les Dernières années de la cour de Tzarskoïe-Selo.* 2 vols. Paris, 1928–29.

————. *Histoire du terrorisme Russe, 1886–1917.* Millwood, N.Y., 1983.

————. *Raspoutine.* Paris, 1935.

————. *Velikaya voina i fevralskaya revolyutsia, 1914–1917 gg.* 3 vols. New York, 1960–62.

Spring-Rice, Sir Cecil. *Letters and Friendships.* 2 vols. Boston, 1929.

Startsev, V. I. *Russkaya burzhuazia i samoderzhavie v 1905–1917 gg.* Leningrad, 1977.

Stavrou, Theofanis George (ed.). *Russia under the Last Tsar.* Minneapolis, 1969.

Stead, W. T. *The United States and Europe on the Eve of the Parliament of Peace.* London, 1899.

Steinberg, Mark D., and Vladimir M. Khrustalëv. *The Fall of the Romanovs.* New Haven, Conn., 1995.

Stephan, John J. *The Russian Fascists.* New York, 1978.

Stevenson, David. *The First World War and International Politics.* Oxford, 1988.

Stieve, Friedrich. *Isvolsky and the World War.* Freeport, N.Y., 1971.

Stolypin: zhizn i smert. Saratov, 1991.

Stolypin, P. A. *Rechi v gosudarstvennoi dume i gosudarstvennom sovete, 1906–1911.* New York, 1990.

Stone, Norman. *The Eastern Front, 1914–1917.* New York, 1975.

Sukhomlinov, V. *Vospominania.* Berlin, 1924.

Summers, Anthony, and Tom Mangold. *The File on the Tsar.* New York, 1976.

Surguchev, Ilya. *Detstvo imperatora Nikolaya II.* Paris, 1953.

Surh, Gerald D. *1905 in St. Petersburg: Labor, Society, and Revolution.* Stanford, Calif., 1989.

Suttner, Bertha von. *Memoirs.* 2 vols. New York, 1972.

Suvorin, A. S. *Dnevnik.* Moscow, 1923.

Svyatoi Chert: Taina Grigoria Rasputina. Moscow, 1991.

Sydačoff, B. von. *Nicholas II: Behind the Scenes in the Country of the Tsar.* London, 1905.

Szeftel, Marc. *The Russian Constitution of April 23, 1906: Political Institutions of the Duma Monarchy.* Brussels, 1976.

Tagantsev, Nikolai S. *Perezhitoe: uchrezdenie gosudarstvennoe dumy v 1905–1906 gg.* Petrograd, 1919.

Tager, Alexander B. *The Decay of Czarism: The Beiliss Trial.* Philadelphia, 1935.

Tan, Chester T. *The Boxer Catastrophe.* New York, 1955.

Tang, Peter S. H. *Russian and Soviet Policy in Manchuria and Outer Mongolia, 1911–1931.* Durham, N.C., 1959.

Tarasov-Rodionov, Aleksei. *February 1917.* New York, 1931.

Tarnovski, Theodore (ed.). *Reform in Modern Russian History.* New York, 1995.

Tarsaidze, Alexandre. *Yetyre mifa.* New York, 1969.

Tate, Merze. *The Disarmament Illusion.* New York, 1942.

Taube, Baron M. de. *La Politique russe d'avant-guerre et la fin de l'empire des tsars (1904–1917).* Paris, 1928.

Taylor, A. J. P. *The Struggle for Mastery in Europe, 1848–1918.* Oxford, 1954.

Tcharykow, N. V. *Glimpses of High Politics.* New York, 1931.

Teffi, N. A. *Vospominania.* Paris, 1931.

Telberg, George Gustav, and Robert Wilton. *The Last Days of the Romanovs.* New York, 1920.

Thaden, Edward C. *Interpreting History: Collective Essays on Russia's Relations with Europe.* Boulder, Colo., 1990.

———. *Russia and the Balkan Alliance of 1912*. University Park, Pa., 1965.

———. (ed.). *Russification in the Baltic Provinces and Finland 1855–1914*. Princeton, N.J., 1981.

Thompson, Arthur W., and Robert A. Hart. *The Uncertain Crusade: America and the Russian Revolution of 1905*. Amherst, Mass., 1970.

Thompson, Ewa M. *Understanding Russia: The Holy Fool in Russian Culture*. Lanham, Md., 1987.

Thurston, Robert W. *Liberal City, Conservative State: Moscow and Russia's Urban Crisis*. New York, 1987.

Timberlake, Charles E. (ed.). *Essays on Russian Liberalism*. Columbia, Mo., 1972.

———. (ed.). *Religious and Secular Forces in Late Tsarist Russia*. Seattle, 1992.

Tisdale, E. E. P. *Marie Fedorovna: Empress of Russia*. New York, 1957.

Tokmakoff, George. *P. A. Stolypin and the Third Duma*. Washington, D.C., 1981.

Trani, Eugene P. *The Treaty of Portsmouth*. Lexington, Ky., 1969.

Treadgold, Donald W. (ed.). *The Development of the USSR*. Seattle, 1964.

———. *The Great Siberian Migration*. Princeton, N.J., 1957.

———. *Lenin and His Rivals*. New York, 1955.

Trewin, J. C. *Tutor to the Tsarevich*. London, 1975.

Trotsky, Leon. *The History of the Russian Revolution*. 3 vols. in 1. New York, 1936.

———. *Trotsky's Diary in Exile*. New York, 1963.

———. *1905*. New York, 1971.

Troyat, Henri. *Daily Life in Russia under the Last Tsar*. Stanford, Calif., 1979.

———. *Nicolas II: Le dernier tsar*. Paris, 1991.

Trubetskoi, Gr. N. *Russkaya diplomatia 1914–1917 gg. i voina balkanakh*. Montreal, 1983.

Trufanoff, Sergei Michailovich (Iliodor). *The Mad Monk of Russia, Iliodor*. New York, 1918.

Tuchman, Barbara W. *The Proud Tower*. New York, 1966.

Tupper, Harmon. *To the Great Ocean: Siberia and the Trans-Siberian Railway*. Boston, 1965.

Tyutyukin, S. V. *Yulsky politichesky krizis 1906 g. v Rossii*. Moscow, 1991.

Ular, Alexander. *Russia from Within*. London, 1905.

Urussov, Prince Serge Dmitriyevich. *Memoirs of a Russian Governor*. New York, 1908.

Van der Kiste, John. *Princess Victoria Melita: Grand Duchess Cyril of Russia, 1876–1936*. Phoenix Mill, Eng., 1991.

Vassili, Count Paul [pseud.]. *Behind the Veil at the Russian Court*. New York, 1914.

Vasyukov, V. S. *Vneshnyaya politika Rossii nakanune fevralskoi revolyutsii, 1916–fevral 1917 g*. Moscow, 1989.

Verner, Andrew M. *The Crisis of Russian Autocracy: Nicholas II and the 1905 Revolution*. Princeton, N.J., 1990.

Vinogradov, K. B. *Bosniisky krizis, 1908–1909 gg*. Leningrad, 1964.

Viroubova, Anna. *Memories of the Russian Court*. New York, 1923.

Vitte, S. Yu. *Vospominania*. 3 vols. Moscow, 1960.

Vogel, Barbara. *Deutsche Russlandpolitik* [1900–1906]. Dusseldorf, 1973.

Volkov, Alexis. *Souvenirs*. Paris, 1928.

Von Laue, Theodore H. *Sergei Witte and the Industrialization of Russia.* New York, 1963.

Von Schoen, Freiherr. *The Memoirs of an Ambassador.* London, 1922.

Vonlyarlyarsky, V. *Moi vospominania, 1852–1939 gg.* Berlin, 1939.

Vorres, Ian. *The Last Grand-Duchess: Olga Alexandrova.* London, 1964.

Voyeikov, V. N. *S tsarem i bez tsarya.* Helsingfors, 1936.

Vucinich, Wayne S. *The Peasant in Nineteenth-Century Russia.* Stanford, Calif., 1968.

Vulliamy, C. E. (ed.). *The Letters of the Tsar to the Tsaritsa, 1914–1917.* London, 1929.

Vyrubova, Anna (comp.). *The Romanov Family Album.* New York, 1982.

Walder, David. *The Short Victorious War: The Russo-Japanese Conflict, 1904–5.* London, 1973.

Walkin, Jacob. *The Rise of Democracy in Pre-Revolutionary Russia.* New York, 1962.

Warner, Denis and Peggy. *The Tide at Sunrise: A History of the Russo-Japanese War, 1904–1905.* New York, 1974.

Warth, Robert D. *The Allies and the Russian Revolution.* Durham, N.C., 1954.

Washburn, Stanley. *On the Russian Front in World War I.* New York, 1982.

Wcislo, Francis William. *Reforming Rural Russia: Local Society and National Politics, 1855–1914.* Princeton, N.J., 1990.

Webb, James. *The Occult Establishment.* La Salle, Ill., 1976.

Weber, Max. *The Russian Revolutions.* Ithaca, N.Y., 1995.

Weigh, Ken Shen. *Russo-Chinese Diplomacy, 1689–1924.* Bangor, Maine, 1967.

Weinberg, Robert. *The Revolution of 1905 in Odessa: Blood on the Steps.* Bloomington, Ind., 1993.

Weissman, Neil B. *Reform in Tsarist Russia: The State Bureaucracy and Local Government, 1900–1914.* New Brunswick, N.J., 1981.

Westwood, J. N. *Russia against Japan, 1904–05.* Albany, N.Y., 1986.

———. (ed.). *Witnesses of Tsushima.* Tokyo, 1970.

White, Andrew Dickson. *Autobiography.* 2 vols. New York, 1905–6.

White, Andrew D. *The First Hague Conference.* Boston, 1912.

White, John Albert. *The Diplomacy of the Russo-Japanese War.* Princeton, N.J., 1964.

Wilcox, E. H. *Russia's Ruin.* New York, 1919.

Wildman, Allen K. *The End of the Russian Imperial Army.* Princeton, N.J., 1980.

Williams, Robert C. *Culture in Exile: Russian Emigres in Germany.* Ithaca, N.Y., 1972.

Williamson, Samuel R., Jr. *Austria-Hungary and the Origin of the First World War.* New York, 1991.

Williamson, Samuel R., Jr., and Peter Pastor (eds.). *Essays on World War I: Origins and Prisoners of War.* New York, 1983.

Witte, Count [Sergei]. *Memoirs.* (Yarmolinsky ed.). New York, 1921.

———. *Memoirs.* (Harcave ed.). Armonk, N.Y., 1990.

Wolfe, Bertram D. *Revolution and Reality: Essays on the Origin and Fate of the Soviet System.* Chapel Hill, N.C., 1981.

———. *Three Who Made Revolution.* Boston, 1948.

Wolkonsky, Prince Sergei. *My Reminiscences.* 2 vols. London, 1925.

Wonlar-Larsky, Nadine. *The Russia That I Loved*. London, 1937.

Woytinsky, W. S. *Stormy Passage*. New York, 1961.

Wrangell-Rokassowsky, Baron C. *Before the Storm*. Ventimiglia, Italy, 1972?

Yefremov, P. N. *Vneshnaya politika Rossii (1907–1914 gg.)*. Moscow, 1961.

Yakovlev, N. N. *Vooruzhenne vosstania v dekabre 1905 goda*. Moscow, 1957.

Yakovlev, S. *Poslednie dni Nikolaya II*. Petrograd, 1917.

Yaney, George. *The Urge to Mobilize: Agrarian Reform in Russia, 1861–1930*. Urbana, Ill., 1982.

Yeltsin, Boris. *Against the Grain*. New York, 1990.

Young, L. K. *British Policy in China, 1895–1902*. Oxford, 1970.

Youssoupoff, Prince Felix. *Lost Splendour*. London, 1953.

Zabriskie, Edward H. *American-Russian Rivalry in the Far East* [1895–1914]. Philadelphia, 1946.

Zaionchkovsky, P. A. *Rossiiskoe samoderzhavie v kontse XIX stoletia*. Moscow, 1970.

———. *The Russian Autocracy in Crisis, 1878–1882*. Gulf Breeze, Fla., 1979.

———. *The Russian Autocracy under Alexander III*. Gulf Breeze, Fla., 1976.

Zaitsev, Kirill. *Pamyati poslednyago tsarya*. Shanghai, 1948.

Zavalishin, Sergei (ed.). *Gosudar Imperator Nikolai II Aleksandrovich*. New York, 1968.

Zenkovsky, Alexander V. *Stolypin: Russia's Last Great Reformer*. Princeton, N.J., 1986.

Zilliacus, Konni. *The Russian Revolutionary Movement*. London, 1905.

ARTICLES AND ESSAYS

Aronsfeld, C. C. "Jewish Bankers and the Tsar." *Jewish Social Studies*, 35 (April 1973), 87–104.

Avdeyev, A. D. "Nikolai Romanov v Tobolske i v Yeketerinburge." *Krasnaya nov*, 5 (May 1928), 185–209.

Avrekh, A. Ya. "Vopros o zapadnom zemstve i bankrotstvo Stolypina." *Istoricheskie zapiski*, 70 (1961), 61–112.

Bark, Sir Peter. "The Last Days of the Russian Monarchy—Nicholas II at Army Headquarters." *Russian Review*, 16 (July 1957), 35–44.

Bazylev, L. "Zagadka i sentyabra 1911 goda." *Voprosy istorii*, 7 (July 1975), 115–29.

Berry, Thomas. "Seances for the Tsar: The Reign of Nicholas II." *Journal of Religion and Psychical Research*, 8 (October 1985), 231–42.

Bounds, Marcella. "The Sino-Russian Secret Treaty of 1896." *Papers on China*, 23 (1970), 109–25.

Cecil, Lamar. "William II and His Russian 'Colleagues.'" Carole Fink et al. (eds.), *German Nationalism* (Norman, Okla., 1985).

Chmielewski, Edward. "Stolypin and the Russian Ministerial Crisis of 1909." *California Slavic Studies*, 4 (1967), 1–38.

———. "Stolypin's Last Crisis." *California Slavic Studies*, 3 (1964), 95–126.

Corrigan, H. S. W. "German-Turkish Relations and the Outbreak of War in 1914: A Re-Assessment." *Past and Present*, 36 (April 1967), 144–52.

Crist, David S. "Russia's Far Eastern Policy in the Making." *Journal of Modern History*, 14 (September 1942), 317–42.

Danilov, General Goury. "How the Tsar Abdicated." *Living Age*, 336 (April 1929), 102–3.

Danilova, Yu. N. "Moi vospominania ob Imperator Nikola II-om i Vel. Knyaz Mikhail Aleksandrovich." *Arkhiv russkoi revolyutsii*, 19 (1928), 212–42.

Doctorow, Gilbert S. "The Fundamental State Laws of 23 April 1906." *Russian Review*, 35 (January 1976), 33–52.

Dubensky, D. N. "Kak proizoshel perevorot v Rossii." *Russkaya letopis*, 3 (1922), 11–111.

Emmons, Terence. "Russia's Banquet Campaign." *California Slavic Studies*, 10 (1977), 45–86.

Enden, M. N. de. "The Roots of Witte's Thought." *Russian Review*, 29 (January 1970), 6–24.

Esthus, Raymond A. "Nicholas II and the Russo-Japanese War." *Russian Review*, 40 (October 1981), 396–411.

Fon-Shtein, VI. "Khodinskaya katastrofa 1896 goda." *Istorichesky vestnik*, 118 (1909), 473–506.

Ford, Thomas K. "The Genesis of the First Hague Peace Conference." *Political Science Quarterly*, 40 (September 1936), 354–82.

Freeze, Gregory L. "Subversive Piety: Religion and the Political Crisis in Late Imperial Russia." *Journal of Modern History*, 68 (June 1996), 308–50.

Gan, L. "Ubiistvo P. A. Stolypina." *Istorichesky vestnik*, 135 (1914), 960–97.

Ganelin, R. Sh. "On the Eve of 'Bloody Sunday' (The Royal Authorities, January 6–8, 1905)." *Soviet Studies in History*, 20 (Winter 1981–82), 96–119.

Gill, Peter, et al. "Identification of the Remains of the Romanov Family by DNA Analysis." *Nature Genetics*, 6 (February 1994), 130–35.

Gleason, William. "Alexander Guchkov and the End of the Russian Empire." *Transactions of the American Philosophical Society*, 73, Pt. 3 (1983).

Godwin, Robert K. "Russia and the Portsmouth Peace Conference." *American Slavic and East European Review*, 9 (December 1950), 279–91.

Gottschalk, Louis. "Leon Trotsky and the Natural History of Revolution." *American Journal of Sociology*, 44 (November 1938), 339–54.

Hasegawa, Tsuyoshi. "Rodzianko and the Grand Dukes' Manifesto of 1 March 1917." *Canadian Slavonic Papers*, 18 (June 1976), 154–67.

Heilbronner, Hans. "Count Aehrenthal and Russian Jewry, 1903–1907." *Journal of Modern History*, 38 (December 1966), 394–406.

Hosking, Geoffrey A. "P. A. Stolypin and the Octobrist Party." *SEER*, 47 (1969), 137–60.

Howorth, Henry H. "Some Plain Words about the Tsar's New Gospel of Peace." *Nineteenth Century*, 45 (February 1899), 202–15.

Jefferson, Margaret M. "Lord Salisbury and the Eastern Question, 1890–1898." *SEER*, 39 (December 1960), 44–60.

———. (ed.). "Lord Salisbury's Conversations with the Tsar at Balmoral, 27 and 29 September 1896." *SEER*, 39 (December 1960), 216–22.

Jones, David R. "Imperial Russia's Forces at War." Allan R. Millet and Williamson Murray (eds.), *Military Effectiveness*; Vol. I, *The First World War* (Boston, 1988).

————. "Nicholas II and the Supreme Command: An Investigation of Motives." *Sbornik* (1985; Study Group on the Russian Revolution), 47–83.

Kokovtzoff Comte W.-N. "La verite sur la tragédie d'Ekaterinbourg." *Revue des deux mondes*, 53 (September–October 1929), 506–31, 847–65.

Kurth, Peter. "The Mystery of the Romanov Bones." *Vanity Fair*, 56 (January 1993), 96–103, 117–25.

Lensen, George Alexander. "The Attempt on the Life of Nicholas II in Japan." *Russian Review*, 20 (July 1961), 232–53.

Levin, Alfred. "June 3, 1907: Action and Reaction." Levin and Alan D. Ferguson (eds.), *Essays in Russian History* (Hamden, Conn., 1964).

————. "Peter Arkadevich Stolypin: A Political Reappraisal." *Journal of Modern History*, 37 (December 1965), 445–63.

Lieven, Dominic. "Pro-Germans and Russian Foreign Policy, 1890–1914." *International History Review*, 2 (January 1980), 34–54.

Long, James William. "Russian Manipulation of the French Press, 1904–1906." *Slavic Review*, 31 (June 1972), 343–54.

Lopukhin, V. B. "Lyudi i politika." *Voprosy istorii*, 9 (September 1966), 120–36; 10 (October 1966), 110–22; 11 (November 1966), 116–28.

Lyubimov, D. N. "Gapon i 9 yanvaria." *Voprosy istorii*, 8–9 (August-September 1965), 121–30, 114–21.

McNeal, Robert H. "The Fate of Imperial Russia." Samuel H. Baron and Nancy W. Heer (eds.), *Windows on the Russian Past* (Columbus, Ohio, 1977).

Maisky, B. Yu. "Stolypinshchina i konets Stolypina." *Voprosy istorii*, 1 (January 1966), 134–44; 2 (February 1966), 123–40.

Massie, Robert K. "The Last Romanov Mystery." *New Yorker* (August 21–28, 1995), 72–95.

Matsui, Masato. "The Russo-Japanese Agreement of 1907: Its Causes and the Progress of Negotiations." *Modern Asian Studies*, 6 (January 1972), 33–48.

Melancon, Michael. "The Ninth Circle: The Lena Goldfield Workers and the Massacre of 4 April 1912." *Slavic Review*, 53 (Fall 1994), 766–95.

Mordvinov, A. "Otryvki iz vospominany." *Russkaya letopis*, 5 (1923), 65–177.

Morrill, Dan L. "Nicholas II and the Call for the First Hague Conference." *Journal of Modern History*, 46 (June 1974), 296–313.

Mosely, Philip E. "Russian [Foreign] Policy in 1911–12." *Journal of Modern History*, 12 (March 1940), 69–86.

Mosse, W. E. "Imperial Favourite: V. P. Meshchersky and the *Grazhdanin*." SEER, 59 (October 1981), 529–47.

————. "Stolypin's Villages." SEER, 43 (June 1965), 257–74.

Neilson, Keith. " 'My Beloved Russians': Sir Arthur Nicolson and Russia, 1906–1916." *International History Review*, 9 (November 1987), 521–54.

Oppel, Bernard. "The Waning of a Traditional Alliance: Russia and Germany in the Portsmouth Peace Conference." *Central European History*, 5 (December 1972), 318–29.

Pares, Bernard, "Alexander Guchkov." SEER, 15 (1936–37), 121–34.

Radzinsky, Edward. "Rasstrel v Yekaterinburg." *Ogonok*, 2 (1990), 25–33.

Renzi, William A. "Great Britain, Russia, and the Straits, 1914–1915." *Journal of Modern History*, 42 (March 1970), 1–20.

Rodichev, F. "The Liberal Movement in Russia (1891–1905)." *Slavonic Review*. 2 (1923–24), 249–62.

Rodzyanko, M. V. "Gosudarstvennaya duma i fevralskaya 1917 goda revolyutsia." *Arkhiv russkoi revolyutsii*, 6 (1922), 5–80.

Rogger, Hans. "Russia in 1914." *Journal of Contemporary History*, 1 (October 1966), 95–119.

Romanov, A. F. "Imperator Nikolai II i yevo pravitelstvo." *Russkaya letopis*, 2 (1922), 1–38.

Romanov, B. "Kontsessia na Yalu." *Russkoe proshloe*, 1 (1923), 87–108.

———. "Likhunchangsky fond." *Borba klassov*, 1–2 (1924), 77–126.

"Romanovs Find Closure in DNA." *Nature Genetics*, 12 (April 1996), 339–40.

Ruzsky, N. V. "Telegrammi i razgovori po telegrafu mezhdu Pskovom, Stavkoyu i Petrogradom. . . ." *Russkaya letopis*, 3 (1922), 112–60.

Savickij, Nicholas. "P. A. Stolypin." *Monde Slave*, 11–12 (November–December 1933), 227–63, 360–83.

Schapiro, Leonard. "The Role of the Jews in the Russian Revolutionary Movement." SEER, 40 (December 1961), 148–67.

Seraphim, Ernest. "Zar Nikolaus II. und Graf Witte: Eine historisch-psychologische Studie." *Historische Zeitschrift*, 161 (1939–40), 276–308.

Snow, George E. "The Peterhof Conference of 1905 and the Creation of the Bulygin Duma." *Russian History*, 2 (1975), 149–62.

Sokolova, K. "Popytka osvobozhdenia tsarskoi semi." *Arkhiv russkoi revolyutsii*, 17 (1926), 280–92.

Sontag, John P. "Tsarist Debts and Tsarist Foreign Policy." *Slavic Review*, 27 (September 1968), 529–41.

Spendelow, Howard R. "Russia's Lease of Port Arthur and Talien." *Papers on China*, 24 (December 1970), 146–69.

Spring, D. W. "Russia and the Franco-Russian Alliance, 1905–14: Dependence or Interdependence?" SEER, 66 (October 1988), 564–92.

Strakhovsky, Leonid I. "Count Paul Ignatiev's Efforts to Save the Monarchy of Nicholas II." *University of Toronto Quarterly*, 23 (1953–54), 64–81.

———. "The Statesmanship of Peter Stolypin: A Reappraisal." SEER, 37 (June 1959), 348–70.

———. "Stolypin and the Second Duma." *Canadian Slavonic Papers*, 6 (1964), 3–17.

Struve, Peter. "My Contacts with Rodichev." SEER, 12 (1933–34), 347–67.

Svyatopolk-Mirskaya, Ye. A. "Dnevnik." *Istoricheskie zapiski*, 77 (1965), 236–93.

Sworakowski, Withold S. "The Authorship of the Abdication Document of Nicholas II." *Russian Review*, 30 (July 1971), 277–86.

Szeftel, Marc. "Nicholas II's Constitutional Decisions of October 17–19, 1905 and Sergius Witte's Role." *Album J. Balon* (Namur, 1968).

Tcharykow, N. V. "Reminiscence of Nicholas II." *Contemporary Review*, 134 (October 1928), 445–53.

Thaden, Edward C. "Charykov and Russian Foreign Policy at Constantinople in 1911." *Journal of Central European Affairs*, 16 (April 1956), 25–44.

Tokmakoff, George. "P. A. Stolypin and the Second Duma." SEER, 50 (1972), 49–62.

———. "Stolypin's Assassin." *Slavic Review*, 24 (June 1965), 314–21.

Tuck, Robert L. "Paul Miljukov and Negotiations for a Duma Ministry, 1906." *American Slavic and East European Review*, 10 (1951), 117–29.

Turnbull, Daniel. "The Defeat of Popular Representation, December 1904: Prince Mirskii, Witte, and the Imperial Family." *Slavic Review*, 48 (Spring 1989), 54–70.

Turner, L. C. F. "The Russian Mobilisation in 1914." Paul M. Kennedy (ed.), *The War Plans of the Great Powers, 1880–1914* (London, 1979).

Vilchkovsky, S. N. "Prebyvanie gosudarya imperatora v Pskov 1 i 2 marta 1917 goda." *Russkaya letopis*, 3 (1922), 161–87.

Vinogradoff, Igor. "The Emperor Nicholas II, Stolypin, and Rasputin: A Letter of 16 October 1906." *Oxford Slavonic Papers*, 12 (1965), 112–16.

[Vonlyarlyarsky, Vladimir]. "Why Russia Went to War with Japan: The Story of the Yalu Concession." *Fortnightly Review*, 87 (1910), 816–31.

"Vzryv na Aptekarskom ostrov." *Byloe*, 5–6 (November–December 1917), 212–27.

Waldron, Peter. "Stolypin and Finland." SEER, 63 (January 1985), 41–55.

Walsh, Warren B. "The Romanov Papers: A Bibliographic Note." *The Historian*, 31 (February 1969), 163–72.

Warth, Robert D. "Before Rasputin: Piety and the Occult at the Court of Nicholas II." *The Historian*, 47 (May 1985), 323–37.

———. "Rasputin, Gregory Efimovich." George Jackson and Robert Devlin (eds.), *Dictionary of the Russian Revolution* (New York, 1989).

Williams, Beryl J. "The Revolution of 1905 in Russian Foreign Policy." C. Abramsky (ed.), *Essays in Honour of E. H. Carr* (London, 1974).

———. "The Strategic Background to the Anglo-Russian Entente of 1907." *Historical Journal*, 9 (1966), 360–73.

Witte, Count Sergius. "The Czar and the Czarina and Occultism at the Russian Court." *World's Work*, 41 (November 1920), 39–63.

———. "My Meetings with Roosevelt and Morgan." *World's Work*, 41 (April 1921), 587–93.

Wohlforth, William C. "The Perception of Power: Russia in the Pre-1914 Balance." *World Politics*, 39 (April 1987), 353–81.

Wortman, Richard S. " 'Invisible Threads': The Historical Legacy of the Romanov Tercentenary." *Russian History*, 16 (1989), 389–406.

———. "Moscow and Petersburg: The Problem of Political Center in Tsarist Russia, 1881–1914." Sean Wilentz (ed.), *Rites of Power* (Philadelphia, 1985).

Zakharova, L. G. "Krizis samoderzhavia nakanune revolyutsii 1905 goda." *Voprosy istorii*, 8 (August 1972), 119–40.

Index

About the Author

ROBERT D. WARTH is Professor Emeritus of History at the University of Kentucky.

ISBN 0-275-95832-9

EAN

90000>

9 780275 958329

HARDCOVER BAR CODE